Unfurling Dragon

The Multicultural Art of Vietnam

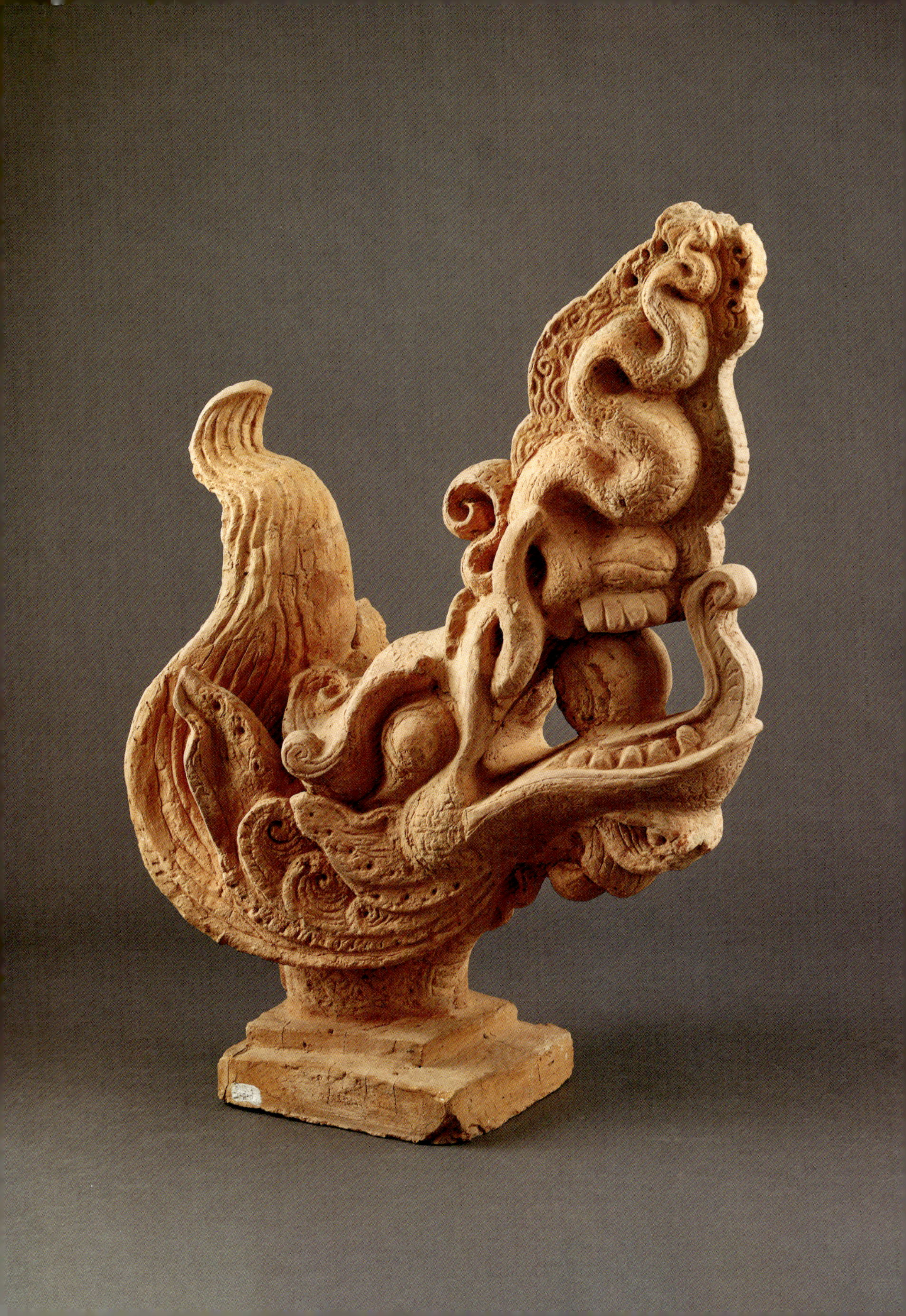

Unfurling Dragon

The Multicultural Art of Vietnam

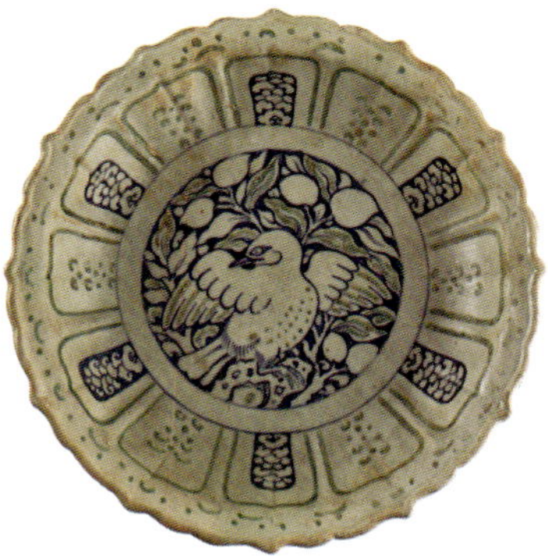

Edited by

Peter D. Sharrock • Pierre Baptiste • Hoàng Anh Tuấn

RIVER BOOKS

First published in Thailand in 2025 by
River Books Press Co., Ltd
396/1 Maharaj Road, Phraborommaharajawang,
Bangkok 10200 Thailand
Tel: (66) 2 225-0139, 2 225-9574
Email: order@riverbooksbk.com
www.riverbooksbk.com
@riverbooks riverbooksbk Riverbooksbk

Publisher: River Books Press Ltd., Bangkok, Thailand
EU Authorised Representative: Easy Access System Europe Oü,
16879218 - Mustamäe tee 50, 10621 Tallinn, Estonia,
gpsr.requests@easproject.com

Editor: Peter D. Sharrock
Text editor: Narisa Chakrabongse
Design: Ruetairat Nanta

ISBN 978 616 451 106 4

Previous page: Dragon head architectural antefix: Terracotta, Hà Nội, Trần Dynasty, 14th century CE
H: 62 cm, W: 43.5 cm, BTLS.23210

Cover & Back cover: Emperor's robe with dragon: Silk brocade,Yellow silk, mid-19th century
L: 133 cm, W: 250 cm, BTLS.4381

Printed and bound in Thailand by Sirivatana Interprint Public Co., Ltd

Contents

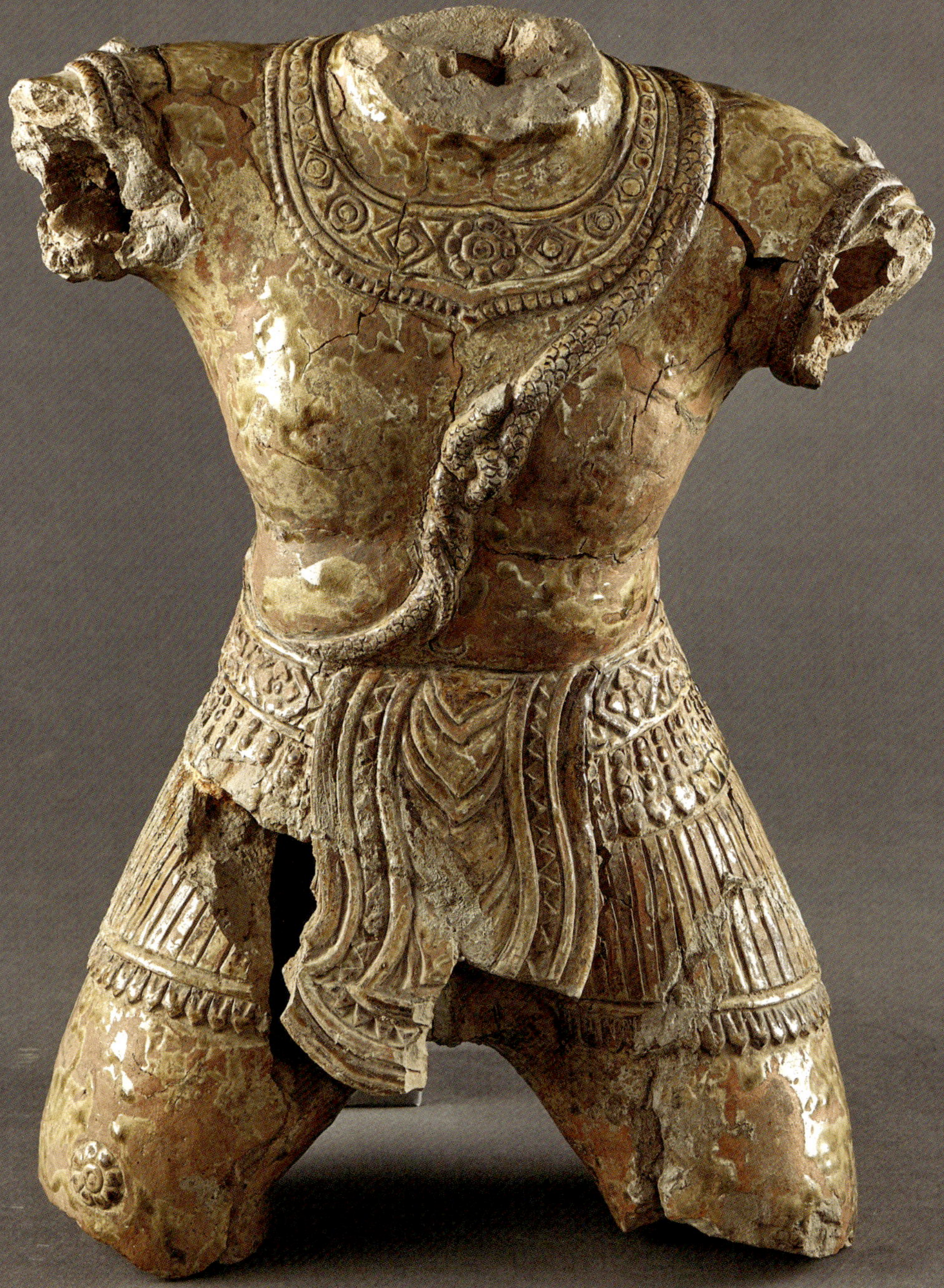

Yang Mum enameled glazed stoneware statue of Śiva
Stoneware, Yang Mun, Gia Lai province, 14th-15th centuries
H: 41 cm, L: 31 cm, BTLS.1294

Foreword

Peter D. Sharrock

The slow unfurling of two millennia of Vietnam's history has woven an extraordinarily rich and heterogeneous cultural tapestry. The warp was set by Bronze Age sinicized lowlanders who settled the Red River Valley in the far north. The weft was progressively threaded after this technologically advanced people stopped a Chinese fleet and declared its sovereignty in a tenth-century Buddhist state that would eventually expand southwards to dominate the long established and artistically advanced Hindu, Buddhist then Islamic culture of multiple ethnic Cam coastal settlements. Finally, in the eighteenth century, the Nguyễn Dynasty reached and absorbed the ancient Khmer-Camic 'Óc Eo' culture of the Delta of the Mekong River in the south and cut long, hand-dug canals linking the rivers to turn it into a tropical rice bowl. A century later in the 1850s the French colonisers built a road network to fully exploit the agriculture.

Much of the long, historical *Nam tiến* ('movement south') is recorded in state annals in an old demotic script, and in the meticulously recorded discoveries of early twentieth-century French colonial archaeologists, who constructed and curated a chain of magnificent museums in Hanoi, Đà Nẵng and Hồ Chí Minh City. Today the museums are being extended and enhanced to capture the full context and coherence of this fascinating and complex and national history.

The early Việt settlers along the diked banks of the Red River in the north developed their distinctive contribution to the bronze skills of southern China in ritual vessels and weapons. In 111 BCE, a 100,000 strong Han army crossed the Trường Sơn mountains and extended Chinese dynastic rule over what they called Nan Yue and the Việts called 'Nam Việt' for most of the first millennium CE. The Việt craftsmen perfected the piece-mould bronze casting of large, engraved Đông Sơn drums that eventually became the prized emblem of chieftainship and exchange far down the coasts as far as the Nusantara archipelago. Their elegant ceramic vessels, moulded from the pure Red River clay, inspired sophisticated ceramic technologies throughout the region.

Independence from China

The golden age of the great Tang Dynasty collapsed in 907 CE, and by 939 CE the Việt commander Ngo Quyen defeated a Chinese fleet and declared the independence of the first Việt Ngo Dynasty. Buddhist scholar-soldier Lý Công Uẩn consolidated the territory of the Đại Cồ Việt province around a new capital called Thăng Long ('soaring dragon') and became

King Lý Thái Tổ, the first ruler of the Lý Dynasty, who established a single administration based on Buddhism and the rule of law rather than autocracy.

Mahāyāna Buddhist pagodas with tiered roofs of glazed ceramic tiles curving upwards at the edges began to arise beside mountain lakes. Their interiors were richly ornamented with guardian figures, refined wooden Buddhas and arrays of ceramic and bronze ritual vessels. From that time on, the renamed Đại Việt fought successfully several times to defend its territory against the Chinese Song Dynasty. By the late thirteenth century, their armies and fleets defeated three invasions by the Mongol Yuan dynasty.

Language and historical annals

The core of the Vietnamese language had been forged by some 40 generations of city-dwelling Han-Tang Chinese speakers who developed a provincial Chinese dialect. After the state's links with the giant northern neighbour loosened into independent vassalage, this merged with the autochthonous Mon-Khmer language of the coastal plain into Old Vietnamese, written in a demotic Chinese script called *chữ Nôm*. This language of the non-Chinese speaking lowland inhabitants developed into the Mon-Khmer group of Austroasiatic languages and is known to linguists as Proto-Việt-Mường.[1] The 54 ethnic minorities of Vietnam today share some cultural traditions with the sinicized lowland early Việt people, who still today call themselves 'kinh', the people of the capital.

Dynastic annals, a legacy from the Chinese period, present a core historical narrative that is unique in this southeastern region. While the north acquired Han culture, further down the narrow coastal plain a long chain of settlements emerged that the Chinese first called 'Linyi' and 'Xitu' and which the inhabitants called Nagara Campā. The narrow coastal strip below the Annamite Mountain chain was studded with riverine ports settled by ship-borne migrants probably from Borneo. In the world before the rise of rice-based agricultural empires, these migrants from the islands grew prosperous through their maritime skills and support for the surging private sea trade between Song China, India and the Arab and European worlds.

Ceramics

John Stevenson, the late authority on Vietnamese ceramics, in Chapter 13 defines what he characterises as 'a happy freedom, almost an anarchy, of creativity' that is distinctive of the local tradition and a pole away from the mathematical precision of Chinese wares to the north. Technical innovations include jars inlaid with a dark brown iron oxide in designs of 'luxuriant vegetation, elephants, and tropical birds.' Phạm Ngọc Uyên, in Chapter 14, analyses the large, representative collection of the History Museum-Hồ Chí Minh City (HC-HCMC), tracing the innovations of the

1 Taylor, K. W. 2013. *A History of the Vietnamese* Cambridge U.P.: 5.

Lý Dynasty potters that expanded to meet the world demand for blue and white Chinese porcelain when the Minh Dynasty banned exports in the fifteenth century. Bui Minh Tri's evaluation (Chapter 15) of the scale of the kilns in Campā at this time, which were producing large jars for transporting commodities, with Cam designs but often today misidentified as 'Martaban' jars from southern Myanmar. He concludes the high production kilns must have been designed, financed and owned by Đai Việt entrepreneurs in Thăng Long (now Hanoi), who sent ceramic technologists to profit from the long-established Cam links to the shipping network around Maritime Asia and with the Arab world.

Campā, Cambodia and 'the movement south'

John Whitmore, the late authority on Campā, devotes his last work (Chapter 17) to the entangled history of the twelfth century. With their growing wealth from the maritime trade, the Cams built high, dramatically shaped brick temple towers to the Hindu god Śiva, utilizing elements from contemporary Karṇāṭaka in west India. Some of these still dot central Vietnam's coastal strip. Cam-style brick and stone temple architecture, including octagonal sanctuaries, formed the early markers of the world-renowned later architecture of the Khmer Empire.

The conquering Vaiṣṇava King Suryavarman II of Kambujadeśa (Cambodia) marched north to briefly enter Thăng Long – the court withdrew in advance – then in the 1140s allied himself with the Cams of Vijaya on the central coast to help construct the new blue water port of Śrī Banoy/Thị Nại for the ocean-going ships of the burgeoning Song trade. The Song were cut off from the overland routes and were dependent for trade on shippers who were developing monsoonal navigation directly across the seas, abandoning the slower old coastal route, that made Campā a prime stopover for all shipping to and from China.

A Khmer prince, sent to Vijaya to cement the alliance with a Buddhist Cam monarch, would decades later drive out of Angkor the army of a rival Śaiva Cam king, who had invaded and killed Suryavarman's younger Buddhist brother and successor King Tribhuvanādityavarman. This Khmer prince became Angkor's greatest King Jayavarman VII, who, after fortifying the city and its fast-growing population against future attack, sent armies to Vijaya to bring Campā into his empire. Jayavarman VII's 'Bayon style' architecture left a strong imprint on Cam sacred art in the early decades of the 13th century when he brought the Cams into his empire, but his successor withdrew, removing one likely resistance to the ongoing Nam tiến of the Việts, which would eventually reduce the Cams to ethnic minority status in Pāṇḍuraṅga (now Phan Rang) in the south.

Royal Cam Silver

As well as the vast ruined temples of Nagara Campā at Mỹ Sơn, Đồng Dương, Po Klong Garai, some of them devastated by bombing in the wars of the 20th century, a collection of Cam royal silver has been found hidden in caches created during uncertain times and retrieved from farmers and archaeological digs and now housed in the History Museum-Hồ Chí Minh City. Anne-Valérie Schweyer (Chapter 10) translates the inscriptions engraved in Sanskrit and Old Cam on the beautifully worked offering vases, plates and candle holders, which were offered to divinities by kings or members of the court in Hồ Chí the cults exercised in the temples over several centuries.

Óc Eo, 'Funan' and the ancient Mekong Delta

Our volume opens in the ancient deep south, where Óc Eo afforded a well-supplied stopover for coastal merchant marine traders. Nguyễn Khánh Trung Kiên (Chapter 1) says finds of rice grains at An Sơn, some 50 km northwest of HCMC indicate the ancient inhabitants ate rice there by around 3500 BP and produced both a distinctive form of pottery with a wavy rim and some cast bronze. The first settlements were circular with a high outer wall (against wild animals), a deep inner moat and simple houses with thatch and wooden pillars. Maritime traders introduced glassmaking, jewelry and face masks crafted from thin sheets of gold.

Between the third and sixth centuries CE, Chinese imperial histories written under the dynasties of the Jiankang Empire (ca. 220-589 CE) record the name of this allied polity in the region as 'Funan'. Andrew Chittick (Chapter 3) also records non-official Chinese reports that give glimpses of the early court life by Kant Tai, an envoy of the third-century kingdom of Wu. By the sixth century Liang Emperor Wu commended Funanese King Jayavarman I as the pacifier of the south. Funan native Buddhist monk Sanghabhara (460-524 CE) became a top adviser to this Emperor. In the late seventh century, when the Chinese name for the region changed to 'Zhenla', the travelling Chinese monk Yijing reported that the Buddhist community had been dispersed by an evil king. Kunthea Chhom and Arlo Griffiths, in their full account of the Delta epigraphy (Chapter 5) however say the epigraphical and archaeological evidence suggests a smooth transition from Funan into the larger polity of Zhenla.

Le Thi Lien (Chapter 8) traces the demand for luxury goods and specialties from Chinese, Roman, Central and Western Asian people increasing in the early centuries CE, as multiple trading centres developed in coastal Hà Tiên and Ba Thê-Óc Eo. By the mid first millennium CE, these blossomed into urban centres with monuments for adopted Buddhist and Hindu sculptures and long rows of stilted urban houses. Large and graceful Buddha images were sculpted from local hard woods and excavated at Gò Tháp in a variety of styles and once reaching 291 cm in height.

The Brahmanical deity Viṣṇu arrived from India probably in the fifth century CE, and was soon revered in what Paul Lavy (Chapter 7) calls a universalist message of a cosmic order created, maintained, and protected by the deity and localized in the power and sovereignty of the king as the supreme devotee. Evidence of the deity's growing presence is found in Sanskrit inscriptions, small gold foil plaques and an array of stone sculptures that bring the god and the king into direct correspondence through recurring references to Viṣṇu in meditation, resting on the giant serpent Ananta on the ocean and creating the universe. These icons evolved from a 500 CE standing figure with 'conch-on-the-hip' from Chaiya in the Peninsula and an imposing seventh century image from Gò Tháp.

Buddhism

Buddha images and inscriptions were also early and rare, including what Pierre Baptiste calls a 'flagship image', an exceptionally well-preserved, probably sixth century Buddha image seated in meditation *dhyānamudrā* from Linh Sơn Cổ Tự, Vũng Tầu. In the seventh century, as countless merchant vessels plied the seas from the eastern Indian coast to the ports of Tang China, Chinese monks reported on Buddhist communities in Campā. Then in the ninth century, only decades after Tang Emperor Wuzong's unleashed his devastating Huichang persecution of Buddhism in China in 841-5 CE, Buddhism was taken to unprecedented heights in Campā by King Jaya Indravarman, who built a 1.4 km long vihara at Đồng Dương on the central coast. It was by far the most important centre of Chinese-influenced Tantric Buddhism in the region and it likely fuelled the rise of Tantric Buddhism in neighbouring Cambodia in the 10th century. Trần Kỳ Phương and Nguyễn Thị Tú Anh (Chapter 18) record the large sandstone Đồng Dương Buddhas excavated by the French archaeologist Henri Parmentier in the 1900s, including a headless Mahāvairocana, seated in characteristic *bodhyangī-mudrā*.

Nguyễn Dynasty annexes Mekong Delta

In the 16th century the Vietnamese Nguyễn lords persuaded their court rivals, the Trịnh lords, to agree to their moving down to rule over the central frontier lands that were the conquered and declining Cam territories of central Vietnam. Vũ Hồng Liên (Chapter 2) traces the Nguyễn advance to control the southern Cam polity of Pāṇḍuraṅga in 1694 and then move into the sparsely populated mangrove swamps of the Mekong Delta, which was then ruled remotely from the post-Angkorian Cambodian capital of Oudong. The Khmer king granted Lord Nguyễn Phúc Nguyên permission to install customs posts at Bến Nghé on the Saigon River that were to benefit both sides. With Khmer and Cam labour, supported by an influx of Chinese fleeing Minh China, the Nguyễn slowly began an ambitious water

Opposite page:
Avalokiteśvara with child. Gilded and lacquered wood, 19th century. H: 86 cm, W: 53 cm, D: 41 cm, BTLS.9770

management programme, building canals linking rivers and developing the Delta into a rice bowl. Over time the Nguyễn prospered and the Trịnh declined, and a Nguyễn Dynasty ruled over the whole country under powerful Emperors Gia Long and Minh Mang from 1818-24. The Delta became a major rice producer, which Liên says fed the south, the centre and some of the North Vietnam and still had a surplus for export. South Vietnam was ceded to France in 1867 and renamed Cochinchina, when more canals and a large road system were constructed.

The art of the Nguyễn Dynasty included the construction of the enormous and graceful citadel of Huế, modelled on the Forbidden City in Beijing, and adorned with large dynastic bronze urns carved with landscapes of the empire and defended by giant ceremonial cannons. The yellow silk imperial robe that graces our cover has the emperor represented as a dragon surrounded by clouds and 'flanking the sun', all of this rendered in fine, elaborate and continuously variegated silk embroidery. Hoàng Anh Tuấn (Chapter 12) says that as well as symbolising royal power, the aerial dragon also expresses the desire for a favourable environment for agriculture, farmers and artisans. Celebrated 'bleu de Huế' porcelains with dragon motifs in bright blue cobalt were manufactured at scale under close supervision by Vietnamese masters at the Jingdezhen imperial kilns in China. Masterpieces in wood include sacred cabinets, inlaid with mother-of-pearl and bone, and icons of Buddhas and the female Bodhisattva Quan Am holding a child, some of which achieved special renown for the dramatic roles they played in historical conflicts.

This volume is an output of a collaborative Summer Programme of the SOAS University of London with the History Museum-Hồ Chí Minh City (HCMC), organized to create a new catalogue of the Museum's growing collection of artifacts recovered from Vietnam's extensive archaeological programmes. The catalogue *From the Red River to the Mekong Delta: Masterpieces of the History Museum-Hồ Chí Minh City* is published by River Books, Bangkok, and launched at Hồ Chí Minh City University this year, with a Vietnamese language version to follow shortly thereafter.

The SOAS Southeast Asian Art Academic Programme is generously funded by the Alphawood Foundation in Chicago to bring students from Southeast Asian universities for postgraduate study in London and to annual research Summer Programmes in the Region.

BẢO TÀNG LỊCH SỬ

SOAS University of London

ALPHAWOOD FOUNDATION CHICAGO

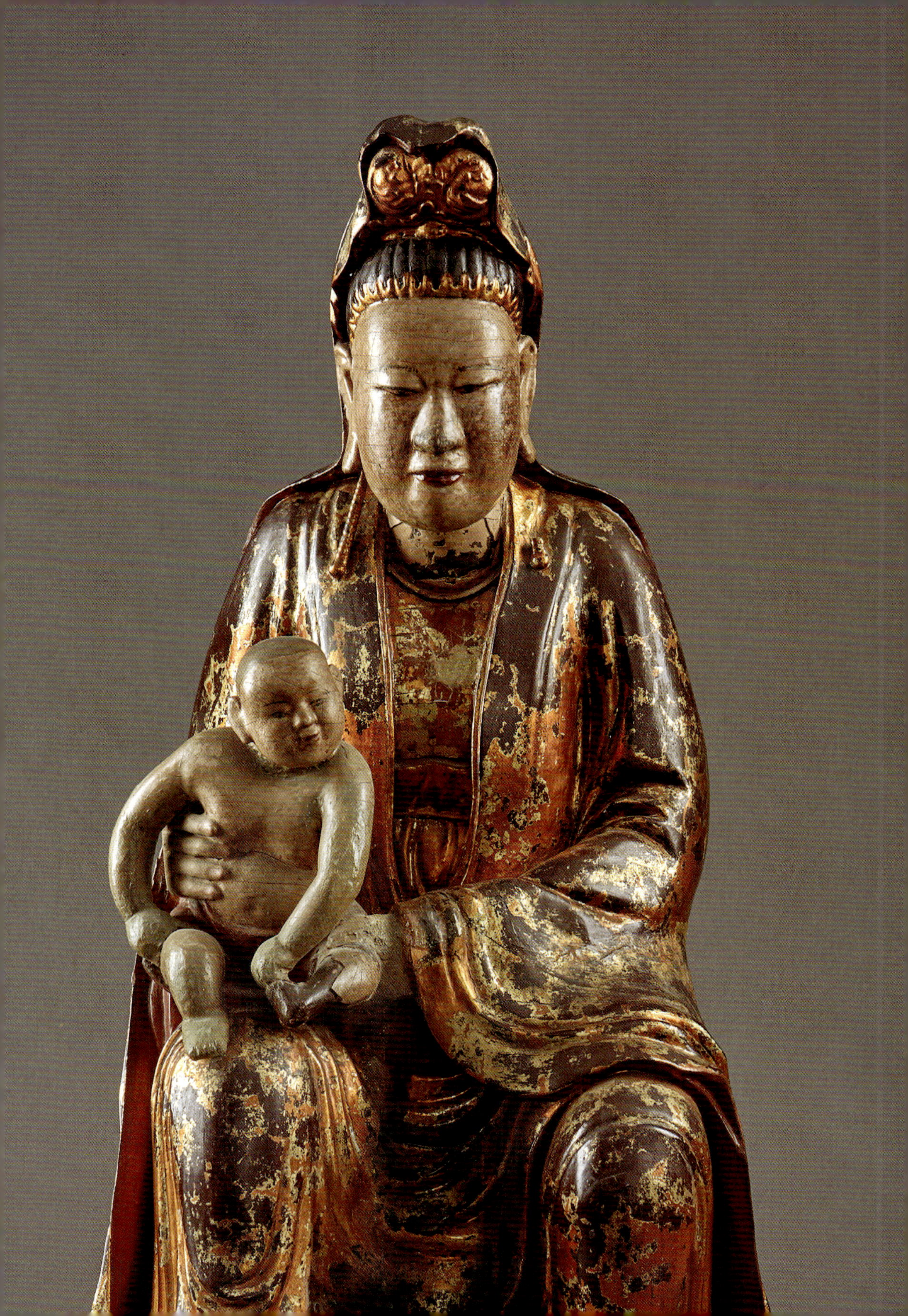

1 | Pre-history of Southern Vietnam

Nguyễn Khánh Trung Kiên

Introduction

This paper briefly introduces the Southern region of Vietnam in prehistoric times from 4,500 to 2,500 years ago, as recorded in recent archaeological publications. The geographical zone is determined by the basalt plateau and ancient alluvial soil along the basin of the Đồng Nai, the Bé and the Vàm Cỏ rivers, including the Vàm Cỏ Tây (west) and Vàm Cỏ Đông (east). To this younger land has been added by coastal mangroves.

From the late 19th century, most of the monuments and archaeological sites found in the southern region of Vietnam were recorded by French scholars at Cù lao Rùa, Mỹ Lộc, An Sơn and circular fortified settlements in Bình Phước province. Other sites were then detected in the Biên Hòa area. Later the French archaeologists became aware of the archaeological sites in the area of Óc Eo, in An Giang province. These sites were surveyed and excavated from 1942 and recorded in publications in the years 1959-63.

Since the late 1970s until today, Vietnamese archaeologists have conducted many programmes surveying, excavating and researching in Southern Vietnam to reach new perceptions and to define the settlement process of ancient communities as they expanded their areas of residence on the land.

Very few traces of the prehistoric appearance of humans in this Southern zone preceded the findings of Edmond Saurin, who found a number of stone tools at the Hàng Gòn-6 (Nhân Gia) and the Dầu Giây-2 sites, located on the red basalt soil of Xuân Lộc in Đồng Nai province and dated to the Early Palaeolithic period c. 600000-700000 BP. Cutting tools were collected on the surface of some sites in the Xuân Lộc area such as Dốc Mơ (or Gia Tân) with a date of c. 250000-300000 BP. However, due to the uncertain archaeological stratigraphy or palaeontology of those finds, it is not possible to determine their absolute age (Lê Xuân Diệm et al. 1991: 121).

For an extended period of the Early Neolithic, archaeology has produced no data on prehistoric human habitation of the land of Southern Vietnam until about 4500 BP. Since then, this region began to shift strongly and rapidly with changes emerging at a series of archaeological sites formed during the transition period between the Late Neolithic and Early Metal Ages.

The first settlements of the Late Neolithic in Southern Vietnam dating to c. 5000-3000 BP

Traces of human habitation in the hinterland are first recorded in the archaeological data of this period. They include the ancient alluvial terraces along the flow of the Đồng Nai and the Vàm Cỏ river systems in the provinces of Đồng Nai, Bình Dương, Bình Phước and the highlands of Long An province.

The earliest evidence of human settlement has been found at sites dating back to the late Neolithic around 4500 to 4000 BP, in locations such as An Sơn, Lộc Giang, on the right bank of the Vàm Cỏ Đông river, as below.

The earliest traces of human habitation at An Sơn site date back to c. 4200-2500 BP, according to results obtained by the Accelerator Mass Spectrometry (AMS) technique (Bellwood et al. 2011). Archaeological evidence collected between 1977 and 2013 indicates that the settlement process started between 2200-2000 BP and the residence time lasted for more than 1,200 years.

Lộc Giang is a site located on a mound about 3 m in height, with an area of about 500 m^2. Ancient Indic-style architecture was first recorded by Louis Malleret (1963) from bricks on the mound surface. Recently, four samples from different layers were subjected to the AMS technique and indicated habitation process from about 4000-3000 BP (Piper et al. 2017).

At both An Sơn and Lộc Giang sites, the ancient residents knew how to build houses with wooden columns on clay foundations and with roofs covered with leaves. Hunting to supplement daily food procured mammals such as deer. There is evidence that from about 4000 BP pigs and dogs were domesticated by the inhabitants (Piper et al. 2017). Rice grains found in layers of soil suggest that rice was usable as a food by the ancient An Sơn inhabitants by around 3500 BP. This was perhaps domesticated rice (*Oryza sativa*) of the genus *japonica* as reported by gene analysis techniques (Peter Bellwood et al. 2011). Rice husk is not only found in the cultural layers but also used as an addition to clay for strengthening earthenware, as indicated by the micro-CT techniques (Barron et al. 2017).

The ancient An Sơn inhabitants have been identified as probably Austroasiatic language speakers based on the study of ancient human remains found there by anthropologists (Matsumura et al. 2017). It should also be added that archaeologists have found an area of many earth graves with burial items located at the foot of the hill, apparently an ancient 'cemetery', which may signal a belief in an afterlife in this community.

Prehistoric 'circular earthworks' or 'round villages' in the plateau basalts

In 1959 Louis Malleret published a map of the distribution of 17 'circular earthworks' or 'round village' sites. Twelve sites were in Bình Long and Phước Long, now Bình Phước province, and six in Kampong Cham province in Cambodia.

Some 70 sites were identified within Vietnam's territory from 1980 to 2019 (Nguyễn Khánh Trung Kiên, Nguyễn Nhựt Phương 2020), and more than 30 sites of a similar type have so far been found in Cambodia. Thus, more than 100 'circular earthworks' sites built with similar construction techniques, have been found within an area some 160 km in the east-west and 60 km in the north-south direction in southern Peninsular Indochina.

Some recent publications have pointed to differences in type and scale in these circular earthworks. Their diameters range from 100-250 m to about 360 m, so the habitable area ranges from 4-6 hectares to about 10 hectares – for example, the Lộc Tấn-2 site, with an estimated population of 300-500 people.

The inhabitants of these centres may have had a relationship with other communities such as the An Sơn-Lộc Giang sites, which may be indicated by the types of pottery with a wavy-rim which is strongly associated with the An Sơn-Lộc Giang sites. They have also found in 'round-villages' in Bình Phước province such as An Phú, Long Hưng-1, Thuận Phú-2 and they have a similar date range of 3500-3300 BP (Nguyễn and Nguyễn 2020). In addition, stone tools indicate that the inhabitants of such villages in Bình Phước may also have used products from a workshop located about 80-100 km downstream on the Bé river (Nguyễn Khánh Trung Kiên 2017).

The characteristics of these settlements are a circular closed space with a high outer wall and deep inner moat. These structures are thought to be intended to prevent wild animals from intruding from the surrounding old-growth forests, rather than to prevent attack by other communities. The AMS results showed a habitation lasting from 3,500 to 3,200 years BP based on coal ash samples in the cultural layer at a depth of one metre from the Long Hưng-1 'round-village' site.

Ancient stone tool workshops along the Bé river

Tool workshop sites have been identified in the sites of Hàng Ông Đại and Hàng Ông Đụng in Bình Dương province and beside the Bé river in the south-eastern region of Vietnam.

An open-pit quarry on both sides of the Bé river with an estimated area of 5,000 m^2 may have been the source of raw materials for the tool workshops. Small excavation pits have been reported to contain thousands of fragments and stones that have been shaped but not sharpened. A huge number of scrapers formed a thick layer with a density of about 10,000 pieces/m^2 together with countless waste products damaged in the manufacturing process, or tools that have been shaped but with unsharpened edges (Nguyễn Khánh Trung Kiên 2017). Long-term habitation has not yet been established in these sites.

Products from these workshops may have been exchanged with many different regions. For example, tools from the downstream sites of the Đồng Nai river or the small stream systems along the Bé river, are also found in the 'circular earthworks' in Bình Phước province (Nguyễn Khánh Trung Kiên 2017). And notably, a piece of a lithophone instrument was found at Hàng Ông Đụng site.

The Hàng Ông Đại site is located on the right bank of the Bé River, with mainly shoulder-axe tools. The stone knives made in large quantities indirectly show the development of agricultural cultivation in the area at that time. Stone tool workshops may have partly contributed to the development of agriculture in southern Vietnam between 3500 and 3000 BP (Bùi Chí Hoàng et al. 2017).

Conquering the lowlands close to the sea

The Rạch Núi site is located in the mangrove area in Cần Giuộc district, Long An province, close to the confluence of the Vàm Cỏ Đông and Vàm Cỏ Tây rivers in the south-east coastal region, where the earliest traces of human habitation were found. The Rạch Núi site was first excavated in 1978 by the Institute of Social Sciences in Hồ Chí Minh City (later the Southern Institute of Social Sciences/SISS); the excavation was then continued by the National Museum of History (Hanoi) in 2003. The most recent excavation was coordinated by SISS, the Australian National University (ANU) and the Long An Museum in 2012.

Palaeontologists reported cultural layers at this site with rice and millet along with bones of fish, monkeys, pigs and dogs (Castillo et al. 2017; Piper et al. 2017). However, the micro-CT techniques found no rice husk in the terracotta samples from the Rạch Núi site (Barron et al. 2017). This may indicate the natural environment was not favourable for rice cultivation in the Rạch Núi area at that time and that the inhabitants traded for rice from other places.

Archaeological evidence indicates that the residents lived in simple houses with wooden pillars raised on a flat clay base to support a roof covered with leaves, similar to those a few centuries earlier in the An Sơn and Lộc Giang sites.

In 2012, a cooperative research programme was implemented at this monument, conducted by ANU and the Centre of Archaeology of SISS. From cultural layers up to 0.5 metres thick, about 13 tons of ceramic pieces of all kinds have been collected. They are simple in type, design and decoration. These studies looked at 14 samples taken in multiple layers using the AMS technique and reached the conclusion that habitation lasted only about 200 to 300 years in this area, c. 3600 to 3400 BP (Oxenham et al. 2015). In 2013, a similar case was recorded by the same group at Lò Gạch site in Vĩnh Hưng district, Long An province, on the right bank of the Vàm Cỏ Tây river, which dated to 3000-2700 BP.

There is also evidence that residents were aware of bronze casting techniques, dating to 3500 to 3000 BP at Rạch Lá, Cái Vạn, and Nhơn Trạch mangrove area in Đồng Nai province. The wetlands may have had important copper smelting workshops with the sites at Bưng Bạc, Bưng Thơm in Bà Rịa-Vũng Tàu province today. ANU reported that bronze tools excavated were dated 2555 ± 28 BP (804-747 cal. BC) from the wooden handle of a bronze axe found at Bưng Bạc.

Cần Giờ is another prehistoric site dated to c. 2500 BP not far from HCMC. Evidence from excavations in the 1990s in Giồng Cá Vồ, Giồng Phệt, Giồng Đất Đỏ, and Núi Đất Lớn suggested contacts with the outside world via the growing maritime trade routes. It has been called an 'early port' (Nguyễn Thị Hậu 1997). New technology introduced to the local residents included glassmaking and jewelry with a unique aesthetic.

The spiritual life of the ancient inhabitants of Giồng Cá Vồ may have formed at this time for the concept of an afterlife appears implied in burying the dead in large spherical jars – these are different from the cylindrical jars without any remains in the Sa Huỳnh culture. The spherical jar style and the ritual of burying human remains were also recorded at Hòa Diêm site in Khánh Hòa province, another coastal site.

A special discovery at Giồng Lớn site northeast of Gành Rái bay, opposite the Giồng Cá Vồ site and in Bà Rịa-Vũng Tàu province is a burial site dated to the 3rd century BCE to 2nd century CE by C^{14} dating and artifact comparison. Unique finds were three human face masks crafted from a thin sheet of gold, one of which is believed to be local and the others imports, possibly from a southern island (Trương Đắc Chiến 2018).

The lack of fresh water in Cần Giờ makes it a harsh environment for food crops. The settlement near the estuary area was therefore probably chosen because it was favourable for commerce with the outside world. As such it promoted the rapid social and spiritual development of the inhabitants.

Prehistoric archaeology in the Southern part of Vietnam – A journey of more than 2,500 years

Many archaeological discoveries have contributed to bringing clearer awareness about prehistory in the Southern region in recent decades. This is the output of Vietnamese archaeology combining with international cooperation.

From 4000 BP, the first human communities lived along the great rivers in the highlands of the Mekong Delta. The livelihoods of these communities include exploitation of natural resources, rice and vegetable agriculture, and animal husbandry with pigs and dogs.

From 3500-3000 BP, settlements increased rapidly and handicraft workshops began to form for stone labour tools for agricultural production on both banks of the Bé river.

From 3000 to 2500 BP, bronze tools were made and widely used notably in Dốc Chùa (Bình Dương province), Bưng Bạc and Bưng Thơm (Bà Rịa-Vũng Tàu province). The spiritual and artistic life of the ancient residents also developed. Along with bronze tools, they cast animal statues of pangolins (Long Giao), predators (Dốc Chùa), and a musical lithophone.

In the marshy wetlands along the coast, the inhabitants may have lived in stilted houses at Bưng Bạc, Bưng Thơm (Bà Rịa-Vũng Tàu), Cái Vạn, Cái Lăng (Đồng Nai), and Phú Chánh (Bình Dương). Weaving may have started at the Phú Chánh site, where evidence of seated looms were found.

The inhabitants of the coastal areas appeared to have participated in the sea trade routes that were growing active at that time. Such commercial activities contributed to the increasing cultural and technological diversity that produced the renowned Óc Eo culture in the early Common Era centuries in the southern part of Vietnam, which this catalogue will cover in detail.

References

Báo cáo khai quật khảo cổ học. 2009. Hai di tích An Sơn và Lộc Giang thuộc địa bàn huyện Đức Hòa tỉnh Long An ngày nay, đã được khai quật nhiều lần bởi các nhà khảo cổ học Việt Nam vào năm 1978, 2004, 2008 và trong các chương trình hợp tác quốc tế giữa Viện Khảo cổ học và Nhật Bản (năm 1997) và Viện Khoa học Xã hội vùng Nam Bộ, Bảo tàng Long An phối hợp với Đại học Quốc gia Úc (năm 2009).

Barron, Aleese, M. Turner, L. Beeching, P. Bellwood, P. Piper, E. Grono, R. Jones, M. Oxenham, Nguyen, K. T. Kien, T. Senden, T. Denham, (2017). 'Micro CT reveals domesticated rice (*Oryza sativa*) within pottery sherds from early Neolithic sites (4150-3265 cal BP) in Southeast Asia'. *Scientific Reports*. Available at: https://www.nature.com/articles/s41598-017-04338-9.

Bellwood, P., M. Oxenham, Bùi Chí Hoàng, Nguyễn Kim Dzung, A. Willis, C. Sarjeant, P. Piper, H. Matsumura, K. Tanaka, N. Beaven-Athfield, T. Higham, Nguyễn Quốc Mạnh, Đặng Ngọc Kính, Nguyễn Khánh Trung Kiên, Võ Thanh Hương, Văn Ngọc Bích, Trần Thị Kim Qúy, Nguyễn Phương Thảo, F. Campos, Yo-Ichiro Sato, Nguyễn Lân Cường, N. Amano. 2011. 'An Sơn and the Neolithic of Southern Vietnam'. *Asian Perspectives* 50 (1 & 2), Spring/Fall 2011.

Bùi Chí Hoàng (chủ biên). 2017. *Khảo cổ học Nam Bộ thời tiền sử*. NXB Khoa học Xã hội, Hà Nội.

Castillo, C. C., D. Q. Fuller, P. J. Piper, P. Bellwood, M. Oxenham. (2017). 'Hunter-gatherer specialization in the Late Neolithic of southern Vietnam – the case of Rạch Núi'. *Quaternary International.* Available at http://dx.doi.org/10.1016/j.quaint.2016.11.034.

Lê Xuân Diệm, Phạm Quang Sơn, Bùi Chí Hoàng. 1991. *Khảo cổ Đồng Nai*. NXB Đồng Nai.

Malleret, Louis, (1959). 'Ouverages circulaires en terre dans L'Indochine Méridionale'. *Bulletin de l'École Française de l'Extrême-Orient* 49: 409-34.

Matsumura, H., M. Oxenham, T. Simanjuntak, M. Yamagata. 2017. 'The biological history of Southeast Asian populations from Late Pleistocene and Holocene cemetery data'. *First Islanders: Prehistory and Human Migration in Island Southeast Asia*. Wiley Blackwell.

Nguyễn Khánh Trung Kiên, Nguyễn N. Phương. 2020. 'Di tích đất đắp dạng tròn ở Đông Nam Bộ: không gian phân bố, quy mô và niên đại'. *Khảo cổ học*, số 5.

Nguyễn Khánh Trung Kiên. 2017a. *Loại hình xưởng chế tác đá thời tiền sử ở Đông Nam Bộ.* Luận án tiến sỹ. Hà Nội (tài liệu chưa công bố).

Nguyễn Thị Hậu. 1997. *Di tích mộ chum miền Đông Nam bộ - những phát hiện mới tại Cần Giờ TP.HCM*. Luận án PTS. Khảo cổ học. Thư viện BTLS-TP. HCM.

Oxenham, Marc F., Philip J. Piper, P. Bellwood, Bùi C. H., Nguyễn, K.T. Kiên, Nguyễn, Q. Mạnh, F. Campos, C. Castillo, R, Wood, C. Sarjeant, Noel Amano, A. Willis, J. Ceron, (2015). 'Emergence and Diversification of the Neolithic in Southern Vietnam: Insights from Coastal Rạch Núi'. *The Journal of Island and Coastal Archaeology*. Available at DOI: 10.1080/15564894.2014.980473.

Phạm Đức Mạnh. 1996. *Di tích khảo cổ học Bưng Bạc (Bà Rịa - Vũng Tàu)*. NXB Khoa học Xã hội, Hà Nội.

Piper, Philip J., Nguyễn Khánh Trung Kiên, Trần Thị Kim Quý, R. Wood, C. Castillo, A. Weisskopf, F. Campos, Đặng Ngọc Kính, C. Sarjeant, Armand S. B. Mijares, M. Oxenham, P. Bellwood. 2017. 'The Neolithic settlement of Lộc Giang on the Vàm Cỏ Đông River, southern Vietnam and its broader regional context'. *Journal Archaeological Research in Asia* (2017). Available at http://dx.doi.org/10.1016/j.ara.2017.03.003

Susumu, Tanabe, Tạ Thị Kim Oanh, Nguyễn Văn Lập, Masaaki Tateishi, Iwao Kobayashi, Yoshiki Saito. 2003. 'Delta Evolution Model Inferred from the Holocene Mekong Delta, Southern Vietnam'. *Tropical Deltas of Southeast Asia – Sedimentology, Stratigraphy, and Petroleum Geology* (eds F. Hasan Sidi, Dag Nummedal, Patrice Imbert, Herman Darman, Henry W. Posamentier):175-188. Available at DOI: 10.2110/pec.03.76.0175.

Trương Đắc Chiến. 2018. 'Di tích Giồng Lớn (Bà Rịa - Vũng Tàu) với vấn đề nghiên cứu quá trình hình thành văn hóa Óc Eo ở vùng ven biển Đông Nam Bộ'. *Khảo cổ học*, số 6.

2 | The Nguyễn Delta

Vũ Hồng Liên

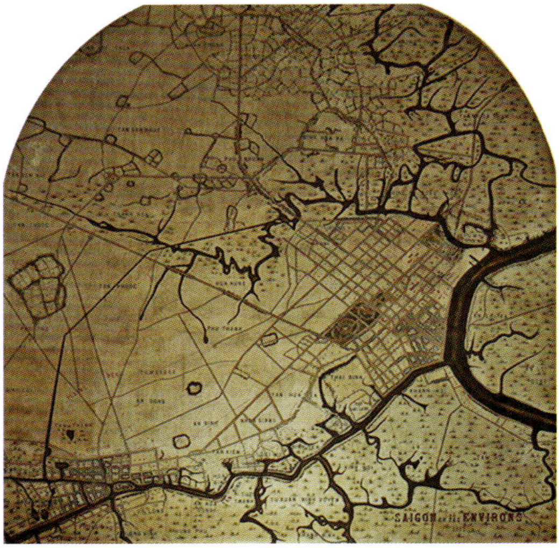

Old Saigon, today's Ho Chi Minh City, on the wall of the Saigon Post Office.

With historical hindsight, it is apparent that the Nguyễn Dynasty would not have existed without the Mekong Delta and the Mekong Delta would not be what it is today without the Nguyễn. Similarly, the Mekong Delta would not have become an important part of Vietnam without the establishment of Gia Định, previously Saigon and today's Hồ Chí Minh City. The development and maintenance of Gia Định required an efficient network of supply and a rear base for the Nguyễn as they faced their enemies on two fronts, the Trịnh from the north and the Tây Sơn from the western mountains of Central Vietnam throughout the 17th and 18th centuries. After an enormous and demanding pioneering effort by the Nguyễn, the Mekong Delta served both functions well, although sometimes more by necessity than design.

The Nguyễn was the last Dynasty of Vietnam, a Royal House that ruled in Huế from 1802 until 1945 CE when they handed over to the revolutionary government of Hồ Chí Minh. The mutual dependency between the Nguyễn and the southern land of Vietnam, however, began much earlier, in 1558 CE. In this year, a dispute arose between Lord Nguyễn Hoàng and his more powerful brother-in-law, Lord Trịnh Kiểm, at the Lê Court in Đông Kinh, today's Hanoi, where they both served behind the throne. The sharing of power inevitably brought about a struggle for supremacy that came to a head in 1558. To escape a perceived imminent purge by the Trịnh, Lord Nguyễn Hoàng asked the Lê Emperor and the Trịnh Lord to allow him to move south, to the wild frontier area of Thuận Hóa (DVSKTT, 1967, vol. 4, p. 231), a sparsely populated land but rich in natural resources (Phan Huy Chú,1992, pp. 157-60). The area is today's Quảng Trị and Thừa Thiên provinces but was previously the Cam territories of Ô and Lý that the Trần annexed to Đại Việt in 1307 (DVSKTT, vol. 4, p. 144). The agreement was that Nguyễn Hoàng would develop the land and pay taxes to the Lê Court, effectively to the Trịnh Lords.

All was well at first as the Nguyễn grew richer and more influential in their international trade across the entire East-West maritime route, amid a commercial boom later termed the 'Age of Commerce' (Reid, 1988). In 1568, the Nguyễn were granted Quảng Nam to the south of Thuận Hóa and now traded successfully through their two international ports of Hội An and Đà Nẵng. Merchant ships from East and Southeast Asia, as well as from India and Europe called regularly to trade (Taylor, 1993, pp. 49-50). Overseas trade became the engine propelling the Nguyễn into modern maritime commerce and became 'a matter of life and death' for the early Nguyễn in the south (Li Tana, 1998, p. 63). During this initial period, Nguyễn Hoàng carefully maintained good relations with the Lê/Trịnh, he even paid several visits to Đông Kinh and stationed himself there for several years to help the Lê against the Mạc usurpers. When the Lê were restored, Nguyễn Hoàng went back to the south to again focus on trade and the development of his land. Success and wealth made Nguyễn Hoàng's successor, Lord Nguyễn Phúc Nguyên, secured enough to stop paying taxes to the Lê/Trịnh (DVSKTT, vol. 4, p. 360, note 25).

War broke out in 1627, when Lord Trịnh Tráng sent an army south to demand their dues (DVSKTT, p. 360, note 25), only for them to return empty-handed. The event marked the beginning of an intermittent civil war that lasted 161 years, from 1627 to1788 CE, when the Trịnh succumbed to a third warring party, the Tây Sơn. The long war did not deter either the Trịnh or the Nguyễn Lords from proclaiming themselves Royal Lords. In the south, Lord Nguyễn Phúc Khoát called himself Vũ Vương in 1744 and established a line of royal Nguyễn Lords who ruled as either *Chúa* (supreme lord) or *Vương* (king) (Trịnh Hoài Đức, 2004, pp. 4-5). The Nguyễn's land was now called Đằng Trong as a viable alternative to Đằng Ngoài, the northern region ruled by the Trịnh behind the Lê Emperor.

As the Trịnh-Nguyễn war progressed, the Nguyễn gradually edged southward toward the former Cam land of Kauthara, today's Khánh Hòa. Thousands of Trịnh prisoners of war were settled on this newly developed land, now called the Việt frontier post *Trấn Biên*, in 1648 (Đại Nam Thực Lục Tiền Biên, 1961, p. 78). Still gradually, the Nguyễn took over the whole of Kauthara in 1653. By then, the only land the Cam still controlled was the southern kingdom of Pāṇḍuraṅga, today's Bình Thuận province, but it wasn't for long. Several skirmishes occurred in this region between the Cam and the Nguyễn; each time, the Nguyễn won a little more land. In 1694, the Nguyễn took over the whole of Pāṇḍuraṅga and changed its name to *Trấn* Thuận Thành with a Cam administrative official ranked *Khám Lý*, who was loyal to them. Three years later the area was renamed the Việt province of Bình Thuận. Binh Thuan was thus the southernmost province of the Nguyễn that shared a border with the Khmer land further south, the Mekong Delta.

The Mekong Delta at the time was a sparsely populated zone of mangrove swamps and was ruled by a Khmer king who resided in his capital Udong by the Tonle Sap river in what is today's Cambodia. For most of the 17th century, relations between the Khmer court and the Nguyễn were cordial and were further strengthened by a marriage between a Nguyễn Princess and the Khmer king Chey Chettha II (Phoeun & Dharma, 1984, Vol. 73, pp. 285-318, p. 292). Through this connection Lord Nguyễn Phúc Nguyên obtained a five-year agreement from the Khmer king to establish as early as 1623 two custom-posts Prei Nokor and Kas Krobei at today's Bến Nghé, overlooking the Saigon River. The two posts quickly became convenient stop-over locations for merchants plying their trade overland and by river routes across today's Cambodia, Thailand and southern Vietnam. The provisional five-year-term was never mentioned again as the trading posts prospered and greatly benefited both the Nguyễn and the Khmer.

The intermittent Trịnh-Nguyễn fighting and general unrest in the former Cam territories, meanwhile, drove many people, both Việt and Cam, southward to the area north of these custom-posts, in today's Biên Hòa, to take refuge and to start a new life. Here, the Việt and Cam immigrants shared a muddy, swampy land with the local Khmers and, quite unexpectedly, another group of refugees, the Ming loyalists who came in 1679 to escape the Qing in China. They were part of a larger group of 3,000 former Ming who sailed into the Nguyễn port of Hội An to ask for asylum and were directed to two locations to settle. One was Biên Hòa and the other was today's Mỹ Tho (Đại Nam Thực Lục.., pp. 135-41, Đào Duy Anh, p. 240).

The new migrants started cultivating the land and the Ming group settled on an island on Đồng Nai river called Cù Lao Phố. Together, the Việt settlers, the indigenous Khmers and the Ming loyalists soon brought prosperity to Biên Hòa. Merchant ships from China, Europe, Japan and Java were regular callers. They traded products with people from the hinterland who came by land or river routes, while marine traders came on the East-West maritime route in the Eastern Sea by sailing up the Đồng Nai river to Cù Lao Phố. In a short time, the area was turned into a prosperous trading post called Cảng Đại Phố (the Great Port of Phố).

The custom-posts at the river ports of Kas Krôbei and Prei Nokor, today's Bến Nghé, were included in this busy trading system and brought even more riches to the developing southern land. As the trade expanded, more people moved down to the area further south of Bến Nghé, toward the Mekong. Wherever they went they turned the land into fertile agricultural farms and orchards which attracted even more settlers who, in turn, developed the region further.

Despite their continuing conflict with the Trịnh, by 1688, the Nguyễn under Lord Nguyễn Phúc Tần had won control over a large area of the southern land. In 1693, having won over Pāṇḍuraṅga, the southern territory under Nguyễn Phúc Chu stretched from Bình Thuận down to the province of Long An. The Nguyễn then named this land *Phủ* Gia Định and placed it under the governorship of a trusted general, Nguyễn Hữu Cảnh. Nguyễn Hữu Cảnh quickly established administrative units for the area such as towns, districts and villages and then appealed to more people from northern provinces to move in to settle. The number of people in *Phủ* Gia Định during this time was recorded as over 40,000 households and the area was listed as thousands of square kilometres. (Trịnh Hoài Đức, 2004, pp. 4-5).

For his governing seat, Nguyễn Hữu Cảnh chose to settle in the former Prei Nokor/Bến Nghé, turning this site into a booming commercial hub where products from the mountains and the Mekong Delta were gathered and offered to maritime traders from India, Japan, China and even further in both East-West directions. The produce from the Mekong Delta was transported north via a system of rivers and canals, and from the mountains by foot-porters along the upstream of the Đồng Nai river and then by boat on the calmer lower stretch near Biên Hòa. For most of the 18th century, Bến Nghé continued to thrive and the area was largely expanded.

Trouble at the Khmer court, meanwhile, divided the Khmer royals and weakened the dynasty a great deal. Intrigues at the Khmer court drove some royal factions to ask their neighbours for help. By allying with some Khmer factions and being at war with others, the Nguyễn managed to hold on to the Mekong Delta without much opposition.

The Nguyễn's control of the Mekong Delta then expanded further in 1714 with the annexation of Hà Tiên, Phú Quốc island and Cà Mau. This area was originally granted by the Khmer to another Ming refugee named Mạc Cửu who settled in Hà Tiên in 1708 and turned this area into a thriving port. Seeing that the Nguyễn were now stronger than the Khmer, Mạc Cửu offered his allegiance to the Nguyễn and was appointed governor of Hà Tiên (Đào Duy Anh, 2005, p. 375).

As soon as they secured the entire Mekong Delta, the Nguyễn launched an ambitious water control programme to take advantage of the region's many natural waterways and established a fluid system of irrigation and transport. They cleaned up shallow rivers, widened ditches and motivated soldiers and civilians to build canals to link up the natural rivers with each other. Indeed, for most of the 18th century, canal construction in the Mekong Delta was one of the most important activities of the Nguyễn, for not only did they help to increase the production of foodstuffs, they played a crucial role in getting supplies in and out of Gia Định. They were also necessary for the Nguyễn to control the seasonal floods of the region so that farmers could grow even more rice and produce.

One of the first canals to be developed was the Bảo Định Canal linking Mỹ Tho with Vàm Cỏ Tây River. This canal started life as a defensive ditch in 1705 under Lord Nguyễn Phuc Chu and was widened into a large canal that eventually became one of the most important waterways of the Mekong Delta under Emperor Gia Long in 1819. Another major canal called Ruột Ngựa was created in 1772 by General Nguyễn Cửu Đàm. It was so called because it was 'as straight as a horse gut'. This canal later became L'arroyo de la Poste under French authority. When completed, this canal played an important role in the flow of riverine traffic linking the then Gia Định with the fertile Delta.

Local farmers then dug their own smaller canals to take their products to the larger waterways and then to the markets. Water from the canals, big and small, made it easy for farmers to irrigate their fields and orchards and grow rich from their products. It can be said that in some areas of the Mekong Delta, it was possible to travel totally by water for whatever purpose. The flow of water transport drew more people to settle along the river and canal banks, from the Mekong to Gia Định, bringing with them a variety of skills. In Gia Định, each group of skilled artisans gathered in their own enclave and dug even more canals to link up with the larger ones to transport their products. Side by side, they created a rich tapestry of professional wards along the rivers and canals of southern Vietnam, some of them, such as the potters, stayed in business until the beginning of the 20th century.

Against this background of intense development in Gia Định and the Mekong Delta, the Trịnh-Nguyễn Civil War (1627-1788) rumbled on but the Nguyễn now faced a new enemy from the former Cam Vijaya and Pāṇḍuraṅga, the Nguyễn Tây Sơn, led by three brothers, Nguyễn Nhạc, Nguyễn Lữ and Nguyễn Huệ (Đào Duy Anh, pp. 412-3). The Trịnh meanwhile were weakened by natural disasters and internal rivalry among the Lords.

The Nguyễn Tây Sơn brothers started fighting both the Nguyễn and the Trịnh in 1770 and very quickly became a powerful force. In 1771 the Tây Sơn took Quy Nhơn citadel, in today's Bình Định province, from the Nguyễn, and used it as their main base (Trần Trọng Kim, 2002, p. 370). From there, they launched repeated attacks against the Nguyễn while allying themselves at first with the now much weaker Trịnh. Taking advantage of the now three-way-conflict, in 1771 the Trịnh attacked the Nguyễn and captured their capital Phú Xuân, today's Huế in Thừa Thiên province (Dai Nam Thuc Luc, 1961, pp. 248-51). That was the last major battle between the Trịnh and the Nguyễn. Lord Nguyễn Phúc Thuần escaped by ship to *Phủ* Gia Định with his family, one of them was a teenager called Nguyễn (Phúc) Ánh. They were hotly pursued by the Tây Sơn, on behalf of the Trịnh (Tran Trong Kim, 2002, p. 373). The Tây Sơn caught up with the Nguyễn further south and killed all but one of them in 1777 (Đại Nam Thực Lục, 1963, Vol. 2, p. 28), the survivor Nguyễn Ánh escaped down to the lower Mekong Delta, then to Hà Tiên and Phu Quoc island.

For the next 25 years the Tây Sơn and the last Nguyễn Lord Nguyễn Ánh fought a running battle across southern Vietnam and up and down the Vietnamese coast. Battleships of both sides travelled according to the monsoon winds along the coast to attack each other. The riverine system of the Mekong Delta was regularly blocked or made impassable by submerged stakes. They took turns in winning the land of *Phủ* Gia Định, which changed hands at least five times. Each time, the winning party changed the laws and raised their taxes accordingly.

When he was victorious in *Phủ* Gia Định, Nguyễn Ánh consolidated his base by establishing army plantations all over the Mekong Delta while building up his army and navy. Civilian farmers were recruited and encouraged to form pioneering groups to develop remote areas of the Mekong Delta. Those who were too poor to buy their own equipment and animals were given cattle and agriculture implements which they would pay back with a portion of their crops. Taxes were generally levied by measures of rice. Soldiers and farmers alike were exempted from corvée duty for a year if they paid enough taxes the year before.

When the Tây Sơn took in Gia Định, the Nguyễn under Nguyễn Ánh escaped to the lower Mekong Delta and even to today's Bangkok. By their association with the Nguyễn, the Ming refugees became victims of the Tây Sơn during this period. Their enclave in Biên Hòa was destroyed and many were killed. They eventually regrouped and settled in an area next to Bến Nghé, turning it into a prosperous market town by receiving and distributing goods in bulks from the Mekong Delta. These large consignments of products were conveniently transported on the fluid water system the Nguyễn built. The market town then acquired the name 'Wholesale' or 'Big Sale' Market, Chợ Lớn, a name that is still in use today.

In 1780 Nguyễn Ánh proclaimed himself king in Gia Định but it wasn't long before he faced the Tây Sơn and lost again in 1783. Nguyễn Ánh was chased out of Gia Định and pursued down the Mekong Delta before taking refuge on Phú Quốc island, with his troops in a dire state. The Tây Sơn pursued them for seven years, without success. As needs dictated during this period, the Nguyễn developed the canal system further to accommodate their ships and established farms wherever they took refuge. On Phú Quốc island Nguyễn Ánh appealed to both Siam and the French court of King Louis XVI for help (Manguin, 1978, pp. 1305-1308). Siam did come to help but to no avail (Đại Nam Thực Lục, p. 55). The French king promised help by signing the Treaty of Versailles in 1787 but delivered little. The French court at the time had bigger trouble to deal with as their revolution was raging on (Manguin, 1977-8, pp. 1305-08). Nguyễn Ánh finally got help from a group of French ship captains who were staying in Asia after the French revolution.

With better ships and weapons, Nguyễn Ánh re-took Gia Định in a decisive battle in 1790 and was finally able to establish his capital in Bến Nghé area of Gia Định (Trần Trọng Kim, pp. 414-8). This time, he held the area and started a long-term construction programme for Gia Định and its supply base in the Mekong Delta, while still facing potential attacks from the Tây Sơn further north. The much weakened Trịnh by then were no longer a viable threat to him.

In Bến Nghé Nguyễn Ánh built a huge octagonal fortification commonly called the Turtle Citadel (*Thành Quy)* from its shape, or Ba-gua in the Yijing. This citadel was designed in a mixed French and Vietnamese style by French architect, Théodore Lebrun, and fortified according to the Vauban principles of defence. The building of this citadel later inspired Nguyễn Ánh to create his much more famous citadel in Huế. Thirty thousand soldiers worked day and night under the supervision of Colonel Victor Ollivier, one of Nguyễn Ánh's trusted officers at the time. The Turtle Citadel was surrounded by three natural waterways, the Saigon river to the east, the canal of Thị Nghè to the north and the canal of Bến Nghé to the south. The perimeter of the citadel measured 3,800 metres and there were eight gates, each facing a strategic direction, and each with its own name – Càn Nguyên, Li Minh, Khôn Hậu, Khảm Hiền, Chấn Hanh, Cấm Chí, Tốn Thuận and Đoài Duyệt. Later emperor Minh Mạng would rename them Gia Định, Phiên An, Củng Thần, Vọng Thuyết, Phục Viễn, Hoài Lai, Tĩnh Biên and Tuyên Hóa. Inside, the citadel was served by eight main roads from each gate. There were guard turrets, barracks, a treasury house, an ancestral temple and the royal residence among many other buildings. An army of elephants was kept in Biên Hòa with selected ones in the citadel.

The perimeter walls of the Turtle Citadel were built with packed earth and stones quarried from Biên Hòa, reinforced with gun turrets and guard houses. Each wall was over five metres high. A large shipyard was built at one corner of the citadel, on a bank of the Saigon river where it connected with the canal of Thị Nghè. Here, warships of all shapes and sizes were built for the Nguyễn to continue their war against the Tây Sơn. The interior of the citadel was served by a system of canals, two of which ran out to the Saigon river from its centre point. This point was also the convergence of the main roads linking Gia Định with Phnom Penh, the rice rich Mekong Delta, the strategic location of Biên Hòa and the riverine system leading out to the East-West Maritime Route via the Saigon river.

The citadel became a magnet for people who came to trade and settle. A big market was established on the bank of one of the main canals at the point where it met a corner of the citadel called Bến Thành (Quay by the Citadel). This market was moved under French authority to its present site but still keeps its original name. The rapid expansion of the surrounding area now needed to be controlled and an urban planning programme was entrusted to architect Trần văn Học. He divided the area into square quarters flanked by straight roads, like a chequerboard.

The canal system of the Mekong Delta was also further improved during this time and later under Emperor Gia Long. Many more canals were dug, one of the most important ones was called An Thông, a part of the Bến Nghé canal, linking the two natural rivers Vàm Cỏ Đông and Tây and the Mekong Delta with Chợ Lớn area. This system of waterways helped both Chợ Lớn and Bến Nghé to prosper under the Emperors Gia Long, Minh

Mạng, Thiệu Trị and Tự Đức, before the arrival of the French in the middle of the 19th century.

After 10 years of living in and ruling from the Turtle Citadel, Nguyễn Ánh/ Gia Long finally defeated the Tây Sơn in 1799 in a decisive victory at Quy Nhơn (Đại Nam Thực Lục, p. 316). The Trịnh by then had succumbed to the Tây Sơn in 1786, taking with them the nominal Le emperor. The taking of Quy Nhơn led to a swift final defeat of the Tây Sơn in Bắc Hà, the Tây Sơn's name for today's Hanoi. The year was 1801. The Nguyễn now ruled the entire land of the Việt, from the Chinese border down to Ca Mau. Most significantly, with this final victory, Emperor Gia Long had for the first time created the unified Việt state we know today.

In 1802 Nguyễn Ánh abandoned the Turtle Citadel to resettle in Huế, the original Nguyễn Lords' capital since the late 16th century. The Turtle citadel was downgraded to be a fortress guarding the south. *Phủ* (capital) Gia Định was renamed *Trấn* (town) Gia Định and placed under a military governor, Lê Văn Duyệt. The eunuch Lê Văn Duyệt was appointed Viceroy of the southern region twice, the first time in 1812-16 under Gia Long, and again in 1820-32 under Emperor Minh Mạng. He was known as a powerful Grand Mandarin who was a strict disciplinarian, much feared and respected by the locals and the remnant Cam and Khmer in the south. He had jurisdiction over the entire southern Vietnam. When Emperor Minh Mạng succeeded his father, he apparently did not like to leave so much power in the hands of one man, so he ordered Gia Định to be divided into six smaller administrative units called provinces, much to the resentment of Lê Văn Duyệt's officials and especially his adopted son Lê Văn Khôi, who was imprisoned for voicing his opposition. From then on, the old Gia Định became known commonly as Lục Tỉnh (the six provinces) and the Turtle Citadel was renamed Phiên An.

In 1833, after the death of Lê Văn Duyệt, Lê Văn Khôi rebelled and entrenched himself in the Phiên An Citadel, and tried to establish Gia Định as an autonomous region (Đại Nam Thực Lục, Chính Biên, Vol VI, p. 90). It took nearly three years for the forces from Huế to besiege and recapture the citadel. Lê Văn Khôi died during the siege. The citadel was razed to the ground in 1835 (Lê Thanh Khôi, 1955, pp. 340-1). Lê Văn Duyệt's grave was put under lock and chain as if his remains were being imprisoned. The chains were only removed in 1848 when Emperor Tự Đức pardoned him. Lê Văn Duyệt's tomb then became a place for serious worship for many southerners and remains so to this day.

In 1836, Emperor Minh Mạng decreed that a new citadel be built immediately northeast of the old Turtle Citadel as a fortress guarding the south and named the Citadel of Phoenix, Thành Phụng. The Phoenix Citadel was a more modest version of the Turtle Citadel. It was constructed in a simple square shape with a perimeter of just under 2 kilometres. It had four gates and was surrounded by large moats. In 1859 the French army called it the Citadelle de Saigon when they stormed and destroyed it and occupied the city.

The process of controlling and developing southern Vietnam, including Bến Nghé/Saigon, today's Hồ Chí Minh City, took the Nguyễn over 200 years to complete. As Emperors, the Nguyễn ruled from Huế and continued to develop the southern land by digging more canals to improve the existing water system. One of the major canals of the Mekong Delta was built during this time, under Emperor Gia Long. It was called Thoại Hà linking Rạch Giá with Long Xuyên and was created by enlarging an existing small silted-up canal. The Thoại Hà canal was 31 kilometres long and built under the supervision of the local Governor Nguyễn Văn Thoại. It was completed in 1818 and named in his honour. The location of this canal is interesting for it was built on the edge of the ancient site of Óc Eo. It is still an important transport route today.

Nguyễn Văn Thoại next constructed the major canal called Vĩnh Tế, the largest and longest canal built under the Nguyễn Emperors Gia Long and Minh Mạng from 1818-24. The building of Vĩnh Tế canal was an ambitious project that stretched nearly 90 kilometres over difficult terrain along the Cambodia-Vietnam border, linking Châu Đốc with Hà Tiên on the south coast. This was probably the most troublesome canal built by hand under the Nguyễn. Tens of thousands of soldiers, local civilians both Việt and Khmer, started digging in 1819 but the work had to be paused as it was extremely hard and the death toll was high. In 1824 construction was restarted and the canal completed under Emperor Minh Mạng. This time, the canal was named Vĩnh Tế after the wife of Nguyễn Văn Thoại. The Long An canal was built in 1843-44 to link the two main branches of the lower Mekong River between Tiền Giang and Hậu Giang. This canal led to the Vĩnh Tế canal and then on to the Gulf of Siam.

Many more smaller canals were dug both on official orders and privately by farmers to link farms or factories with natural rivers or larger canals to facilitate transport and irrigation. The entire network of waterways made it possible for travellers to move all around the Mekong Delta by boat – even up to Chợ Lớn/Gia Định. It made the Mekong Delta a rich food basket for Vietnam. This region can feed not only the southern population but also the centre and some of the north and still have a surplus for export.

When Emperor Tự Đức ceded southern Vietnam to France in1867 the region was renamed Cochinchine and many more canals were built. However, without the initial work under the Nguyễn Lords and the Emperors, southern Vietnam would not have evolved into the important role it has in Vietnam today. Much has changed in the centuries since the Nguyễn started moving southward but the most eloquent testament to their legacy is still visible in the thriving cities, the rich market towns, the vast rice fields and fruitful orchards bordering every river and canal of the Mekong Delta. It was an enormous and demanding effort that became an undeniable success due to the pioneering work of the Nguyễn.

Bibliography

Đại Nam thực lục Tiền Biên [Chronicle of the Great South] (1961) Version 1, Vol. 1, trans. Viện Sử Học, Hà Nội

Đại Nam Thực Lục, Chính Biên [Chronicle of the Great South, Official Version] (1963) Vol. 2, trans. Nguyễn Ngọc Tỉnh, ed. Đào Duy Anh, Hà Nội

Đào Duy Anh. 2005. *Đất Nước Việt Nam qua Các Đời [Geography of Vietnam Through the Ages]* Hà Nội

———. 2006. *Lich Sử Việt Nam, từ nguồn gốc đến thế kỷ XIX, [The History of Vietnam, From the Origin to the 19th Century]*, Hà Nội

Khâm Định Việt Sử Thông Giám Cương Mục [Imperial Ordered Annotated Text to Totally Reflect the History of the Viet]. 1998. Tiền Biên. vol. I, trans. Viện Sử Học, Hà Nội.

Lê Thanh Khôi. 1955. *Le Vietnam, Histoire et Civilisation* Paris.

Manguin, Pierre-Yves.1977-8. 'Les Nguyen, Macau et Le Portugal. Aspects politiques et commerciaux d'une situation privilégiée (1773-1802)' in École pratique des hautes études. 4e section, *Sciences historiques et philologiques. Annuaire* Paris: pp. 1305-1308

Ngô Sĩ Liên.1967. Đại Việt Sử Ký Toàn Thư [Complete Book of the Historical records of Great Viet], Vol.4, trans. Cao Huy Giu, ed. Đào Duy Anh, Hà Nội. p. 360, note 25

Ngô Sĩ Liên. 2004. *Đại Việt Sử Ký Toàn Thư [Complete Book of the Historical records of Great Viet)*, vol. 2, trans. Hoàng Văn Lâu, ed. Hà Văn Tấn, Hà Nội

Phan Huy Chú. 1992. *Lịch Triều Hiến Chương Loại Chí [Chart of Court Rituals and Protocols According to Categories]*, Hà Nội

Phoeun, Mak & Dharma, Po. 1984. 'La première intervention militaire Vietnamienne au Cambodge (1658-1659)', *BEFEO* Vol. 73, Paris pp. 285-318, p. 292

Reid, Anthony. 1988. *Southeast-Asia in the Age of Commerce 1450-1680*, New Heaven

Tana, Li. 1998. *Nguyễn Cochinchina: Southern Vietnam in the Seventeenth and Eighteenth Century. Studies in Southeast Asia* 23. Ithaca, Cornell University, New York

Tana, Li, Reid Anthon Eds. 1993. *Southern Vietnam Under the Nguyen: Documents on the Economic History of Cochinchina (Đằng Trong), 1602-1777.* ISEAS Singapore

Taylor, Keith. 1998. 'Nguyen Hoang and Vietnam's Southern expansion' in Anthony Reid, ed. *Southeast Asia in the early modern era: trade, power and belief.* Ithaca, N.Y.: Cornell University Press New York, pp. 49-50

Trần Trọng Kim. 2002. *Việt Nam Sử Lược* [*Concise History of Vietnam*]. Van Hoc Publishing House: Hà Nội.

Trinh Hoai Duc. 2013. *Gia Dinh Thanh Thong Chi* (ebook). Vol. VI, Thanh tri chi.

———. 2004. *Gia Định Thành Thông Chí [Complete Geographical History of Gia Định Region]*, trans, Lý Việt Dũng, ed. Huỳnh Văn Tới, Saigon.

———. 2013. *Gia Dịnh Thanh Thong Chi* (ebook), Vol II. , Son Xuyen Chi pp.10-1

Việt Sử Lược [Historical Annals of Great Viet] (1998), book 1, trans. Nguyễn Gia Tường, HCMC.

Vương Hồng Sển. 1992. *Sài Gòn năm xưa*, (Vols I, II 1960, III. Đồng Nai-2004.

3 | ‘Funan’ and ‘Zhenla’ in Chinese annals

Andrew Chittick

Sinitic writings on Funan come from three principal sources. The first is the official accounts in imperial histories, which survive as intact texts and provide the most information overall. Seven imperial histories address different dynasties of the Jiankang Empire (ca. 220-589 CE, also known as the “Southern Dynasties”), whose capital, Jiankang (modern Nanjing, in the Yangzi delta) was one of the world’s largest cities and a vital river and maritime trading port, and whose court had intensive diplomatic and trade relations with South Seas states. Its imperial annals note visits by Funan emissaries, and its histories include several dedicated accounts of Funan. The two most important are in the *History of the Southern Qi Dynasty (479-501 CE)* and the *History of the Liang Dynasty (502-556 CE)*. These will be called the Southern Qi text and the Liang text, respectively.[1]

The two accounts have different compositional contexts and outlooks. The Southern Qi text was compiled in the early sixth century, when the Jiankang Empire still existed and had close ties to Funan. The account views Funan as an allied Buddhist regime, and includes extensive quotations from diplomatic memorials, as well as material on Funan’s customs, trade products, and craft traditions. The Liang text was compiled in the early seventh century under the Tang Empire, based in inland northern China at Chang’an (modern Xi’an, capital of Shaanxi province). This was well after Jiankang had been conquered, and Funan also was no longer an independent regime. The account draws on diverse source materials to assemble a comprehensive history of Funan from its earliest period, including a sequence of kings and diplomatic missions up to the sixth century. It arranges its sources in ways which are artificially systematizing and in accordance with the Tang regime’s hostility to Buddhism and to the culture and politics of southern regions, which the Tang regime saw as backward and uncivilized.[2]

Another source about Funan consists of excerpts from a variety of non-official works which are mostly no longer extant but are quoted in encyclopedias (compiled in the seventh to tenth centuries) and other sources.[3] The original works were composed in the third to sixth centuries, in some cases by authors who were emissaries with direct experience of Funan. The most important is ascribed to Kang Tai, an emissary to Funan from the court of the third-century kingdom of Wu (220-280, the first of the Jiankang regimes). These excerpts can be difficult to interpret, but offer important glimpses of what was known about Funan in their time. Some of this material was incorporated into the Southern Qi and Liang texts. A third source of information is Buddhist writings, which make frequent if passing mention of Funan, primarily as a place where Buddhist monks from South Asia spent time before travelling on to East Asia.[4]

The first substantive account of Zhenla is in the *History of the Sui Dynasty (581-617 CE)*, which, like the Liang text, was compiled during the early Tang Empire.[5] While shorter than accounts of Funan, it is quite detailed and possibly based on visits by official emissaries.[6] Accounts of Zhenla in official histories of the Tang Empire, which were compiled in the tenth and eleventh centuries, are comparatively meager, probably because Tang diplomacy centered on central and northeastern Asia rather than the maritime south.[7] The passages on Zhenla in encyclopedic works are mostly derived from these sources, suggesting that not much new was learned during this period, but they occasionally include alternative phrasings or additional nuggets of information.[8]

It is helpful to divide the material from these sources chronologically into three clusters: the second and third centuries; the fifth and sixth centuries; and the seventh to tenth centuries.

Funan in records from the second-third centuries

Material dating from the second and third centuries CE, mostly generated by the Kang Tai mission and other early diplomatic and commercial exchanges, makes up the bulk of excerpts from non-official works, much of the Liang text, and a smaller part of the Southern Qi text. It can be sorted into three types: 1) the legend of the "founding union" between Liuye and Huntian; 2) accounts of the early kings, court life, and tribute missions; 3) miscellaneous records of customs.

The legend of the founding union: This has generated a lot of scholarly discussion, but it represents only a small part of the textual corpus. Later encyclopedias ascribe a portion of the tale to Kang Tai's third-century manuscript, which makes it the earliest known Sinitic source for the legend.[9] Versions in the Southern Qi and Liang texts appear to be derived from Kang Tai but include further information, either from unquoted parts of Kang Tai, or from other sources of unknown origin.[10]

The essence of the tale is that a man named Huntian was equipped by his god with a magic bow and guided on a merchant ship to the shores of Funan.[11] The ruler of Funan, a woman named Liuye (literally "willow leaf"), sought to capture him, but he intimidated and defeated her with his bow. According to the Southern Qi and Liang texts, the two were then married and their descendants continued their royal line. The legend is similar to other Southeast Asian legends of warriors or merchants coming from faraway places and influencing local politics (Manguin 1991; Vickery 2003: 110). Based on the Liang text, Cœdès (1968: 17-19, 37-38; also Ishizawa 1995) takes the union of Liuye and Huntian to be a dateable historical event, with the pair founding a "dynasty," but this is not a tenable assertion (Jacques 1979: 376-77; stated more bluntly in Jacques & Lafond 2007: 48). The reference to rule by their descendants is not in the account cited to Kang Tai, and the Southern Qi text just indicates that their children and descendants succeeded them, without naming any particular rulers. Only the Liang text makes an explicit connection to the named ruler Pan Kuang, and even adds the apparent surname "Hun" to emphasize the connection. However, this is likely to be a later, systematizing emendation to make the succession of kings appear more historically valid. The legend does not indicate that Huntian implemented any elements of "Indianization," despite the interpretive efforts of Cœdès and other scholars (Vickery 2003: 105-110).[12]

Succession of early kings: Several sources offer information on the rise to prominence of the first imperial-scale court of Funan in the second to third centuries CE. The information is likely to have come from the Kang Tai mission and other third-century diplomatic embassies, which went in both directions. Since there are no known inscriptions from this early period, this reconstruction is the best record we have (Jacques 1979: 375).

Name of king (Mandarin)	Approximate dates of reign	Noteworthy features
Pan Kuang	late 2nd century	initial founding of Funan "empire" (expanded *mandala*)
Pan Pan	late 2nd century	short-reigning successor to Pan Kuang
Fan Man	late 2nd-early 3rd	further expansion, including overseas; takes *maharaja* title
Fan Zhan	220s-240s CE	first known diplomatic exchange with Jiankang court
Fan Xun	240s-260s CE	Kang Tai mission, Sinitic record of court and local customs

The Liang account, which is more detailed than the Southern Qi account, describes the initial success of Pan Kuang conquering many towns and installing his sons as local "small kings" before dying at 90 years of age. His general Fan Man (or Fan Shiman) took the throne and undertook vigorous expansion, conquering neighboring polities and calling himself the Great King or *maharaja* of Funan.[13] He also built a navy and launched campaigns across the sea against other states, widely understood to have been on the Isthmus of Kra in what is now southern Thailand. The texts report on the struggles to succeed Fan Man, which began with a usurpation by his nephew Fan Zhan and the assassination of Man's son and heir Jinsheng. After nearly two decades in power, including the first known diplomatic exchanges with the Jiankang court, Zhan's reign ended when a much younger son of Fan Man staged a coup and killed him, then was killed by the general Fan Xun, who seized power in his own name. The narrative is similar to frequent succession struggles at Jiankang, which may have been a part of its interest, along with its generally lurid appeal.

In addition to the first known contact with East Asia, two other Sinitic accounts mention direct diplomatic connections between Funan and South Asia during Fan Zhan's reign.[14] After the Wu regime was conquered in 280 by the northern-based Western Jin dynasty (265-317 CE), the Jin court at Luoyang (in modern Henan province) recorded the arrival of several diplomatic missions from the Funan court. Thereafter, relations between Funan and East Asian courts appear to have fallen off, with only a couple records of emissaries, and no other substantial information, for over a century.

Culture: There are numerous stories about court life and customs from this early period. For example, one encyclopedia (in a section on cocks) quotes Kang Tai's work as stating that "Fan Xun makes iron spurs for his fighting cocks, and gambles on fights with his generals," showing that cockfighting was actively practiced as early as the third century CE.[15] Another quotes Kang Tai on crocodiles:

> The largest crocodiles are two or three *zhang* (about five to seven meters) in length. They have four legs, and resemble a *shougong* (house lizard). They often devour people. The King of Funan, Fan Xun, captures them and puts them in the moat around the city. When Xun has someone with whom he is angry, he binds him and feeds him to the crocodiles. Those who have committed a crime punishable by death, the crocodiles eat; if they do not eat him, then he is set free, and is assumed to be without guilt.[16]

The Liang text reworks this passage, adding additional descriptions of crocodiles from other early texts, and uses it to discuss court practices and the penal system in Fan Xun's time. Other parts of the Southern Qi and especially the Liang text may be derived from Kang Tai or other early accounts, though most cannot be explicitly traced.

Funan in records of the fifth-sixth centuries

The dearth of material for the late third and fourth centuries is attributable to several factors: first, the shift of the center of power in 280 CE to the largely land-locked Yellow River plains under the Western Jin dynasty; second, the weakness of the refounded Eastern Jin regime (317-420 CE) which, although based again at Jiankang, was not very assertive and left little record of diplomatic exchange; and third, the general lack of imperial sources throughout the period, which is covered only by the *History of the Jin Dynasty (265-420 CE)*, an especially flawed imperial history not finalized until the seventh century. All we know from this period is that a Funan king named Zhu *Zhan-tan*/Candana sent a tame elephant and a written memorial (the text of which is not recorded) to the Eastern Jin court, an event dated to 357 CE.[17] The surname Zhu suggests someone understood to be of South Asian ancestry. The Liang text further states that a brahman surnamed *Qiao-chen-ru*/Kaundinya, whose ancestors originally came from South Asia, went south to Panpan (Chaiya, in modern southern Thailand), then returned at the head of a popular movement to assume the throne of Funan, after which he changed the regulations to follow those of South Asia.[18] The timing matches the earliest known spread of Sanskritization in Southeast Asia, in the late fourth or fifth century.[19]

We have much better records for the fifth and sixth centuries, when the Jiankang court was stronger and had intensive relations with Funan, beginning when Kaundinya's successor, King *Chi-li-tuo-ba-mo*/Dharidavarman, sent three separate diplomatic missions to the Liu-Song dynasty at Jiankang in the years 434-438 CE. The material from this period can be divided into four types of information: 1) Buddhist connections and the Nagasena mission of 484 CE; 2) Funanese customs; 3) subsequent kings and tribute missions; 4) peripheral materials.

Buddhist connections and the Nagasena mission: By the sixth century Buddhist scholars in the Jiankang Empire had begun to write about Buddhism using biographical and other historical genres common in non-Buddhist Sinitic writing. Numerous monk biographies report that they spent time in Funan prior to coming to Jiankang. *Qiu-na-pi-di*/Gunavrddhi (403-502 CE), a South Asian monk living in Jiankang in the late 5th century, was significant for being close to south seas merchants and using his wealth to found the Zhiguan monastery, which subsequently hosted other monks from the South Seas, including Funan natives *Seng-jia-po-luo*/Sanghabhara (460-524) and *Man-tuo-luo-xian*/Mandrasena. Sanghabhara became a top advisor to Liang Emperor Wu (r. 502-549 CE) as well as an important translator of Sanskrit materials, and was based at the "Funan office," apparently a translation bureau or diplomatic office of some kind.[20]

The early 6th century Southern Qi account devotes about seventy percent of its text to a particularly important diplomatic mission in 484 CE led by the Buddhist monk *Na-jia-xian*/Nagasena, a native of South Asia, who had taken initial passage from Guangzhou towards home on a merchant ship owned by the King of Funan, *She-ye-ba-mo*/Jayavarman. The ship was taken captive by forces from Linyi (the Cam coast of central Vietnam), and Nagasena proceeded to Funan only after some difficulty. After reporting to the king on the piety of the Jiankang ruler, he was sent back on an official embassy to Jiankang. The account incorporates lengthy quotes from memorials sent at the time, probably translations from Sanskrit originals, which are deeply couched in Buddhist ideas.[21]

One interesting coda to this material comes from the late seventh century Buddhist monk Yijing, who reports in detail on the circumstances of Buddhism in South and Southeast Asia. He notes that the region of Funan, which he reports is now called *Ba-nan*, had once had a flourishing Buddhist community. "But now an evil king has destroyed it, and there have long been no monks, with heterodox beliefs everywhere."[22] As a result, Buddhist monks no longer went there, and Yijing has little else to say about it.

Funan customs: The Southern Qi text offers a substantive account of the customs of the Funan region, generally sympathetic and intended to supplement the extensive information on its Buddhist piety. It begins as follows:

> People of Funan are resourceful, generous, knowledgeable, and skillful. They attack those people of neighboring villages who do not submit and make them slaves. For commerce they use gold, silver, and colored silk. The men of great families use cut lengths of brocade as wraps, and the women to tie their hair. The poor use ordinary fabric to clothe themselves. [They] forge gold rings and bracelets and silver eating utensils.[23]

The discussion of customs in the Liang text is shorter and has quite different information, mostly on religious practices involving the worship of "heavenly gods," with no mention of Buddhism. The tone is highly disparaging and dismissive; for example, "The people's nature is greedy and stingy, lacking ritual or propriety; men and women are unrestrained in their impulses." The Liang text is also ideologically manipulative in subtler ways. For example, it leads off by asserting that the people were originally naked, tattooed, short-haired, and knew nothing of clothing, all of which were standard stereotypes for southern barbarians. This then frames the account of Huntian's arrival, which has a passing mention of people being without clothing in the *legendary* past. The Liang text follows with a claim that Jiankang emissaries in the third century CE first taught them to wear clothes, which is not credible, especially when compared to the Southern Qi text's description of its well-established and distinctive sartorial customs. The Liang text in this way seeks to highlight Funan's barbarian Otherness, and its submissive acceptance of superior customs from the Sinitic world.

Subsequent kings and tribute missions: The Liang text offers a brisk record of nine diplomatic missions sent from the Funan court to Jiankang from 484 to 539 CE, with a variety of gift items, including Buddha images made of coral and Indian sandalwood; gold and gems; storax (a Persian aromatic); and a live rhinoceros. It also includes the brief text of a pronouncement by the newly-enthroned Liang Emperor Wu in 502 CE, commending Jayavarman and pronouncing him King of Funan and General who Pacifies the South. These titles nominally made Jayavarman's court a subsidiary of the greater

Jiankang Empire, at least in the eyes of the Jiankang court. It further records that, upon Jayavarman's death in 514 CE, the designated heir was killed by an elder brother who then took the throne as *Liu-tuo-ba-mo*/Rudravarman. The reigns of Jayavarman and Rudravarman are the earliest that can be verified from local inscriptions (Heng 2016: 500-502).

Peripheral materials: The Liang text includes two other types of material that are only marginally related to the core region of Funan. The first, an extensive account of several peripheral regions across the sea, appears to have been assembled from material in Kang Tai and other textual sources dating centuries earlier. Of these, the account of Dunxun, a subsidiary of Funan located on the isthmus of Kra, is the most substantive.[24] The second is a discussion of revelations linked to the Mauryan Emperor Asoka, which consumes almost half the entire section dedicated to Funan. The focus is on the Jiankang Empire itself; the only direct link to Funan is mention of a Buddha relic (a length of hair) in the Funan court's possession, which the Liang Emperor sent a monk emissary to fetch in 539 CE. Though the reason for its placement in the section on Funan is unclear, one likely purpose of the Tang editors was to associate Jiankang's political use of Buddhism to practices of a "barbarian" South Seas regime, making it appear more alien and inferior.[25]

Zhenla in records of the seventh-tenth centuries

Under the Tang Empire (618-907 CE) diplomatic exchange with and interest in Southeast Asia was much less than it had been under the Jiankang Empire, leading to a significant decline in new information, though considerable energy was expended in compiling and repackaging older information. The Sui Empire (581-618 CE), which briefly preceded the Tang and completed the conquest of Jiankang, was significantly more engaged, and sent several diplomatic missions to the south seas, most famously to the (still unidentified) polity of Chitu. The *History of the Sui Dynasty* offers a lengthy account of a new polity it calls Zhenla, which it says "was originally subject to Funan" but "annexed and possessed it" under King *Zhi-duo-si-na*/Citrasena.[26] The two official Tang histories each have a very brief account of Zhenla; they are obviously stitched together from a miscellany of sources, including the Sui history, and partly duplicate one another.[27] Little of this material was based on first-hand experience, and it is highly susceptible to error. Moreover, in this period archaeological and inscriptional materials from Khmer regions are plentiful and offer a much more reliable (if obviously still incomplete) source for this history (summarized in Jacques & Lafond 2007: 67-99).

Culture. The Sui text primarily discusses Zhenla's culture, particularly the customs of the principal court, perhaps based on reports from diplomatic emissaries. An example:

> Their King holds court once every three days. He sits on a bed of the five fragrant and seven-jeweled [materials]. There is a precious screen arrayed above him, which has balusters of patterned wood and panels of ivory and gold inlay, in the form of a small house. A golden nimbus is hung [around it], similar to the one in Chitu.[28]

The division into two states. The Sui history notes that the principal court of Zhenla was surrounded by other states, whose names (*Cheju* and *Zhujiang*/ Vermilion River) do not obviously correlate to any known polities. Tang histories indicate that people of the region actually called Zhenla by a different name, *Ji-mie*. Both Tang histories have an extended discussion of the division of Zhenla, sometime in the early eighth century, into two courts: a northern "land" Zhenla, called *Wenshan* (or *Wendan*) and also *Poluo*, and a southern "water" Zhenla. Both polities sent embassies to Chang'an at various times, with Wenshan more active, sometimes sending the son of the king, and also a "vice-king" named *Po-mi* and eleven tame elephants in the 760s or 770s. Both polities were bordered by yet other, smaller states, such as *Canban*, a close ally (according to the Sui history) which was northeast of Wenshan and subordinate to it, but which sent an independent embassy to Chang'an in 625 CE before becoming subordinate to Wenshan again. The last recorded embassy, from "water" Zhenla, came to Chang'an in 813 CE, after which all information ceases.

Bibliography

Aspell, William. "Southeast Asia in the Suishu: A Translation of Memoir 47 with Notes and Commentary." *Asia Research Institute Working Paper Series*, no. 208 (2013).

Chen Xiansi. *Zhongguo gujizhong de Jianpuzhai shiliao*. Zhengzhou: Henan renmin chubanshe, 1985.

Chittick, Andrew. *The Jiankang Empire in Chinese and World History*. Oxford: Oxford University Press, 2020.

Cœdès, G. *The Indianized States of Southeast Asia*. Translated by Susan Brown Cowing. Canberra: Australian National University, 1968.

Fang Xuanling. *Jinshu (History of the Jin Dynasty)*. Beijing: Zhonghua shuju, 1974.

Haw, Stephen. "The Maritime Routes Between China and the Indian Ocean During the Second to Ninth Centuries C.E." *Journal of the Royal Asiatic Society Series 3*, 27 no. 1 (2017): 53-81.

Heng, Piphal. "Transition to the Pre-Angkorian Period (300-500 CE): Thala Borivat and a Regional Perspecitve." *Journal of Southeast Asian Studies* 47, no. 3 (2016): 484-505.

Huijiao. *Gaoseng Zhuan (Accounts of Eminent Monks)*. Edited by Tang Yongtong. Beijing: Zhonghua shuju, 1997.

Ishizawa, Yoshiaki. "Chinese Chronicles of 1st-5th Century AD Funan, Southern Cambodia." In *South East Asia & China: Art, Interaction & Commerce*, edited by Rosemary Scott and John Guy, 11-18. Colloquies on Art & Archaeology in Asia 17. London: Percival David Foundation of Chinese Art, University of London, 1995.

I-Tsing (Yijing). *A Record of the Buddhist Religion as Practised in India and the Malay Archipelago (A.D. 671-695)*. Translated by J. Takakusu. Oxford: Clarendon Press ; Oxford University Press, 1896.

Jacques, Claude. "'Funan','Zhenla': The Reality Concealed by These Chinese Views of Indochina." In *Early South East Asia: Essays in Archaeology, History and Historical Geography*, edited by R.B. Smith and W. Watson, 371-79. Oxford: Oxford University Press, 1979.

———. *The Khmer Empire: Cities and Sanctuaries from the 5th to the 13th Century*. Bangkok: River Books Press, 2007.

Kulke, Hermann. "Indian Colonies, Indianisation, or Cultural Convergence? Reflections on the Changing Image of India's Role in South-East Asia." In *Onderzoek in Zuidoost-Azie: Agenda's Voor de Jaren Negentig*, edited by H. Schulte Nordholt, 8-32. Leiden: Rijksuniversitiet te Leiden, 1990.

Li Daoyuan. *Shuijing zhu jiaoshi*. Edited by Chen Qiaoyi. Hangzhou:

Hangzhou daxue chubanshe, 1999.

Li Fang. *Taiping yulan*. Beijing: Zhonghua shuju, 1963.

Li Yanshou. *Nanshi (History of the Southern Dynasties)*. Beijing: Zhonghua shuju, 1975.

Liu Xu. *Jiu Tangshu (Old History of the Tang Dynasty)*. Beijing: Zhonghua shuju, 1997.

Mabbett, I.W. "The 'Indianization' of Southeast Asia: Reflections on the Historical Sources." *Journal of Southeast Asian Studies* 8, no. 2 (1977): 143-61.

Manguin, Pierre-Yves. "Introduction." In *Early Interactions between South and Southeast Asia: Reflections on Cross-Cultural Exchange*, edited by Pierre-Yves Manguin, A. Mani, and Geoff Wade, xiii–xxxi. Singapore: Institute of Southeast Asian Studies, 2011.

———. "The Merchant and the King: Political Myths of Southeast Asian Coastal Polities." *Indonesia* 52 (1991): 41-54.

Ouyang Xiu. *Xin Tangshu (New History of the Tang Dynasty)*. Beijing: Zhonghua shuju, 1975.

Ouyang Xun. *Yiwen leiju*. Shanghai: Shanghai guji chubanshe, 1999.

Pelliot, Paul. "Le Fou-Nan." *Bulletin de l'École Française d'Extrême-Orient* 3 (1903): 248-303.

Pollock, Sheldon. "The Sanskrit Cosmopolis, 300-1300: Transculturation, Vernacularization, and the Question of Ideology." In *Ideology and Status of Sanskrit: Contributions to the History of the Sanskrit Language*, edited by Jan E. M. Houben, 198-247. Leiden; New York: E.J. Brill, 1996.

Vickery, Michael. "Funan Reviewed: Deconstructing the Ancients." *Bulletin de l'École Française d'Extrême-Orient* 90/91 (2004 2003): 101-43.

Wan Zhen. *Nanzhou yiwuzhi jigao*. Edited by Chen Zhifu. Hong Kong: Chen Zhifu jiaoshou jiu zhi rong qing men ren zhuhe weiyuanhui, 1987.

Wei Zheng. *Suishu (History of the Sui Dynasty)*. Beijing: Zhonghua shuju, 1973.

Wheatley, Paul. *Nagara and Commandery: Origins of the Southeast Asian Urban Traditions*. Chicago: Dept of Geography, University of Chicago, 1983.

———. *The Golden Khersonese: Studies in the Historical Geography of the Malay Peninsula before AD 1500*. Kuala Lumpur: University of Malaya Press, 1961.

Xiao Zixian. *Nan Qishu (History of the Southern Qi Dynasty)*. Beijing: Zhonghua shuju, 1972.

Xu Yunqiao. *Kang Tai Wushi waiguo zhuan jizhu*. Singapore: Dongnanya yanjiusuo, 1971.

Yao Silian. *Liangshu (History of the Liang Dynasty)*. Beijing: Zhonghua shuju, 1973.

Yu Shinan. *Beitang shuchao*. 2 vols. Taipei: Wenhai chubanshe, 1962.

Zurcher, E. "Tidings from the South: Chinese Court Buddhism and Overseas Relations in the Fifth Century CE." In *Buddhism in China; Collected Papers of Erik Zurcher*, 587-607. Leiden: Brill, 2013.

Endnotes

1 Xiao Zixian, *Nan Qishu (History of the Southern Qi Dynasty)* (Beijing: Zhonghua shuju, 1972), chaps. 58: 1014-17; Yao Silian, *Liangshu (History of the Liang Dynasty)* (Beijing: Zhonghua shuju, 1973), chaps. 54: 789-93. There are accounts in two other official histories, but they are mostly recapitulations and abbreviations of information in the Southern Qi and Liang texts, with small amounts of additional material: Fang Xuanling, *Jinshu (History of the Jin Dynasty)* (Beijing: Zhonghua shuju, 1974), chap. 97: 2547; Li Yanshou, *Nanshi (History of the Southern Dynasties)* (Beijing: Zhonghua shuju, 1975), chaps. 78: 1951-57. The same is true for other sources from the Tang period (seventh-tenth centuries), such as the *Tongdian*, whose section on Funan is just a revision of prior textual information. The Southern Qi and Liang texts are translated into French in Pelliot 1903: 248-303. Parts are also translated in to English in Wheatley 1961 and Wheatley 1983.

2 For further discussion, see below under 5th-6th century customs.

3 Modern Chinese scholars have assembled these quotes together in edited volumes. Three of the most helpful are Xu Yunqiao, *Kang Tai Wushi waiguo zhuan jizhu* (Singapore: Dongnanya yanjiusuo, 1971); Chen Xiansi, *Zhongguo gujizhong de Jianpuzhai shiliao* (Zhengzhou: Henan renmin chubanshe, 1985); Wan Zhen, *Nanzhou yiwuzhi jigao*, ed. Chen Zhifu (Hong Kong: Chen Zhifu jiaoshou jiu zhi rong qing men ren zhuhe weiyuanhui, 1987).

4 These are best accessed through an online searchable database, such as the one at cbeta.org.

5 Wei Zheng, *Suishu (History of the Sui Dynasty)* (Beijing: Zhonghua shuju, 1973), chaps. 82: 1835-37. The Sui text is fully translated into English in Aspell 2013.

6 However, Jacques & Lafond 2007: 68-73 casts considerable doubt on whether they could be eyewitness observations, based on comparison with archaeological evidence.

7 Liu Xu, *Jiu Tangshu (Old History of the Tang Dynasty)* (Beijing: Zhonghua shuju, 1997), chaps. 197: 5271-72; Ouyang Xiu, *Xin Tangshu (New History of the Tang Dynasty)* (Beijing: Zhonghua shuju, 1975), chaps. 222B: 6301-02.

8 For this material, see Chen Xiansi, *Zhongguo gujizhong de Jianpuzhai shiliao*.

9 Yu Shinan, *Beitang shuchao* (Taipei: Wenhai chubanshe, 1962), chap. 125; Li Fang, *Taiping yulan* (Beijing: Zhonghua shuju, 1963), chap. 347: 1599.

10 There are also versions in the *Jinshu* and *Nanshi*, which offer some variant readings.

11 Different versions give several graphical variants of the second character in Huntian's name. The encyclopedia quotes of Kang Tai's text identify Huntian's country of origin as Mofu, which cannot be confidently identified; other versions just say "a borderland country." Another item quoted from Kang Tai's text says Huntian set sail from Niaowen, which is located in south Asia; the country of Hengfu, also mentioned by Kang Tai, is graphically similar to Mofu and may be what is intended. Efforts to place these countries by taking literally the statement that they are 5,000 li from India (e.g. Vickery 2003: 106-07, following Pelliot) are misguided; figures for distance in these Chinese records are notoriously unreliable.

12 For more recent views on "Indianization," the spread of Sanskrit and south Asian religious and political influence, see Mabbett 1977; Kulke 1990; Pollock 2006; Manguin 2011.

13 The Chinese term for "polity" used here (*guo*) would refer to a somewhat autonomous, often fortified, and potentially rival state or political unit, rather than the small unincorporated "settlements/ towns" (*yi*) conquered during Pan Kuang's reign.

14 Li Daoyuan, *Shuijing zhu jiaoshi*, ed. Chen Qiaoyi (Hangzhou: Hangzhou daxue chubanshe, 1999), chap. 1; Yao Silian, *Liangshu*, chap. 54: 798.

15 Quoted in Ouyang Xun, *Yiwen leiju* (Shanghai: Shanghai guji chubanshe, 1999), chap. 91: 1585. The Southern Qi text just says "They enjoy cock and pig fights."

16 Quoted in Li Fang, *Taiping yulan*, chap. 938: 4168.

17 The event is dated in Fang Xuanling, *Jinshu*, chap. 8: 202.

18 This occurred only a generation prior to the resumption of regular information flows between Funan and Jiankang, and is likely to have historical basis. It is not clear from what place Kaundinya fled south; the most likely explanation is that he was in Funan and was forced to exile to Panpan before his triumphant return. In early texts, the isthmus is always listed as "south" of Funan, even though in reality it lies due west.

19 Coedès 1968: 46 called this Funan's "second Indianization," but the "founding union" story is fundamentally ahistorical and cannot be considered evidence of a "first Indianization." See n.12.

20 Huijiao, *Gaoseng Zhuan (Accounts of Eminent Monks)*, ed. Tang Yongtong (Beijing: Zhonghua shuju, 1997), chaps. 3: 138-39. Other monks who passed through Funan include Qiyu (late 3rd century); *Po-luo-mo-tuo*/Paramartha, also known as Zhendi (499-569); and *Xu-pu-ti*/ Subodhi (late 6th century).

21 The Liang text has only a brief reference to this mission. For English translations of some parts of the memorials, see Zurcher 2013, as well as the French translations of the complete text in Pelliot 1903.

22 Yijing, *Nanhai jigui neifa zhuan*, T54n2125-0205a18; Takakusu 1896: 12.

23 Translation by author, with reference to Pelliot 1903.

24 For a translation and interpretation of this section, see Stephen G. Haw, "The Maritime Routes Between China and the Indian Ocean During the Second to Ninth Centuries C.E.," *Journal of the Royal Asiatic Society, Series 3* 27, no. 1 (2017): 56-60.

25 This section, one of very few discussions of Buddhism in the official histories of Jiankang, has complex religious and political significance not immediately relevant to the study Funan. For more, see Chittick 2020: 269-323.

26 Wei Zheng, *Suishu*, chaps. 82: 1835-36; Aspell 2013: 17-18.

27 Liu Xu, *Jiu Tangshu (Old History of the Tang Dynasty)*, chaps. 197: 5271-72; Ouyang Xiu, *Xin Tangshu (New History of the Tang Dynasty)*, chaps. 222B: 6301-02.

28 Translation adapted from Aspell 2013.

4 | Óc Eo Culture's Rise and Fall

John Miksic

Prelude to the History of the Lower Mekong

Approximately 2,000 years ago,[1] a new culture sprang up in the Mekong Delta,[2] an environment in which land fights for existence against annual floods. An inscription erected by a sixth-century king describes the hard work of reclaiming a kingdom from mud (Cœdès 1931). During the lifetime of this culture, the Mekong Delta became a major center of world trade, renowned from the plains of north China to the shores of the Mediterranean Sea. Scholars now call this Óc Eo culture, after a major archaeological site in the delta.

Óc Eo culture shared characteristics with other "ports of trade" (societies which lie at the margins of continental empires, struggling to maintain autonomy as cosmopolitan, even hybrid cultures by exploiting commerce). Singapore and Hong Kong are modern examples (Polanyi 1957, Miksic 2004). The Mekong Delta is now one of the best-known areas of Protoclassic Southeast Asia, the importance of which for world history is only now becoming appreciated.

Óc Eo culture's rise was closely linked to the emergence of a network of ports along the entire south coast of Eurasia. The relationships among the ports were complex; they cooperated, for no port can exist in isolation from other ports, but also competed. After a glorious period of 600 years, Óc Eo culture suddenly vanished in the early seventh century. Was its fall due to internal factors, environmental change, or the rise of a new competitor?

Chinese officials thought that a kingdom in the Mekong Delta which they called Funan was conquered by its former vassal Zhenla, which then split into two kingdoms, Land and Water Zhenla. Zhenla became the Chinese name for Cambodia. Historians and archaeologists have become skeptical of the Chinese perception of what happened to Óc Eo culture. Chinese sources are vague; they do not even tell us what the kingdoms of Funan and Zhenla called themselves or what language(s) they spoke. Chinese reports on Funan are useful, but they must be viewed critically rather than accepted literally.

On the bright side, a huge number of recent archaeological discoveries, combined with reevaluations of old texts, have given scholars more colours with which to paint a clearer outline of Óc Eo culture and its relationships with its neighbors. After Óc Eo culture disappeared, no new ports evolved in the Mekong Delta for the next thousand years. Although Óc Eo culture had no local successor, it probably influenced other ports which arose in south-central Vietnam and the Straits of Melaka around the time when Funan disappeared.

Óc Eo was not Southeast Asia's first maritime trading culture. The earliest known ports in Southeast Asia appeared on the Siamo-Malay Peninsula around 350 BCE (Bellina 2017). Soon thereafter, a major port developed at the hinterland edge of the Red River delta in the vicinity of Hanoi. This port was integrated into a sphere of interaction in which hard gemstones, gold jewellery, and pottery styles circulated around the shores of the South China Sea.[3] This coincides with what Vietnamese scholars now call the pre-Óc Eo period in the Mekong Delta (2,500-2,000 years BP; Lê Thị Liên et al 2018). Between 2500 and 2000 BP, a major new port evolved in the Mekong Delta which exemplified a different culture from north Vietnam. This chapter will summarize the features of Óc Eo culture and show how it related to the rest of Southeast Asia, especially Cambodia and Vietnam.

The Role of Deltas in Southeast Asian Development

When sea level stabilized around 6,000 years ago, shallow waters along the coasts of Southeast Asia offered ideal conditions for the formation of river deltas. Settlements just inland from the edges of the deltas were strategically located: their residents could act as middlemen for exchanges between people of the hinterlands and other locations to which they were linked by maritime routes, while being safe from surprise attack from the sea.

Deltas usually have multiple river mouths: the modern Mekong has nine, two of them large enough for big ships to enter (in the thirteenth century only one out of "dozens" was viable; Pelliot 1902: 138). Foreign sailors had difficulty determining which river mouth gave access to the port, making them reliant on local pilots. Adding another complication, the locations of the mouths changed frequently.

Until 4000 BCE, water in the Mekong Delta was too salty for human consumption or rice growing (Penny 2006). In 1950 the water of the delta was still brackish 80 km upstream from the mouth of the Tiền Giang (or Bassac) distributary (Dobby 1967: 302). North of the delta, circular earthworks known as *banteay kou* in Khmer have been discovered in what is known as the "red soil" region of southwest Vietnam and eastern Cambodia. Carbon dates from four of these sites span the period from 4,300 to 2,200 years ago (Malleret 1959; Dega 2001). The Mekong Delta was probably populated by migrants from this area as fresh water gradually penetrated further downstream.

The precise shape of the Mekong delta in premodern times is not known, but recent research suggests that it has not changed greatly in the last 2,000 years (Bourdonneau 2003: 261; Liu et al 2017; Nguyễn Thị Mai Hương et al 2015). This parallels findings in other parts of Southeast Asia (Miksic 1977; Hutangkura 2014; Vayssière et al 2020). Southeast Asian deltas 2,000 years ago probably consisted of habitable islands separated by shallow water which later was filled by sedimentation. Wet-rice cultivation in the deltas began around 2,500 years ago (Ma et al 2020), around the time Óc Eo culture began to form.

The Mekong Delta now covers 40,000 square kilometers (Lê Thị Liên et al 2018: 163) with a coastline 360 km long; the upstream apex of the delta is 280 km inland. The surface of the lower Mekong rises by several meters every year when meltwater from Himalayan glaciers plus seasonal rainfall reaches the delta (though this is now changing due to dams built upstream). The area under water in the delta and the Tonle Sap Lake in Cambodia quadruples during this period, creating special challenges but also opportunities for human habitation.

The Mekong Delta's Original Population

A few locations in the Mekong Delta may have been inhabited as early as 4,000 years ago. Six sites in the delta have yielded Neolithic style artifacts, but five are represented by only one or two artifacts, and the dating of the other is controversial (Reinecke 2012: 246-249). One of these, Gò Ô Chùa, is 140 km from the modern coast. The main occupation was salt-making, probably using brine imported from downstream. Rạch Núi, dated by radiocarbon to the period from the second millennium BCE to about 1000 BCE, is very close to the modern coast (Reinecke 2012: 243). Detailed analysis of pottery from An Sơn, 100 km inland, occupied between about 2300 and 1200 BCE, showed that south Vietnamese Neolithic pottery shares traits with northeast and central Thailand (Sarjeant 2012: 159). Only three possible Bronze Age artifacts have been found in the delta, and they may have been deposited during the Óc Eo period (Reinecke 2012: 249).

Pottery of the "Pre-Óc Eo period" (2500-2000 BP) is similar to that of Óc Eo culture (Lê Thị Liên et al 2015: 161), suggesting continuity between the prehistoric population and Óc Eo people. Pottery is the diagnostic type of artifact for identifying sites of Óc Eo culture (Lê Thị Liên et al 2015: 162).

A second type of pottery indicates the presence of another cultural element in the people of Vietnam's southeast coast. Their customs of cremating the dead and burying their ashes in jars are found at late prehistoric sites in the eastern part of the Mekong delta. These ceramics in a style known as Sa Huỳnh represent the prehistoric aspect of what in historic times became known as Cham culture. Similar pottery has been found in the Philippines, so archaeologists often call it Sa Huỳnh-Kalanay. People who created Sa Huỳnh pottery were active traders. Chinese coins have been found at some sites in the Mekong Delta with Sa Huỳnh pottery (Lê Thị Liên et al: 165). Hàng Gòn, just east of Ho Chi Minh City, was occupied between 400 BCE and 100 BCE (Higham 1989: 228-229). Burial jars found there contain imported beads and ear ornaments known as *ling-ling-o* which are found in a broad area where Austronesian languages are now spoken (Solheim 1992: 199; Srisuchat 1996: 228; Glover 1996: 74). *Ling-ling-o* have also been found at Óc Eo (Nguyen Kim Dung 2014). Jar burials found at Giồng Cá Vồ (Cần Giờ) combine artifacts typical of both Sa Huỳnh and Óc Eo Culture (Manguin 2009). Roof tiles used in Óc Eo were flat like those of Campa rather than Cambodia, where roof tiles were curved (Malleret 1950: LIII).

Vickery (1998: 64-65) suggested that the early Mekong Delta population spoke not Khmer, but either another Mon-Khmer language, or Chamic. The oldest inscriptions in Mon and Khmer are found in Thailand and Cambodia respectively and date from the seventh century (Higham 1989; Vickery 1998:19) when the centre of power in the Mekong shifted to the hinterland. This suggests that Óc Eo culture's disappearance might have been correlated with a changing balance of power between ethno-linguistic groups. The Mon ethnolinguistic group was distributed over a broad area of mainland Southeast Asia at the dawn of history (Shorto 1979: 277). They were later absorbed by Khmer, Thai, and Burmese speakers, and many of their kingdoms vanished, although they retained power in Myanmar until the seventeenth century.

Linguistic and archaeological data prove that Mon-Khmer/Vietnamese speakers[4] had close contact with Austronesian speakers in late prehistory. There is a recent analogy for this situation. In the early twentieth century, the Mekong Delta was inhabited by Khmer speakers who lived and planted trees and gardens on levees and sandy ridges (*giồng* in Vietnamese). Vietnamese lived on lagoons between the *giồng*, exploiting them for rice fields, and at river mouths (Malleret 1963: 7-8).

At the dawn of the historic period, the population of the delta may have exhibited a similar pattern, but with Austronesian speakers occupying the ecological niche which Vietnamese later filled. Óc Eo culture may have constituted a specific adaptation to the Mekong Delta in which local inhabitants speaking a Mon-Khmer language coordinated the extraction of resources from the Mekong hinterland which were exchanged for commodities from the lands around the South China Sea, Indian Ocean, and Mediterranean Sea, by seafarers speaking an Austronesian language. Óc Eo culture may have emerged out of a symbiotic relationship between Khmer and Cham (later replaced by Vietnamese speakers).

Óc Eo Culture was probably a unique hybrid of Mon-Khmer and Austronesian origin, enabling Mekong Delta society to exploit both terrestrial and maritime environments. This model best accounts for the diversity of Óc Eo culture and economy.

Late Prehistory and Protohistory (1-600 CE) of Southeast Asia

Early References to Vietnam

By the late third century BCE, north Vietnam was a node on a trading network encompassing the seas and beyond. Archaeological research confirms the complex nature of a sphere of trade which unified Vietnam, the Java Sea, and eastern Indonesia. Evidence includes bronze drums produced in north Vietnam, more than 60 of which have been found in Indonesia (Bernet Kempers 1988).

Chinese merchants in the Qin Dynasty were well aware of a port in Giao Chỉ (Tonkin) which was connected with the South Sea trading zone and provided luxuries in demand among Chinese nobles and scholars (Wang 1958: 17-26; Schaeffer 1967). The "first emperor" sent half a million men (including merchants) to conquer the Yüeh ("Việt") people, because of the economic lure of tropical items to be obtained in the markets there (Wang 1958: 7). The climate of south Vietnam was beyond the pale of what the Chinese could bear (Yang 2010), so Giao Chỉ was the southern limit of their expansionist ambition.

Around the time that Qin conquered Tonkin, its sphere of interaction expanded to the Bay of Bengal; Indian artifacts began to appear in Southeast Asia. Two hundred years later, artifacts from Rome began to reach the Mekong Delta. For the next six centuries the Mekong Delta was the most cosmopolitan and sophisticated region in Southeast Asia. The Mekong Delta provided China with a combination of regional products and re-exports from the west (Wang 1958: 48). Wolters (1967: 39-40) believed that the Chinese were mainly interested in the Mekong Delta for its western produce.

Trade between Southeast Asia, India, and China began centuries before written sources and Indian art styles spread eastward. The first written references to Southeast Asia appeared in India and the Mediterranean at the start of the Protoclassic period (1-600 CE). Around 400 CE, temples built of brick or stone and Indic statues began to appear in both Southeast Asia and India. The Protoclassic period ended with the foundation of the first Southeast Asian kingdoms for which a coherent history can be reconstructed using indigenous sources (Miksic and Goh 2017a: 12-14).

Southeast Asia was not a passive recipient of foreign influences during the Protoclassic period. Southeast Asians travelled to China, India, the Persian Gulf, and Madagascar. The Mekong Delta was no doubt one of the main Southeast Asian areas where economic, political, technological, artistic, and philosophical evolution took place.

Óc Eo's Hinterland

Some sites in Thailand such as Phromthin Tai and Ban Don Ta Phet have archaeological sequences beginning around 3,000 years ago, from the Bronze Age to the Dvāravatī period beginning around 600 CE. These sites display a continuous sequence of development, suggesting *in situ* evolution (Lertcharnrit 2014; Clark 2014).

At the beginning of the Protoclassic period, artifacts from Rome, India, and the South China Sea, combined with items possibly made in Óc Eo, were available to people living in central and eastern Thailand, far from the coast (Miksic 2003: 25-28). Boisselier (1968) suggested that U-Thong in west-central Thailand might have been Funan's capital. Other important sites in this belt include Nakhon Pathom (Khunsong et al 2011), Tha Muang, Ban Tha Kae, Chansen, Ban Khu Muang (Higham and Thosarat 1998: 183), and Muang

Phra Rot (Bacus 2004: 263, fig. 11.4; Glover 1996: 64; Solheim 1984: 144, fig. 31, Bronson 1979: 323-325). These were significant centers of economy, art, and ritual, but there is no evidence that they were politically or culturally part of Funan.

At approximately the same time, i.e. 200 BCE to 200 CE, numerous ramparts, reservoirs, and moats were constructed in the area between the Chao Phraya and the Mekong (Welch 1984, Moore 1988, Higham 1989: 208-210). Salt was made there on an industrial scale by the early Funan period, no doubt for trade over a broad area. Phimai, an important site during the Angkor period, was first occupied over 600 years BCE, but the nature of that occupation is still obscure (Higham 1989: 215).

The portion of the Mekong valley near the Dangrek Mountains which form the Thai-Cambodian border played an important but as yet poorly understood role in the development of civilization in the lower Mekong. There is little evidence of early long-distance trade, and no Funan style artifacts in the region, though a style of pottery known as Phimai Black Ware is found in a fairly extensive area (Welch 1989), suggesting regional cultural development. Inscriptions show that this region had some sort of relationship with Funan during the Protoclassic period. It became known to the Chinese, who thought it overthrew Funan, as Land Zhenla.

Many inscriptions from the late Óc Eo period have been found east of the Dangrek Mountains, whereas only three inscriptions from the Óc Eo culture area survive (all from the terminal period of Óc Eo culture in the early seventh century; Vickery 1998: 37). The oldest inscription in the Khmer-speaking region was carved in Sanskrit around 450-500 CE (Cœdès 1956: 211) at the order of a *mahārājādhirāja* ("Great King of Kings") named Śrī Devānīka. Sixteen other inscriptions attributed to him are found in the same area (Lorillard 2014). Śrī Devānīka came from "far away" to be enthroned there (Cœdès 1968: 65). Some believe that he came from Funan (Lorrillard 2014: 204); Vickery concluded that he came from the Dangrek area; Guy (2009) speculates that he may have come from Mỹ Sơn, Campā, which is connected to Wat Phu by a mountain pass. His son Īśānavarman I (reigned ca 612-637) established his court at Sambor Prei Kuk, northeast Cambodia, but his successors during the period 637-680 went back to the Wat Phu region (Lorrillard 2014: 207).

The first Southeast Asian coins were made of silver in the mid-fifth century. Many were decorated with images of a conch shell or a "rising sun" (Wicks 1992: 86). These coins have been found in Thailand, Cambodia, and the Mekong Delta. The largest known hoard of ancient Southeast Asian coins was found in south Thailand, an area supposed to have experienced strong influence from Funan (Wicks 1992: 108, 221). Some scholars associate similar coins made during the Early Classic period (600-900 CE) with Dvāravatī, a problematic name which scholars variously use to refer to a kingdom, a period, and an art style, roughly identified with the area of modern Thailand (Revire and Murphy 2014).

Coinage was an important part of the trading system of the Mon-Khmer/Vietnamese region of Southeast Asia at the time of Óc Eo culture, but not in insular Southeast Asia. There is no proof that coins were made in the Mekong Delta, but no other location for their production has yet been discovered. Without historical evidence, we have no way of knowing how they were actually used. The distribution of these coins along with Indian and Roman artifacts suggests that Óc Eo was not only a maritime trading culture; the Mekong Delta also served as a major link between the people of the middle Mekong, the Khorat Plateau, the Chao Phraya valley, and even the Ayeyarwady, in other words most of mainland Southeast Asia, with more distant parts of the world.

Southeast Coastal Vietnam

The oldest known inscription in Southeast Asia was found at Võ Cạnh, 300 km northeast of the Mekong Delta. It was probably set up by a ruler in what became Campā, populated by Malayo-Polynesian speakers. Like those of the delta, it was written in Sanskrit and so gives us no hint of the local language.

The first of several Southeast Asian kingdoms to use the name Singapura was a contemporary and probably trading partner of Funan, founded in the valley of the Thu Bồn River around 400 CE. An inscription written in Cam at Đông Yên Châu in this valley is the oldest in any Southeast Asian language (Wheatley 1983: 394). The inscription was set up by king Bhavavarman, who built a palace on a hill now called Bửu Châu. Archaeological research there has yielded much information on the early Protoclassic (Glover 1996: 67; Glover and Yamagata 1995: 156). Excavations at Gò Cấm, 3.5 km east of Bửu Châu , revealed another site where a Protoclassic stratum overlies a Sa Huỳnh layer, the first such sequence yet found in central Vietnam, supporting the hypothesis that Sa Huỳnh was ancestral to Cam culture (Yamagata 2011; Southworth 2004; Prior and Glover 2003).

The Malay Peninsula and Indonesia

The Chinese believed that Funan conquered ten kingdoms, some on the Malay Peninsula. Dunsun, a Chinese name for one of them, could be a transcription of "Five Cities" in proto-Mon (Wheatley 1961: 15-21). The Chinese were impressed by Dunsun's trading connections: "At this mart East and West meet together…Precious goods and rare merchandise, there is nothing which is not there" (Wheatley 1961: 16). Archaeologists have unearthed the probable remains of this port in southern Myanmar. Some ceramics found here are similar to Óc Eo and Sa Huỳnh types (Bellina et al. 2018: 4).

The oldest Southeast Asian statue in Indian style may be a Viṣṇu of the fourth century CE found in peninsular Thailand (O'Connor 1972: 39). Similar statues are found in southeast Cambodia and southern Vietnam, one of which may have come from Óc Eo. Óc Eo was probably a member of a network of Southeast Asian ports linked in part by the popularity of Viṣṇu (Dalsheimer and Manguin 1998).

A popular Buddhist icon called *dharmacakra* was sometimes made of stone. Several have been found in the Funan area, which Indorf (2014) considers to display a special local style that spread to other parts of Funan's sphere of influence (Indorf 2014: 304). One was found at Óc Eo (Malleret 1959 pl. LXXXIVb). A *cakra* in the Funan collection in the Museum of History, Hồ Chí Minh City, is very similar to one found in the upper Malay Peninsula supposedly conquered by Funan (Indorf 2014: 273). Two Funan-style *cakra* have been found in the isthmian region of the Malay Peninsula, another west of Bangkok, and one south of Sambor Prei Kuk, northeast Cambodia (Indorf 2014: 300, map 1).This example is notable because it was found in a Śiva temple; Indorf suggests that *cakra* were associated with royal graves of Funan rulers who were devotees of Viṣṇu (Indorf 2014: 274).This is another indication of the syncretic quality of Óc Eo culture.

The oldest known Buddhist texts composed in Southeast Asia are inscriptions of the late fourth and fifth centuries found in Kedah, peninsular Malaysia (Christie 1990: 48). One contains a prayer for safety by a ship captain from "Red Earth Land". Chinese envoys visited a kingdom of this name in 607-609 on the east coast of the peninsula. Red Earth Land was Buddhist and according to the Chinese formed part of Funan (Wheatley 1961: 26-36, 105).

Port sites contemporary with Óc Eo culture have been found on Java, Sumatra, Bali, and east Kalimantan (Borneo; Miksic and Goh 2017a: 207-218). The most complex sites are located on northwest Java. Romano-Indian rouletted ware made in India imitating Roman style around 2,000 years ago has been found in this area (Walker and S. Santoso 1977, 1980) and in Sembiran, north Bali, as well as a burial, DNA analysis of which indicates that the skeleton probably belongs to a person from India (Ardika 1997).

Severely looted sites have been found in southeast Sumatra where another kingdom was visited by the Chinese in the third century. Indian beads, a Chinese ewer provisionally assigned to Han dynasty China (206 BCE-220 CE), Romano-Indian rouletted ware, and a large rudder from a ship have been found in this region in association with radiocarbon dates ranging between the third and the sixth centuries (Budisantoso and Tri Marhaeni S. 2002, 2005, 2007; Manguin, Soeroso, and Charras 2006; Nurhadi Rangkuti 2008; Tri Marhaeni 2010: 40-44; Adhyatman and Arifin 1993: 28-29).

A kingdom in Java probably located in the delta of the Cibuaya River east of Jakarta sent ambassadors to China six times between 430 and 452 (Wolters 1967: 165). The delta has yielded an early Viṣṇu image which closely resembles those from south Thailand, and brick and stone foundations and clay votive tablets depicting Buddhist motifs similar to others found in Thailand, and a gold duodecahedron-shaped bead of Greek style similar to examples in Óc Eo (Manguin and Agustijanto Indrajaya 2011).

Funan's Indian Connection

Although Funan is much closer to China than India, artifacts of Indian origin outnumber Chinese artifacts in the Mekong Delta (Le 2015). Even Mediterranean objects are more common than Chinese at Óc Eo (Malleret 1963: 395). Temples made of stone or brick, and statuary of important gods appear in Funan around the same time as in India (Ray 2014). Many of the earliest Buddhist images in Southeast Asia, made of wood, have been found at Angkor Borei and its environs where the waterlogged soil has preserved them (Miksic 2003: 25; Lê Thị Liên 2014: 9). Chinese Buddhist monks visited Funan on their way to and from India. One was on a ship with Funanese traders when they were wrecked on the Cam coast (Mabbett 1986: 295). Funanese monks also visited China. Tribute sent by Funan included Buddhist "holy things" (Wang 1958: 48; 56 note 32).

The oldest statues of Viṣṇu from Ba Phnom, near Angkor Borei, display strong Gupta influence. They are normally assumed to date from the sixth century (Dowling 1999). Early Chinese records described Funan people as worshippers of Śiva (Cœdès 1968: 61). Statues of Śiva in the Mekong Delta are found in different areas from Viṣṇus. It has been proposed that this distribution was connected with different ethnic groups and polities until the end of the Protoclassic, when Harihara (half Śiva, half Viṣṇu) appeared, possibly in a political effort to reconcile these divisions (Lavy 2003).

The Mekong Delta: Earliest History

Our earliest report about the Mekong Delta comes not from Asia, but from a Greek scholar living in Alexandria, Egypt: Klaudios Ptolemaios. Around 150 CE he wrote a book which mentions many places in Southeast Asia. Ptolemaios' book contains a fair amount of geographical information about Southeast Asia (Wheatley 1961: 138-176; Pagani 1990). One toponym in Ptolemaios' book, Kattigara, may have been Óc Eo (Cœdès 1968: 277 n. 20; Malleret 1962: 421-54). People from *Zabai* (south Sumatra and Java; Laffan 2005) sailed to Kattigara (Berggren and Jones 2000: 75-76, footnote 51). A very long river, perhaps the Mekong, reaches a mountain range about where the Himalayas should be. Several more towns appear along the southern Vietnamese coast, north of which a river (perhaps the Thu Bồn) enters the "Great Bay", the East Sea. Several more ports appear, then the Serus River, possibly the Red River.

Chinese authors first mentioned Funan in the third century. The *History of the Liang Dynasty* (502-56 CE) says that Funan conquered more than ten kingdoms. Historians of the early 20th century assumed that Funan "encompassed southern Vietnam, the central Mekong, and a large part of the Menam Valley and the Malay peninsula" (Cœdès 1968: 36). Historians now doubt that Funan's organization resembled China. Vickery (1998: 43) defined Funan as "the coastal and delta-based polity or polities of the pre-seventh century period known from Chinese records and probably identifiable on the ground at Óc Eo, in the canal network of southern Cambodia and Vietnam, and in some of the early pre-Angkor sites such as Angkor Borei and Phnom Bayang."

There is archaeological evidence for contact between the Malay Peninsula and the Mekong Delta at this time. Probably commerce and cultural exchange were the main factors which led to a close relationship between these two areas. Pottery from Funan has been discovered at two sites in Peninsular Malaysia (Evans 1927: 94; illustrated in Miksic 2003: 71; Malleret 1960: plate LXXIII).

The Mekong Delta is one of the most metal-deficient areas in Southeast Asia. Chinese sources note that Funan obtained metal objects and ores from islands across the Sea; this was probably an important activity during Funan's period of greatness (Wolters 1967: 39, 61).

Some Funan products in demand in China at this time[5] included marine products obtained from other parts of Southeast Asia, including cowrie shells, tortoiseshell, and coral. Funan also imported gold and silver from other parts of Southeast Asia to make jewellery. Some gold ornaments from Óc Eo bear strong resemblances to artifacts found in other parts of Southeast Asia (Miksic 2011: 110). Other export commodities came from Funan's own hinterland, including aromatic wood, ivory, peacock-feathers, and tortoiseshells, and resin used as incense. There was probably considerable trade and communication along the Mekong.

Funan sent a mission to the Chinese kingdom of Wu around 231 CE, which advertised Funan's role as a link to suppliers of luxury products from the Southern Seas and Indian Ocean. Around 250 CE two Chinese ambassadors visited Funan, the Malay Peninsula, and the Indonesian archipelago. In Funan, the ambassadors met an Indian diplomat. During the Southern Dynasties (420-589 CE), Funan sent 17 missions to China with commodities like incense, ivory and sandalwood stupas and statues, and glass vessels (Wang 1958: 51). Two Buddhist monks from Funan, expert translators of Sanskrit, moved to China. An office for Funan music was set up just outside Wu's capital Nanjing in 244 CE (Wang 1958: 35). Funan music was still played in China nearly 400 years later (Wang 1958: 41 note 44).

Several features of Funan described in Chinese sources hint at a close cultural relationship with Khmer culture. The *History of the Liang* says that "Several scores of families have a pond in common where they draw water" (Cœdès 1968: 59). It seems likely that these ponds were important socio-political units in ancient times. The Angkor kingdom intensified this system in the area north of the Tonle Sap (Vickery 1998: 19).

The *History of the Liang Dynasty* says that Funan had ships propelled by up to 100 paddlers (Wang 1958: 38). These were probably not meant for oceanic travel, but would have been suitable for the Mekong. Another source, *Nan Zhou Yi Wu Zhi,* described other, much larger sailing ships around the end of the third century, called *po,* perhaps from the Malay word for ship, *perahu* (Wang 1958: 38). Malayo-Polynesians may have connected the Funanese coastal settlements, creating a symbiotic relationship with the land dwellers.

Settlement Patterns in Funan

Funan inscriptions mention several settlements designated by the Sanskrit word *pura*, which usually meant a walled town or city with administrative functions. Óc Eo may have been known as *Samudrapura* ("City of the Sea", mentioned in inscription K.137) found in the delta. Funan-period inscriptions from the Delta mention two other *pura* but more than 20 outside the delta, suggesting that the majority of Funan's population lived upstream.

The discovery of Funan's palace would give us important insight into Funan's culture. Most scholars believe that the capital was at the inland edge of the Delta. The *Liang Shu* says the "enclosed settlement" (*pura/*capital?) of Funan was 500 *li* (200 kilometers) from the sea (Cœdès 1968: 37). This could refer to Angkor Borei or Ba Phnom (now known as Banteay Prei Nokor; Vickery 1998: 36-37), which are in southeast Cambodia. Another Chinese record says that the capital was once at *Temu*, but after that city was captured by Zhenla in the late sixth century, it moved to *Nafuna* (Naravaranagara; Cœdès 1968: 65). Two inscriptions from Angkor Borei (K.557 and K.600) imply that the last king of Funan lived there. Cœdès (1968: 68; 1943-46: 3) believed that Naravaranagara was Angkor Borei's ancient name. Vickery (1998: 45) agrees that Funan's capital must have been at Angkor Borei. Higham (1989: 252) calls Angkor Borei Funan's "pre-eminent centre". Whether Angkor Borei was always the capital of Funan, and what precisely the significance of the capital may have been for the people of Funan (i.e., how highly centralized Funan's government was), are vital questions awaiting further study.

The Archaeology of Óc Eo Culture

Óc Eo Culture was adapted to life in the swampy delta. Its people lived in dwellings built on stilts. Shellfish were a common source of food. More than 300 sites of this culture have been discovered in the Delta, and over 20 have been excavated. Several trading communities already existed in the Delta at the very beginning of the Protoclassic. At Gò Hàng for example, Indian beads were associated with a radiocarbon date of 54 BCE-130 CE. At Gò Tháp, a mound covering one hectare contained brick-lined pits, ashes, gold discs, and traces of wooden stilts with a radiocarbon date of 400-600 CE (Vo 2003). Some scholars inferred that ashes found in subterranean brick chambers are cremated human remains, but it is more likely that these were consecration deposits buried as part of rituals at the founding of temples (Ślączka 2007, 2011). This practice is known from Indian texts. The deposits found in the Mekong Delta are among the oldest examples known.

The most important site in the delta, Óc Eo, covers 450 hectares enclosed by five moats and four ramparts bisected by a canal. Remains of brick buildings on granite foundations may have been built in the fifth century, among the first brick structures built in Southeast Asia. Louis Malleret was the first archaeologist to conduct extensive research at this site, in 1944 (Cœdès 1947, Malleret 1959-1963). Óc Eo's inhabitants were employed in many specialized occupations using imported raw materials including various kinds of metal. Pottery-making was probably a full-time profession, judging from discoveries of kiln supports and potter's wheels (Malleret 1960: 11, 101, 127-131). Coins, some perhaps locally made, as well as imported examples, indicate the existence of a monetized economy. Óc Eo has yielded the largest number of glass beads recorded at any archaeological site in Southeast Asia (Bellina 2003), most if not all imported from India.

Numerous deposits of dammar (amber-like tree resin) were recovered, especially near the central canal. Some of this resin may have been used for boat caulking (Malleret 1960: 11, 85-87) but other varieties were extremely valuable in China as incense. Dammar was available in the Mekong hinterland. It was probably one of the important trade items which attracted traders to the delta.

Óc Eo may have been a centre of trade and industry, but scholars believe that the political capital may have been located at Angkor Borei, a large site (300 hectares) at the inland edge of the delta. Radiocarbon dates from Angkor Borei span the period from the fourth century BCE to the seventh century CE (Stark 1988: 194). The two oldest dated inscriptions in the delta, K.557 and K.600, carved in 611 CE, were found at Angkor Borei. Another inscription, K.53, dated 667 CE and found at the nearby sacred hill Phnom Da, suggests that Funan's last ruler lived in Angkor Borei in the seventh century (Vickery 1998: 45-46). Angkor Borei is surrounded by one wall, irregular in shape. Inside it are pools, canals, and at least 15 ancient structures. Its population has been estimated at 20,000 (Stark 2006a: 419). Angkor Borei was abandoned at the end of the Protoclassic, at about the same time as other sites of Óc Eo culture declined.

Pottery at Angkor Borei resembles that found at other parts of the Mekong Delta, especially the Vietnamese area, but is not closely related to contemporary sites in northwest Cambodia or northeast Thailand, where Khmer culture later became well developed (Stark 2006b: 100; Fehrenback 2009). One important variety found at Angkor Borei, Fine Buffware, was mainly used to make water ewers called *kendi.* This ware has been found at Óc Eo and other sites in the delta, and Trà Kiệu, central Vietnam (Glover and Yamagata 1994: 89). Similar kendis have been found in many later sites including Dvāravatī period sites in central Thailand, and in Indonesia and the Philippines (Miksic and Yap 1992). After the disappearance of Óc Eo culture, the main site of production may have been Pa-O in south Thailand (Srisuchat 2003). This distribution of this ware is sufficiently extensive to consider it a marker of a ceramic interaction sphere, comparable to bronze drums or *lingling-o* of the Preclassic and early Protoclassic. It may be considered one of Óc Eo culture's major legacies to later Southeast Asia.

Banteay Prei Nokor is northeast of the Mekong Delta, near the source of one of the small rivers which flow into the bay where Ho Chi Minh City is located. This site has "the most complete group of ruins probably of the Funan Period" (Briggs 1951: 53). In the Early Classic it became one of the biggest sites in Cambodia. At the nearby site of Prohear, archaeologists discovered the richest burials from the transitional period from Protoclassic to Early Classic of any site in Southeast Asia. Villagers reported finding almost 20 Đông Sơn drums there, and at least 79 gold and silver objects, mainly jewellery. Sources of gold are known in Cambodia, but it is suspected that Prohear like Óc Eo obtained most of its gold from abroad. One other site in this region yielded a similar quantity of gold: Giồng Lớn in Vietnam, where gold masks were found as well as beads and earrings (Reinecke et al 2009). Similar masks are found in Protoclassic Indonesia (Miksic 2011: 100-101).

Major sites of Óc Eo culture in the delta such as Óc Eo and Angkor Borei were linked by canals, almost certainly constructed to facilitate transport. Some of the canals were built around 2,000 years ago. Several networks were built in different parts of the Delta at different periods. Parts of the canal system at Angkor Borei began to deteriorate in the fifth century, but canals in the Óc Eo area were built in the late fifth and early sixth century. Possibly construction of Óc Eo's canals began simultaneously with the abandonment of the Angkor Borei canals, but it is premature to draw conclusions (Bishop et al. 2003; Bourdonneau 2003; Stark 2006b: 100; Manguin and Vo 2000).

The End of Óc Eo Culture

Funan sent embassies to China until the early seventh century; thereafter, no more. Not only were cities such as Óc Eo and Angkor Borei deserted; very few remains of any sort appear in the Mekong Delta during the next 1,000 years (Malleret 1962: 355). Both Funan the kingdom and Óc Eo culture came to a sudden and utter end. At the same time that Funan vanished, inscriptions record the erection of many *liṅgas* by rulers of Khmer polities north of the Dangrek Mountains. These have been interpreted as evidence of the rise of Zhenla, conqueror of Funan. Whereas Óc Eo religion was characterized by a range of Buddhist and Hindu deities, during the Angkorian period the rulers of the Dangrek area were devotees of a cult of the Śivaliṅga. The market economy of Óc Eo culture was replaced by a rigid agrarian bureaucracy.

Rather than a unified kingdom, recent interpretations of Chinese records conclude that "Water Zhenla" was a collection of warring kingdoms. Northwest Cambodia was divided into five principalities, four of which sent rival diplomatic missions to China in 638 CE (Vickery 1998: 19-21). Seventh-century Cambodian rulers competed for status by founding temples and reservoirs rather than acquiring wealth from trade and industry.

Modern Sambor Prei Kuk in northeastern Cambodia was the site of Īśānapura, which was probably given this name by Īśānavarman, who reigned from c. 616 to c. 635 CE, and left many inscriptions. His territory stretched from southeastern Cambodia to northeastern Thailand. He sent an embassy to China in 616. Īśānavarman thus lived at a time when the Chinese thought that Funan was conquered by Zhenla. His inscriptions suggest evolution rather than violence. They indicate that he established hegemony over strategic areas and appointed a son to rule in the west but there is no mention of an attack on the Mekong Delta.

If we discard conquest as the reason why Óc Eo culture vanished, what then explains the transfer of the center of power and people from the Delta to northern Cambodia? Malleret (1962: 355, note 4) believed that changes in the coastline had something to do with it. However, geomorphological research indicates that theories about rapid coastal change in historic times in Southeast Asia in general are not true (Miksic 1977; see also *supra*).

Mercantile factors could account for the collapse of what had been a thriving civilization, not only in the lower Mekong but across central Thailand and Burma. The breakup of a Mon thalassocracy may have coincided with the genesis of separate Mon and Khmer identities (Keyes 1976; Brown 1996: 39), and the end of symbiosis between the Mon-Khmer speakers and the Cam. Charles Higham suggested that when Funan became the main source of prestige goods from the west, the groups of the hinterland intensified the use of overland routes to the west (Higham 1989: 315). This may have undermined Funan to some extent, but the hinterland polities never became major trading centres.

During the Tang and Song Dynasties, Campā profited from trade with China. It is possible that one factor causing the disappearance of Óc Eo culture is that Cam and Malay sailors began to take new routes through the Straits of Melaka which reduced the role of portages across the Malay Peninsula. At the same time that Óc Eo culture disappeared, ports in the upper Malay Peninsula such as Dunsun also declined. Simultaneously ports along the Straits of Melaka became new centres of long-distance maritime trade. This represented a move to the heartland of Malay culture. Funan people do not seem to have been sailors; the maritime transportation network was probably operated by Malays, Javanese, and Filipinos, who were specialized sailors.

Why did the old symbiosis disappear? The Malays of the Straits of Melaka may have benefited from more efficient and intensive trade patterns which emerged during the fifth and sixth centuries, particularly after 581 CE, when

China was reunified under the Sui Dynasty. Meanwhile the Cam began to develop their own ports closer to China (which archaeologists have not yet studied intensively). These hypotheses however do not entirely explain why the old economic system disappeared. The effects of its disappearance were striking. No densely-populated cosmopolitan commercial zones appeared in Cambodia during the Angkor period. Coins were no longer used in Southeast Asia; Indonesia only developed its own coinage system 200 years later.

Historians have tended to favour narratives which emphasize dramatic struggles and reliance on external factors to explain the collapse of kingdoms. Chinese and later historians may have been mistaken in perceiving Funan's disappearance as the result of a clash between two civilizations, one in the lower Mekong, the other in the hinterland. It seems that in many cases, the decline of civilizations may have been due to internal rather than external factors. It may be more appropriate to view Funan's disappearance as a sign of a gradual shift in popularity from maritime trade in swampy lowlands to intensive agriculture in fertile plains. In the early seventh century, while Óc Eo culture still survived, the centre of political activity and settlement already had begun to shift into the hinterland. Inscriptions were thenceforth written not in Sanskrit, but in Khmer. Buddhism and worship of Hindu deities including Viṣṇu, Durgā, and Harihara were replaced by Śivaliṅga. This focus had previously been associated mainly with north Cambodia and the Dangrek Mountains. The "conquest" of Funan by Zhenla may not have been military but cultural. At the same time that the Mekong Delta was abandoned, the Khmer who lived in the vicinity of Cambodia's great lake created a new religious cult associated with Śiva, and a new irrigation system. The migrants from the Delta may have found the new ideology and agrarian lifestyle more congenial.

Although few scholars now believe that the deposed ruler of Funan fled southward and founded new empires such as Śrīvijaya (Vickery 1998: 6), the people of island Southeast Asia may have benefited from their experience as transport agents between Óc Eo and other proto-industrial cities of the Mekong Delta in developing the prosperous ports which later evolved in Java, Sumatra, and the Malay Peninsula.

Bibliography

Cœdès, George. 1954. *Inscriptions du Cambodge VI.* Collection de textes et documents sur l'Indochine, 3.6. Hanoi, Paris: École française d'Extrême-Orient.

Endnotes

1 According to Vietnamese archaeologists, sites related to the culture of Óc Eo in the Mekong delta appeared around 500 BCE. The oldest settlement in the *Óc Eo* plain is dated to 170 ± 40 BCE (Vo Si Khai 1997: 213).

2 The southernmost part of Vietnam consists of two deltas: Cửu Long or Mekong on the west, and Đồng Nai on the east. Twelve provinces in the Vietnamese portion of the delta are collectively known as Đồng bằng Sông Cửu Long, "Nine Dragon River Delta". Ho Chi Minh City is located on the Sai Gon River, a tributary of the Đồng Nai. Though not technically part of the Mekong delta, the Đồng Nai delta formed an integral part of Óc Eo culture.

3 On early Hanoi's importance, see Wang 1958. On the meaning of the term "interaction sphere" , see Miksic and Goh 2017b. On the South China Sea Sphere of Interaction, see Bellina 2018.

4 Khmer, Mon, and Vietnamese all belong to the language family known as Austroasiatic.

5 See Wang 1958: 48 for a list of Funan's exports to China.

5 | Early Inscriptions from the Mekong Delta

Kunthea Chhom,
Arlo Griffiths

Introduction

In this article, the region of the Mekong Delta is defined as covering eight provinces of present-day Vietnam, viz. An Giang, Bạc Liêu, Đồng Tháp, Lâm Đồng, Long An, Tây Ninh, Trà Vinh and Vĩnh Long, and six Cambodian provinces, viz. Kampot, Kandal, Kompong Speu, Prey Veng, Svay Rieng and Ta Keo.[1] The region has been inhabited since prehistoric times. Between the 3rd and 7th centuries CE, Chinese sources record the name of the region's polity as Funan.[2] Little is known with certainty about this Funan and the Funanese people. To the historian Michael Vickery (1998, 2003), Funan was 'a group of allied ports' (rather than a unified polity) the population of which was mostly Khmer in ethnic and linguistic terms.

Since the prehistoric period, the local population had probably practiced trade, more than agriculture. The most important trading centre was located at the site now known as Óc Eo (An Giang province, Vietnam) which was linked to a port on the coast and to the city of Angkor Borei by a system of canals. Angkor Borei (Ta Keo province, Cambodia), with its rich urban infrastructure, is believed to have been the Funanese capital.[3] Neither the ancient name of Óc Eo nor that of Angkor Borei is known with certainty from local inscriptions. However, the name Tamandarapura is found in four inscriptions, viz. K. 9 (639 CE, from Đồng Tháp), K. 604 (627 CE, Kompong Thom), K. 1235 (627 CE, Ta Keo) and K. 1426 (7th century CE An Giang). In a recent article, Dominic Goodall (2019), on the basis of K. 9, K. 604 and K. 1235, proposes that this Tamandarapura may have been located in the Mekong Delta.[4] The mention of the same name in the Sanskrit part of the newly discovered stela K. 1426 seems to support his hypothesis. The stela was found during excavations at Óc Eo archaeological site in October 2019. While *pura* means 'city' in Sanskrit, the element *tamandara* is hard to explain in Sanskrit or Khmer and may perhaps reflect an indigenous language of the Austronesian family: in Malay, for instance, *taman darat* could mean 'flatland garden', and it is likely that a very similar expression also existed in the ancient Cham language.[5] So the name may be an indication that the ethnolinguistic profile of the ancient Mekong Delta, and the polity of Funan, included other people beside Khmers.

Around the 3rd century CE, an increased influx of Indian cultural facets can be observed in the region's archaeological record. From the 5th century onwards, this influence becomes visible more clearly and through a greater variety of evidence: the Funanese rulers started to use

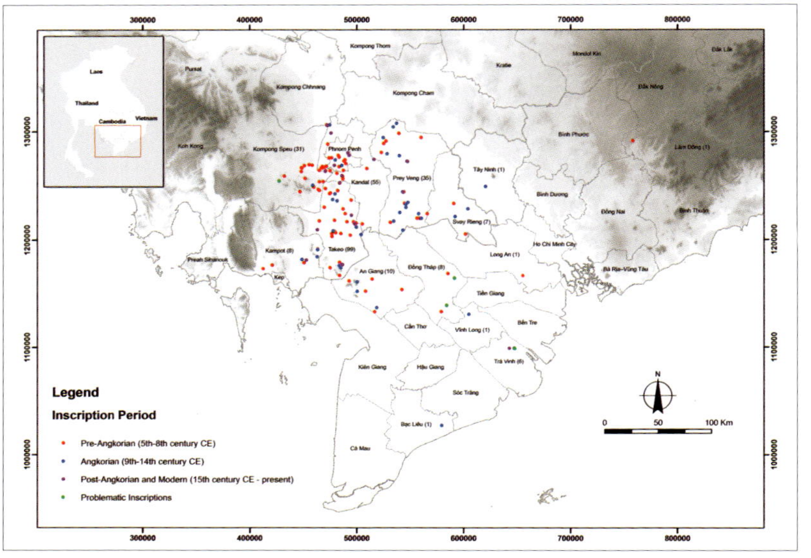

Map prepared by Socheat Chea showing the provinces of Cambodia and Vietnam that make up the Mekong Delta region and the findspots of pre-Angkorian, Angkorian, post-Angkorian and modern inscriptions.

Sanskrit in their inscriptions, worship Brahmanical and Buddhist deities, build temples, claim Indian roots and apply an Indian model of government, etc. The Sanskrit inscription K. 5 (5th century CE) of Prasat Pram Loveng (Đồng Tháp province),[6] for example, praises King Guṇavarman as "a moon" of the lineage of the legendary Indian Brahmin named Kauṇḍinya. The purpose of the inscription was to record the installation of a statue of the Vaiṣṇava deity Cakratīrthasvāmin, worshiped by the king.[7]

In the 7th century CE, the name Zhenla replaces that of Funan in the Chinese records.[8] The number of inscriptions noticeably increases and it is possible to argue that increased epigraphic production reflects significant social changes at the local level; the changed perception among Chinese visitors would then reflect these changes. The inscriptions of King Bhavavarman I and of his brother, King Citrasena-Mahendravarman, rarely contain a date or other information sufficiently clear to locate and date these kings with any precision. Nevertheless, the provenance of their inscriptions suggests that they lived in cities relatively farther inland.[9]

The first capital city to be mentioned in inscriptions is Īśānapura, founded by King Īśānavarman I (616-637 CE). It is identifiable as the present-day Sambor Prei Kuk, about 280 kilometers north of Angkor Borei, far away from the Mekong Delta. Consequently, trade relied more on the Mekong river and its tributaries than on the sea, and agriculture (mostly wet and dry rice-planting) played a more important role than in the Funanese period. Whereas the Chinese records describe Zhenla as a vassal state which overthrew its suzerain Funan, the local epigraphical and archaeological evidence suggests a rather smooth transition from Funan to Zhenla.[10] In whatever way the entities named Funan and Zhenla by the Chinese are to be mapped onto the political actors and polities about which we read in local inscriptions, the Chinese sources refer to them as successive kingdoms, naming many kings. Jayavarman (c. 470-514? CE) and Rudravarman (514?-539? CE) are two Funanese kings in the Chinese sources who can be identified in local inscriptions (Pelliot 1903: 270-271). A strong indication of Funan to Zhenla continuity is found in the Sanskrit inscription of Kdei Ang (Ba Phnom, Prey Veng province), dated 667 CE (K. 53). It records a high-ranking official family serving five kings including the last king of Funan, Rudravarman, and the Zhenla kings Bhavavarman I, Citrasena-Mahendravarman, Īśānavarman I, and Jayavarman I.

The 7th century CE was also the time when the writing of inscriptions not only in Sanskrit, but also in vernacular languages, started to spread throughout Southeast Asia. In the 5th and 6th centuries CE, a nascent epigraphic tradition made exclusive use of Sanskrit. From this early phase of history in the Mekong Delta, a total of six inscriptions (K. 5, K. 40, K. 875, K. 924, K. 1270 and K. 1515) have so far been discovered. Later, when the vernacular Khmer language starts to be used, it is for recording details of religious endowments (donations of land, servants, etc.), often following after a passage in Sanskrit with invocations of gods plus eulogies and genealogies of kings or other members of the social elite.

To date, 150 inscriptions datable from the 5th to the 8th century CE have been discovered in the Mekong Delta, if we take the region to comprise the aforementioned eight Vietnamese and six Cambodian provinces. The inscriptions are composed in Sanskrit, Old Khmer, a combination of both the languages, and much more rarely in a Middle Indo-Aryan ('Prakrit') language that is quite similar but not identical to Pali – quite possibly the canonical language of the Buddhist Saṁmitīya school;[11] and only once in Pali proper. In **table 1** below, they are presented with their inventory ("K.") number, a chronological indication and their language profile.

Table 1

Century CE	Language(s)	Items	K. numbers
5th	Sanskrit	2	5; 875
5th-6th	Sanskrit	4	40; 924; 1270; 1515
6th-7th	Khmer; Sanskrit; Sanskrit+Khmer;	17	25; 41; 46; 48; 548; 559; 710; 764; 785; 810; 918; 939; 1003; 1032; 1215; 1216; 1413
7th	Khmer; Sanskrit; Prakrit; Sanskrit+Khmer; Sanskrit+Prakrit	83	1; 8; 9; 13; 21; 22; 24; 28; 30; 37; 38; 44; 49; 50; 51; 53; 54; 55; 60; 66; 73; 74; 76; 77; 78; 79; 80; 416; 422; 423; 424; 426; 427; 483; 493; 561; 562; 563; 582; 599; 600; 652; 654; 666; 670; 709; 711; 712; 719; 748; 755; 759; 761; 762; 765; 784; 787; 788; 820; 858; 860; 877; 884; 903; 910; 940; 946; 1004; 1028; 1235; 1239; 1247; 1266; 1267; 1322; 1352; 1396; 1419; 1426; 1429; 1455; 1460; 1465
7th-8th	Khmer; Sanskrit; Pali; Prakrit; Sanskrit+Khmer;	22	3; 6; 7; 11; 419; 560; 664; 689; 789; 811; 851; 956; 1010; 1031; 1148; 1176; 1254; 1275; 1298; 1330; 1355; 1412
6th-8th	Khmer; Sanskrit; Sanskrit+Khmer	12	421; 796; 1147; 1261; 1416; 1484; 1511; 1512; 1534; 1537; 1553; 1560
8th	Khmer; Sanskrit; Sanskrit+Khmer	10	18; 20; 29; 154; 1029; 1214; 1236; 1241; 1242; 1451

Out of these 150, no less than 134 inscriptions cluster in or around the 7th century (including 53 inscriptions that we can date only approximately to the 6th-7th, 7th-8th or 6th-8th centuries). Among the 134, 74 are wholly formulated in Khmer, 29 are in Khmer preceded by a portion in Sanskrit (see table 1 above), while 27 items are exclusively formulated in Sanskrit, two exclusively in Prakrit (K. 820 and K. 1330), one in Sanskrit combined with Prakrit (K. 1455), and only one in Pali (K. 1355). Most of them belong to the reign of two prolific kings, namely Īśānavarman I (616-637 CE) and Jayavarman I (654-694 CE).

King Īśānavarman's own royal inscriptions (mostly in Sanskrit) are generally found in the vicinity of his capital Īśānapura (Sambor Prei Kuk), whereas the inscriptions discovered in the Mekong Delta and some northeastern provinces of Thailand were issued by influential persons but not by the king himself. This may suggest that the king, ruling in the North, had established governors who ruled in his name in the Delta region.[12] For example, the recently discovered inscription K. 1419 from Kompong Speu records the installation of several divine images and donations of paddy-fields and cattle by a courtier namely Vrau Etta, after first praising King Īśānavarman as the king of kings ruling a kingdom that extends as far as the ocean (*samudraparyanta-*).[13]

Under the reign of King Jayavarman I, the Khmer-language inscriptions, including those formulated with portions in Sanskrit and in Khmer, come to outnumber the single-language Sanskrit records. Unlike his predecessor's records which were concentrated around his capital Sambor Prei Kuk, King Jayavarman I's inscriptions have been found in the northern provinces as well as in the Mekong Delta. This wide distribution makes it difficult to determine where his centre of power was situated, let alone to identify his capital. Michael Vickery (1998: 350-352), noting especially K. 44 from Kampot, suggested that the king may have ruled in the South while benefiting from good connections also in the North.

After his death in circa 694 CE,[14] there follows a century with only few inscriptional records. One of the rare inscriptions of the 8th century is K. 904 (713 CE, Sanskrit and Khmer) from Siem Reap mentioning Queen Jayadevī, King Jayavarman I's daughter, as ruling in the Angkor region.[15] In addition, three inscriptions of the second half of the 8th century are attributed to a king known to scholars as Jayavarman 'I^{bis}'. Two of them, viz. K. 1236 (763 CE, Sanskrit) and K. 1254 (7th-8th century CE, Sanskrit) are from the Mekong Delta province of Ta Keo,[16] whereas K. 1417 (probably 775 CE) comes from the more northerly province of Kompong Thom. The distribution of these inscriptions conforms to some extent with a gradual shift of the economic and political centre from the South to the North, which began around the end of the 6th century and seems to have continued in the 7th and 8th centuries, before being completed in the early 9th by King Jayavarman II and his successors.

Language, Script and Decoration

As shown in **Table 1**, four different languages were used in the inscriptions: Sanskrit, Old Khmer, Pali and Prakrit. Unlike in some other regional epigraphic cultures (such as the one of Arakan and the one of Tamil Nadu) where different scripts were used to inscribe different languages, only a single script was used during most of the history of Cambodian epigraphy.[17] The script is commonly referred to in modern publications as "Pallava" or "Pallava-Grantha". Arlo Griffiths (2014: 54) has argued to call it "Late Southern Brāhmī" (4th/5th century through to about 800 CE).[18] The forms of the letters show a high degree of consistency even between sites separated by long distances. The inscription K. 9 (639 CE), from the Vietnamese province Đồng Tháp, for instance, bears letters that are distinctly similar to those of K. 749 (674 CE) from Siem Reap province, far to the North, in Cambodia, and K. 505 (639 CE) from the even more northerly province of Prachin Buri, in Thailand. We are tempted to speculate that this consistency may be due to a very small circle of scribe-artisans having been involved in the production of these inscriptions.

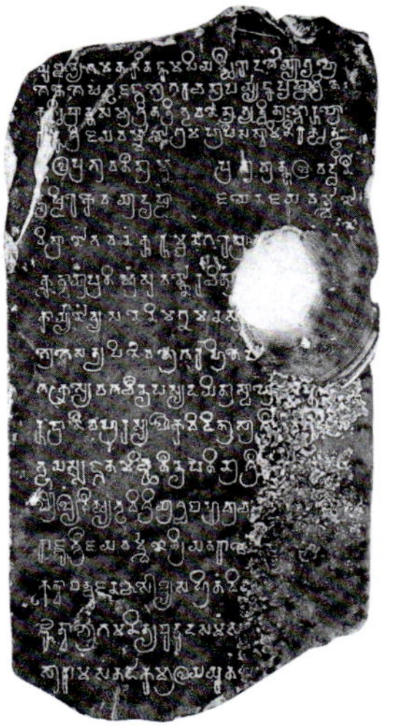

Fig. 1 *The EFEO estampage n. 1135 for inscription K. 875. National Museum of Cambodia, Phnom Penh (ក 23077).*

Some inscriptions reveal an attempt at particularly ornate writing, that may be called calligraphic (K. 8, K. 423, K. 875, K. 1254, K. 1270 and K. 1515);[19] others show a style that may be called cursive (K. 73, K. 424, K. 548, K. 561, K. 1247 and 1266); while others still seem to reflect a sloppy engraver (K. 77, K. 654 and K. 670). See **figs. 1, 2 and 3**.

A remarkable characteristic of the pre-Angkorian inscriptions is the frequent presence of floral decoration on the top of the engraved stelae. Such decoration is discernible, for instance, in K. 9, K. 426, K. 563, K. 940, K. 1148, K. 1352 and K. 1426. The stela K. 940, on the other hand, contains a figure of Śiva's vehicle, the bull (often, though wrongly, called Nandin in modern publications[20]) on a lotus above the text. K. 9 presents an exceptional decoration where a lotus is carved on the top, another lotus in the middle of the Sanskrit text, while a horizontal string of pearls separates the text in Sanskrit from the one in Khmer (**fig. 4**).

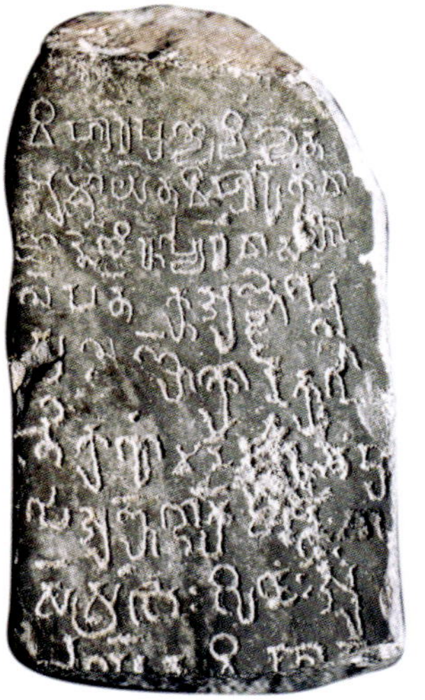

Fig. 2 *Stela of Angkor Borei, Ta Keo Province, inscription K. 1266. Photo Ka7 01. National Museum of Cambodia, Phnom Penh (ក 2058).*

The layout of the inscriptions itself reflects the language(s) they deploy: texts written in columns are in Sanskrit (or Pali or Prakrit) whereas the Khmer texts occupy the full breadth of each inscribed surface. This layout reflects the fact that while the Khmer texts are composed in prose (infra p. 107, Contents), the Sanskrit (Pali and Prakrit) ones are in verse. One exception is the Sanskrit-Khmer inscription K. 493:[21] its Sanskrit text consists of seven stanzas in the *anuṣṭubh* meter followed by a prose portion of four lines and a half. The stanzas are divided in columns whereas the prose is written with left and right justification (**fig. 5**). If the four and a half lines had been intended to be in verse, they would have been inscribed with a space between the verse quarters.

Materials and Object Types

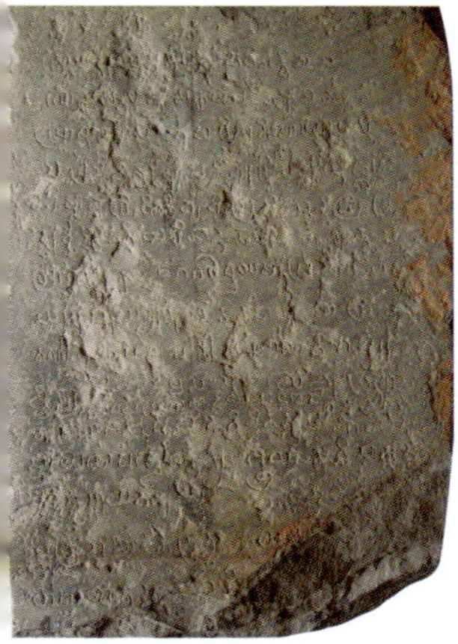

Fig. 3 *Stela of Vat Sre Ampil, Kandal province, inscription K. 77. Photo AMPP 001817. National Museum of Cambodia, Phnom Penh (ក3131).*

Three exceptional items are a text engraved on gold leaf (K. 1330, 7th-8th century, Long An), a gold coin (K. 1322, 7th century, Ta Keo) and a gold plate (K. 1451, 8th century, Lâm Đồng), but the overwhelming majority of the early inscriptions of the Mekong Delta are engraved on stone artifacts, about 80% of them fashioned from sandstone and about 20% from schist. A brief survey of the whole Khmer epigraphic corpus shows that inscriptions in sandstone far outnumber those in schist, presumably because the former material was not only easier to carve but also more widely available.[22] Almost all the inscriptions that are engraved on schist originate from the delta, suggesting that quarries of schist existed in the region.

Regardless of the type of stone, the majority of the texts are inscribed on doorjambs, the architectural element of Cambodian temples typically chosen as support for inscription. Some of the stones originally carved as doorjambs have subsequently been reused as lintels in ancient temples (e.g. K. 40, 5th-6th century?, Ta Keo) or as thresholds in modern houses (e.g. K. 875, 5th century, Ta Keo; see **fig. 1**).[23] A fragment of an inscription that may date to the same period (K. 1270, 5th-6th century, Ta Keo), whose original use can no longer be discerned, was reused as a conduit for libations (a so-called *somasūtra*) in a brick temple that was erected not more than one or two centuries later

Fig. 4 *Stela from Phú Hựu, Đồng Tháp province, inscription K. 9. Museum of Vietnamese History, Hồ Chí Minh City (BTLS 5548).*

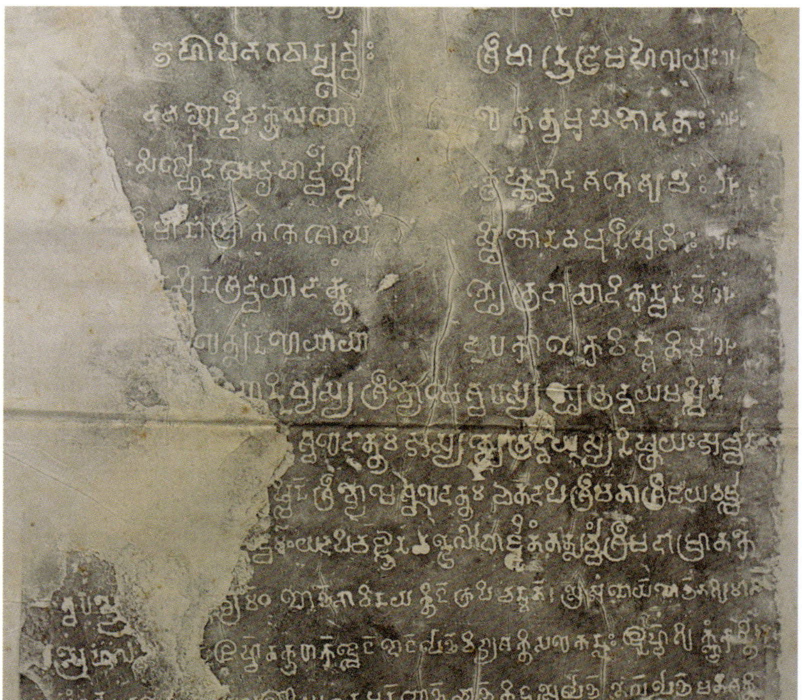

Fig. 5 *The middle segment of EFEO estampage n. 250 for inscription K. 493.*

(**figs. 6 and 7**). The other common object type is the freestanding stela, several of them carved not only with text but also with decorations (see above). Rarer object types include pedestals (e.g. K. 755, 7th century, Ta Keo and K. 884, 7th century, Trà Vinh), slabs of stone (K. 1216, 6th-7th century, Ta Keo and K. 956, 7th-8th century, Prey Veng), a Buddha statue (e.g. K. 820, 7th century, Kompong Speu), a grinding stone (K. 1215, 6th-7th century, Ta Keo) and a baked clay tablet (K. 1355, 7th-8th century, Ta Keo).

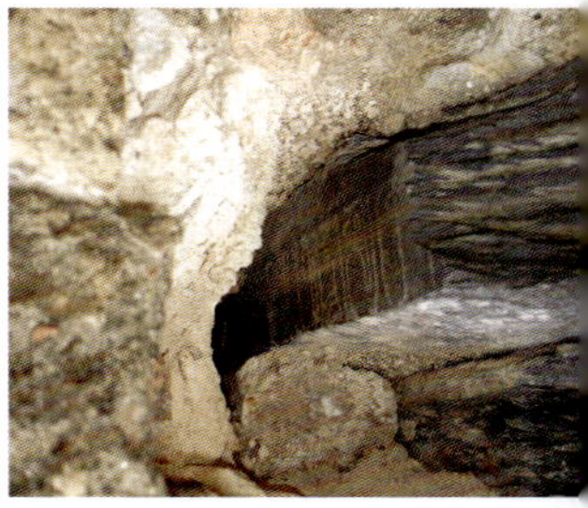

Fig. 6 *Inscription (K. 1270) on a fragment of a schist artifact at Prasat Preah Ko, Ta Keo province. Photograph Dominque Soutif.*

Contents

As mentioned above, the Sanskrit inscriptions (as well as those formulated in Prakrit and Pali), with only one partial exception (K. 493), are in verse and the Khmer ones in prose. The inscriptions are relatively short: the Sanskrit texts have an average of five stanzas and the Khmer ones do not on average extend over more than ten lines. The entirely Sanskrit inscription K. 483 with its 29 stanzas and the double-language inscription K. 1247 containing 45 lines in its Khmer text are the longest texts in this corpus.

Generally, the Sanskrit inscriptions open with an invocation to one or more gods, give a eulogy and genealogy of kings or other members of the social elites, and declare a work of merit (installing a divine image, etc.), whereas the Khmer texts give details of religious endowments (donations of land, servants, etc.) as already mentioned (see p. 57).[24] Often, at the end of the inscriptions, a formula of malediction and benediction is found. One of the earliest examples of a praise of a king is found in the Sanskrit inscription of Prasat Pram Lveng (K. 5, see above p. 104). In addition to the purity of lineage, King Guṇavarman was eulogized for his intelligence and valor. At the end of the inscription, the warning that misuse of the foundation shall be punishable in hell (stanza XI) opposed to the promise that proper use shall be rewarded by attaining the supreme abode of Viṣṇu and felicity (stanza XII) are the first formulae of malediction and benediction recorded to date:

dattaṁ ya[d] guṇavarmmaṇā bhagavate dharmmārtthinā śaktito
viprair bhāgavatair anātha-kṛpaṇais tat-karmma-kārais tathā
tat sarvvair upayujyatāṁ samayato yair anyathā bhujyate
yujyantāṁ narake yamasya patitās te pañcabhiḥ pātakaiḥ / / XI / /
Abhivarddhayatīha yo mahātmā bhagavad-dravyam idaṁ guṇāhva[yas](ya)[25]
*sa tu yat-ku[*śa*]laṁ labheta viṣṇoḥ paramaṁ prāpya padaṁ mahad yaśaś ca*
/ / XII / /

'Whatever is given to the Lord (*bhagavant*, i.e. Viṣṇu) by [King] Guṇavarman, with Dharma in view, in conformance with [his] capacity, is to be enjoyed in accordance with the rules by the Bhāgavata Brahmins (or the Bhāgavatas and the Brahmins), those who are poor and without protection as well as those who officiate there. Those who

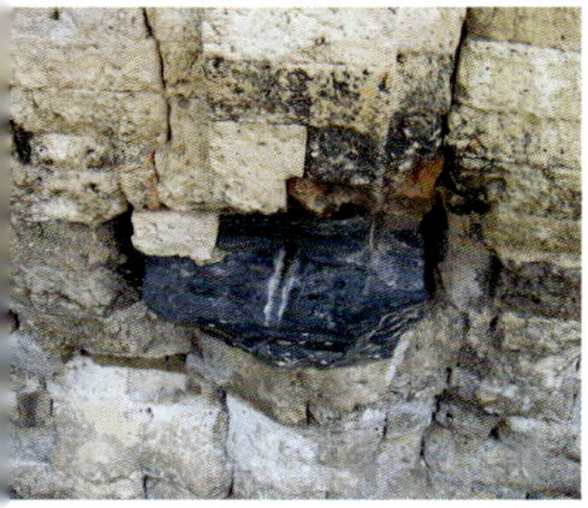

Fig. 7 *Reuse of the same fragment at Prasat Preah Ko as a conduit for libations. Photograph Dominque Soutif.*

otherwise make use of it must, [being considered as] fallen because of the five cardinal sins, be brought to Yama's hell.'

'May any great soul who increases this property of the Lord, [donation] of the one named Guṇa[varman], having attained the supreme abode of Viṣṇu, obtain the same merit and great glory as he.'

To illustrate the way language and contents go hand-in-hand, we now furnish two summaries of complete texts:

- K. 1426, from Óc Eo, 7th century with one face in Sanskrit, one in Khmer
  - Face A contains seven Sanskrit stanzas in *anuṣṭubh* meter. The first is an invocation to the Buddha. Stanzas II and III praise the fieriness and righteousness of the ruling King Jayavarman I. The *raison d'être* of the inscription is mentioned in stanzas IV and V: the grant of King Jayavarman I to a monastery called Candanavihāra to fund the annual procession of the image of the Buddha on the full moon day of the month of Vaiśākha (April-May). Stanza VI records the donation of slaves, cows, buffaloes, gardens, fields, servants, etc., to the image. The last stanza states that the protection of the god's property shall be the responsibility of the Governor of Tamandarapura.
  - Face B is a fourteen-line text in Khmer. It echoes the Sanskrit text vis-à-vis the annual procession of the Buddha's statue of Candanavihāra on the full moon day of Vaiśākha as an order of king Jayavarman I. It also provides details of the management of the wealth of the monastery including servants, slaves, cows, buffaloes etc. The last two lines warn that those who flout the order of the king shall be punished.

- K. 600, from Angkor Borei, entirely in Khmer (612 CE)[26]
  - The text consists of a list of servants,[27] cattle, buffaloes, goats, coconut trees, paddy fields donated by Poñ Uy, Jaṁ Añ and Mratāñ Antāra to four gods, namely Kpoñ Kamratāñ Añ, Kamratāñ Teṁ Kroṁ, Mahāgaṇapati and Maṇīśvara.

In the context of enumerating the servants and the tracts of land which were offered to gods, a dozen Khmer texts (K. 1, K. 9, K. 22, K. 28, K. 44, K. 49, K. 66, K. 79, K. 424, K. 600, K. 785, K. 884) contain numerous honorific titles of personal names, many of which seem not to be Khmer and may be of Malay or Cham origin.[28] Among them, the titles coined with the term *pu* "lord" are particularly common and intriguing. While the title *pu yāñ* could be fully Cham (its close English translation would be 'Lord God'), the compound *pu caḥ añ* contains two Khmer terms: *caḥ* 'old' and *añ* 'I'. The latter appears to be a term of address to a Buddhist monk. A variant of this title, *po cas*, is found in K. 884, an inscription engraved – curiously, upside-down, see **fig. 8** – on the pedestal of a Buddha statue.[29] The text which was edited by Cœdès (1954: 69) as *po cas sūryyadat* should instead be read as *po cas āryyadat* "Venerable Āryadatta". In addition to the titles *pu yāṅ* and *pu caḥ añ* which can be understood with some certainty, many titles such as *pu neṅ*, *hap añ* and *kvaḥ añ* still defy interpretation in terms of meaning and linguistic origin. A detailed study of the titles is a desideratum as it may help to reveal which other ethnolinguistic groups were in contact with the Khmer in the delta region and to learn more about the nature of such contact, whether religious, economic or otherwise.

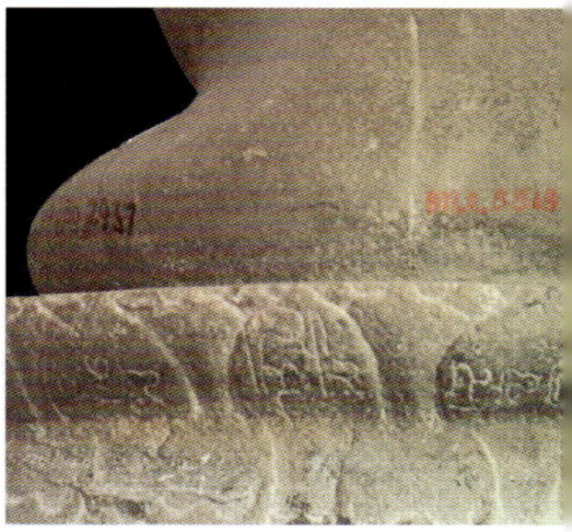

Fig. 8 *Inscription K. 884 on the pedestal of the Buddha statue. Photo 6707, rotated 180°. Museum of Vietnamese History, History Museum, HCMC (BTLS 5519/ Kp 30, 3).*

The Delta in later times

The 9th century CE marks the conventional date for the beginning of the Angkorian period. Khmer kings established their capital city in the region known as Angkor (Siem Reap province, Cambodia) and it remained there until the fall of the empire in the 14th century (except for a shift that lasted only about 20 years to the city called Koh Ker to the northeast of Angkor, at the behest of King Jayavarman IV). Although the capital city was thus moved to the northern region, the Mekong Delta was still important and the north-south connectivity even seems to have been reinforced. The production of inscriptions was one of the major concerns of the ruling kings. About 700 items have been identified as belonging to the period between the 9th and the 12th centuries CE for the Khmer kingdom as a whole. While the distribution of the inscriptions is densest in the north, the production of inscriptions continued in the southern region but at a noticeably reduced intensity. To date, 74 inscriptions have been discovered in the following provinces of the Mekong Delta: An Giang, Bạc Liêu, Vĩnh Long, Tây Ninh, Trà Vinh, Đồng Tháp, Long An, Kampot, Ta Keo, Kompong Speu, Kandal, Prey Veng and Svay Rieng. Three provinces, Bạc Liêu, Vĩnh Long and Tây Ninh seem to correspond to an area of territorial expansion of the Khmer kingdom, as no inscription from the pre-Angkorian period was ever found there. As mentioned in **table 2** below, 29 out of the 74 inscriptions are dated and 45 are datable with some accuracy.

However, after the reign of King Jayavarman VII (1181-1218 CE), there was a sharp decrease in the production of inscriptions. Only about two dozen inscriptions were issued during the period of a century that corresponds to the reigns of the last four Angkor kings. Only two of them, K. 549 and K. 756, datable to the 13th century, are from the Mekong Delta whereas others have been found in the northern region, especially in Siem Reap.

Century CE	Language(s)	Items	K. numbers
9th	Sanskrit; Sanskrit+Khmer; Khmer	15	14; 15; 36; 42; 45; 47; 56; 57; 69; 70; 71; 655; 853; 861; 1370
9th/10th	Sanskrit	1	35
10th	Sanskrit; Khmer; Sanskrit+Khmer;	28	2; 4; 17; 19; 43; 52; 58; 61; 62; 67; 68; 72; 111; 425; 556; 653; 735; 760; 849; 854; 859; 862; 863; 950; 1397; 1398; 1422; 1555
10th-11th	Khmer	6	492; 911; 1258; 1274; 1328; 1401
11th	Khmer; Sanskrit+Khmer; Sanskrit	6	31; 33; 34; 63; 865; 913
11th-12th	Khmer; Sanskrit+Khmer;	2	516; 736
12th	Sanskrit; Sanskrit+Khmer; Khmer	11	12; 32; 418; 830; 850; 852; 864; 912; 1036; 1439; 1523
13th	Khmer	2	549; 756
9th-13th	Sanskrit+Khmer; Khmer	3	518; 1399; 1400
16th	Khmer+Pali; Khmer	2	27; 39
17th	Khmer	2	65; 75
19th	Khmer; Thai	7	23; 26; 59; 804; 1211; 1212; 1213
20th /Modern	Khmer; French	22	10; 747; 763; 771; 803; 1376-1392
Unknown	Unknown	7	16; 64; 112; 698; 758; 798; 919

Table 2

Interestingly, K. 549 which was found in the vicinity of Angkor Borei, alludes to the last king of Funan, namely Rudravarman, having installed a statue called Harikamvujendra, which seems to mean something like 'Hari (i.e. Viṣṇu) as King of Cambodia'.[30]

In the post-Angkorian period (15th-18th centuries), Cambodia shrank in the almost permanent turmoil because of wars with the neighboring kingdoms, especially Campā (which was eventually integrated into Vietnam) and Siam.[31] Consequently, the capital city was moved from Angkor in the North back to the Delta region, on the site of the current capital Phnom Penh. The practice of inscribing texts on stone continued, but on a much smaller scale than during the Angkorian period and was almost entirely limited to what is now Siem Reap province. Between the 16th to the 18th centuries, kings, members of the royal family, courtiers and common people, now Theravāda Buddhists, commissioned inscriptions in Khmer in the originally Vaiṣṇava Angkor Wat temple to commemorate their pious acts of freeing slaves, ordaining their relatives, installing divine statues and donating various objects, etc. As far as we know, only four inscriptions of this period were found in the Mekong Delta. In the modern period (19th century-present), about forty stone inscriptions are recorded, roughly half of them now from the Delta. They are generally short Khmer texts of Buddhist faith.

Acknowledgements

The authors are collaborating on the study of inscriptions from Cambodia and Vietnam in general, and on those of the Mekong Delta in particular, in the context of the project 'The Domestication of "Hindu" Asceticism and the Religious Making of South and Southeast Asia' (DHARMA), funded from 2019 to 2025 by the European Research Council (ERC) under the European Union's Horizon 2020 research and innovation programme (grant agreement no. 809994). On the project, see https://dharma.hypotheses.org. We thank Dominic Goodall, Nicolas Revire and William A. Southworth for their comments on the first draft of this paper.

Bibliography

Bhattacharya, Kamaleswar. 1964. 'Hari Kambujendra.' *Artibus Asiae* 27 (1/2): 72-78.

Bourdonneau, Éric. 2003. 'Culturalisme et historiographie du Cambodge ancien: A propos de la hiérarchie des sources de l'histoire khmère.' *Moussons* 7: 39-70.

———. 2007. 'Réhabiliter le Funan: Óc Eo ou la première Angkor.' *Bulletin de l'École française d'Extrême-Orient* 94: 111-58.

Chhom, Kunthea. 2018. *Le rôle du sanskrit dans le développement de la langue khmère: une étude épigraphique du VIe au XIVe siècle*. Phnom Penh: Sāstrā.

———. 2019. 'សិលាចារឹកវត្តគីរីស្តេចគង់ K. 1419 សេចក្តីប្រែនិងសេចក្តីអត្ថាធិប្បាយ [silacārik vatt girī stec gaṅ' K. 1419 secktī prae niṅ secktī atthādhippāy] Edition and Annotated Translation of K. 1419.' *Kambuja Suriyā* Special volume 2019: 35-54.

Chhom, Kunthea, Dominic Goodall, and Arlo Griffiths. 2025. 'A Buddhist Procession Inaugurated in a Seventh-Century Inscription from Óc Eo (K. 1426) and the Ancient Toponym Tamandarapura'. The Journal of the Siam Society 113: 141-64.

Cœdès, George. 1931. 'Études cambodgiennes XXV: Deux inscriptions sanskrites du Fou-nan.' *Bulletin de l'Ecole française d'Extrême-Orient* 31: 1-12.

———. 1937–1966. *Inscriptions du Cambodge*. 8 vols. Collection de textes et documents sur l'Indochine 3. Hanoi; Paris: Imprimerie d'Extrême-Orient [vol. I]; EFEO.

———. 1968. *The Indianized States of Southeast Asia*. Edited by Walter Francis Vella. Translated by Susan Brown Cowing. The University Press of Hawaii. Honolulu.

Dalsheimer, Nadine. 2001. *L'art du Cambodge ancien: Les collections du musée national de Phnom Penh*. Paris: École française d'Extrême-Orient; Magellan.

Dimitrov, Dragomir. 2016. *The Legacy of the Jewel Mind: On the Sanskrit, Pali, and Sinhalese Works by Ratnamati*. Series Minor 82. Napoli: Università degli studi di Napoli "L'Orientale", Dipartimento Asia Africa e Mediterraneo.

Gerschheimer, Gerdi & Dominic Goodall. 2014. '« Que cette demeure de Śrīpati dure sur terre... ». L'inscription préangkorienne K. 1254 du musée d'Angkor Borei.' *Bulletin de l'École française d'Extrême-Orient* 100: 113-46.

Goodall, Dominic. 2015. 'Les influences littéraires indiennes dans les inscriptions du Cambodge: l'exemple d'un chef-d'œuvre inédit du VIIIe siècle (K. 1236).' In *Migrations de langues et d'idées en Asie*, edited by Jean-Louis Bacqué-Grammont, Pierre-Sylvain Filliozat, and Michel Zink, 67-80. Paris: Académie des inscriptions et belles-lettres.

———. 2018. 'Rudragaṇikās: Courtesans in Śiva's Temple? Some Hitherto Neglected Sanskrit Sources.' *Cracow Indological Studies* 20 (1): 91-143.

———. 2019. 'Nobles, Bureaucrats or Strongmen? On the "Vassal Kings" or "Hereditary Governors" of Pre-Angkorian City-States: Two Sanskrit Inscriptions of Vidyāviśeṣa, Seventh-Century Governor of Tamandarapura (K. 1235 and K. 604), and an Inscription of Śivadatta (K. 1150), Previously Considered a Son of Īśānavarman I.' *Udaya: Journal of Khmer Studies* 14: 23-85.

———. 2020. 'Nandirāśi's Pāśupata Monastery: K. 1352 (590 śaka), a non-royal Sanskrit inscription in Kampot from the reign of Jayavarman I.' In *LIBER AMICORUM Mélanges réunis en hommage à / in honor of Ang Chouléan*, edited by Grégory Mikaelian, Siyonn Sophearith, and Ashley Thompson, 325-43. Paris, Phnom Penh: Péninsule / Association des Amis de Yosothor.

Griffiths, Arlo. 2005. 'La stèle d'installation de Śrī Tribhuvaneśvara: une nouvelle inscription pré-angkorienne du musée national de Phnom Penh (K. 1214).' *Journal Asiatique* 293 (1): 11-43.

———. 2014. 'Early Indic Inscriptions of Southeast Asia.' In *Lost Kingdoms: Hindu-Buddhist Sculpture of Early Southeast Asia*, 53-57. New York, United States of America: The Metropolitan Museum of Art.

Griffiths, Arlo & D. Christian Lammerts. 2015. 'Epigraphy: Southeast Asia.' In *Brill's Encyclopedia of Buddhism*, edited by Jonathan A. Silk, Oskar von Hinüber, and

Vincent Eltschinger, 1: 988-1009. Leiden: Brill.

Griffiths, Arlo & William A. Southworth. 2007. 'La Stèle d'installation de Śrī Satyadeveśvara: Une Nouvelle Inscription Du Campā Trouvée à Phước Thiện.' *Journal Asiatique* 295 (2): 349-81.

Jacques, Claude. 1972. 'Études d'épigraphie cambodgienne: VIII. La carrière de Jayavarman II.' *Bulletin de l'École française d'Extrême-Orient* 59: 205-20.

Pal, Pratapaditya. 2009. 'Revisiting the "Vṛṣa/Nandi" Issue.' In *Prajñādhara: Essays on Asian Art History, Epigraphy and Culture in Honour of Gouriswar Bhattacharya*, edited by Gerd J.R. Mevissen and Arundhati Banerji, 413-17. New Delhi: Kaveri Books.

Pelliot, Paul. 1903. 'Le Fou-nan.' *Bulletin de l'École française d'Extrême-Orient* 3: 248-303.

Skilling, Peter. 2015. 'The Circulation of Artefacts Engraved with "*Apramāda*" and Other Mottos in Southeast Asia and India: A Preliminary Report.' *Annual Report of the International Research Institute for Advanced Buddhology at Soka University for the Academic Year 2014* 18: 63-77.

Tournier, Vincent. 2023. 'A 4th/5th-Century *Sūtra* of the Saṁmitīya Canon? On the so-Called 'Continental Pāli' Inscription from Devnimori.' In *Proceedings of the Third International Pali Studies Week – Paris 2018*, edited by Claudio Cicuzza, 403-70. Bangkok; Lumbini: Fragile Palm Leaves Foundation; Lumbini International Research Institute.

Vickery, Michael. 1998. *Society, Economics and Politics in Pre-Angkor Cambodia: The 7th-8th Centuries*. Tokyo: The Centre for East Asian Cultural Studies for Unesco, The Toyo Bunko.

———. 2003-2004. 'Funan Reviewed: Deconstructing the Ancients.' *Bulletin de l'École Française d'Extrême-Orient* 90-91: 101-43.

———. 2010. 'Cambodia and Its Neighbours in the 15th Century.' In *Southeast Asia in the Fifteenth Century: The China Factor*, edited by Geoff Wade and Sun Laichen, 271-303. Singapore; Hong Kong: NUS Press; Hong Kong University Press.

Endnotes

1 In the Pre-Angkorian period (5th-8th century CE), Cambodian inscriptions are found in only four Vietnamese provinces. However, the territory covered by inscriptions includes three more Vietnamese provinces in the Mekong Delta region during the Angkorian period (9th-14th century CE), viz., Bạc Liêu, Vĩnh Long and Tây Ninh (see p. 63). It may be noted that, depending on the context, we use the word 'Cambodian' to designate either the contemporary nation state or in a historical sense as the English equivalent of the indigenous term Kamvujā, in much the same way as speaking about medieval 'France' implies a rather different polity with a rather different territory from that of contemporary France.

2 The names 'Funan' and 'Zhenla' (see below) are found exclusively in Chinese records. They do not figure in any inscriptions.

3 Some scholars, for instance G. Cœdès (1968: 36-37, 68) and C. Jacques (1972: 213), believed Vyādhapura ('Hunter-ville'), which may have been located in Ba Phnom district (Prey Veng province, Cambodia), to have been the Funanese capital city. However, the poor archaeological vestiges at Ba Phnom compared to those of Angkor Borei cast doubt on this hypothesis. E. Bourdonneau (2007: 146) proposes that Angkor Borei and Óc Eo were the capitals in tandem.

4 The "K." numbers cited here and throughout this article are those of the inventory of inscriptions of the Khmer cultural sphere, begun more than a century ago by G. Cœdès on behalf of the EFEO and still maintained by that institution. The current version of the inventory can be found at https://cik.efeo.fr/.

5 The word *taman* is not recorded in any known Old Cham inscriptions, but this is not necessarily meaningful, as we have only very few Cham records, with a very limited vocabulary, for this early period, and even for later centuries, the Cham inscriptions preserve only a small fraction of the entire lexicon that must have been in active use. The word is also not recorded in dictionaries of modern Cham, but this is not necessarily significant either, as the word may have existed in Old Cham and since been lost.

6 The edition of the inscription by G. Cœdès (1931) has now been improved and furnished with an English translation. Along with the other inscriptions mentioned here, this will be made available in due course in the online epigraphic database of the DHARMA project.

7 The term 'king' is our interpretation; the inscription states that Guṇavarman was the son of a king.

8 According to the Chinese records, Zhenla was divided into two realms: Water Zhenla (associated to the Mekong Delta) and Land Zhenla (associated to the area north of the delta up to the later Wat Phu in the South of modern Laos). The designation Zhenla was still in use by the Chinese envoy to Cambodia Zhou Daguan in 1296 CE.

9 The reign of Bhavavarman I was in the late 6th century and that of Citrasena-Mahendravarman in the late 6th or early 7th century. For discussion of the dates of the rulers of Zhenla, see Vickery 1998: 22. The inscriptions which belong to Bhavavarman's reign were found in the central and Western parts of the kingdom, whereas those mentioning Citrasena-Mahendravarman were discovered in the Northern and Eastern parts.

10 Vickery (2003: 135-136) holds that 'the Chinese interpretation of the Funan-Chenla transition was simply wrong, no doubt because

the Chinese, mainly interested in trade and ports, were poorly informed about internal politics.' However, Bourdonneau, in his article on the '*hiérarchisation*' of the sources of Khmer history (2003), offers important qualifications to this statement and cautions not to dismiss the Chinese records as merely sinocentric and lacking any value as historical documents.

11 On the possibility that the Prakrit language in question is a trace of the presence of monks of this school in the Mekong Delta, see Skilling 1999: 176. For an up-to-date review of the canonical language and extant works of the Saṁmitīya school, see Dimitrov 2016 and Tournier 2023.

12 On the role of such governors, see Goodall 2019.

13 The inscription contains the intriguing term *suvarṇabhūmi* 'gold-earth' which has stirred up quite a bit of interest in Cambodia recently. For its edition and translation, see Chhom 2019: 35-54.

14 The date of the end of Jayavarman I's reign is controversial. Cœdès (1968: 72) first states that the king's reign ended after 690 CE, probably basing himself on the Sanskrit-Khmer inscription K. 1004 from Tuol Kuhear, Kandal province, which mentions the name Jayavarman and the date 612 Śaka (= 691 CE). However, in his 'Genealogy of the Kings of Cambodia' at the end of the same book, he gives '657-681 CE' as the dates of the king's reign. The year 681 CE is the conversion from 602 Śaka which is the date of the Khmer inscription K. 451 from Siem Reap province. This text refers to King Jayavarman I by his posthumous name Śivapura; hence Cœdès' later assumption in his genealogy that the king could not have been alive after 681 CE. Recently discovered inscriptions which belong to the king's reign suggest that the king might have ruled from 654 to 694 CE. For detailed discussion of the dates of King Jayavarman I, see Chhom et al 2025.

15 In addition to the royal inscription K. 904, some inscriptions of the 8th century CE are non-royal and have been discovered in the southern provinces of Cambodia. One of them, K. 1214, was published by A. Griffiths (2005).

16 They were published by D. Goodall (2015) and G. Gerschheimer & D. Goodall (2014) respectively.

17 It is to be noticed that in the reign of King Yaśovarman I (889-c. 915 CE), a new script of the Siddhamātr̥kā type was introduced in the Sanskrit epigraphic compositions to coexist with the usual script of the Khmer called Kambujākṣara 'script of the Kambujas', the identification of which is controversial (see Chhom 2018: 25, n. 3). The new script is used in at least 27 inscriptions; most of them belong to the king's reign. Griffiths (2014: 54) points out that the Siddhamātr̥kā script is closely linked with the dominion of the Pālas, who ruled a large area of northeastern India from about the mid-eighth century onward and was also used to write Sanskrit in Java in the 8th and 9th centuries.

18 P. Skilling (2015: 65) has proposed "Southeast Asian Brāhmī" as an alternative.

19 For a discussion of calligraphic writing in early Southeast Asia, see Griffiths & Southworth 2007: 352-353.

20 On this issue, see Pal 2009.

21 To date, the corpus comprises three Sanskrit inscriptions which are considered to contain some prose: K. 365 (5th century, Champassak, Laos), K. 493 (657 CE, Prey Veng) and K. 162 (8th century, Kompong Thom).

22 We thank Chhunteng Hun for pointing out to us that schist is a very challenging material (personal communication, January 2020). While a scribe could easily make a beautiful line to draw the shape of a letter on sandstone, he would need more patience to carve letters into schist, hole by hole, because it disintegrates so easily into flakes.

23 Goodall 2015: 67-68.

24 A. Griffiths and Ch. Lammerts (2015: 988) list the subject-matter of the inscriptions of Southeast Asia as follows: 1. the date of the work of merit; 2. the name(s) of the donor(s); 3. the name(s) of the recipient(s) of the gift; 4. a list of the property transferred; 5. the motivation for the gift; and 6. an admonition warning others against nullifying or injuring the gift.

25 We tentatively restore the last syllables *yasya*, and translate accordingly, but other restorations are imaginable.

26 It is the earliest known dated Old Khmer inscription.

27 Among the servants were three female dancers with names ending in *-senā* 'army', viz. Priyasenā, Samarasenā and Madhurasenā. Their names suggest that they were probably courtesans. For a discussion of the courtesans' names, see Goodall 2018: 99-103.

28 For further analysis of such titles, see Vickery 1998: 220-223.

29 For a description of the seated image and a brief discussion of the inscription, see Revire in this (cat. 123).

30 The inscription is believed to be a late Angkorian attempt to replicate an early pre-Angkorian text (Vickery 1998: 45). The large (1.8 m) statue in question represents an eight-armed deity carved with exceptional delicacy and power. It is on display at the National Museum of Cambodia (inv. no. 1635). See Bhattacharya 1964 and Dalsheimer 2001 (no. 30).

31 For details on the history of 15th-century Cambodia, see Vickery 2010.

6 | Buddhist icons of the Delta

Pierre Baptiste

It is not an easy task to evoke the development of Buddhism in the Mekong Delta, a region of nearly 39,000 km^2 essentially characterized by vast marshy plains, punctuated by slightly elevated areas where agglomerations have been concentrated, probably since the earliest days of human occupation. What is more, the impressive agricultural work developed since the reunification of Vietnam, transforming these vast spaces into the rice granary of the country, considerably disturbed large Delta tracts. Intensive rice cultivation, supporting a massive increase in the population to 17 million by the 2011 census, has generated significant urban spread precisely in areas archaeology would probably have found most fruitful. However, many authors, since the beginning of the 20th century, have studied the subject and provided various answers on which we will base this brief introduction. But our approach, will start from the artifacts and archaeological documents themselves which, like the clues in a police investigation, will allow us to sketch the outline of a landscape whose contours can be defined in the light of the more general context of process of absorption of Indic religious and artistic conceptions in emerging states along the Asian southern rim.

The first clues in our investigation: epigraphic evidence. It will be recalled here that it was the inscriptions – dedicatory texts written in Sanskrit and/or in Old Khmer on the piers of temples, on stelae, bricks or votive plaques associated with religious foundations – which made it possible to write the early days of the history of ancient Cambodia and that of other peoples of Southeast Asia, by associating them with texts devoted to foreigners in classical Chinese literature. It is clear that these epigraphic testimonies are not abundant in the region.

Of the 1,360 inscriptions recorded from ancient Cambodia, only 33 have been found in the Mekong Delta stricto sensu, that is to say in territories now in Vietnam[1]. Moreover, many of these are only fragments in a few lines. In this group, 13 inscriptions date with certainty to the period that interests us and range between the 5th and the 8th century (K1; K3; K5 to K9; K419; K884; K918 and 919; K924 and K1330). They are mainly Brahmanic, sometimes alluding, more or less explicitly, to Śaiva or Vaiṣṇava foundations. A single inscription (K. 884) appears on a clearly Buddhist artwork, the Buddha of Trapeang Veng from the village of Nhị Trường, district of Cầu Ngang, province of Trà Vinh. But the text only mentions the donor or the recipient of the gift (?), a certain Sūryadatta with an obscure title (Cœdès 1954: 69, Guy 2014: 99). Nothing about the historical or even religious context can be drawn from this.

In this very limited corpus, only the inscription of Gò Xoài, Long An province, can, in fact, be considered as a real epigraphic testimony to the presence of Buddhism in the Mekong Delta. Preserved at the Long An Provincial Museum, this beautiful inscription, carefully written in five lines on a thin gold leaf once folded in four, has been published many times because of its exceptional character (Lê Xuân Diệm; Đào Linh Côn; Võ Sĩ Khai 1995; Skilling 1999 p. 171-87; Skilling 2002: 169-72; Lê Thị Liên 2005; Tingley: 2009: 166-7). It was found with a set of 26 small plaques with various iconographies, visibly associated with a foundation deposit (Lê Thị Liên 2005: 148). We will only deal here with the major aspects of this inscription allowing us to enrich our more general discussion on the developments of Buddhism in the Mekong Delta. The first part of the text is indeed the famous formula *'ye dhammā'*, which recalls the notion of causality as it was expounded by the Buddha. Dating from around the 7th century, the inscription written in a Pāli form may have come from a Theravādin context. However, Peter Skilling, who has devoted a large number of works to these inscriptions, reconciles this first part of the text with the same formula written on the back of the Buddha unearthed in 1935 Tuol Preah Theat (a small pre-Angkorian site in the Kompong Speu province in Cambodia) and now in the Guimet museum (Baptiste et Zéphir 2008, p. 27-28). From a palaeographic and linguistic point of view, the two inscriptions are indeed apparently very close and dated to around the 7th century. Above all, they differ from the inscriptions in Pāli in that they present elements of Sanskritization which make them a form of prakrit. If one is to believe Peter Skilling, indeed, 'the language of the inscriptions on the Gò Xoài gold plate and Tuol Preah Theat Buddha image reveals the presence of a Buddhist school other than the Theravāda. What school cannot be said, but that more than one school was active in the region is not surprising' (Skilling 2002, p. 172).

In summary, the inscription of Gò Xoài can be considered as part of a Buddhist foundation deposit, from a significantly different tradition from Theravāda. It was carefully arranged in an architectural structure of which only the brick foundations have been preserved, almost square in plan (15.2 by 15.5 m), which could be accessed by steps in the centre of the east side (Lê Thị Liên 2005: 148): very probably a stupa whose bricks on the upper levels were undoubtedly reused long after the monument was abandoned, perhaps in the early days of the Vietnamese presence in the region. Peter Skilling moreover evokes the ritual dimension of some of these *'ye dhammā'* verse inscriptions in their association with ceremonies for the foundation and consecration of *caitya* and Buddhist images of all kinds (Skilling 2002, p. 173. See also Skilling in Baptiste and Zéphir (Eds) 2008, p.108). This implies, in the case of the Gò Xoài inscription, that it could have been arranged in this sense in association with the other repoussé gold plaques unearthed on the same site.

Moreover, it is not uninteresting to compare the Gò Xoài *'ye dhammā'* inscription with those unearthed in the surroundings and beyond that date back to the same chronological period. Their evocation provides a more general panorama of ritual practices participating in traditions common in the larger sector of continental Southeast Asia in the period of interest. Thus, a Buddhist inscription in Pāli , notably containing the '*ye dhammā*' verse was found in Angkor Borei, Ta Keo, Cambodia (Skilling 2002, p. 159), written in a so-called 'Pallava' scripture on a brick that Peter Skilling also compares to those found in Thailand in the Dvāravatī art of Phra Pathom Chedi of Nakhon Pathom, and on the back of a standing Buddha statue at Wat Mahathat in Ratburi (Baptiste and Zéphir (Eds) 2008, p. 108-9). The links between the pre-Angkorian city of Angkor Borei and the sites of the Mekong Delta have been highlighted for a very long time (see Stark 1991-2001 and 2003 and Baptiste 2021). Eric Bourdonneau more recently proposed a particular link between the two cities in his essay devoted to the 'Rehabilitation of Funan' (Bourdonneau 2007: 146). It is in this perspective that we will compare the Buddhist statuary unearthed in the Mekong Delta to the pieces found in the vicinity of Angkor Borei and more generally in the southern part of Cambodia.

As for the early days of Dvāravatī art, it is evident that it offers a number of points of comparison with the works unearthed in the Mekong Delta (see Dupont 1955). It is regrettable that the only other '*ye dhammā*' inscription to have been found in the territories corresponding to present-day Vietnam, further north than the Mekong Delta, in Cam territory, has been lost (Skilling 2003: 285). Be that as it may, a large Buddhist network was loosely woven between the Mekong Delta, the region of Angkor Borei and the cities of Dvāravatī. We will find these links again by studying the remains of the statuary.

If we ignore the content of the K. 924 inscription, a fragment of which was discovered in 1936 in Tráp Đá (An Giang province), ten kilometers northeast of Óc Eo (Malleret 1959a: 110 and Malleret 1963: 309; Dupont 1955: 16), George Cœdès was able to relate its writing to the famous stele of Tháp Mười (K. 5). Although it has no Buddhist references, it is interesting to specify that this venerable stele emanates from an important site of the Mekong Delta, Tháp Mười, which has yielded several important Buddhist remains dating back to the Funan period; we will soon come back to this. In many ways, if we are to believe the epigraphists, these two inscriptions can be linked to another one, found a little further north, in present-day Cambodia, beyond the current border between Vietnam and Cambodia, in the ruins of the Vat Bati temple (Ta Keo province) where this stela was reused. The Sanskrit text, dated to the 5th century *śaka*, (K. 40, see Cœdès 1931: 8) presents a brilliant homage to the Buddha, to his victory, to the worship of relics and to the three jewels: the Buddha, the Law (Dharma) and the Community (Saṅgha): 'This master whose holy relics, left in view for the production of the happiness of creatures, still cause the happiness of everybody today' (Cœdès 1931: 11).

To this homage responds the eulogy of Rudravarman (c.514-39) and his father Jayavarman (c.484-514), considered by many historians to be the last two kings of Funan. Admittedly, the content of the inscription remains very incomplete. But its Buddhist character is undeniable, as is its clear association with King Rudravarman, introduced as 'extremely devoted to Dharma'. We know, moreover, that the names of these last two kings of Funan appear in Chinese dynastic chronicles, of the 6th century, under the transcription 闍耶跋摩 Sheyebamo and 留陁跋摩 Luotuobamo. This is why we shall now follow this direction to find our next clues.

It will be useful to recall here that the Chinese tradition of the reigning dynasty taking responsibility for compiling the historical documents of the previous dynasty has long been an inexhaustible source of information for historians of the Chinese world and its margins. At the end of the 19th century and the beginning of the 20th century, the translation of these more or less explicit mentions in these texts enabled researchers to reconstruct the early stages of the history of certain peoples of South Asia that had regular relationship with the empire of China, in particular through the system of tribute regularly sent by the sovereigns pledging allegiance, in an often symbolic way, to the son of Heaven. The very name of Funan 扶南 comes from this literature which refers to it between the 3rd and 7th centuries CE. Fortunately, the French sinologist Paul Pelliot (1878-1945) gathered the passages devoted to this region of the world that he could find in the Chinese chronicles and translated them in 1903 in a remarkable article, soberly entitled 'Le Fou-Nan' (Pelliot 1903), yet unmatched to this day. In addition to a lot of information on the daily life of its inhabitants, one finds here information on customs, laws, rulers, and religion. In this regard, we can quote the passage specifying, in the Liang Shu 梁書 (*History of Liang*, 502-57) compiled at the beginning of the 7th century, that the inhabitants of Funan adore 'the spirits of the sky [Brahmanism]. Of these spirits of the sky, they make bronze images; those with two faces have four arms; those with four faces have eight arms. Each hand holds something, sometimes a child, sometimes a bird or a quadruped, or the sun, the moon'. No doubt, as epigraphy and archaeology testify today, Funan was first and foremost a Hindu kingdom. However, Buddhism is not absent from these relationship with China. Thus, the same source informs us that King Jayavarman (Sheyebamo) sent an embassy to the Chinese ruler Qi Wudi 齊武帝 (483-93) and that a few years later, in 503, he offered to the emperor Liang Wudi 梁武帝 (502-49) 'an image of the Buddha made in coral' (Pelliot 1903: 269), before his successor, King Rudravarman, proposed in 539 CE a holy relic of the Buddha in the form of a hair of exceptional length (Pelliot 1903: 271). As we can see, the relics of the Buddha were appreciated, and we find, in this Chinese mention, an echo of the stele of Vat Bati and the cult of relics mentioned in it.

Finally, Chinese chronicles even attest to the presence of Funanese Buddhist monks, at the court of Qi and Liang, translating sutras into Chinese, in particular in an office named 'Funan Bureau' (Funanguan 扶南館) (Pelliot: 284-5), which affords strong testimony to the liveliness of the Buddhist communities of the Mekong Delta in the 5th and 6th centuries. If some of these translator monks seem to originate from Funan, such as Saṅghapāla who made a large number of translations between 506 CE and 521 CE (Pachow 1958: 205), others like Paramārtha were Indians who lived in Funan and went to China in the same circumstances. In the notice dedicated to the monk Saṅghapāla in the *Xu Gaoseng Zhuan* 續高僧傳 'Continued Biographies of Eminent Monks' compiled in the 7th century under the Tang but including many biographies dating back to the time of the Three Kingdoms and Six Dynasties (220-580), we learn that the texts he translated were essentially devoted to Mahāyāna Buddhism (Pachow 1958: 205).

However, if we are to believe the Chinese pilgrim Yijing 義淨 who travelled in these regions from 671-95 CE, Buddhism, once flourishing there, had by then completely disappeared: 'People there worshiped very much the *devas* [Brahmanism]. Then the law of the Buddha flourished and spread. But today an evil king has completely destroyed it, and there are no more monks at all' (Pelliot 1903: 284). Is it possible to see there, as George Cœdès envisioned, a link between this disappearance of Buddhism and the coming to power of new Hindu rulers, from a more northern origin, replacing Funan by the name of Zhenla 真腊 in Chinese Sources (Cœdès 48: 129)? In this perspective, the chronological indices at our disposal would invite us to conceive of a relatively late development of Buddhism in the history of Funan, corresponding to the reigns of the last two rulers (late 5th-6th century), a rather ephemeral development which would have experienced a rapid decline, or even a violent disappearance during the integration of Funan into the Khmer kingdom of Zhenla, if we are to believe Yijing. Or, if we are to believe Michael Vickery, this could have occurred during the dynastic continuity which marks the passage, in Chinese annals, from Funan to Zhenla (Vickery 1994). It's not impossible. However, some Buddhist sculptures discovered in the Mekong Delta seem to date stylistically to the middle, or even the end of the 7th century. Perhaps it is appropriate to relativize this assertion.

We must now rely on new clues to illustrate the fragile elements that epigraphy brings us. These are the Buddhist works themselves, unearthed in the Mekong Delta. We therefore benefit from a very exceptional situation to which few sites in Southeast Asia can be compared. On the one hand, it is the very precise inventory that Louis Malleret carried out in the 1940s, which he scrupulously recorded the results of in the various volumes of *L'Archéologie du delta du Mékong*. But it is also, on the other hand, the extraordinary work carried out from the second half of the 1970s and continued to this day by Vietnamese archaeologists among whom Ms Lê Thi Liên can be considered as the leader. This enormous task was enriched by the contribution of Pierre-Yves Manguin, Vo Sĩ Khài and Dào Linh Côn within the framework of the Franco-Vietnamese mission 'Archaeology of the Mekong Delta' under the aegis of the French School of the Far East (EFEO) and the Institute of Social Sciences of Ho Chi Minh City. In parallel and in the continuity of the work conducted by Pierre Dupont on pre-Angkorian sculpture (Dupont 1955: 189 ff.), Louis Malleret has indeed carried out on this subject a very detailed synthetic study which will serve here as a basis. This is based on a double analysis. The first is geographic and fits into his meticulous inventory of sites in the Mekong Delta, which he classifies by major geographic areas: the Transbassac, the Cisbassac. His second approach to the works is mainly based on modes of dress. We can add a stylistic analysis to this that can be completed both by the discoveries that have taken place since the end of the war in 1975, and by a vision better known today of the broader context of Buddhism in Southeast Asia between the 5th and 7th centuries (Malleret 1963: 173-187).

Since we are dealing with the testimonies of a religion which, by nature, was an import, we will briefly mention, in the preamble, the few pieces which precisely appear to be of foreign origin. Unearthed by Louis Malleret on the Óc Eo site, they were studied on numerous occasions by this scientist and Vietnamese archaeologists (Malleret 1960a: 201-212; Malleret 1960b: pl. LXXXIV-LXXXV) in that they appeared as eloquent testimony to the links that this culture had been able to forge with the West and the Far East. If we can hardly go into Malleret's analysis of the small bronze stele, unfortunately very eroded, depicting a Buddha seated with his legs folded and dressed in a monastic robe apparently covering both shoulders, with symmetrical folds in a way he saw as connected with the art of Gandhāra, we can add, however, that this small sculpture is very similar to pieces transported over long distances by pilgrims. We would not be surprised if it had travelled from Gandhāra or Central Asia along the Silk Road from China, before reaching the Mekong Delta. The same could be said of the small head known as the 'Gandhāran Buddha' found in a rock shelter on Mount Ba Thê, near the main Óc Eo site, the dating of which is still as difficult today as it was in 1960. In our opinion, this work like the previous one, probably testifies more to the adaptation of the Buddhist iconographies of Gandhāra and Central Asia by the China of the Six Dynasties, and their transfer from China to the coasts of Vietnam, than to direct contacts with Western India, Pakistan and Afghanistan. Among these Indo-Gandhārian iconographies adopted and adapted in China, the most famous is undoubtedly the gilded bronze Buddha from the Avery Brundage collection, dated 338 CE and kept in the Asian Art Museum in San Francisco (see Rhie 1999: 133-, fig. 2.26abc; fig. 2.28 a, b; fig. 2.32h), or the Jingchuan Xian 涇川縣 Buddha (Gansu, China) discovered in 1975/6 and remarkably studied by Marylin Martin Rhie (Rhie 2010: 29 sqq,

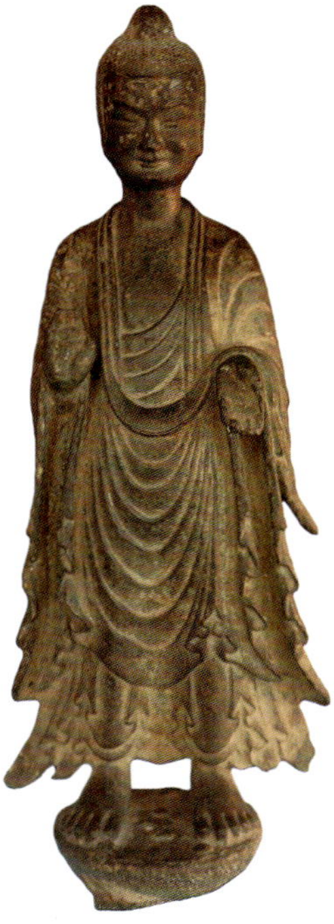

Fig.1 *Chinese, Wei dynasty standing Buddha, bronze, from Vọng Thê, Thoại Sơn, An Giang province, 6th century, An Giang provincial Museum.*

pl.I and fig. 1.1). But probably even more interesting is the bronze image of the Chinese Buddha found in Óc Eo (notice 58, see Malleret 1960a: 202-8 and Malleret 1960b: pl. LXXXV) in which Malleret saw a work dating from the Northern Wei period 北魏 (386-534 CE) but which we agree today to relate to the art of Northern Qi 北齊 (550-77). It was in 1979 that Vietnamese archaeologists also found a second piece of Chinese origin, this time indeed a Northern Wei Buddha, now kept in the An Giang Provincial Museum (Lê Xuân Diệm 1995: 284) (Fig. 1).

The earliest evidence of the adoption of Buddhism in the region and perhaps even throughout the Indochinese peninsula to have been produced locally, is in our opinion, the impressive pillar unearthed in 1994 at the Mount Gò Ông Địa (Mount of the god of the Soil) in the village of Lạc Quới, Tri Tôn district, An Giang province (Fig. 2). This small hillock is one of the few elevations that continue to Phnom Ba Thê, the Phnom Bayang massif in Cambodia, the last buttress of the Damrei mountains. Now lying in the entrance courtyard of the An Giang Provincial Museum, this granite bas-relief of very rough appearance but of undeniable power, was studied by Ms. Nguyễn Thị Tú Anh who has shown how its iconography is part of a tradition at the transition between aniconism and the first representations of the Buddha, as they appear in India in the art of Amarāvatī in the 2nd century of our era, and which possibly dating from the 3rd-4th centuries. The particular proportions of the figures and the rustic appearance of the highly expressive sculpture are reminiscent of early Śrīkṣetra Pyu art (see Gutman & Hudson 2012). The large pipal leaf evokes the Bodhi tree (*Bodhivṛkṣa*), under which the Buddha attained Awakening. The pillar surmounted by the Wheel of the Law (*Dharmacakrastambha*) recalls the Buddha's first sermon in the deer park of Sārnath and, if we are to believe the interpretation proposed by Ms. Nguyễn Thị Tú Anh, the lower register represents the teaching of the Doctrine to his mother, which the Buddha made in the Heaven of the Thirty-three Gods (Trāyastriṃśa).

To tell the truth, this pillar, the use of which has yet to be determined (an element of a portal/toraṇa, balustrade/vedikā, column bordering an entrance door or a pillar supporting a wheel of the Law...), is the only architectural fragment that can truly be linked to a Buddhist monument that once stood in the region. All the other remains – wood and stone statuary – are, at best, associated with brick foundations whose superstructures have been levelled and which archaeologists hesitate to identify as 'tombs', 'temples', or 'stūpas', to which are sometimes added wooden pillars whose initial use is not always clear. Like Anna Aleksandra Ślączka (Ślączka 2011), we would, however, like to propose the hypothesis that small fragments of gold sheet are elements of the foundation deposits of Buddhist and Hindu structures. These were unearthed in 1982-3 in Nền Chùa (Hòn Đất district, Kiên Giang province), in 1982, 1993 and 1996 in Gò Tháp (Tân Kiều village,

Tháp Mười district, Đồng Tháp province), in 1985 in Đá Nổi (Thạch Đông village, Tân Hiệp district, Kiên Giang province) and especially in Gò Xoài (Long An province) of which we spoke above. The Buddhist character of the architectural remains of Nền Chùa and Gò Xoài is evident. We can in particular interpret the brick structures with a square plan, unearthed at lower levels in the central part of the remains, which are sometimes described as 'tombs' by archaeologists, as chambers for foundation deposits and/or for relics (Lê Thị Liên 2005). Among many examples, we can compare them with the structures unearthed on the site of Nāgārjunakoṇḍa stupa (Andhra Pradesh, India), dating from the 3rd to 4th centuries and that of the 6th century Khin Ba in Śrīkṣetra, central Myanmar (Guy 2014: 78-81, cat. 26-27). In Malleret's time, one could still see some architectural remains. In Trung Điền, for example, the little Buddha comes from a place where Malleret could still make the following observations: 'The sanctuary [a small Christian church] is established on a mound strewn with large bricks which seems to correspond to the site of an old Khmer building'. So it is for the Buddha of Hiếu Tử we shall study later: 'A piece of slab which seems to correspond to half of an ablution tank which remained in the state of a rough outline was lying in the enclosure of the pagoda and would come from a mound located to the east of the enclosure where the sanctuary stands'. Today, the extensive scale of rice cultivation in the Delta no longer allows such observations.

But despite this gradual erasure, the Buddhist statuary unearthed in the Delta since the beginning of the 20th century confirms our point convincingly. The variety of sites in which Buddhist images have been found testifies to the wide spread of Buddhism throughout the Delta, a spread which also appears to have been more abundant than further north, along the coasts of Vietnam, or more upstream along the Mekong in present-day Cambodia. Be that as it may, it is certain that these images of Buddhas and Bodhisattvas in stone and wood are found along the coasts of the Delta, from the bay of Rạch Giá to Cape Vũng Tàu as well as along the banks of the Mekong and its outlets, the Sông Hậu, the Vietnamese continuation of the Bassac and the Cổ Chiên, Hàm Luông and Mỹ Tho rivers. Whether it spread from India or China, or from both of these inputs, Buddhism arrived by water. Some parts of the Delta seem to have been particularly active, such as the present province of Trà Vinh – the ancient Preah Trapeang of the Khmers – where many Buddhist pagodas are still concentrated today and where the modern districts of Trà Cú and Cầu Ngang have delivered the most numerous statuary testimonies.

The stylistic approaches of Pierre Dupont (1955: 189), Louis Malleret (Malleret 1963: 173-87), Jean Boisselier (1966: 262) and Lê Thị Liên (in Guy 2014: 118-9), based on the iconography, the costume, the position of the Buddha or the place of discovery, demonstrate above all a wide variety of production in a chronological framework that is nevertheless relatively limited (the 6th and 7th centuries, essentially). To those we can add a more global

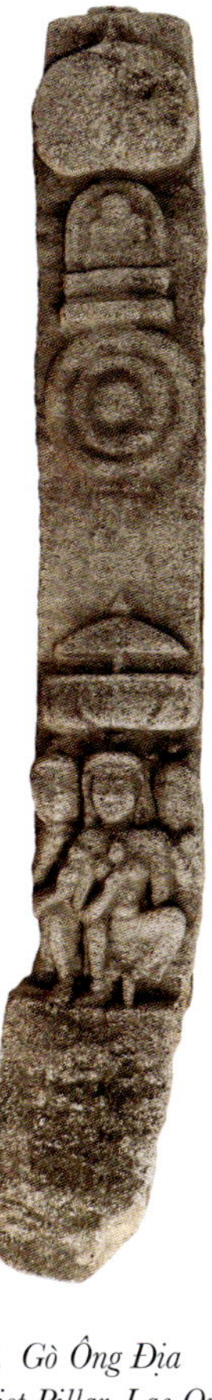

Fig. 2 *Gò Ông Địa Buddhist Pillar, Lạc Quới village, Tri Tôn district, An Giang province (H. 238 x 30 x 34 cm), granite, c.4th century (?), An Giang Museum: BTAG. 2773/D*

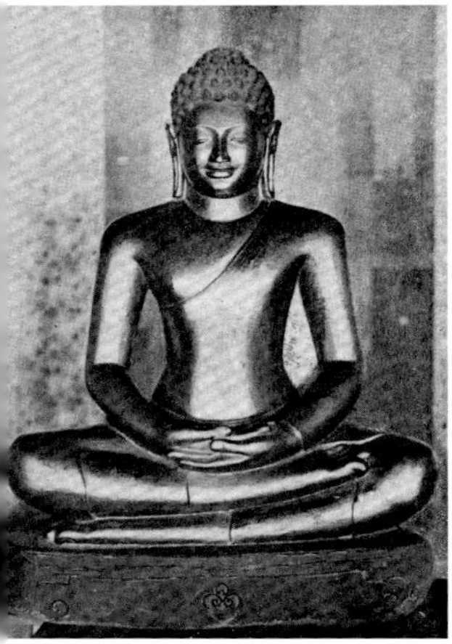

Fig. 3 *Seated Buddha, Linh Sơn Cổ Tự, Thắng Tam, Vũng Tầu, Bà Rịa – Vũng Tàu, sandstone, 6th century.*

approach, attempting to unite these images within more or less coherent sets, perhaps reflecting workshop habits or their influence in the region.

The first set is structured around a flagship work now preserved in Linh Sơn Cổ Tự pagoda in Vũng Tầu[2] (see fig. 3). It is the statue of a Buddha, seated in *vīrāsana* on an undecorated base, his hands resting in *dhyānamudrā*, the *uttarāsaṅgha* of his monastic robe leaving the right shoulder uncovered. We believe the work is revealing not only of the spread and development of Buddhism in the region, but also of the rediscovery of this history in the 19th century, as well as the continuity of places of worship in contemporary Vietnam. It was published for the first time by Henri Parmentier in 1924 under the designation of 'Buddha du Cap Saint-Jacques', the French name of the Vũng Tàu peninsula (Parmentier 1924: 293-5 and pl. XVII-XVIII). Preserved in an exceptional state of conservation, this statue was found by chance by sailors who came from central Vietnam to look for wood at the beginning of the 19th century at the top of Núi Lớn, the 'Great Spur' which dominates the bay of Gành Rái and the city of Vũng Tàu. A pagoda was built for it, whose name and location have changed somewhat over time. If it was once covered with a rich polychromy allowing the statue to harmonize with those surrounding it on the main altar of the modern pagoda (see Võ Văn Tường 1994: 66), it has since been cleaned and found again its archaeological aspect, although it is not easy to photograph at the top of the Mahāyānic pantheon over which it presides.

The work carried out jointly with Thierry Zéphir within the framework of teaching at the Louvre School (Art course: 'Art and archaeology of India and the countries of the Indianized world' 2009-12) and together with the proposals developed by John Guy and highlighted in his exhibition 'Lost Kingdoms' (Metropolitan Museum of Art, New York, 2014, see Guy 2014) allowed us to glimpse modes of diffusion, progressive, flexible and indirect, it is true, but nevertheless undeniable, from India to Southeast Asia. The image indeed appears to us as the local expression of Indic models inherited from the Gupta and post-Gupta traditions but retransmitted in particular by the Buddhist traditions of the art of Anurādhapura in Sri Lanka. The famous 'Samadhi Buddha', dating back to the 6th century and exhibited outdoors in the Mahamevnāwa gardens of Anurādhapura, can be considered as an archetype of this school of art (Schroeder 1990). John Guy has shown the milestones between India, Ceylon and Southeast Asia, that punctuate this transfer of images. This is the case with the inscribed Buddha from Kan Whet Khaung Gon, in the Pyu art of Śrīkṣetra (Thiri Khittaya Archaeological Museum, Myanmar, Guy 2014: 91-92) and with the Buddha of Wat Phra Borromathat (Chaiya district, Surat Thani province, Thailand, now in the National Museum, Chaiya, Guy 2014: 92-93). We need not mention the key role the Malay peninsula and the city of Chaiya played in the context of the maritime trade between West and East in the era of coastal navigation. In the demonstration given by John Guy, we are missing the Vũng Tàu Buddha in which we would be tempted to see the oldest Buddhist image in the region, dating back to the 6th century, found on the highest eminence of the region. Overlooking the sea at 245 m altitude, its role in the context of trade by cabotage from the sea as well as through the vast and complex network of the Mekong outlets (the Cổ Chiên, Hàm Luông and Mỹ Tho rivers) but also the Vàm Cỏ Đông and Vàm rivers Cỏ Tây and the network of rivers Soài Rạp, Đồng Nai, Thị Vải, Long Tàu, must have been fundamental.

A whole ensemble of works, can be considered as following in the direct wake of the Vũng Tàu Buddha and as such can be dated to around the end of the 6th and 7th centuries. First of all the Phnom Cangek Buddha, near Wat Trapeang Veng[3] can be linked to a fairly coherent group unearthed in this same region of the Trà Vinh province and today kept in the museum of History of Vietnam in Hồ Chí Minh City, unless otherwise indicated: the Hiếu Tử Buddha[4], the two Buddhas from Vat Trapeang Veng[5], the so-called Vat Char Buddha[6], the Vat Svay Xiem Cas Buddha[7] and the Vat Laca Cas Buddha[8]. To this group of works which testify to the activity of a Buddhist monastery undoubtedly important in this region and well placed between the outlets of the Mekong Sông Hậu and Cổ Chiên, we can add the Tân Thanh Buddha unearthed in the district of Giồng Trôm, present-day Bến Tre province, in an area precisely halfway between the Trà Vinh discoveries and the city of Vũng Tàu.[9] Perhaps we can also include the Đức Hòa Buddha, kept at the Long An Museum (Khoo 2003: 136, fig. VI-5) and the very eroded small Buddhas unearthed at Đá Nổi (Phúc Hùa, An Giang province) and kept at the An Giang Province Museum. On the other side of the current border, in Cambodia, we should include the Phum Thmei Buddha which appears to be one of the most northerly examples of this fairly cohesive group[10].

The images depicting the standing Buddha seem, for the most part, to stem from somewhat distinct traditions, apart from the Nền Chùa Buddha, whose face presents all the characteristics belonging to our 'Vũng Tầu Buddha family'[11]. The fine and hooked nose, the nobility of the open and smiling face are indeed neighbours of the Phnom Cangek Buddha mentioned above. This sensitivity is also reflected in the treatment of the body, marked by a strong swaying which testifies to the persistence of post-Gupta Indian models, of which we find few examples in the region, with the notable exception of the very beautiful Vat Romlok Buddha, in Cambodia, also very probably dated to the end of the 6th or the very beginning of the 7th century.[12] The Trung Điền Buddha seems to us to be a continuation of this small group.[13] But it shows a slight evolution by its more frontal position and the more synthetic treatment of the relief. It seems to announce tendencies which are those of the middle and the end of the 7th century, and which one finds on both sides of the current border (frontality, monastic costume revealing a body a little more schematic, face more square, etc. …), to which the Buddhas from Hòn Sóc[14], and, in Cambodia, from Tuol Lean[15], Tuol Ta Hoy[16] and Tuol Preah Theat testify[17].

With regard to the wooden representations of the Buddha, which probably constitute the most exceptional part of Buddhist art in the Mekong Delta, the analysis is less easy, in particular because of the fragmentary or very altered character of the preserved images. But the carbon-14 dating confirms their adherence to the chronological period in which we place the stone images (Malleret 1963: 155-172; Nghi – Tuấn 2004). Likewise, the places where they were unearthed are closely related to epigraphic evidence and stone statuary. Thus, the site of Tháp Mười (Đồng Tháp province), the importance of which has already been stressed, provided an exceptional example which is among the most impressive remains of all the Buddhist statuary of Southeast Asia.[18] Its slender proportions are undoubtedly related to the technique of direct carving in a single tree trunk. As for the Phong Mỹ Buddha, unearthed not far away, it appears as the wooden transcription of the group of stone works, more frontal and characterized by the more synthetic model, that we described in the previous paragraph[19]. The many wooden images from Gò Tháp were accidentally uncovered in 1969/1970 at a nearby site of Tháp Mười, which would later benefit from the archaeological work of Lê Thi Lien.[20] But the whole delta is really concerned by these discoveries of wooden statues which are the oldest unearthed in all the territories of continental and island Southeast Asia, because they were found in the Northeast, in Bình Hòa[21] and in the West, near the Rạch Giá bay, in Đá Nổi[22], as near the Phnom Ba The in the rice fields of Giồng Xoài.[23]

This quick overview cannot be completed without discussing the importance of Bodhisattva representations in this context. Less numerous, they are nonetheless very significant, first of all in that they testify to the importance of the cult devoted to the Bodhisattva Lokeśvara, then because their treatment allows them to be brought closer to the pre-Angkorian statuary of the Prei Kmeng and Prasat Andet styles (second half-late 7th century). This is notably the case with the images from Vat Khbal Tuk[24], Vat Chetdei[25], and especially with the masterpiece that is Lokeśvara from Lưu Nghiệp Anh[26] which, decidedly, emanates from a particularly rich region for Buddhist art in the delta. As for the famous Lokeśvara by Tân Long[27], kept at the Guimet museum, it brilliantly expresses the multiplicity of Indian influences that have irrigated the delta after being enriched, along the way, by multiple contributions which nevertheless participate in the singularity of an art of great spirituality.

Bibliography of quoted works

Baptiste, Pierre. 2021. 'Expressing Royal Magnificence: the city of Angkor Borei and the temple of Phnom Da', in Sonya Rhie Mace et al., *Revealing Krishna: Journey to Cambodia's Sacred Mountain*, Cleveland Museum of Art, 2021: 117-39.

Baptiste, Pierre and Zéphir, Thierry.2008. *L'Art khmer dans les collections du musée Guimet*, Réunion des musées nationaux, Paris.

Baptiste, Pierre and Zéphir, Thierry. 2008. (Eds) *Dvāravatī aux sources du Bouddhisme en Thaïlande*, Réunion des musées nationaux / Musée national des arts asiatiques – Guimet, Paris, 2008

Bourdonneau, Eric. 2007. 'Réhabiliter le Funan. Óc Eo ou la première Angkor' *Bulletin de l'École française d'Extrême-Orient*, Tome 94: 111-58.

Cœdès, George. 1948. *Les États hindousiés d'Indochine et d'Indonésie*, Nouvelle édition revue et mise à jour, E. de Boccard, Paris, 1964 [1948]

Cœdès, George.1954. Collection de textes et documents sur l'indochine, III, *Inscriptions du Cambodge*, Volume VI, École française d'Extrême-Orient, Paris, 1954

Dupont 1955: P. Dupont, La Statuaire préangkorienne, *Artibus Asiae*, Supplementum XV, Ascona, 1955

Guy, John (ed.). 2014. *Lost Kingdoms, Hindu-Buddhist Sculpture of early Southeast Asia,* The Metropolitan Museum of Art, New-York

Gutman, Pamela & Hudson, Bob. 2012. 'A First-Century Stele from Sriksetra' *Bulletin de l'École française d'Extrême-Orient* 99(1), janvier 2012 :17-46

Ledgerwood, J., Dega M., Mortland, C., Dowling, N., Bayman, J., Sovath, Bong, Van, Tea, Chamroeun, Chhan & D. K. Latinis, D.K. 1999. 'Results of the 1995-1996 Field Investigations at Angkor Borei, Cambodia', *Asian Perspectives* 38, 1, p. 7-36

Lê Thị Liên. 2005. 'Gold plaques and their cultural contexts in the Oc Eo culture', *Indo-pacific Prehistory Association Bulletin*, 25, (Taipei Papers, Volume 3): 145-54

Lê Thị Liên . 2006. 'Excavations at Minh Su Mound, Go Thap site, Dong Thap Province, South Vietnam, 2000-2003', Bacus, Elisabeth A., Glover, Ian C., Vincent C. Pigott, Vincent C. (eds) *Uncovering Southeast Asia's Past: Selected papers from the 10th International Conference of the European Association of Southeast Asian Archaeology,* National University of Singapore, Singapore: 232-44

Lê Thị Liên .2006b. *Nghệ thuật Phật giáo và Hindu giáo ở Đồng bằng sông Cửu Long trước thế kỷ X* Nhà xuất bản Thế giới, Hà Nội

Lê Xuân Diệm; Đào Linh Côn; Võ Sĩ Khai. 1995. *Văn hóa Óc Eo: Những khám phá mới* Nhà xuất ban Khoa học xã hội, Hà Nội

Mã Thanh Cao et al. 2010. *Tượng cổ (thế kỷ IV-XII) ở Nam Bộ Việt Nam tại Bảo tàng Mỹ thuật TP. Hồ Chí Minh, Ancient Statues (from 4th-12th century) in the Southern Vietnam at the Fine Arts Museum of Ho Chi Minh City*, Bảo tàng Mỹ thuật TP. Hồ Chí Minh

Malleret, Louis. 1937. *Musée Blanchard de la Brosse Saigon, Catalogue général des collections*, Tome I «Arts de la famille indienne », Imprimerie d'Extrême-Orient, Hà Nội

Malleret, Louis. 1959a. *L'Archéologie du delta du Mékong*, Tome I « L'Exploration archéologique et les fouilles d'Oc-Èo », Texte, École française d'Extrême-Orient, Paris

Malleret, Louis. 1959b. *L'Archéologie du delta du Mékong*, Tome I « L'Exploration archéologique et les fouilles d'Oc-Èo », Planches, École française d'Extrême-Orient, Paris

Malleret, Louis. 1960a. *L'Archéologie du delta du Mékong*, Tome II « La Civilisation matérielle d'Oc-Èo », Texte, École française d'Extrême-Orient, Paris

Malleret, Louis. 1960b. *L'Archéologie du delta du Mékong*, Tome II « La Civilisation matérielle d'Oc-Èo », Texte, École française d'Extrême-Orient, Paris

Malleret, Louis. 1963. *L'Archéologie du delta du Mékong*, Tome IV « Le Cisbassac », École française d'Extrême-Orient, Paris

Hoàng Nghị, Nguyễn Anh Tuấn. 2004. Tượng Phật gỗ văn hóa Óc Eo, Những bảo vật của văn hóa Việt Nam, Cổ vật tinh hoa, 2004, số 9, tr. 28-9.

Pachow, Wang.1958. 'The voyage of Buddhist missions to Southeast Asia and Far East' *University of Ceylon Review* 18(3/4): 195-212 (1960 Reprint)

Rhie, Marylin Martin. 1999. *Early Buddhist Art of China & Central Asia, Later Han, Three Kingdoms and Western Chin in China and Bactria to Shan-shan in Central Asia*, Volume One, Brill, Leiden Boston, Köln

Rhie, Marylin Martin. 2010. *Early Buddhist Art of China & Central Asia, The Western Ch'in in Kansu in the Sixteen Kingdoms Period and Inter-relationships with the Buddhist Art of Gandhāra,* Volume Three, Brill, Leiden Boston

Schroeder, Ulrich von. 1990. *Buddhist Sculptures of Sri Lanka*. Hong Kong: Visual Dharma Publications

Skilling, Peter. 1999. 'A Buddhist inscription from Go Xoai, Southern Vietnam and notes towards a classification of ye dharmā inscriptions' in *80 pi sasatrachan dr. prasert na nagara: ruam botkhwam vichakan dan charük lae ekasan boran* [80 Years: A collection of articles on epigraphy and ancient documents published on the occasion of the celebration of the 80th birthday of Prof. Dr. Prasert Na Nagara], Bangkok, 21 mars 2542: 171-87

Skilling, Peter. 2002. 'Some Citation Inscriptions from Southeast Asia' *Journal of the Pāli Text Society*, 27: 159-75

Skilling, Peter. 2003. 'Traces of the Dharma' *Bulletin de l'Ecole française d'Extrême-Orient*. Tome 90-91: 273-87

Ślączka, Anna Aleksandra. 2011. 'The Brick Structures of Go Thap – Tomb or temples?' *Bulletin of the Indo-Pacific Prehistory Association*, 31: 108-16

Stark et al. 1999 : M. T. Stark, P.B. Griffin, Chuch Phoeurn, J.

Stark, M. T. 2001. 'Some Preliminary Results of the 1999-2000 Archaeological Field Investigations at Angkor Borei, Takeo Province', *Udaya Journal of Khmer Studies*, n°2: 19-35

Stark, M.T. 2003. 'Angkor Borei and the Archaeology of Cambodia's Mekong Delta' in J.M. Khoo, *Art and Archaeology of Fu nan, Pre-Khmer Kingdom of the Lower Mekong valley*, The Southeast Asian Ceramic Society, Orchid Press, Bangkok: 87-105

Tingley, Nancy. 2009. *Arts of Ancient Viet Nam, from River Plain to Open Sea*, Asia Society, New York, Museum of Fine Arts, Houston

Vickery, M. 1994. 'What and where was Zhenla?' in F. Bizot (ed.), *Recherches nouvelles sur le Cambodge*, École française d'Extrême-Orient, Paris: 197-212

Võ Văn Tường (ed.). 1994. *Những ngôi chùa nổi tiếng Việt Nam – Vietnam's Famous Pagodas*, Nhà xuất bản văn hóa thông tin – Eds Culture-Information Publishing House, Hà Nội

Endnotes

1 Corpus des Inscriptions Khmères (CIK), EFEO/EPHE. https://cik.efeo.fr/

2 Linh Sơn Cổ Tự is in Thắng Tam, Vũng Tầu, Bà Rịa – Vũng Tàu, today in the 2nd district of the city Vũng Tầu (Malleret 1963: 125 et 176 et pl. XXXII ; Võ Văn Tường 1994 : 66).

3 Nhị Trường village, Cầu Ngang district, Trà Vinh province (see notice 63, see also Malleret 1963: 20 and 177, pl. XXIX and Guy 2014: 99-100).

4 Found in the Vat Canchong Phno Don temple, today Chùa Ô Đùng, in the hamlet of Ô Đùng, Hiếu Tử village, Tiểu Cần district, Trà Vinh province (Malleret 1963: 12 and 175 and pl. XXVII, current localization unknown).

5 The Vat Trapeang Veng or Vat Sơn Thọ in today Chùa Bông Veng, Nhị Trường village, Cầu Ngang district, Trà Vinh province. One of the two images found there is in Guimet Museum (Malleret 1963: 18 and 177, pl. XXXI; Baptiste et Zéphir 2008: 24-5) and the second, seated 'in Western style', but stylistically similar, is in the MVH-HCMC (Malleret 1963: 18 and pl. XXXIV; Tingley 2009: 148-149 ; Guy 2014: 196-7, see notice).

6 The Vat Char is today Chùa Chà, Thanh Sơn village, Trà Cú district, Trà Vinh province (see Malleret 1963: 24 and 177, pl. XXXIII).

7 Today Chùa Xoài Xiêm Cũ, Ngãi Xuyên village, Trà Cú district, Trà Vinh province. This statue is preserved in the Museum of Fine Arts, HCMC (Malleret 1963: 23 et 177, pl. XXXIV; Mã Thanh Cao et al. 2010: 32-4).

8 Today Chùa La Ca Củ, Nhị Trường village, Cầu Ngang district, Trà Vinh province (Malleret 1963: 16 and 177, pl. XXX). It received a post-angkorian pedestal. Current localization unknown.

9 Malleret 1963: 49 and 177, pl. XXXIII.

10 Preserved in the National Museum of Cambodia, it was found about 50 km South-West from Phnom Penh, in the Kong Pisei district, Kompong Speu province, Cambodia (See Lobo et al. 2007: 48-9).

11 Found in Nền Chùa, Hòn Đất district, Kiên Giang province (Lê Thị Liên in Guy 2014: 119, fig. 87).

12 Though armless, this Buddha preserved in the National Museum of Cambodia can be considered as the most explicit expression of post-Gupta traditions inherited in Cambodia. See Giteau 1965: 39-42 ; Dalsheimer 2001: 64-6, n°15. From the same site come a Buddha head and a standing Buddha showing the same influences, together with the vitality of a Buddhist center in the city of Angkor Borei (Baptiste 2021).

13 We were unable to find this village today. It could be Trung Hiếu, Vũng Liêm district, Vĩnh Long province, six kilometers South-West from the right bank of the river, halfway between Trà Vinh and Vinh Long. (Malleret 1937: 78; Malleret 1963 :39 and 174-175 and pl. XXVIII). The catholic church Mai Phốp is probably the modern position of the former archaeological mound.

14 The site of Chùa Crak, núi Hòn Sóc, Hòn Đất district, Kiên Giang province, is in the vicinity of Rạch Giá bay where are also situated Nền Chùa and Đá Nổi sites. The Buddha is now in the collection of the Museum of Fine Arts HCMC (Malleret 1959: 443-4 and 1959b: XCVII, Malleret 1963: 175; Mã Thanh Cao et al. 2010: 26-28).

15 Tuol Lean site is close to Angkor Borei (Ta Keo province, Cambodia). See Dupont 1955: pl. XLIV, Dalsheimer 2001 : 68.

16 Tuol Ta Hoy is in Oudong district, Kompong Speu province, Cambodiaa. It is preserved in the National Museum of Cambodia (Guy 2014: 49-51).

17 Tuol Preah Theat, Kompong Speu province, Cambodia. It is preserved in Guimet Museum (Baptiste and Zéphir 2008: 27-8).

18 Tháp Mười wooden Buddha, Đồng Tháp province (Malleret 1963: 77 and 156, pl. XXI), found in1943 close to the inscriptions mentioned above.

19 Phong Mỹ wooden Buddha, Cao Lãnh, Đồng Tháp province, (Malleret 1963: 63 and 155, pl. XXVI), found in 1937.

20 Gò Tháp, Tân Kiều, Tháp Mười district, Đồng Tháp province (Higham 2002: 237; Khoo 2003: 25; Lê Thị Liên 2006: 232-3 and Lê Thị Liên 2006b).

21 The two wooden Buddhas from Bình Hòa, Đức Huệ district, Long An province, were found in 1945 and entered the museum in 1947. (Malleret 1963: 59-60 and 157, pl. XXII-XXV).

22 Đá Nổi wooden Buddha, Thạch Đông, Tân Hiệp district, Kiên Giang province, is preserved in

the Museum of Fine Arts HCMC (Malleret 1949: 130, Malleret 1963: 158, Mã Thanh Cao et al. 2010: 24-5).

23 Wooden Buddha found in 1986 in the rice fields of Giồng Xoài, Vọng Thê village, Thoại Sơn district, An Giang province, close to Phnom Ba The, in the North-West (Võ Văn Tường 1994: 67), An Giang provincial museum. Another one, kept in the same museum is published in Khoo 2003: 44.

24 Vat Khbal Tuk (Malleret 1963: 25 and 180, pl. XXXVI) could be nowadays Chùa Ba Cụm, Ngọc Biện, Trà Cú district, Trà Vinh province. In any case, it is in its vicinity.

25 Vat Chetdei, Trà Vinh province (Malleret 1963: 14 and 180, pl. XXXV).

26 Lưu Nghiệp Anh, Trà Cú district, Trà Vinh province (Malleret 1963: 21-2 and 180, pl. XXXV; Tingley 2009: 175; Guy 2014: 229-30).

27 Tân Long, Hậu Giang province. Louis Malleret mentions that 'The main statue is said to have been found at a depth of about five feet, leveling the top of a mound for the construction of a stable, a mound adjacent to a canal' (Malleret 1959a: 134). This site is located ten kilometers west of Sông Hậu, the Vietnamese continuation of the Bassac, the most important deltaic outlet of the Mekong, nearly 70 km upstream from the mouth of the river (Baptiste and Zéphir 2008: 29-33).

7 | Viṣṇus of the Delta

Paul Lavy

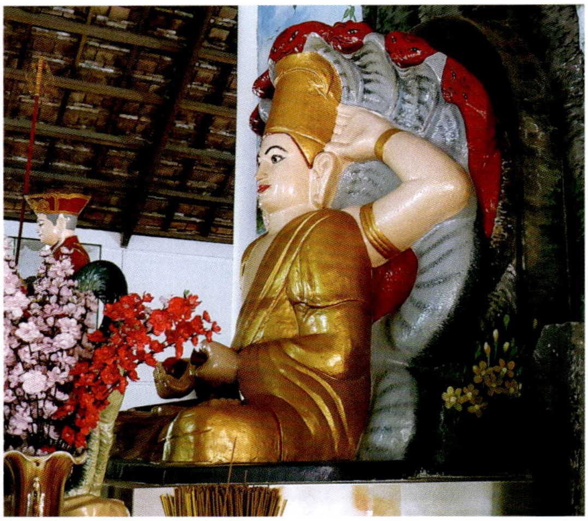

Fig. 1 *Preangkorian Viṣṇu Anantāśāyana converted to a seated Buddha, Chùa Linh Sơn, Núi Ba Thê, An Giang province, Vietnam. (Photo: Paul A. Lavy)*

By the mid-first millennium CE worship of the Brahmanical deity Viṣṇu became widespread in a pan-Southeast Asian Vaiṣṇava network that spanned much of the region, particularly coastal areas that were closely tied to commerce with South Asia across the Bay of Bengal (Manguin 2010; 2019). Sea merchants and brahmans contributed to the dissemination of Vaiṣṇavism (or an early form called Bhāgavatism) from what is today India, but it arrived in a highly receptive climate in which elements of Indic culture were being selectively appropriated by Southeast Asian elites (Lavy 2003; Manguin 2019: 64-66). With its universalist message of a cosmic order created, maintained, and protected by Viṣṇu, the philosophical principles of Vaiṣṇavism were localized to articulate newly imported concepts of power and sovereignty centering on the king as the supreme devotee and, in 'bearing a portion of Viṣṇu', the god's representative on earth (Gonda 1954: 164-167; 1966: 24-33). In the Mekong Delta region, a range of evidence indicates a strong, but not exclusive, Vaiṣṇava religious orientation from the late fifth or early sixth century through the seventh, which, at least to some extent, seems to have included 'public and collective' forms of devotionalism (Manguin & Stark 2021: 650). This evidence includes Sanskrit inscriptions; small gold foil plaques portraying Viṣṇu, his *avatāra*s, or his iconographical attributes; and, most prominently, the stone sculptures of Viṣṇu that are the focus of this essay.[1]

In Southeast Asia, the linkage of royal authority with Viṣṇu occurs in early inscriptions, including a couple that are associated with the polity called 'Funan' in ancient Chinese sources and known as Văn hóa Óc Eo in recent Vietnamese scholarship. Inscription K. 5, from Tháp Mười (Đồng Tháp province) and dating approximately to the late fifth or early sixth century, celebrates the foundation of countless sanctuaries to Bhāgavat (i.e. Viṣṇu) by a king whose son, Guṇavarman, dedicated a shrine containing Bhāgavat's footprints (Cœdès 1931). Sculptures of Viṣṇu's footprints (i.e. Viṣṇupada) reference his most characteristic deed in Vedic texts in which his three strides encompass the universe, establish order, and 'create space and a place for people to live and move' (Brereton & Jamison 2020: 100-101).[2] This deed was later associated with Viṣṇu's dwarf *avatāra* (incarnation) Vāmana, who assumes a colossal form, Trivikrama, and in three enormous steps reclaims the earth, sky, and heavens from demonic control (Sharma 1968: 323-327).[3] Beyond the Mekong Delta region and the area associated with Funan, similar ideas are referenced in the *Prasati Ciaruteun* – a late fifth or early sixth century inscription from the kingdom of Tārumānagara in West Java, ruled by a king named Pūrṇavarman.[4] Accompanying a small pair of footprints said to belong to the king, the inscription describes Pūrṇavarman as 'the great king, ruler of the world, whose footprints are the same as those of Lord Viṣṇu' (Vogel 1925; Guy 2014: 11-12).

An approximately contemporary inscription (K. 875), from Ta Keo province in Cambodia, records the foundation of a hermitage apparently dedicated to Viṣṇu by Kulaprabhāvatī, a queen perhaps of Funan (Cœdès 1937). For her protection, it invokes Viṣṇu, lying on the coils of the serpent Śeṣa (also known as Ananta) with the god containing the three worlds within his body and a lotus rising from his naval to initiate a new cosmic cycle of creation (Goodall 2012: 345-348; Parimoo 1983: 1-16). Probably post-dating Funan, a later inscription (K. 1254) from Angkor Borei, also in Ta Keo province, similarly describes Viṣṇu as resting on the serpent, absorbed in meditation, and creating the universe. It goes on to say that, after taking the form of several *avatāra* to save the world and maintain cosmic order, Viṣṇu partially incarnates himself as the king [Jayavarman] whose bed is the serpent Ananta and whose strides are honored (Gerschheimer & Goodall 2014: 114-126). The king and god are thus brought into direct correspondence through recurring references to the world-snake and the three strides. It is noteworthy that a colossal sculpture of Anantāśāyana (Viṣṇu reclining upon the serpent Ananta) was discovered on a hill near Mount Ba Thê, which overlooks Óc Eo, An Giang province. Of indeterminate date, but likely Preangkorian (pre-ninth century CE), it has been modified and installed as a seated Buddha image in the modern pagoda of Linh Sơn, Ba Thê (**Fig. 1**).[5]

While Viṣṇu Anantāśāyana would become a prominent fixture in Khmer art of the Preangkorian and Angkorian periods (Bénisti 1965; Feneley 2013), the most ubiquitous representation of Viṣṇu in early historical Southeast Asia portrayed him as a cosmic king and perhaps as a world sovereign (Skt: *cakravartin*), a concept that had become increasingly 'Vaiṣṇavized' during the Gupta period of India (ca. fourth-fifth centuries CE) (Sinha 2019: 688).[6] The notable characteristics of these Southeast Asian Viṣṇus include: a frontal standing position (Skt: *sthānaka* or *samabhaṅga*) with a rigid body and evenly placed feet, a smooth cylindrical crown or mitre (Skt: *kirīṭamukuṭa*), four arms (Skt: *caturbhuja*), a bare torso, and a hip-wrapped garment secured by various sashes, knots, and pleats. In the great majority of them, the configuration of the attributes in the hands is, proceeding clockwise from the lower proper right hand, a spherical object (the earth), discus or wheel (Skt: *cakra*), conch (Skt: *śaṅkha*), and mace or club (Skt: *gadā*).[7] An auspicious aquatic symbol associated with creation, the conch relates to Viṣṇu more specifically as a battle trumpet (Taddei 1991: 647-655). Together with the *cakra* and mace, it signifies his universal power as the divine warrior-king, while the sphere refers to his all-encompassing protection (Krishna 1980: 30-59; Parimoo 2000: 141-146). With this iconography, Viṣṇu's role as supreme warrior and universal ruler persisted for many centuries in Khmer art, at least through the sixteenth century, and most famously in the bas-reliefs of Angkor Wat. A different configuration of attributes, however, initially preceded his fully developed form.

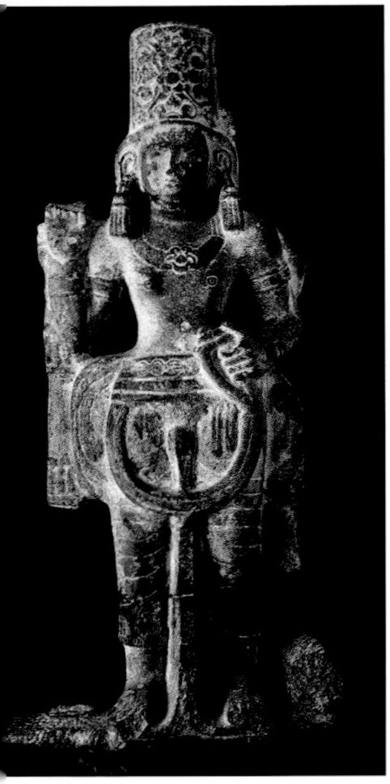

Fig. 2 *Vāsudeva-Kṛṣṇa, found at Wat Sala Thueng, Chaiya district, Surat Thani province, Thailand, ca. 500 CE, Bangkok National Museum, inv. no. S.V. 18. (Photo: © River Books)*

The Early Conch-on-hip Image Type

The oldest mitred Vaiṣṇava image from Southeast Asia, likely dating to circa 500 CE, is probably a well-known sculpture (**Fig. 2**) from Chaiya, Thailand, that can be identified as an incipient form of Viṣṇu named Vāsudeva-Kṛṣṇa on the basis of its iconography: the anterior proper right hand raised with the palm outward in either the gesture of *abhayamudrā* or *vyāvṛttamudrā*, the mace or club (*gadā*) held in the posterior right hand, the conch held against the hip by the anterior left hand, and the now missing posterior left hand most likely holding a *cakra* (discus or wheel) (Lavy 2014: 152-173; O'Connor 1972: 20-21, 39).[8] Although the possibility of pre-Pallava stylistic influences from Andhra Pradesh cannot be completely dismissed, its closest stylistic and iconographic relationships are probably with late fifth-early sixth century northern Indian sculpture from sites including Bhinmal, Mandsaur, and Bhumara (Brown 1992: 46-47; Lavy 2014: 158-164). As one of the few early Brahmanical sculptures carved in Southeast Asia that can be closely tied to Indian prototypes, the Chaiya Vāsudeva-Kṛṣṇa is likely the earliest of a group of about a dozen sixth to seventh century Southeast Asian sculptures distinguished by the conch-on-hip iconography. It was soon followed by several conch-on-hip stone Viṣṇu sculptures in peninsular Thailand and the Mekong Delta, none of which can be so closely related to specific examples of Indian art as the Chaiya image (Lavy 2014: 154-156). The Mekong Delta region has yielded (1) the Viṣṇu from Tuol Koh in Ta Keo province, Cambodia, now in the National Museum, Phnom Penh (Dalsheimer 2001: 44-45, cat. no. 1); (2) a Viṣṇu from Óc Eo in An Giang province, Vietnam BTLS.5528 and (3) a Viṣṇu found near Mount Ba Thê, also in An Giang province BTLS.5529. Additional possible candidates with the same conch-on-hip iconography include (1) a small and badly damaged stone sculpture from Nhơn Thành near Cần Thơ, Vietnam, now in the Cần Thơ Museum (Lê 2014: 120, fig. 91) and (2) a stone sculpture from Trapeang Veng, Trà Vinh province, Vietnam, known to the present author only through a drawing (Malleret 1963: 17-19, fig. 3, no. 151).

The available evidence does not permit precise dating of these images, but in Southeast Asia, conch-on-hip images seem all to have been early in date, i.e., confined to the sixth and perhaps early seventh centuries CE. Beyond peninsular Thailand, the earliest of them is probably the Tuol Koh Viṣṇu (**Fig. 3**), which, despite the loss of its head and all four arms, shares some stylistic features with the Chaiya Vāsudeva-Kṛṣṇa. Both the Chaiya and Tuol Koh sculptures are thin, front to back, and conceived more as relief rather than sculpture in-the-round. The flat backs are largely devoid of carving save for indications of the spine and, on the Tuol Koh image, indications of the belt around the waist. Both images, furthermore, wear a comparable – though not identical – garment and a flat necklace with a prominent central flower, while the presence of a bracelet on the right wrist of the Viṣṇu of Tuol Koh hints at the numerous armlets worn by the Chaiya image (Lavy 2004: 247-248). The stylistic similarities suggest that these two sculptures cannot be too far apart in date.

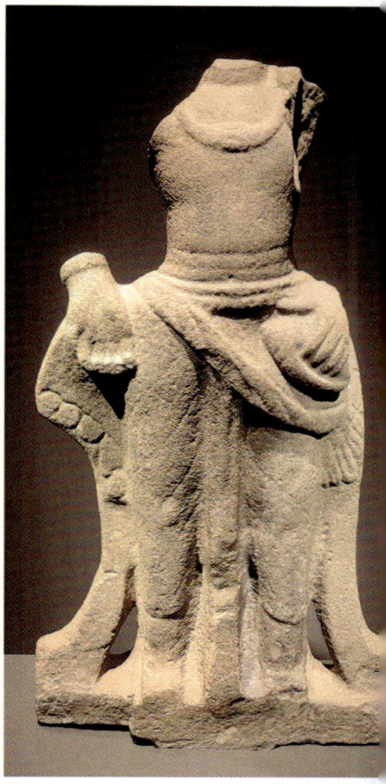

Fig. 3 *Viṣṇu, Tuol Koh, Ta Keo province, ca. 6th cent. CE, Cambodia, National Museum of Cambodia, Phnom Penh, Ka. 1599. (Photo: Paul A. Lavy)*

While they share many stylistic features, their iconography slightly differs. Like the Chaiya Vāsudeva-Kṛṣṇa, the now missing posterior and elevated hands of the Tuol Koh image probably held a *gadā* and a *cakra* but, given the fragmentary state of the image, the precise arrangement cannot be determined with absolute certainty. Both images hold a conch shell against the proper left hip, but unlike the raised open-palm gesture of the Vāsudeva-Kṛṣṇa, the comparable hand of the Tuol Koh Viṣṇu is lowered to the right hip with outward palm and downward fingers in a gesture resembling *varadamudrā*. This hand likely held a small smooth-surfaced orb or a flat disc, now lost (Dupont 1955: 133-134). Inscriptions from Cambodia dating from the seventh through the eleventh centuries indicate that this object represents the earth (Skt: *bhū*, *mahī*, *pṛthivī*, or *dhāraṇī*).[9]

In earlier Indian art, however, the spherical object has been variably identified as a variety of fruit; a lotus flower, seed, or bud (Skt: *padma* or *kamala*); or a ball of ashes (Skt: *vibhūti*) (Gail 2009: 83-84).[10] The first appearance of the spherical object has been associated with a shift from images of Vāsudeva-Kṛṣṇa towards those of Viṣṇu during the late Kuṣāṇa and Gupta periods (ca. third-fifth centuries CE) of northern India, the period over which the iconography and concept of the Purāṇic deity Viṣṇu was becoming concretized (Härtel 1987: 586-587, cf. fig. Xa). But the precise nature and timing of this transition is poorly understood, as is the possible persistence of a distinct Vāsudeva-Kṛṣṇa iconography in Southeast Asia through perhaps the eighth century (Lavy 2014: 157-158). Based on the hypothetical reconstruction of its iconography, it is indeed possible that, like the Chaiya image, the Tuol Koh image should be recognized as Vāsudeva-Kṛṣṇa. Yet the change to the downturned hand, probably holding an earth attribute, also relates the Tuol Koh image to several Viṣṇus from peninsular Thailand which may have shared similar iconography, and which have been argued to date to the early-to-mid sixth century, slightly after the Chaiya Vāsudeva-Kṛṣṇa (Lavy 2014: 165-169, figs. 3-8). The weight of the stylistic and iconographic evidence therefore indicates that the Tuol Koh image dates slightly after the Chaiya image.

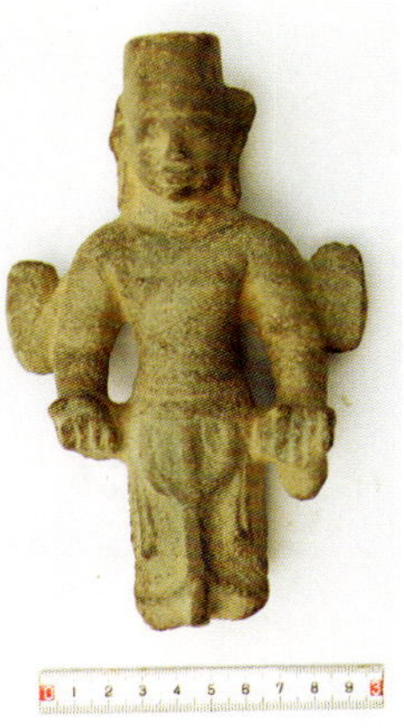

Fig. 4 *Viṣṇu, Nhơn Nghĩa, Cần Thơ province, Vietnam, ca. late 6th or 7th cent. CE, Cần Thơ Province Museum, 685/II.N.246. (Photo: Lê Thị Liên)*

In the Mekong Delta, they were followed by the small Nhơn Thành Viṣṇu now in the Cần Thơ Museum, although its minute size (H. 23.5 cm) and battered state allow only tentative observations. A fifth-century date with Gupta stylistic relationships has been suggested for this image, as well as for other small Viṣṇu sculptures (without the conch-on-hip) from the Cần Thơ area and a Viṣṇu from Gò Miếu (Tây Ninh province) (Lê 2006: 64-66, 198, 226, figs. 43-52; Lê 2014: 120, fig. 91) (**Fig. 4**). However, comparisons to early fifth century Viṣṇu images from Udayagiri (Begley 1973: figs. 3-4) and occurring on late fifth century pillars (Biswas & Jha 1985: 39-41, pl. VIII-IX) are unconvincing because all these fifth century Indian examples are rendered in the typical Gupta presentation of Viṣṇu (Krishna 1980: figs. 7-9). Whereas Kuṣāṇa and Gupta Vāsudeva-Kṛṣṇa images held the *gadā* and *cakra* aloft in their rear arms, now, in what may be regarded as the fully established image of Viṣṇu, the arms were lowered so that all four hands were at or below waist-level (Härtel 1987: 586-587). The rear hands were placed on top of the *gadā* and *cakra*, which rest on the ground, and which were sometimes personified as *āyudhapuruṣa* ("weapon-man") (Mani 1985: 9-14). While characteristic of the Gupta period, the lowered arms, configuration of attributes, and *āyudhapuruṣa* are extremely rare in Southeast Asia and unknown in the Mekong Delta region (Lavy 2004: 285-294; Lavy & Clarke 2015: 43, figs. 15-16). The Cần Thơ and Gò Miếu sculptures have elevated rear arms and therefore probably could not have resulted through direct and unmediated Gupta influence. Instead, their composition and iconography reflect further developments that occurred during the late sixth century (discussed below). The long median fold and looping sash of these images, moreover, persisted well beyond the fifth century as can be seen, for example, on a ca. late sixth-early seventh century Viṣṇu from Prasat Don Tha Em (Tây Ninh province) which retains the thin physique and flat depth of the conch-on-hip images but, although fragmentary, seems to exhibit the new iconography as well (Malleret 1963: pl. IV; Lê 2006: figs. 53-54). Overlapping the iconographic shift, the last of the conch-on-hip Viṣṇus are probably the two images from the Óc Eo area, which can be dated ca. late sixth or seventh centuries on the basis of their anatomy, technical features, and garment styles BTLS.5528 and BTLS.5529.

The Four-Armed Mitred Viṣṇu

During the late sixth and early seventh centuries, the conch-on-hip iconography was replaced by, or evolved into, a new iconographical type. The conch was no longer placed on the left hip but was instead elevated in the raised left hand with the *cakra* mirroring it in the raised proper right hand. Thus, the new arrangement of the attributes became, clockwise from the lower proper right hand: orb, *cakra*, conch, and mace. The elevation of the conch and *cakra* may have been the result of artistic influences from southern India, where the new iconography appeared in late sixth century

Early Western Cāḷukyan art, for example Badami Cave 3, and soon after in Pallava art, for example the Madugula Viṣṇu (Tarr 1970: figs. 28-29; Krishnakumari 2010: 43-44, pl. 9; Lavy 2020: 228). However, the emphasis on the earth orb (rather than a fruit or lotus) and the reliance on the mace for structural support seem also to indicate local Southeast Asian innovation (Brown 2000: 10; Lavy 2014: 165-170).

The production of these mitred Viṣṇu sculptures rapidly proliferated after the mid-sixth century in a complex web of interconnected stylistic relationships primarily involving peninsular and eastern Thailand, Cambodia, and southern Vietnam (Lavy 2004: 302-360). Many, if not most, of the mitred Viṣṇus from the Mekong Delta region probably date to the late sixth and early-to-mid seventh centuries. In the absence of absolute dates, however, various methods emphasizing different technical and stylistic factors have been used to establish a relative chronology for these images. The first and most influential emphasized a relatively steady transition from relief to freestanding sculpture-in-the-round through the gradual elimination of supplemental stone structural elements (e.g., supporting arches, braces, etc.) (Dupont 1936; 1941; 1955: 37-42). Some art historians have questioned whether this occurred in a straightforward chronological succession and have raised the possibility that various configurations of supplemental stone elements may have co-existed and could also have resulted from aesthetic and iconographic reasons or various levels of artistic skill (Boisselier 1966: 229-230; Woodward 2005: 46; Lavy 2004: 206-211; Lavy 2022: 96-100). Nevertheless, classification based largely on technical aspects has been a useful index for studying the development of the mitred Viṣṇu sculptures (O'Connor 1972: 45-48; Jacq-Hergoualc'h 2002: 120-124; Lê 2006: 63-79, fig. 81), particularly if one does not attach specific dates or a rigid chronological sequence based on technical considerations alone. Another factor that has been used to postulate a chronological development of early mitred Viṣṇus is the progressive shortening of the garment from a long robe (*paridhana*) in the earlier images to a short *sampot* in later ones (Dupont 1955: 123-132; Dalsheimer & Manguin 1998: 94; Dalsheimer 2001: 54-58).

The Viṣṇus that may be considered to be among the earliest are distinguished by a low and relatively wide mitre that flares slightly towards the top; a round face; a solid and muscular figure; a long median fold of cloth falling from the central knot of the robe just beneath the naval, and, in most cases, joining with the socle between the legs; and a sash, sometimes coiled, worn horizontally over the robe, around the hips, and tied with a large knot or bow at the proper right hip (Dupont 1941: 233-244; 1955: 124-128).[11] The right hand rests on or against this knot while the left hand is placed against the left hip on the handle of the mace that rests obliquely against the body. The strut on the right, extending downwards beneath the large knot and visually balancing the mace, is typically disguised as a long flowing panel of cloth.

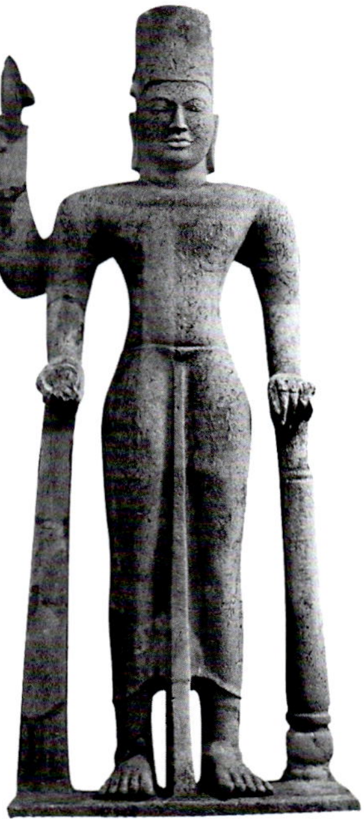

Fig. 5 *Viṣṇu, Gò Tháp, Đồng Tháp province, Vietnam, ca. 7th cent. CE, Đồng Tháp Province Museum. (Photo: Lê Thị Liên)*

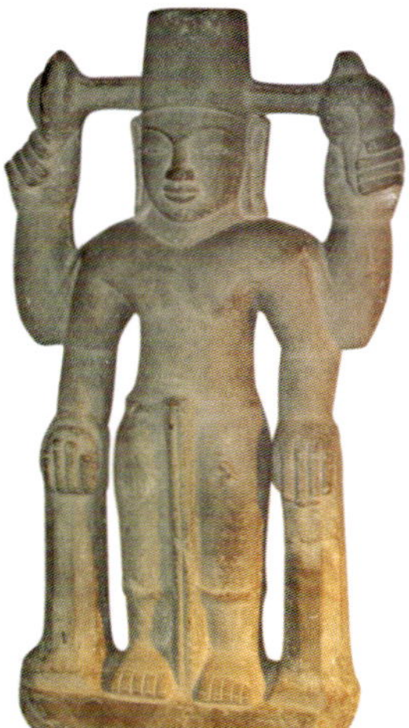

Fig. 6 *Viṣṇu, Gò Thành, Tiền Giang province, Vietnam, ca. 7th cent. CE, Tiền Giang Province Museum, BTTG 590. (Photo: Paul A. Lavy)*

The figures are thus supported by five points of contact with the base: the brace on the proper right, the legs with a panel of cloth between them, and the mace on the left, with the intervals carved out between each of them (Dupont 1955: 127). Viṣṇus exhibiting these features have come from peninsular and eastern Thailand, Cambodia, and southern Vietnam, including one from Hưng Thạnh Mỹ, Tiền Giang province (Dupont 1941: pl. XXXVIA) and another, with only the lower body remaining, from Vĩnh Tân, Đồng Nai province (Lê 2006: 68, fig. 57).[12] Both of them likely date to the first half of the seventh century. At about the same time, the horizontal sash around the hips was eliminated, as can be seen on an incomplete sculpture from Long An province[13] and a badly damaged Viṣṇu from Ô Lâm, Châu Đốc,[14] both in the History Museum HCMC.

More common in the Mekong Delta region are Viṣṇus of a different type dating, for the most part, to the early-to-mid seventh century with some perhaps continuing into the eighth.[15] Unlike the previous type, these images all lack the horizontal sash and the accompanying large bow on the right hip. The right lateral strut, supporting the hand with the sphere, is not rendered as a panel of drapery, but instead, as an undecorated or minimally decorated rectilinear pillar mirroring the mace on the proper left. Rather than resting on the bow and the conjoined hip and mace, the lower hands are disengaged from the body, and the lower arms and their braces constitute a separate, unified unit. An example of this composition can be seen in a rare bronze sculpture which preserves features perhaps more appropriate to stone carving BTLS.1585. Often small in size, numerous stone examples survive from the Mekong Delta region and, depending on their condition, many retain reinforcements (or their vestiges) in the form of cross-pieces bridging the attributes held in the upper hands (*cakra* and conch) and the mitre. For the lower body, the larger figures tend to rest on five points of contact with the pedestal, as described above, while the legs and robe of the smaller figures are often carved as a single stone block, thus providing three points of contact.

Particularly noteworthy among the large images is the elegant sculpture found by archaeologists at Gò Tháp in 1998, one of very few early Viṣṇus to have come to light through controlled excavation (**Fig. 5**).[16] Others, of various sizes, have been found at (1) Vat Cetdei, Trà Vinh province,[17] (2) Gò Thành, Tiền Giang province (**Fig. 6**),[18] (3) Thân Cựu Nghĩa, Tiền Giang province,[19] (4) Prasat Don Tha Em, Tây Ninh province,[20] and (5) Vat Ek, Trà Vinh province.[21] In contrast to the rather slender Gò Tháp Viṣṇu, these images share similar stocky bodily proportions, muscular shoulders, short legs, and rounded abdomens with a small bulge of fat above the waistband (Dalsheimer 2011: 117). Arranged in this sequence, their garments become progressively shorter.

Around the same time, there emerged a distinct style of Brahmanical and Buddhist images distinguished by a short garment (*sampot*) with triangular pleating known variously as "dovetail" or "anchor" folds (Dupont 1955: 58; Boisselier 1955: 22-64). This group includes (1) a second Viṣṇu excavated in 1998 at Gò Tháp that retains vestiges of a supporting arch, conch, and mace (**Fig. 7**);[22] (2) another four-armed figure from Gò Tháp, fragmentary but probably also a representation of Viṣṇu;[23] and (3) a completely intact Viṣṇu from Gò Trâm Qùy, Long An province, where the dovetail fold is doubled (**Fig. 8**).[24] They can be loosely associated with what has been called the Phnom Da style B, a term used to designate images from Cambodia and southern Vietnam with close stylistic connections to the highly accomplished sculptures from the vicinity of Phnom Da (style A) and Angkor Borei in Ta Keo, Cambodia (Dupont 1955: 42-48, 51-70).[25] The date of Phnom Da style A remains one of the most vexed issues in Southeast Asian art history; suggestions range from the early-to-mid sixth to the eighth century with an early-to-mid seventh century date seeming most plausible.[26] Without a firmer chronology, the precise relationships between the style of Phnom Da A and related images remains unclear; rather than all of them following Phnom Da A, some stylistically related images were likely part of the developmental sequence leading to it, while others probably represent regional variations on shared stylistic themes. A conservative view is that they span the greater part of the seventh century.

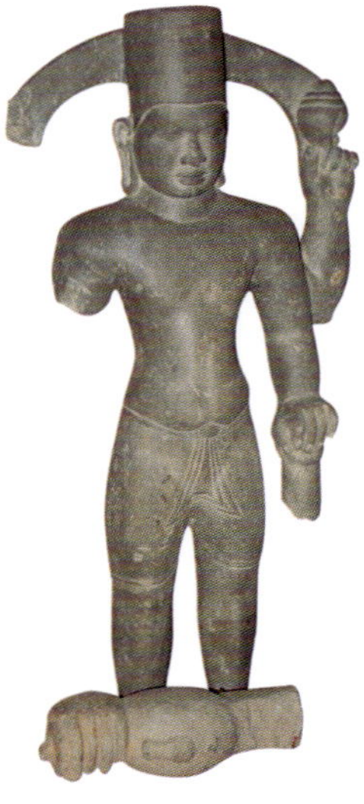

Fig. 7 *Viṣṇu, Gò Tháp, Đồng Tháp province, Vietnam, ca. 7th cent. CE, Đồng Tháp Province Museum, BTĐTCV-451/ Đ78. (Photo: Paul A. Lavy)*

By the mid-seventh century at the latest, the dovetail fold began to evolve into a new configuration of drapery. The lower of two dovetail folds was carved to appear slackened with a fold of fabric curving upward across the proper left thigh before being cinched at the waist. This development is perhaps most clearly evident on the beautiful Viṣṇu from Tuol Dai Buon (Prei Veng province, Cambodia)[27] and on a nearly identical image discovered in the Đồng Nai riverbed near Bình Hòa (Đồng Nai province) in 1976 (**Fig. 9**).[28] The further development of this style can be seen on a large fragmentary male figure, Viṣṇu in all likelihood, from Cổ Lâm Tự (Tây Ninh province) where a fully developed "pocket-fold" appears incised on the proper left thigh.[29] A key defining feature of the Prasat Andet Style, the pocket-fold suggests a date at the end of the seventh century or early in the eighth (Dupont 1955: 166-179; Boisselier 1981). Towards the end of the sequence of mitred Viṣṇus from the Mekong Delta region is a particularly handsome sculpture found in 1938 among temple ruins at Prasat Chót Mạt (Tây Ninh

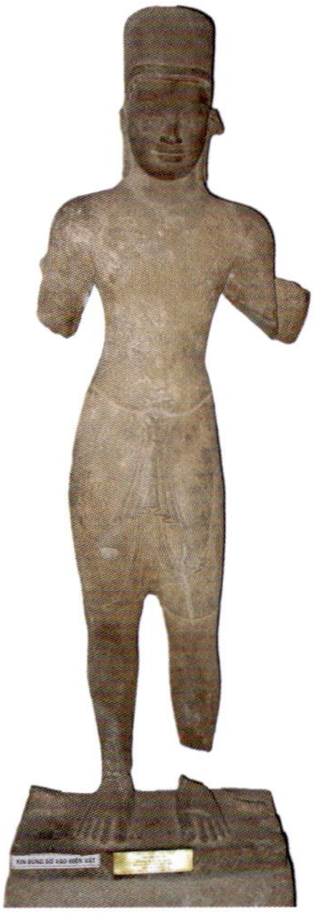

Fig. 9 *Viṣṇu, Bình Hòa, Đồng Nai province, Vietnam, ca. 7th cent. CE, Đồng Nai Province Museum, BTĐN 02. (Photo: Paul A. Lavy)*

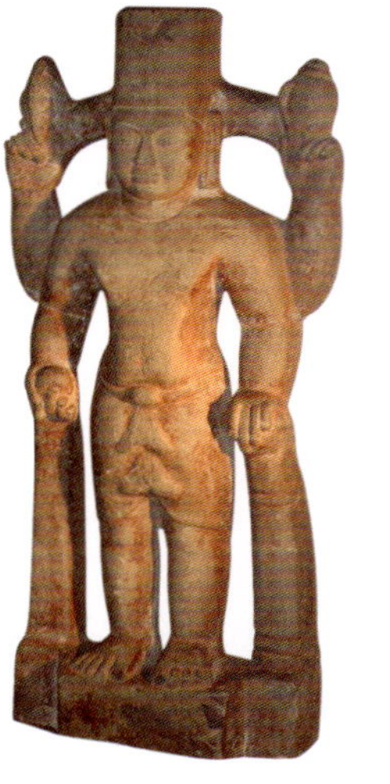

Fig. 8 *Viṣṇu, Gò Trâm Qùy, Long An province, Vietnam, ca. 7th cent. CE, Long An Province Museum, BTLA.Đa.40. (Photo: Paul A. Lavy)*

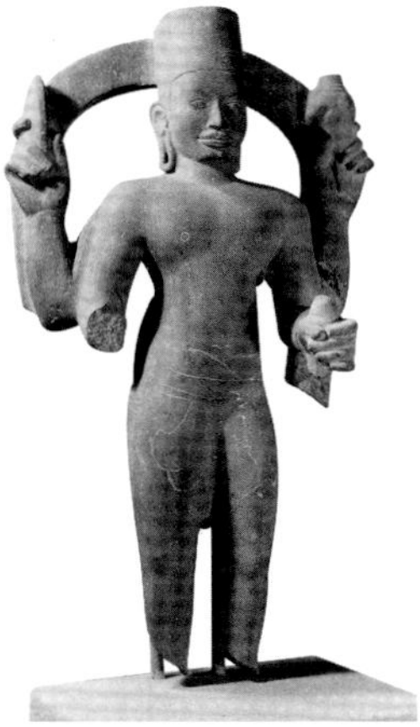

Fig. 10 *Viṣṇu, Prasat Chót Mạt, Tây Ninh province, Vietnam, ca. 8th cent. CE, Fine Arts Museum, Hồ Chí Minh City, BTMT 187. (Photo: fonds d'archives de l'École française d'Extrême-Orient: EFEO_CAM20198_1)*

province) (**Fig. 10**).[30] It is relatively well-preserved, having survived with its body, head, the upper portion of its supporting arch, and three arms and hands intact together with the *cakra*, conch, and the pommel of the mace. Like Prasat Andet style images, it has a mustache, and the garment is outfitted with a perfunctory pocket-fold, but in this case, it is moved to the right thigh. The mitre, however, lacks the characteristic Prasat Andet style angled protrusion over the temples, and the rendering of the details of the garment with incisions rather than modeling suggests relationships with the subsequent style of Kompong Preah in the eighth century (Dupont 1955: 179).

Over the course of the seventh century, Vaiṣṇava devotion and religious dedications increasingly gave way to worship of the god Śiva. The rising popularity of Śaivism can be witnessed through stone inscriptions (Sanderson 2003/2004), the appearance and spread of figural images of Śiva (Guy 2018), and in the importance of Harihara, a deity consistently portrayed in Khmer art with a bilateral division between the proper left side, with the attributes of Viṣṇu (Hari), and the hierarchically superior, proper right side with the attributes of Śiva (Hara) (Lavy 2003; Lê 2014: 120). Mitred Viṣṇu images would continue to be made in Cambodia through the ninth century style of Kulen, and Viṣṇu would remain an important feature of Khmer art for centuries to come. But, by the late seventh century, Viṣṇu's domination of the Mekong Delta had come to an end.

References

Bénisti, Mireille. 1965. 'Représentations khmères de Viṣṇu couché'. *Arts Asiatiques* 11, 1: 91-117.

Bakker, Hans. 1991. 'The Footprints of the Lord'. In: Diana L. Eck & Françoise Mallison (eds.), *Devotion Divine: Bhakti Traditions from the Regions of India: Studies in Honour of Charlotte Vaudeville*. Groningen: Egbert Forsten: 18-37.

Begley, W.E. 1973. *Viṣṇu's Flaming Wheel: The Iconography of the Sudarśana-Cakra.* New York: New York University Press.

Bhattacharya, Gouriswar. 2007. 'Vāsudeva-Viṣṇu Images from Bengal: Development and Innovation: Is Lotus an Essential Attribute?' In: G. Bhattacharya *et al.* (eds.), *Kalhār (White Water-Lily): Studies in Art, Iconography, Architecture and Archaeology of India and Bangladesh (Professor Enamul Haque Felicitation Volume)*. New Delhi: Kaveri Books: 99-108.

Bhattacharya, Gouriswar. 2011-2012. 'The Lotus Attribute of Viṣṇu'. *Jñāna-Pravāha Research Journal* XV: 11-22.

Bhattacharya, Kamaleswar. 1961. *Les religions brahmaniques dans l'ancien Cambodge: d'après l'épigraphie et l'iconographie*. Paris: École française d'Extrême-Orient.

Bidyabinod, Pandit B.B. 1920. 'Varieties of the Vishnu Image'. In: *Memoirs of the Archaeological Survey of India* no. 2. New Delhi: Archaeological Survey of India: 23-33.

Biswas, T.K. & Bhogen Dra Jha. 1985. *Gupta Sculptures: Bharat Kala Bhavan*. New Delhi: Books & Books.

Boisselier, Jean. 1955. *La Statuaire khmère et son évolution*. Saigon: École française d'Extrême-Orient.

Boisselier, Jean. 1966. *Le Cambodge*. Manuel d'archéologie d'Extrême-Orient, pt. 1, Asie du Sud-Est, vol. 1. Paris: Editions A. et J. Picard.

Boisselier, Jean. 1981. 'The Avalokiteśvara in the Museum's Wilstach Collection'. *Bulletin of the Philadelphia Museum of Art* 77, no. 333: 11-24.

Brereton, Joel P. & Stephanie W. Jamison. 2020. *The Rigveda: A Guide*. New York: Oxford University Press.

Brown, Robert L. 1992. 'Indian Art Transformed: The Earliest Sculptural Styles of Southeast Asia'. In: Johannes Bronkhorst (ed.), *Panels of the VIIth World Sanskrit Conference*. Leiden: E. J. Brill: 40-53.

Brown, Robert L. 2000. 'The Early Viṣṇu images from Southeast Asia and their India Relationships'. A paper presented at *Crossroads and Commodification: A Symposium on Southeast Asian Art History*, University of Michigan, 25-26 March. [Unpublished]

Cœdès, George. 1931. 'Études cambodgiennes: XXV. Deux inscriptions sanskrites du Fou-Nan'. *Bulletin de l'École française d'Extrême-Orient* 31, 1/2: 1-8.

Cœdès, George. 1937. 'A New Inscription from Fu-Nan'. *Journal of the Greater India Society* 4, 2: 117-121.

Dalsheimer, Nadine. 2001. *Les collections du musée national de Phnom Penh: l'art du Cambodge ancien*. Paris: École française d'Extrême-Orient.

Dalsheimer, Nadine. 2011. *Le corps des*

dieux: contribution à l'étude de la formation de l'art khmer. Paris: L'Harmattan.

Dalsheimer, Nadine & Manguin, Pierre-Yves. 1998. 'Visnu mitrés et réseaux marchands en Asie du Sud-Est: nouvelles données archéologiques sur le Ier millénaire apr. J.-C.'. *Bulletin de l'École française d'Extrême-Orient* 85, 1: 87-123.

Đỗ Bá Nghiệp & Võ Sĩ Khải. 1977. 'Tượng cổ bằng đá ở lòng song Đồng Nai (Đồng Nai)'. *Những phát hiện mới về khảo cổ học năm 1977*: 189-192.

Dowling, Nancy H. 2011. *The Measured Art: A Proportional Analysis of Early Khmer Sculpture*. Bangkok: White Lotus Press.

Dupont, Pierre. 1936. 'La statuaire en ronde-bosse dans l'Asie du sud-est'. *Revue des arts asiatiques* 10, 2: 97-106.

Dupont, Pierre. 1941. 'Viṣṇu mitrés de l'Indochine occidentale'. *Bulletin de l'École française d'Extrême-Orient* 41: 233-254.

Dupont, Pierre. 1955. *La statuaire préangkorienne*. Ascona: Artibus Asiae Supplementum.

Feneley, Marnie. 2013. 'The context of the West Mebon Viṣṇu'. In: Marijke J. Klokke &Veronique Degroot (eds.), *Materializing Southeast Asia's Past: Selected Papers From the 12th International Conference of the European Association of Southeast Asian Archaeologists* 2: 140-155.

Gail, Adalbert J. 2009. 'The Earth and the Lotus: A Contribution to Viṣṇu's Iconography in India'. *Pandanus: Nature in Literature, Art, Myth and Ritual* 3, 1: 83-91.

Gerschheimer, Gerdi and Dominic Goodall. 2014. "Que cette demeure de Śrīpati dure sur terre...': L'inscription préangkorienne K. 1254 du musée d'Angkor Borei'. *Bulletin de l'École française d'Extrême-Orient* 100: 113-146.

Gonda, Jan. 1954. *Aspects of Early Viṣṇuism*. Utrecht: A. Oosthoek.

Gonda, Jan. 1966. *Ancient Indian Kingship from the Religious Point of View*. Leiden: E. J. Brill.

Goodall, Dominic. 2012. 'Les influences littéraires indiennes dans les inscriptions du Cambodge: l'exemple d'un chef-d'œuvre inédit du VIIIe siècle (K. 1236)'. *Comptes rendus de l'Académie des inscriptions et belles-lettres* I (January-March): 345-357.

Goodall, Dominic. 2020. 'Two Inscriptions from Liṅgaparvata (Vat Phu), One Dating to Jayavarman I's Reign (K. 1059) and the Other to Jayavarman II's (K. 1060), Along with a Re-edition of K. 762'. *Udaya: Journal of Khmer Studies* 15: 3-38.

Griffiths, Arlo. 2014. 'Early Indic Inscriptions of Southeast Asia'. In: John Guy (ed.), *Lost Kingdoms: Hindu-Buddhist Sculpture of Early Southeast Asia*, New York: The Metropolitan Museum of Art: 53-57.

Gupta, Vinay Kumar. 2019. 'Vṛṣṇi in Ancient Art and Literature'. In: Corinna Wessels-Mevissen & Gerd J.R. Mevissen (eds.), *Indology's Pulse: Arts in Context: Essays Presented to Doris Meth Srinivasan in Admiration of Her Scholarly Research*. New Delhi: Aryan Books International: 71-92.

Guy, John (ed.). 2014. *Lost Kingdoms: Hindu-Buddhist Sculpture of Early Southeast Asia*. New York: Metropolitan Museum of Art.

Guy, John. 2014. 'Introducing Early Southeast Asia'. In: John Guy (ed.), *Lost Kingdoms: Hindu-Buddhist Sculpture of Early Southeast Asia*. New York: The Metropolitan Museum of Art: 3-13.

Guy, John. 2018. 'Shiva's Land: Understanding the Religious Landscape of Early Southeast Asia'. In: Shyam Saran (ed.), *Cultural and Civilisational Links between India and Southeast Asia: Historical and Contemporary Dimensions*. Singapore: Palgrave Macmillan: 253-274.

Härtel, Herbert. 1987. 'Archaeological Evidence of the Early Vāsudeva Worship'. In: Edenda Curaverunt *et al.* (eds.), *Orientalia Iosephi Tucci Memoriae Dicata. Volume 2*. Rome: Istituto Italiano per il Medio ed Estremo Oriente: 573-587.

Jacq-Hergoualc'h, Michel. 2002. *The Malay Peninsula: Crossroads of the Maritime Silk Road*. Leiden: Brill.

Jessup, Helen & Thierry Zéphir (eds.). 1997. *Sculpture of Angkor and Ancient Cambodia: Millennium of Glory*. Washington, D.C.: National Gallery of Art.

Krishna, Nanditha. 1980. *The Art and Iconography of Vishnu-Narayana*. Bombay: Taraporevala.

Krishnakumari, Myneni. 2010. *Iconography and Art of Andhra: Lesser Known Facets*. New Delhi: Harman Publishing House.

Kuiper, F. B. J. 1962. 'The Three Strides of Viṣṇu'. In: Ernest Bender (ed.), *Indological Studies in Honor of W. Norman Brown*. New Haven: American Oriental Society: 137-151.

Lavy, Paul A. 2003. 'As in Heaven, So on Earth: The Politics of Viṣṇu, Śiva and Harihara Images in Preangkorian Khmer Civilisation'. *Journal of Southeast Asian Studies* 34, 1: 21-39.

Lavy, Paul A. 2004. *Viṣṇu and Harihara in the Art and Politics of Early Historic Southeast Asia*. Doctoral Dissertation. Los Angeles: University of California.

Lavy, Paul A. 2014. 'Conch-on-Hip Images in Peninsular Thailand and the Beginning of Vaiṣṇava Sculpture in Southeast Asia'. In: Nicolas Revire and Stephen A. Murphy (eds.), *Before Siam: Essays in Art and Archaeology*. Bangkok: River Books & The Siam Society: 152-173.

Lavy, Paul A. 2020. 'Early Vaiṣṇava Sculpture in Southeast Asia and the Question of Pallava Influence'. In: Robert DeCaroli and Paul A. Lavy (eds.), *Across the South of Asia: A Volume in Honor of Robert L. Brown*. New Delhi: DK Printworld: 213-250.

Lavy, Paul A. 2022. 'An Isolated Viṣṇu Sculpture from Sathing Phra, Thailand'. In: Nicolas Revire and Pitchaya Soomjinda (eds.), *Decoding Southeast Asian Art: Studies in Honor of Piriya Krairiksh*. Bangkok: River Books & The Piriya Krairiksh Foundation, 90-103.

Lavy, Paul A. & Wesley Clarke. 2015. 'Integrating the Phong Tuek Viṣṇu: The Archaeology and Art History of a Forgotten Image'. *Journal of the Siam Society* 103: 19-62.

Lê Thị Liên. 2005. 'Gold Plaques and Their Cultural Contexts in the Oc Eo Culture'. *Bulletin of the Indo-Pacific Prehistory Association* 25: 145-154.

Lê Thị Liên. 2006. *Nghệ thuật Phật giáo và Hindu giáo ở Đồng bằng sông Cửu Long trước thế kỷ X* (*Buddhist and Hindu Art of the Mekong Delta before the Tenth Century*). Hanoi: Thế Giới.

Lê Thị Liên. 2011. 'Hindu Deities in Southern Vietnam'. In: Pierre-Yves

Manguin, A. Mani & Geoff Wade (eds.). *Early Interactions between South and Southeast Asia: Reflections on Cross-Cultural Exchange*. Singapore: Institute of Southeast Asian Studies: 407-431.

Lê Thị Liên. 2014. 'Hindu-Buddhist Sculpture in Southern Vietnam: Evolution of Icons and Styles to the Eighth Century'. In: John Guy (ed.), *Lost Kingdoms: Hindu-Buddhist Sculpture of Early Southeast Asia*, New York: The Metropolitan Museum of Art: 118-121.

Lê Thị Liên. 2015a. 'History of Maritime Contacts between Vietnam and India: Archaeological Evidence from Oc Eo Culture in Southern Vietnam'. In: Sila Tripati (ed.), *Maritime Contacts of the Past: Deciphering Connections Amongst Communities,* New Delhi: Delta Book World: 95-123.

Lê Thị Liên. 2015b. 'Hindu Beliefs and the Maritime Network in Southern Vietnam during the Early Common Era'. *Journal of Indo-Pacific Archaeology* 39: 1-17.

Lê Xuân Diệm, Đào Linh Côn & Võ Sĩ Khải. 1995. *Văn hóa Óc Eo: Những khám phá mới*. Hanoi: Nhà xuất bản khoa học xã hội.

Liebert, Gösta. 1976. *Iconographic Dictionary of the Indian Religions: Hinduism–Buddhism–Jainism.* Leiden: E. J. Brill.

Mace, Sonya Rhie & Bertrand Porte (eds.). 2021. *Revealing Krishna: Essays on the History, Context, and Conservation of Krishna Lifting Mount Govardhan from Phnom Da*. Cleveland: The Cleveland Museum of Art.

Malleret, Louis. 1937. *Catalogue général des collections du Musée Blanchard de la Brosse, Saigon*, vol. 1, *Arts de la famille indienne*. Hanoi: Imprimerie d'Extrême-Orient.

Malleret, Louis. 1959. *L'archéologie du Delta du Mékong*, vol. 1, *L'exploration archéologique et les fouilles d'Oc-Èo*. Paris: École française d'Extrême-Orient.

Malleret, Louis. 1960. *L'archéologie du Delta du Mékong*, vol. 2, *La civilisation matérielle d'Oc-Èo*. Paris: École française d'Extrême-Orient.

Malleret, Louis. 1963. *L'archéologie du Delta du Mékong*, vol. 4, *Le Cisbassac*. Paris: École française d'Extrême-Orient.

Manguin, Pierre-Yves. 2010. 'Pan-Regional Responses to South Asian Inputs in Early Southeast Asia'. In: Bérénice Bellina, Elisabeth A. Bacus, Thomas Oliver Pryce & Jan Wisseman Christie (eds.), *50 Years of Archaeology in Southeast Asia*. Bangkok: River Books: 171-181.

Manguin, Pierre-Yves. 2019. 'The Transmission of Vaiṣṇavism Across the Bay of Bengal: Trade Networks and State Formation in Early Historic Southeast Asia'. In: A. Schottenhammer (ed.), *Early Global Interconnectivity across the Indian Ocean World*, vol. 2, *Exchange of Ideas, Religions, and Technologies*. Cham, Switzerland: Palgrave Macmillan: 51-68.

Manguin, Pierre-Yves & Miriam T. Stark. 2022. 'Mainland Southeast Asia's Earliest Kingdoms and the Case of 'Funan''. In: C. F. W. Higham & Nam C. Kim (eds.), *The Oxford Handbook of Early Southeast Asia*. New York: Oxford University Press: 637-659.

Mani, V.R. 1985. *The Cult of Weapons: The Iconography of the Āyudhapuruṣas*. Delhi: Agam Kala Prakashan.

Nguyễn Công Bình, Lê Xuân Diệm & Mạc Đường. 1990. *Văn hóa và cư dân đồng bằng sông Cửu Long*. Hanoi: Nxb: Khoa học xã hội.

Nigam, M.L. 2000-2001. 'Identification of Vasudeva/Krishna Images in Early Indian Art'. *Kalā* 7: 109-116.

O'Connor, Stanley J., Jr. 1972. *Hindu Gods of Peninsular Siam*. Ascona: Artibus Asiae Supplementum.

Parimoo, Ratan. 1983. *Sculptures of Śeṣaśāyī Viṣṇu: Survey, Iconological Interpretation, Formal Analysis*. Baroda: Maharaja Sayajirao University of Baroda.

Parimoo, Ratan. 2000. 'Vishnu's Weapons and Their Representation in Indian Arts'. In: *Studies in Indian Sculpture (Regional Genres and Interpretations)*. New Delhi: Books & Books: 138-157.

Piriya Krairiksh. 1987. *A History of the Visual Arts in Thailand: The Prehistoric and Protohistoric Periods*. Bangkok: Amarin.

Piriya Krairiksh. 2012. *The Roots of Thai Art*. Bangkok: River Books. [First published in Thai as *Rakngao haeng sinlapa thai*, 2553 (2010 CE)].

Porte, Bertrand. 2016. 'Sculptures transformées, du Phnom Da au Núi Ba Thê'. *Arts Asiatiques* 71: 141-158.

Sanderson, A. 2003/2004. 'The Śaiva Religion among the Khmers, part 1'. *Bulletin de l'École française d'Extrême-Orient* 90-91: 349-462.

Sharma, Brijendra Nath. 1968. 'Viṣṇu-Trivikrama in Literature, Art and Epigraphs'. *East and West* 18, 3/4: 323-334.

Sinha, Kanad. 2019. 'Purāṇic Vaiṣṇavism and the Guptas: A Study of Kingship, Legitimacy and Religion'. In: Kunal Chakrabarti & Kanad Sinha (eds.), *State, Power and Legitimacy: The Gupta Kingdom*. Delhi: Primus Books: 684-690.

Soutif, Dominique. 2009a. *Organisation religieuse et profane du temple khmer du VIIe au XIIIe siècle*. Doctoral Dissertation. Paris: Université Sorbonne nouvelle–Paris 3.

Soutif, Dominique. 2009b. 'À propos de trois possibles attributs mobiles dans les inscriptions khmères'. *Siksācakr* 11': 22-42.

Taddei, Maurizio. 1991. 'Reflections on Śaṅkha in Vaiṣṇava Iconography'. In: Adalbert J. Gail & Gerd J.R. Mevissen (eds.). *South Asian Archaeology 1991*. Stuttgart: Franz Steiner Verlag: 647-658.

Tarr, Gary. 1970. 'Chronology and Development of the Chāḷukya Cave Temples'. *Ars Orientalis* 8: 155-184.

Tingley, Nancy (ed.). 2009. *Arts of Ancient Viet Nam: From River Plain to Open Sea*. New York: Asia Society.

Vogel, Jean Philippe. 1925. 'The Earliest Sanskrit Inscriptions of Java'. *Publicaties van den Oudheidkundigen Dienst in Nederlandsch-Indië* 1: 15-35.

Võ Sĩ Khải. 2003. 'The Kingdom of Fu Nan and the Culture of Oc Eo'. In: James C. M. Khoo (ed.), *Art and Archaeology of Fu Nan: Pre-Khmer Kingdom of the Lower Mekong Valley*. Bangkok: Orchid Press: 35-85.

Võ Sĩ Khải & Đào Linh Côn. 1998. 'Về hai pho tượng Vishnu mới phát hiện tại Gò Tháp Mười (Đồng Tháp)'. *Những phát hiện mới về khảo cổ học năm 1998*: 732-734.

Woodward, Hiram. 2005. *The Art and Architecture of Thailand: From Prehistoric Times through the Thirteenth Century*, 2nd ed. Brill: Leiden.

Endnotes

1 For discussion and images of the gold foil plaques, see Lê 2005: 149-151; 2006: 131-136; 2011: 415-417. In addition, sculptures of Kṛṣṇa-Govardhana were a prominent aspect of the Preangkorian art of Phnom Da in Cambodia's Ta Keo province (Mace & Porte 2021).

2 For Viṣṇu's three strides, see Kuiper 1962. For Viṣṇu's footprints, see Bakker 1991.

3 Trivikrama can be translated as 'taking three steps' or 'he who strode over the three worlds in three steps' or 'conqueror of the three worlds' (Liebert 1976: 307).

4 Griffiths (2014: 53-54) dates the Pūrṇavarman inscriptions to the sixth century.

5 See Malleret 1959: 85, 403-407, pl. LXXXVIa-b; Porte 2016: 137-138, figs. 17a-c.

6 Lê Thị Liên has inventoried over forty-five Viṣṇu sculptures (including reliefs, fragments, and incomplete carvings) from southern Vietnam alone (Lê 2006: 198-200, Table 2.2; 2015a: 116; 2015b: 5). This list, however, does not include sculptures in private and public collections outside of Vietnam, and further examples have come to light in Vietnam in recent years, for example in Vĩnh Long in 2002 and at Gò Tháp in 2018.

7 With a lotus (*padma*), rather than- or synonymous with- the orb, this configuration is identified in the Indian iconographical texts that enumerate the twenty-four forms of Viṣṇu as either Janārdana or Vāsudeva (Bidyabinod 1920: 23-33).

8 For the Vāsudeva-Kṛṣṇa identification, I follow Piriya 1987: 111-112 and Brown 2000: 2-6. For the development of this iconography in India, see Härtel 1987; Nigam 2000-2001; Gupta 2019.

9 Relevant inscriptions include K. 21, K. 165, K. 262, K. 263, K. 275, K. 762, K. 1264. See Dupont 1955: 143-146; K. Bhattacharya 1961: 103-105; Gail 2009: 84; Soutif 2009b: 22-23; Goodall 2020: 20.

10 It has been suggested that the lotus first appears in Viṣṇu's hand during the fourth century, but this is unproven, and others have argued that the lotus does not seem to become an attribute of Viṣṇu until the sixth or seventh century (G. Bhattacharya 2007: 99-104; 2011-2012; Gail 2009: 83-89).

11 Dupont's 1941 and 1955 publications rely on a similar image typology but with adjustments to the groups, their constituents, and the chronology. A detailed summary and critique can be found in Lavy 2004: 205-250.

12 The captions for drawings "A" and "B" are reversed in Dupont 1941, pl. XXXXVI. The mistake is noted in Dupont 1955: 124, n. 11. See also Malleret 1963: 57-58, 144.

13 Long An Viṣṇu (BTLS.5525): Lê 2006: 69, fig. 61.

14 Ô Lâm Viṣṇu (MBB.2984): Malleret 1959: 397-398, pl. LXXXIII-c; Lê 2006: 71, figs. 66-67.

15 Dupont 1941: 237; 1955: 130-132; Lavy 2004: 354-359; Dowling 2011: 69-74.

16 H. 149 cm. It is now in the Đồng Tháp Museum, Cao Lãnh. See Võ & Đào 1998; Võ 2003: 36, 54, figs. II-1, II-19-20; Lê 2006: 62, fig. 40, 69-70, fig. 60; Guy 2014: 131-132, cat. no. 59.

17 Vat Cetdei Viṣṇu (H. 60 cm), carved in high relief: Malleret 1963: 14-15 (no. 146), 146, pl. III (bottom).

18 Gò Thành Viṣṇu (H. 44 cm): See Lê 2006: 70, fig. 62. Now in the Tiền Giang Museum.

19 Thân Cựu Nghĩa Viṣṇu (H. 105 cm): Dupont 1941: 241, pl. XXXVIB; Dupont 1955: 124, 130-132; Malleret 1963: 55, no. 219, 145, pl. III (top).

20 Prasat Don Tha Em Viṣṇu (with head, H. 40 cm): Malleret 1963: 92-93; no. 2948, pl. IV; Lê 2006: 71, fig. 65. Since its first publication by Malleret, its head and upper hands/attributes have gone missing. Now in the Fine Arts Museum, Hồ Chí Minh City. To this list may also be added another Viṣṇu (H. 38 cm) from Prasat Don Tha Em (Malleret, 1963: 92, 147, pl. IV).

21 The Vat Ek Viṣṇu (H. 90 cm with tenon) is almost entirely intact: Malleret 1963: 30-31, no. 176, pl. II; Lê 2006: 70-71, fig. 64.

22 This second Gò Tháp Viṣṇu (H. 55 cm) is also in the Đồng Tháp Museum. See Võ 2003: 47, 53, pls. II-13, II-17; Lê 2006: 72-73, figs. 69-70.

23 This figure (H. 53 cm), now headless and missing the better part of all four arms, was found at Prasat Pram Loveng and now resides in the Fine Arts Museum, Hồ Chí Minh City. See Malleret 1937: 81-2, pl. XVII; Dupont 1955: 58-59.

24 The Viṣṇu from Gò Trâm Qùy (H. 42 cm) is in the Long An Museum. See Lê, Đào & Võ 1995: 287, 290; Lê 2006: 74-75, fig. 76.

25 For the sculptures from Phnom Da, see Dupont 1955: 21-42 and Mace & Porte 2021.

26 The various viewpoints are summarized in Lavy 2004: 227-232, 287-301 and Tingley 2009: 158; see also Mace & Porte 2021.

27 National Museum of Cambodia, Phnom Penh, Ka. 1597. See Jessup & Zéphir 1997: 163-164, cat. no. 15.

28 The stylistic development is discussed in Dupont 1955: 43-48. The Bình Hòa Viṣṇu (H. 1.67 m) is housed in the Đồng Nai Museum (BTĐN 02). See Đỗ & Võ 1977; Lê, Đào & Võ 1995: 286-288; Tingley 2009: 148-159, cat. no. 45; Lê 2006: 74, fig. 74.

29 Now in the Tây Ninh Museum (H. 2.20 m). See Lê 2006: 74, fig. 75.

30 H. 56 cm. Now in the Fine Arts Museum, Hồ Chí Minh City (BTMT 187). See Malleret 1963: 82, pl. IV (bottom right); Tingley 2009: 146-147, cat. no. 39; Guy 2014: 140, cat. 67.

8 | Art of Óc Eo in the Đồng Tháp Mười style

Lê Thị Liên

Introduction

From the second half of the first millennium BCE, the development of maritime trade between India and Southeast Asia made it possible for Buddhism and Hinduism to be drawn into Southeast Asian coastal and island communities. Evidence has been found from the sites around the Gulf of Siam and on both sides of the Malay peninsular, Java and along the central and southern coast of Vietnam (Bellina and Glover: 2004; Glover and Bellina 2011; Bellina et al. 2014; Manguin and Indradjaja 2011; Lâm Thị Mỹ Dung 2011; Trương Đắc Chiến 2018; Lê Thị Liên 2018). The evidence was unearthed in the contexts of local communities adopting and sharing not only technology and materials but also locally made products conferring symbol status (Bellina 2017). In the early centuries CE, the demand for luxury goods and specialties from Chinese, Roman, Central and Western Asian people increased. As a result, the maritime network that was already active among Southeast Asian communities, vibrantly impacted emerging states (Borell et al. 2014, Ardika 2015). As a result, religious structures, sculptures and symbolic objects appeared. The brick architecture SB1B in the Bujang valley on the peninsula was among the earliest (Chia and Watson 2011: 36, 37).

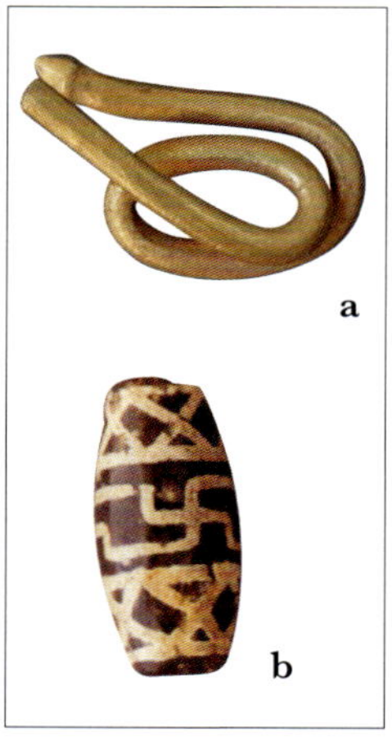

Fig. 1 **a** *Gold artifact as realistic Linga, 1st BC-1st century CE, Giong Lon site (Bà Rịa Vũng Tàu Museum);* **b** *Bead with Swastika symbol, Go Hang site (Long An Museum) (Photo: a-Trương Đắc Chiến; b-Vương Thu Hồng)*

The Mekong Delta, with its favorable geographic location, soon became engaged in these activities. Local prehistoric communities had a fairly high level of development in agriculture, stone and bronze tool-making techniques from the late Neolithic and Metal Age. Their pottery tradition was well preserved and innovated to meet the demands of new markets (Bellwood et al. 2011; Nishimura 2005). Along with the recession of the coastline from 4,000 years ago, especially the decreased sea level at one metre lower than today, a large young alluvial plain was formed by the Mekong River. As a result, several groups of people from the higher terraces created by the low fertile red basalt hills quickly came down to exploit the newly formed lands. The river systems were crisscrossed, having many river mouths opening to the sea, which facilitated exchange and contact with the outside world from the second half of the first millennium BCE. Important trading centres were active in the first centuries BCE-CE in Cần Giờ, coastal Hà Tiên and Ba Thê-Óc Eo areas (Trương Đắc Chiến 2017; Nguyễn Quốc Mạnh 2018; Lê Thị Liên et al. 2018). The exploitation of the new delta made for a boom in agriculture. In addition, the active integration into the maritime trading system brought great opportunities for local people to develop a complex society – called Funan in Chinese annals. The evidence of their society was unearthed from hundreds of archaeological sites of Óc Eo culture (Malleret 1962: 307-456; Lê Xuân Diệm et al 1995; Manguin 2009).

The development of the local communities into the urban sites of early Funan was a process of forming a main centre that played the prominent role in the economy, polity, culture and religion in each region. Works of art found in these centres, reflect a general trend of adopting elements of Indian civilization, mainly in forms of Buddhist and Hindu art, simultaneously combined with indigenous beliefs in a new society that changed gradually from the rural villages into civilized urban centres. In the early period of Óc Eo culture (the first few centuries CE), the vestiges only appeared in a few areas, mainly Óc Eo-Ba Thê, Gò Tháp and some places in Long An province. However, by the middle of the first millennium CE, there was a blossoming of monuments and sculptures across the Delta, along with the prosperous development of the Funan polity (Lê Thị Liên 2006b: Maps I, II). In particular, the excavation results at key sites, such as Óc Eo-Ba Thê, Đá Nổi, Nền Chùa, Gò Tháp, etc. provided important evidence on the relationship between the archaeological sites and art works. The function and significance of the unearthed artifacts contribute greatly in defining the chronological frame of many works of art in the museum collections and to the understanding of the formation and development trends of Óc Eo art in the first millennium CE.

The formation and development of the Óc Eo – Funan art

The art of the Óc Eo culture, as in many other Southeast Asian regions, was mainly Buddhist and Hindu, with a unique combination of indigenous beliefs. The symbols related to these two religions existed very early (around the first centuries BCE-CE) in the societies of pre-Óc Eo communities in South Vietnam, such as Giồng Lớn (Bà Rịa-Vũng Tàu City), Gò Cao Su (Long An province), Giồng Nổi (Bến Tre province) etc.

Being the earliest polity-owned trading centre in Southeast Asia, Óc Eo-Ba Thê was also the site where the largest number of art objects was found, including the earliest ones. Tablets or amulets bearing Brāhmī characters of different periods show many symbols and images of gods and goddesses. The moulds bearing the Buddhist symbol of their owners clearly demonstrate how religions and their artistic themes were propagated and adopted (Malleret 1960: Pls. Pl. XV, XVI, XLI, CI-CIII, CVIII-CXI).

Likewise, the presence of small Buddhist images with various early art styles and origins indicate frequent contacts of Óc Eo people with diverse art schools during their early art history (Malleret 1960: Pl. LXXXIV, LXXXV; Lê Thị Liên 2006b: Ills. 28-33). Merchants, craftsmen and monks played important roles in the diffusion of religions and art to inland and riverine areas, as indicated by vestiges of religious ceremonies and various types of beads, coins, jewelry, and figurines found in the inland sites. These artifacts indicate that they came from or were related to various different regions

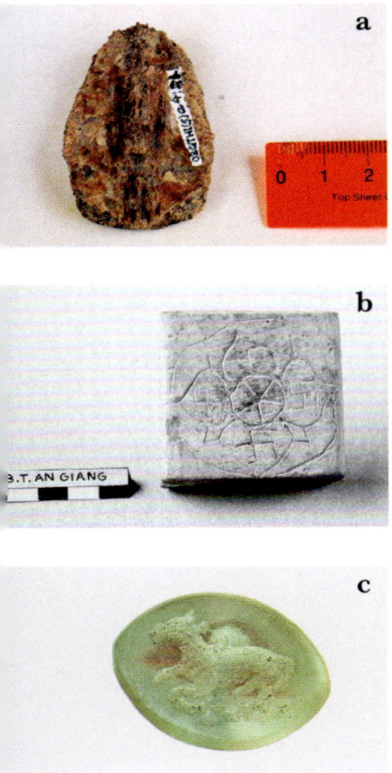

Fig. 2 **a** Linga, *tortoiseshell, Go Thap site (Dong Thap Museum);* **b** *Image of lotus flower with* swastikas *on a stone mould for jewellery casting, Oc Eo site (An Giang Museum);* **c** *Seal with image of Nandin, quartz, Canh Đền site (Kien Giang Museum) (Photo: a, c- Lê Thị Liên; b- Nguyễn Hữu Thiết)*

of the Indian subcontinent, most notably Northwest and South India, the Mediterranean, Central Asia and China (as in the Đồng Tháp Mười area that will be discussed later).

Before sizeable and solid temples were built, the knowledge and worship practice of the people towards the gods of Indian origin was reflected in the uptake of new elements that were combined with an existing tradition, as witnessed by the presence of phallic or naturalistic types of small *liṅgas*, which were made of terracotta at Óc Eo site, of tortoiseshell or small pebbles in Gò Tháp site, of stone in Gò Cao Su and Nhơn Thành sites, of earthenware in Giồng Nổi site, and various religious symbols appeared on potteries, molds, beads and so on (Malleret 1960: 378, Pl. XLII; Lê Thị Liên 2015b: Figs. 5-7; Nguyễn Quốc Mạnh 2020: 31-3, Fig. 4).

Modest temples in the form of houses on stilts with wooden columns and thatched with coconut leaves or other lightweight materials might have been in vogue in the villages, as one image on a piece of gold in Gò Tháp suggests (Lê Thị Liên 2006b: Table. 2.5, No. 6). Thus, the dawn of Óc Eo art history was also the period of development of goods exchange activities on a larger scale than in the first few centuries CE. Adopting and selecting imported models and creating simple products that served the needs of the local community were preparatory steps for the higher development of art in the next period.

From the early centuries CE, there might have been some brick temples built on high ground. They are indicated by terracotta human figurines, *kūḍu* with a *maithunā* couples and A-type tiles, according to Manguin, or Arikamedu style discovered in Óc Eo-Ba Thê site (Malleret 1959: Pl. LXX; LXXXa; Manguin 2006; Lê Thị Liên 2012-personal survey). Early fragments of Indian-type tiles have also been discovered in the context of religious architecture (brick ruins 2018.LSB.KT23) on the slopes of Ba Thê mountain, in the earliest stage of construction in the 1st-3rd centuries CE (Nguyễn Gia Đối et. al. 2020: 13-14). While Groslier (1966: 38-39) claims that the wooden statues in South Vietnam are the earliest sculptures made in the 4th-5th centuries, it is reasonable to believe that the first wooden Buddha images in *tribhaṅga* posture began to appear in the first few centuries CE, given the variety of sizes, styles and C-14 results of wooden statues discovered in Phong Mỹ, Đá Nổi and Gò Tháp (Malleret 1963: 165; Lê Thị Liên 2017: 65-66). A few sculptures from Ba Thê, Gò Tháp and Mỹ Thạnh Đông also suggest that Óc Eo people might have worshipped stone images from before the 5th century, which were probably influenced by Kushana-Gupta art (Nguyễn Gia Đối et al. 2020: Ill. 2; Lê Thị Liên 2006: 51, Ill. 24). Hindu art began with the representation of Hindu symbols on gold fragments, which were probably influenced by punch-marked coins, but soon had its own local character (Lê Thị Liên 2009: Figs. 1-6). Natural and realistic *liṅgas* are the earliest Hindu sculptures available in various shapes and sizes, reflecting the popularity of this belief among different social classes.

The 5th-6th centuries witnessed the flourishing of Óc Eo culture, with the expansion of residential areas, including many economic, cultural and religious centres throughout the Delta and a number of brick temples under construction (Manguin 2004: 296-300). This reached the pinnacle of Óc Eo art (Lê Thị Liên 2006: 60, 186, Maps I, II). The profound influences of Gupta and Pallava art are recognized, not only in art works but also the Brāhmī inscriptions and the small objects found from the major centres and widely spread in many sites in the lower Delta, including Đá Nổi, Nhơn Thạnh, Nền Chùa, Cạnh Đền, Kè Một ... (Lê Thị Liên 2015a: Fig. 11).

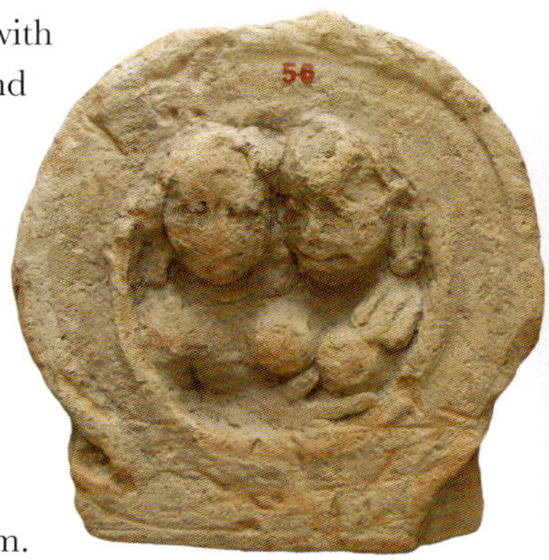

Fig. 3 Kudu, *terracotta, 2nd-4th century CE, Óc Eo site (An Giang Musem). (Photo: Lê Thị Liên)*

The artistic themes are represented in a variety of materials and form. Gold pieces engraved with religious symbols and images were popularly used in temple building rituals. Those discovered from Đá Nổi represent a more complex development in terms of techniques and themes in comparison with those from Gò Tháp in the earlier period (Lê Thị Liên 2011a: Fig. 20.12). Wood sculptures were mainly Buddha images (more details will be discussed later). Delicate decorative carvings of architectural components unearthed from major sites of Óc Eo, Nền Chùa, Gò Tháp, Tráp Đá, and Giồng Xoài, provided authentic evidence for the Chinese accounts on the splendid wooden palaces of the Funan people (Pelliot 1903: 254). Terracotta art works are few in number and found mainly in Óc Eo and Phụng Sơn Tự (Hồ Chí Minh City), in the form of decorative architectural reliefs (lion head reliefs, and *kūḍu* with male and female heads). Bronze sculptures are small in size and number, although some pieces are among the most beautiful works of art (Lê Thị Liên 2014: 121, Fig. 92).

The artists went through a process of receiving, imitating, selecting and finaly fixing the iconographic elements from Indian prototypes to create their own art for the Hindu sculptures in stone. The basic feature of this period is the combination of realistic elements, localization, and standardization of iconographical elements. The presence of various gods and goddesses represented the update and understanding in the development of Hindu pantheon.

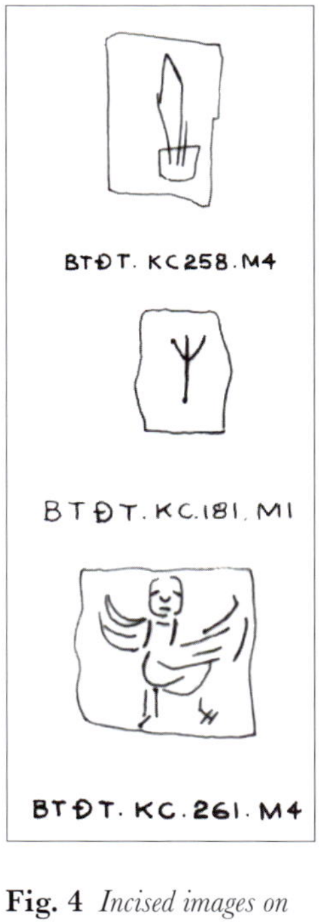

Fig. 4 *Incised images on gold plaques found from Sanctuaries at Go Thap* **a** Linga *in railing,* **b** Vajra; **c** Garuda, *2nd-4th century CE, (Dong Thap Museum) (Drawing: Nguyễn Đăng Cường)*

Buddhist sculptures in stone are smaller in number and represent mainly influences from late Gupta art in North India, although there is a lack of homogeneity in art style (Lê Thị Liên 2014: Fig. 87, Guy 2014: 97, Cat. 45).

Viṣṇu became the most prominent Hindu god in sculptural art, with symbolic criteria typified for the development of art in the next centuries, as observered from many other Hindu gods and goddesses. The small statues discovered at the Nhơn Thành site are considered to be the earliest known works, made on site around the beginning of the 5th century. Their prototypes are believed to be from the sculpture of early Gupta period in the 4th-5th centuries CE (Lê Thị Liên 2006b: 64-66, Ills. 43-45, 49-52; 2014a: Fig. 91). Apart from Nhơn Thành, many stone and wood carving factories might

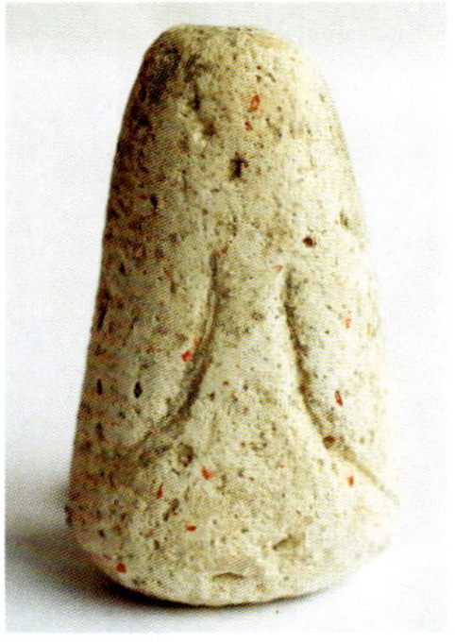

Fig. 5 Linga, *terracotta, Oc Eo site (An Giang Museum). (Photo: Lê Thị Liên)*

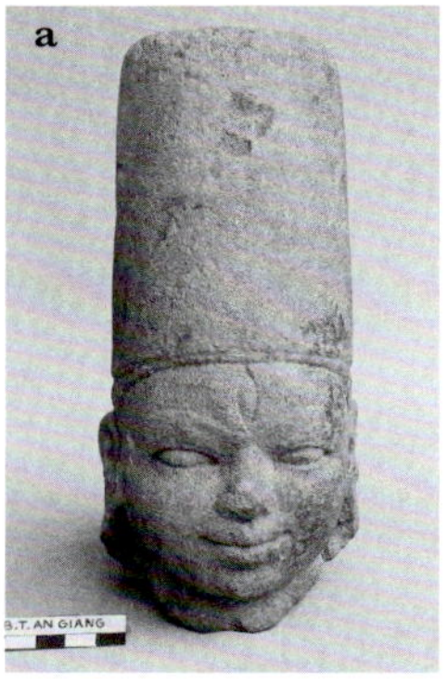

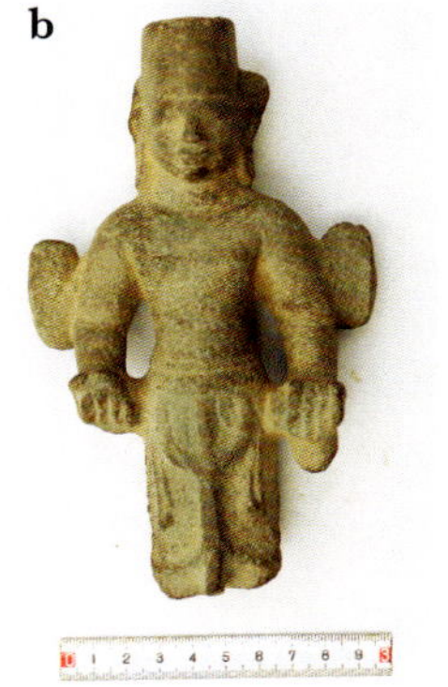

Fig. 6 a *Head of* Harihara, *stone, 5th century CE, Sanctuary A4, Oc Eo site (An Giang Museum);* **b** Visnu, *stone, Nhơn Thành site, early 5th CE (Can Tho Museum) (Photo: a- Nguyễn Hữu Thiết; b- Lê Thị Liên)*

have developed at other sites in the delta. The popularity of Viṣṇu sculptures and the presence of inscriptions, especially K. 5, lead to the viewpoint that Vaiṣṇavism was practiced at the highest level and preponderantly with royal Funanese patronage (Manguin 2014). However, the statistics of the presence of Śivaliṅga, Ekamukhaliṅga and Harihara suggest that not only Vaiṣṇava but also Śaivaism received royal patronage, especially in Ba Thê-Óc Eo, the most important centre that might once have been the capital of Funan in its heyday. At the same time, Śaivism was still popular with many social classes (Lê Thị Liên 2014a: 120; 2015b, 2020).

The 7th-8th century was considered a period of great political upheaval, with the decline of Funan and the rise of Zhenla. However, if there was a sudden change in material infrastructure with the decline or disappearance of Óc Eo cultural centres, then one can still observe a quite seamless continuation in the development of art styles, with some more perfect art works larger in size and in more diverse shrines around the 7th century. In Buddhism, besides Buddha images, there appeared more stone carvings representing the Bodhisattvas Avalokiteśvara and Maitreya. In Hinduism, there are a number of additional deities, notably the goddesses Durga Mahiṣāsuramardinī and Lakṣmī, Gaṇeśa and several fragmented images of male deities. It is worth noting that the places where these sculptures were found were usually in the coastal lowlands or high-lying terraces. From the 8th century, there was a sharp contrast with simultaneous developments in other parts of mainland Southeast Asia, such as Cambodia and Thailand (Hiram Woodward 2014). A small number of Buddhist monuments were still in active use in some coastal regions (mainly in Trà Vinh province). A number of Śiva temples survived, especially in the highlands.

Đồng Tháp Mười art style – Contribution to the formation of Phu Nam art

Đồng Tháp Mười region plays an important role in the formation and development of Óc Eo culture. In terms of geography and topographic features, this is the transition zone between the ancient alluvial terraces in the Southeastern region and the new alluvial zone of the Southwestern region. This is also an ancient shallow bay, with sandy clay mounds popular at the height of 2-2.5 m, the highest one not exceeding 3-5 m above current sea level. These mounds were mostly concentrated in the Gò Tháp area, interspersed with low-lying areas which creates many small natural waterways in the area.

Small fluctuations in sea level during the Óc Eo period had an impact on the environment in this area (Lê Thị Liên et al. 2014). Trading activities that flourished from the second half of the first millennium BCE, through the estuary of Cần Giờ, following the Đồng Nai and the Vàm Cỏ river systems, created chances for contacts and cultural exchanges between the riverine agricultural farmers of the Đồng Tháp Mười area in the Long An and Đồng

Tháp provinces with coastal residents and since then with civilizations outside. As a result, important population communities developed flourishingly in the Pre-Protohistory period (Nishimurta 2005; Reinecke 2012; Lê Thị Liên 2018: 117; Lê Thị Liên et al. 2018: 164-5).

At the dawn of the Óc Eo culture, in the 1st-3rd centuries CE, the imprints of direct or indirect exchanges with neighbouring cultures and other civilizations, such as the Sassanian empire to the West, North and South India and China were visible. The evidence includes ceramics, intaglio, beads, religious symbols on beads and jewellery, and small artifacts discovered from the sites in Bà Rịa-Vũng Tàu and Cần Giờ areas, Gò Ô Chùa, Gò Hàng and Gò Tháp (Trương Đắc Chiến 2018; Vương Thu Hồng 2005; Lê Thị Liên 2015a: Figs. 3, 4a, b, 8, 19). In addition, the innovation of typical pre-Óc Eo traditional ceramics, such as high-footed bowls and dishes with glossy black glazes were used side by side with fine table ware, at the sites in the Đồng Tháp Mười region and the Long Xuyên quadrangle. There was a common development tendency across the whole region, where the agricultural communities transformed themselves into commercial and urban societies with small and large handicraft workshops to serve the new needs in daily life.

Gò Tháp is considered, with its archaeological evidence and inscriptions, as the second most important site of the Óc Eo culture and the most important economic, cultural and political centre of the Đồng Tháp Mười region (Manguin 2004: 298; Lê Thị Liên 2005; Lê Thị Liên et al. 2014). The archaeological vestiges unearthed within the protected area of 300 ha, and also spread widely in the surrounding fields, provide rich information and knowledge on this centre.

This was a residential area formed a few centuries BCE, based on C-14 samples taken from below or in the layer of soil embankment for architecture (Võ Sĩ Khải 2003: 65; Lê Xuân Diệm et al. 1995: 86). The people lived on low hills and along small waterways and were mainly engaged in wet-rice agriculture with many varieties. They raised a wide varieties of poultry and livestock such as pigs, chickens and dogs. Burial customs tended to change from the traditional earth grave to semi-cremation and cremation in the first centuries BCE-CE. Burial of cremated ash in a ceramic jar gradually took over. The metal and glass production, stone and wood carving and ceramic making left rich traces in the excavation pits (Lê Thị Liên 2006c). Right from the first few centuries CE, in addition to intra-regional trade exchanges, Gò Tháp people had already indirectly or directly interacted with other civilizations, based on the presence of Chinese-style figurines and carved human heads, Roman-style gold-inlaid glass beads and dice, along with a terracotta Hanuman figure and numerous objects representing Indic influences. Various types of pottery and wasters showed influence from different regions of India both in form, function and technique (Lê Thị Liên 2005, 2006, 2006c, 2015: 229, Fig. 11.20; Võ Thị Huỳnh Như et. al. 2014). Wood carving developed on a large scale (Lê Thị Liên 2010).

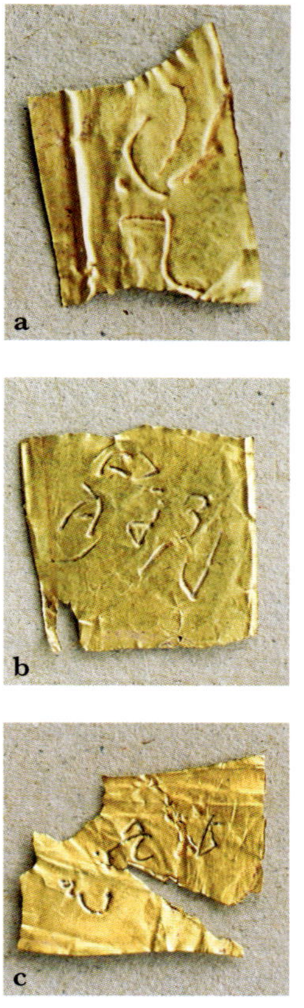

Fig. 7 *Inscriptions on gold plaques found from Sanctuary 93.M1, 2nd-4th century CE, Go Thap site (Dong Thap Museum):* **a** Ya(ṁ) o?; **b** 'Sre chaṁ *ñu*? ra ('Sri chaṁ *ñu*? ra?); **c** Daita(ṁ) div*ā* *(Photo: Lê Thị Liên; Reading: Michel Witzel)*

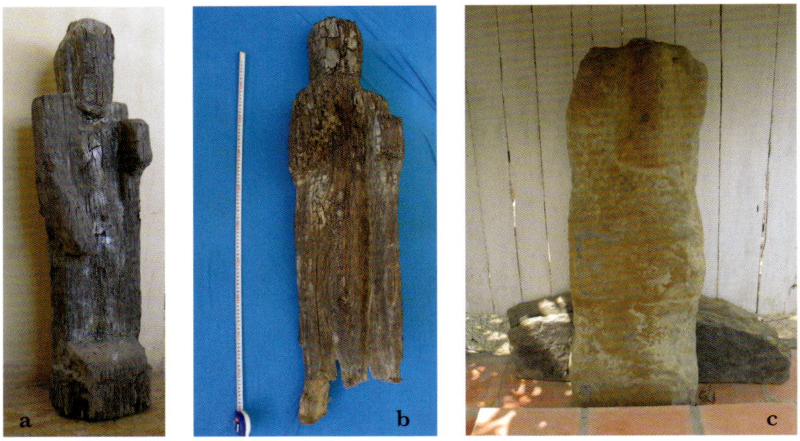

Fig. 8 a, b *Unfinished and damaged Buddha images, wood;* **c** *Unfinished sculpture, stone, Go Thap site (Dong Thap Museum); (Photo: Lê Thị Liên)*

It is possible that stone carving was present in the development period of Óc Eo culture, as suggested by carving waste (Lê Thị Liên et al 2010; Lê Thị Liên, Nguyễn Thị Bé Tư. 2011).

In terms of religion and belief, Gò Tháp people soon had quite a deep understanding of Buddhist and Hindu beliefs and used Brāhmī inscriptions in temple building rituals from the early centuries CE. Several brick temples which are modest in size and simple in plan began to be built in the first half of the first millennium CE in the north-western area of the site, containing pieces of gold representing traditional Indian construction rituals. In the 6th-7th centuries, larger-scale temples were built with very well-reinforced foundations and the layout became more complex (Lê Xuân Diệm et. al. 1995: 86, 243-250; Lê Thị Liên 2005: 851-855; 2015e). In the later period, some previous structures were repaired, replacing the objects of worship (the architectural ruins of Tháp Mười mound and Minh Sư mound). In addition to the main architecture, there are other components that form a diverse complex such as subsidiary buildings, gates, walls, paths and possibly sub-temples. They might have been built and renovated in different stages. Some areas were leveled to expand the ground for religious buildings that overlapped earlier residential areas (Go Bà Chúa Xứ, Go Minh Sư) (Lê Thị Liên et al 2014: 75-78).

Art in Gò Tháp, with its richness and abundance, can represent the art of Đồng Tháp Mười region, which is expressed through a variety of materials. The earliest images are simple drawings depicted on small pieces of gold placed inside the central foundation of the temples built in the first half of the first millennium CE. In addition to the symbols, the owners of these little works had a very good understanding of the symbols, deities, goddesses and incarnations of the Hindu pantheon. At the same time, they chose to create their own style. The earliest Viṣṇu images on gold plaques, while preserving elements of Indian art in their costumes and the *tribhaṅga* standing posture, were adopted as iconographic features that became the general model for almost all the stone images of Viṣṇu of Óc Eo-Funan art (Lê Thị Liên 2006: Color Ill 11; 2009: 71-72, Fig. 1-7).

Terracotta art left very faint imprints through a number of small, fragmented images, mainly in bas-relief. They might have been among the early productions of local art (Lê Xuân Diệm et al. 1995: 304, Ill. XXII, 1; Lê Thị Liên et al. 2014: 79, Ill. 11). There was a concentration of stone sculptures in Gò Tháp, representing mainly Hindu gods and a small number of goddesses. The body a male deity standing with his legs apart and wearing a costume showing some a connection to Gandhara sculptures, is possibly the earliest known sculpture from around 4th-5th century in the area (Malleret 1963: 72; Lê Thị Liên 2006: 105, Ill. 163). The Gò Tháp Surya is the earliest one of four images discovered in Southern Vietnam. The childlike, vivid and roundish face of the god remained a characteristic of the earliest and most beautiful stone sculptures of Óc Eo art which are datable to the 5th century. In the 6th century came fully developed and skilfully executed bodies. (Lê Thị Liên 2006: 102, Ill. 158).

From known statistics, the largest number of Viṣṇu sculptures was found from Gò Tháp – seven images, one head and several fragments. This surpasses the number found in Óc Eo-Ba Thê site. The archaeological context shows that in addition to the most beautiful statues worshipped in the main temple, unfinished products indicate the presence of workshops scattered outside the central area where the temples were concentrated (Lê Thị Liên 2006b: Table 2.2; Lê Thị Liên et. al. 2010; Lê Thị Liên, Nguyễn Thị Bé Tư 2011). The varieties of costumes, the surface treatment techniques, body details and the stone materials used represent a long development history of an art centre with its best works being datable to the 6th-7th centuries. The idealized tendency in the execution of the body and the *samabhaṅga* posture representing the most divine characteristic of the supreme god is also observed (Lê Thị Liên 2006b: Ills. 161, 158, 69-73; Guy 2014: Cat. 59). These features have been followed by other Viṣṇu images in the surrounding area during the end of 7th and 8th centuries, with decreased art quality (Lê Thị Liên 2006b: Ills. 62, 64, 65, 76).

Wood sculptures were the most unique product of Gò Tháp and the Đồng Tháp Mười region as a whole. They constituted a distinctive art style for Óc Eo culture and also for Funan.With more than 30 art works discovered so far along with other archaeological evidence, it can be confirmed that this was the centre of Buddhist worship and also the site of the earliest, largest production workshop. The sculptures were produced in a variety of styles and sizes (the smallest is about 20 cm, the largest one, the Tháp Mười Buddha, is 291 cm high). Most of the sculptures are broken with hands generally missing. The remaining sculptures are shown in standing position and all hands have been lost. A common feature is a thin, plain and fitted *uttarāsaṅga* upper body robe exposing the right shoulder. From the few pieces of hands that have been discovered, it is possible that these statues are mainly in the posture of assurance

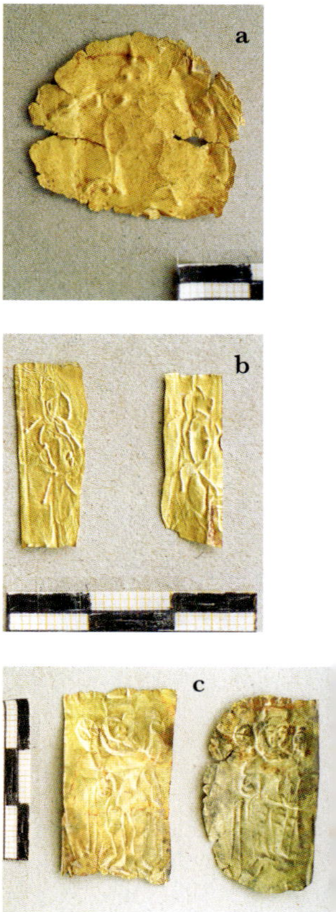

Fig. 9 *Images of* **a** Garuda, **b** Varaha; **c** Visnu *on gold plaques found from Sanctuary, 2nd-4th century CE, Go Thap site (Dong Thap Museum); (Photo: Lê Thị Liên)*

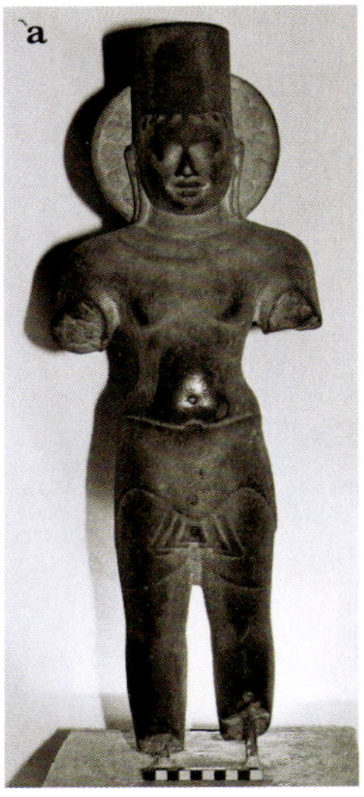

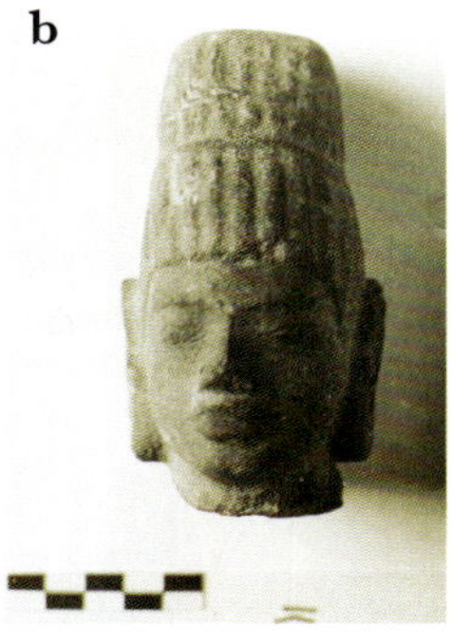

(*abhaya mudrā*) and a few in the teaching posture (*vitaka mudrā*). The sculptures that are in *tribhaṅga* standing posture have the most attractive artistic qualities and were perhaps widely worshipped in large temples. Smaller ones were perhaps erected in village temples, and even in private houses (Malleret 1963: Pl.XXI Lê Thị Liên 2006b: Ills. 6, 11-13). The physical features reveal some influence from Amarāvatī art, especially on reliefs depicting secular characters (Robert Knox 1992). *Mahāpuruṣa* Buddha images were found in the *abhaṅga* standing posture in slightly larger than life size. However, this group of Buddha images in Gò Tháp as well as in the Đồng Tháp Mười area is mainly naturalistic with vivid face details and slim bodies (Lê Thị Liên 2006b: Ills. 15-17). Elements that show the influence of late Gupta art are seen in a number of works with full faces, broad chins, strong chests and sturdy legs firmly planted in the *samabhaṅga* posture (Lê Thị Liên 2006b: Ill. 19).

The large number of artifacts, including wood and stone sketches discovered in Gò Tháp, indicates that these workshops were in operation through the Óc Eo period, and possibly the post-Óc Eo period for the stone statues. Despite the changes in shape and posture as the art evolved, Đồng Tháp Mười artworks, especially wooden sculpture, basically preserved its distinctive naturalistic characteristics. They made an enormous contribution to what is called the Óc Eo art of Funan.

Fig. 10 **a** Surya *Tháp Mười, 6th-7th century CE History Museum-HCMC;* **b** *Head of goddess, stone, 6th-7th century CE, Go Thap site (Dong Thap Museum) (Photo: a- Dong Thap Museum; b- Nguyễn Hữu Thiết)*

Fig. 11 *Buddha images, wood, Go Thap site (***a** *History Museum-HCMC;* **b, c** *Dong Thap Museum;* **d** *Missing) (Photo: a, b, c- Lê Thị Liên; d- Dong Thap Museum)*

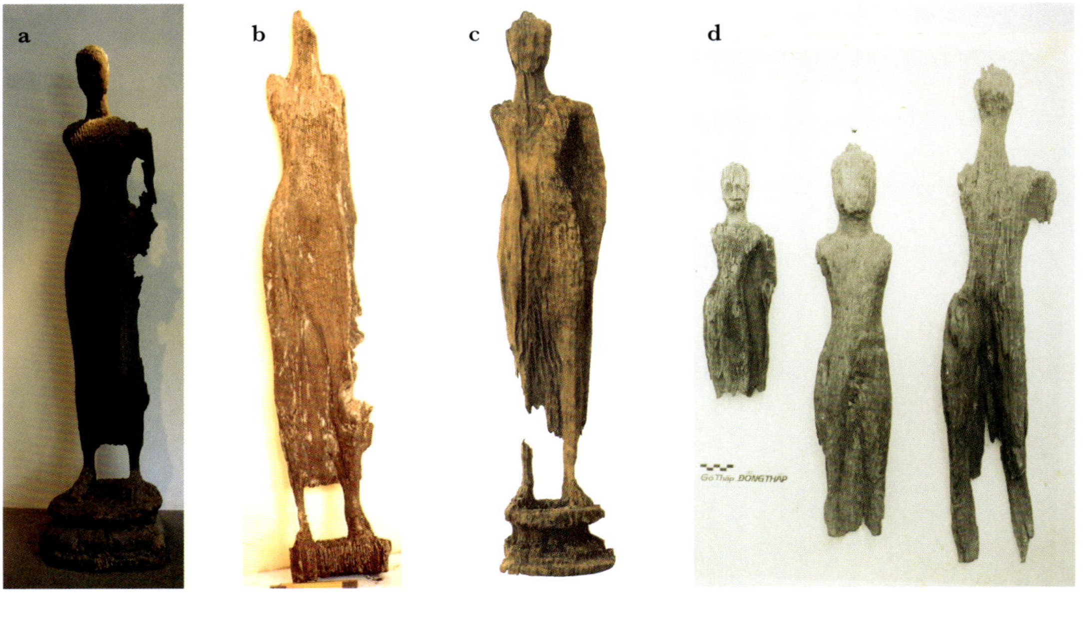

References (with English translation)

Ardika, I Wayan 2015. Early Contacts between Bali and India, in *ASEAN-India Cultural Links: Historical and Contemporary Dimensions*; Proceedings of the International Conference, RIS and ACT, New Delhi, 23-24 July 2015, pp. 28-37.

Bellina B. 2017. Development of maritime Trade Polities and diffusion of the "South China Sea Sphere of Interaction pan-regional culture": The Khao Sek excavations and industriess studies contribution, Archaeological Research in Asia (2017), http://dx.doi.org/10.1016/j.ara.2017.06.004

Bellina, Berenice and Glover, Ian 2004. The Archaeology of early contact with India and the Mediterranean world, from the fourth century BC to the fourth century AD, *Southeast Asia from Prehistory to History*, Ian Glover and Peter Bellwood (edited), Routlegde, pp. 68-88.

Bellina, B. et. al. 2014. The development of Coastal Polities in the Upper Thai-Malay Peninsular, in Nicolas Revire & Stephen A. Murphy (eds.), *Before Siam – Essays in Art and Archaeology*, Narisa Chakrabongse & The Siam Society, pp. 68-89.

Bellwood, Peter, et. al 2011. An Son and the Neolithic of Southern Vietnam, *AP*, Vol. 50 (1&2), Spring/ Fall 2011, 144-175

Borrel, B., Bellina, B., Chaisuwan, B. 2014. Contact between the Upper Thai-Malay Peninsular and the Mediterranian World, In Revire, N. & Murphy S., A. (eds), Before Siam, Essays in Art and Archaeology, River Books & The Siam Society, 98-117.

Chia, Stephen & Barbara Watson Andya 2011. *Bujang Valley and Early Civilizations in Southeast Asia*" Department of National Heritage, Ministry of Information, Communication and Cultures, Malaysia.

Glover, I. C. and Bellina, B. 2011. Ban Don Ta Phet and Khao Sam Kaeo: The earliest Indian contacts Re-assessed, in *Early Indian influences in Southeast Asia: Reflection on Cross-cultural Movements*, Edited by Pierre-Yves Manguin, A. Mani and Geoff Wade, Singapore, Manohar Publishers and distributors, 17-46.

Guy, John 2014. *Lost Kingdoms – Hindu-Buddhist Sculpture of Early Southeast Asia*, (ed), The Metropolitant of Art, New York.

Groslier ,B. P. 1966. *Indochina*, The World Publishing company, Clevelancd and New York

Hiram Woodward 2014. Stylistic Trends in Mainland Southeast Asia, 600-800, in *Lost Kingdoms – Hindu-Buddhist Sculpture of Early Southeast Asia*, John Guy (ed), The Metropolitant of Art, New York, 122-129.

Lam Thi My Dzung 2011. Central Vietnam during the period from 500 BCE to CE 500, in *Early Interactions between South and Southeast Asia: Reflection on Cross-Cultural Exchange,* Edited by P. V. Manguin, A. Mani, Geoff Wade, ISEAS, Manoha, India, pp. 3-16.

Lê Thị Liên 2005a. Hình thức và chức năng của một loại hình vòi vẩy trong văn hóa Óc Eo [Form and function of a type of sprinkler in Oc Eo culture], in *NPHMVKCH năm 2004 [New Discoveries in Archaeology of 2004]*, Social Sciences Publishing House, Hanoi, pp. 823-825 (in Vietnamese).

Lê Thị Liên 2005b. "Di tich Go Thap va nhung van de cua van hoa Oc Eo [Go Thap site and issues of the Oc Eo culture]", in *Mot the ki khao co hoc Viet Nam* [One Century of Vietnamese Archaeology], Hanoi: Social Publishing House. Vol. II: 845-869 (in Vietnamese).

Lê Thị Liên 2006a. Về loại hình Kendi ở di tích Gò Tháp (Đồng Tháp) [On Kendi type at Go Thap site], in *NPHMVKCH năm 2005 [New Discoveries in Archaeology of 2005]*, Social Sciences Publishing House, Hanoi (in Vietnamese).

Lê Thị Liên 2006b. *Nghệ thuật Phật giáo và Hindu giáo ở Đồng bằng sông Cửu Long trước thế kỷ 10 [Buddhist and Hindu Art in the Cuu Long River Delta Prior to 10th century A.D.]*, Thế Giới Publishing House, Hanoi.

Le Thi Lien 2006c. Excavations at Minh Su Mound, Go Thap site, Dong Thap Province, South Vietnam, *Uncovering Southeast Asia's past – Selected papers from the 10th International Conference of the European Association of Southeast Asian Archaeologists*, pp. 232-244, Singapore: NUS Press.

Le Thi Lien 2009. Hindu Iconography in Early History of Southern Vietnam, 美術史研究集刊 第二十五期 (民國97年), 69-96.

Le Thi Lien. 2010. Buddhist Heritage: Archaeological evidence from Oc Eo culture (Southern Vietnam), in proceeding of the *First International Conference on Buddhism Heritage in Southeast Asia*, Phnompenh, pp. 174-181.

Le Thi Lien 2011a. Hindu Deities in Southern Vietnam – Images Seen on the Tiny Archaeological Artifacts, in *Early Interactions between South and Southeast Asia: Reflection on Cross-Cultural Exchange,* Edited by P. V. Manguin, A. Mani, Geoff Wade, ISEAS, Manoha, India, pp. 407-32.

Le Thi Lien 2014a. Hindu-Buddhist Sculpture in Southern Vietnam: Evolution of icon and style to the Eighth Century, in *Lost Kingdoms – Hindu-Buddhist Sculpture of Early Southeast Asia*, John Guy (ed), The Metropolitant of Art, New York, 118-121.

Le Thi Lien 2015a. History of Maritime Contacts between Vietnam and India: Archaeological Evidence from Oc Eo culture in Southern Vietnam, in *Maritime Contacts of the Past: Deciphering Connections amongst communities,* 2015. (Ed.), Sila Tripati, Delta Book World, New Delhi: 95-123.

Le Thi Lien 2015b. Hindu beliefs and the Maritimenetwork in Southern Vietnam during the early Common era, Journal of Indo-Pacific Archaeology 39 (2015): 1-17.

Le Thi Lien 2017. Lung Khe and the Cultural Relationship between Northern and Southern Vietnam, *Asian Review of World Histories* 5 (2017) 53-69.

Le Thi Lien 2018. Indian – Southeast Asian Contacts and Cultural Exchanges : Evidence from Vietnam, in *Cultural and Civilisational Links between India and Southeast Asia.* Shyam Saran (ed.), RIS, New Dehli, India : 107-127.

Lê Thị Liên 2020. Bàn thêm về vai trò của di tích Ba Thê – Óc Eo (An Giang) trong sự phát triển của vương quốc Phù Nam [Further discussion on the role of Ba The- Oc Eo site

(An Giang) in the growth of the Funan Empire], in *Khảo cổ học [Archaeology]*, No. 4-2020, pp. 46-53 (in Vietnamese).

Lê Thị Liên, Nguyễn Quốc Mạnh, Nguyễn Thị Mai Hương 2018. "Context of the Port Cities Establishment in the Coast of Southern Vietnam: Understanding from Recent Surveys", in Noel Hidalgo Tan (ed.) *Advancing Southeast Asian Archaeology 2016*; SEAMEO SPAFA Regional Centre for Archaeology and Fine Arts; 160-177, 347-352, Figs: 20.1-20.12.

Lê Thị Liên, Nguyễn Thị Bé Tư 2011. "Chứng tích nghề chế tác điêu khắc đá ở di tích Gò Tháp" [Evidence of stone sculpture manufacturing at Go Thap site], in *NPHMVKCH năm 2010 [New Discoveries in Archaeology of 2010]*, Social Sciences Publishing House, Hanoi, pp. 751-752 (in Vietnamese).

Lê Thị Liên, Nishimura Mashanari, Nguyễn Thị Mai Hương 2014. Di tích Gò Tháp – Những hiểu biết mới qua các cuộc khảo sát nghiên cứu gần đây [Go Thap site – New Understanding from the Recent Surveys, in *Khảo cổ học [Archaeology]*, No. 2/2015, pp. 64-83.

Lê Thị Liên, Trần Văn Nam, Nguyễn Hữu Lý 2010. Thêm các điêu khắc quan trọng mới phát hiện và nhu cầu mở rộng khảo sát khu vực Gò Tháp trên diện rộng [More important sculptures discovered recently and the need of enlarging the survey at the Go Thap area], in *NPHMVKCH năm 2009 [New Discoveries in Archaeology of 2009]*, Social Sciences Publishing House, Hanoi, pp. 724-726 (in Vietnamese).

Lê Xuân Diệm, Đào Linh Côn, Võ Sĩ Khải 1995. *Văn hóa Óc Eo những khám phá mới [Oc Eo Culture – Rcent Discoveries*. Social Sciences Publishing House, Hanoi (in Vietnamese).

Malleret, L. 1959. *L'archéologie du Delta du Mékong*, Tome I, Paris, bản dịch của BT LS Việt Nam, năm 1969.

Malleret L. 1960. *L'archéologie Du Delta Du Mekong*, T. II, Paris, bản dịch của BT LS Việt Nam, năm 1970.

Malleret L. 1962. *L'archéologie Du Delta Du Mekong*, T. III, Paris, bản dịch của BT LS Việt Nam, năm 1970.

Malleret, L. 1963. *L'archéologie du Delta du Mékong*, Tome IV, Paris.

Manguin P. Y. 2006. Les Tuiles de *l' ancienne Asie du Sud-Est: Essai de typologie, Anamorphoses Hommage à Jacques Dumarçay*

Manguin, P. Y. 2009. The Archaeology of Fu Nan in the Mekong River Delta: The Oc Eo Culture of Viet Nam, in *Arts of Ancient Viet Nam – From River Plain to the Open Sea*, Nancy Tingley edited, Yale University Press. New Haven and London, pp. 103-118.

Manguin, P. Y. 2014. Early Coastal States of Souhteast Asia: Funan and 'Srivijaya, in *Lost Kingdoms – Hindu-Buddhist Sculpture of Early Southeast Asia*, John Guy (ed), The Metropolitant of Art, New York, 111-115.

Manguin, Pierre-Yves and Indradjaja, Agustijanto 2011. The Batujaya Site: New Evidence of Early Indian Influence in West Java, in *Early Interactions between South and Southeast Asia: Reflection on Cross-Cultural Exchange*, Edited by P. V. Manguin, A. Mani, Geoff Wade, ISEAS, Manoha, India, pp. 113-136.

Nguyễn Gia Đối, Lê Đình Phụng, Phạm Văn Triệu 2020. Nhận thức về di tích kiến trúc ở các địa điểm khai quật của Viện Khảo cổ học tại khu di tích Óc Eo – Ba Thê [Understanding on the architectural remains at the excavated areas of the Institute of Archaeology at the Ba The – Oc Eo site], in *Khảo cổ học [Archaeology]*, No. 1-2020, pp. 12-24.

Nguyễn Quốc Mạnh 2018. *Các di tích Tiền Óc Eo ở vùng Tứ giác Long Xuyên trong quá trình hình thành văn hóa Óc Eo ở miền Tây Nam Bộ* [Pre-Oc Eo sites in the Long Xuyen Quadrilateral in the formation process of Oc Eo Culture in the Southwestern region], Ph.D. Thesis, Institute of Social Sciences, Vietnam Academy of Social Sciences (In Vietnamese).

Nguyễn Quốc Mạnh 2020. Đồ gốm có khắc các biểu tượng tôn giáo phát hiện tại Lung Lớn (Khu di tích Óc Eo – Ba Thê) [Potteries incised with religious symbols unearthed from the Grand Canal (Oc Eo – Ba The site complex], in *Khảo cổ học [Archaeology]*, No. 6-2020, pp. 25-37 (in Vietnamese).

Nishimura, M. 2005. "Chronology of the Metal Age in the southern Vietnam", *Journal of Southeast Asian Archaeology 25* (2005), 105-147.

Pelliot P. 1903. Le Founan, *BEFEO* III, pp. 248-303, (Vietnamese translated vesion), document of the Institute of Archaeology.

Reinecke, A (2012) The Prehistoric Occupation and Cultural Characteristics of the Mekong Delta during the Pre- Funan Periods. In: ML Tjoa-Bonatz, A Reinecke and D Bonatz (eds.) *Crossing Borders in Southeast Asian Archaeology: Selected papers from the 13th International Conference of the European Association of Southeast Asian Archaeologists, Berlin 2010*. Singapore: NUS Press, 239-256.

Trương Đắc Chiến 2017. Di tích Giồng Lớn và vai trò của nó với sự hình thành văn hóa Óc Eo ở vùng ven biển Đông Nam Bộ [Giong Lon site and its role in the formation process of the Oc Eo Culture in the Southeastern region], Ph.D. Thesis, Hanoi University of Social Sciences and Humanities (in Vietnamese).

Trương Đắc Chiến 2018. The Giồng Lớn site (Bà Rịa – Vũng Tàu) and research on Óc Eo Culture Formation in the Eastern Coastal Area of Southern Vietnam, *Archaeology*, 2018 (13), 50-72.

Vo Si Khai 2003. The Kingdom of Fu Nan and the culture of Oc Eo. In J. C. M. Khoo (ed.), *Art & Archaeology of Fu Nan: Pre-Khmer Kingdom of the Lower Mekong Valley*, pp. 35-86. Bangkok: Orchid Press.

Võ Thị Huỳnh Như, Ngô Thị Phượng, Cao Thu Nga 2014. Hai hạt xúc xắc (xí ngầu) thuộc văn hóa Óc Eo tìm thấy ở khu di tích Gò Tháp (Đồng Tháp) [Two dices of Oc Eo Culture found from Go Thap site (Dong Thap province), in NPHMVKCH năm 2013*[New Discoveries in Archaeology of 2013]*, Social Sciences Publishing House, Hanoi, pp. 723-726 (in Vietnamese).

Vương Thu Hồng 2005. Sưu tập hạt chuỗi bằng đá ngọc ở Đồng Tháp Mười, tỉnh Long An [Collection of semi-precious beads in Dong Thap Muoi region, Long An province], in *Một thế kỉ Khảo cổ học Việt Nam* [One Century of Vietnamese Archaeology], Hanoi: Social Publishing House. Vol. II: 814-834 (in Vietnamese).

9 | Gold in Óc Eo culture

Bùi Thị Thúy[1], Nguyễn Thị Tú Anh[2], Nguyễn Hoàng Bách Linh[3]

The Óc Eo culture was named after the archaeological site excavated by Louis Malleret in the 1940s (1959: 1-5). A multitude of artifacts, including gold, was collected from the site and transferred to the 'Musée de Blanchard de la Brosse'[4] in Saigon (1962, III: 3). Following the wars years 1954-75, Óc Eo cultural issues have been actively studied by Vietnamese archaeologists. Archaeological surveys and excavations were undertaken in the 1980s and 1990s and many reports of findings have been published. By the end of the 1990s, a total of 90 archaeological sites from the Óc Eo culture had been recorded. This fieldwork had three main goals:

1. Reassessment and documentation of earlier work by the École française d'Extrême-Orient (EFEO) in the colonial period (Malleret 1951: 75-88);
2. Field surveys to evaluate archaeological sites reported by local residents;
3. Excavations of sites at risk of being destroyed (Lê Xuân Diệm et al. 1995: 16-17).

This paper will focus on the Óc Eo gold collections on display at the An Giang Museum (AGM) that were excavated during the 1980s-90s (Lê Xuân Diệm et al. 1995: 237, 338-65). Comparisons will also be made with the earlier finds in the collection of the Museum of Vietnamese History Museum-HCMC and the gold antiques stored at the other provincial museums in the Mekong Delta. The paper will strive to place the Óc Eo gold collection of AGM in the context of early Maritime Asia. The material finds are related to the inscriptions found in the Transbassac region that give some indications of how natural resources were controlled and of the ritual and courtly needs that were served with precious metals. It will consider how local production was combined with imported raw materials to manufacture gold products for Óc Eo residents and their religious practices.

The origin of the gold collection of AGM

The 1995 Vietnamese language work *Văn hóa Óc Eo: Những khám phá mới* (Óc Eo culture: Recent discoveries) published some of the new archeological data collected in post-war excavations at Óc Eo cultural sites. It concentrates on the achievements of the Southern Institute of Social Sciences Hồ Chí Minh City (Lê Xuân Diệm et al. 1995: 13-14).

Most of the provinces in the Delta were first surveyed by French scholars and 14 Óc Eo cultural features were recorded in An Giang (Lê Xuân Diệm et al. 1995: 17-42). In 1997-8 a cooperation project between Vietnam and France undertook excavations at the Óc Eo and Ba Thê sites (Manguin

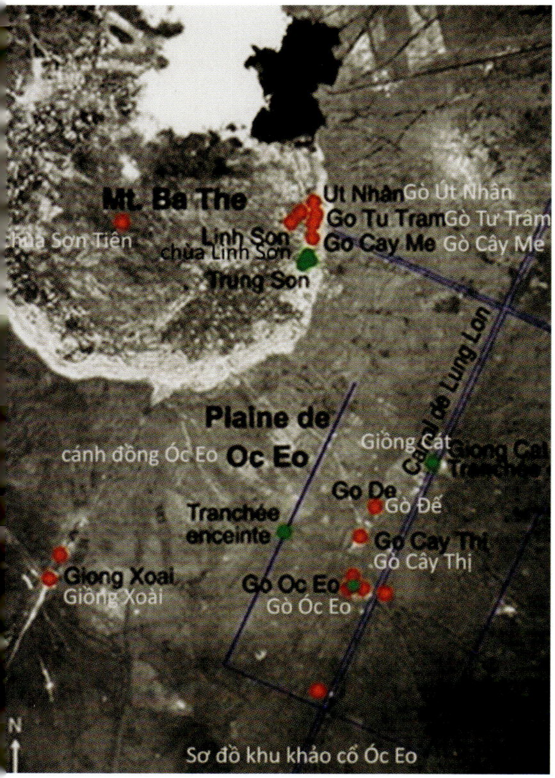

Fig. 1 *Map of the archaeological sites belonging to Óc Eo culture. Available at: https://nghiencuulichsu.com/2013/08/29/theo-doi-cuoc-khao-cuu-van-hoa-oc-eo/. Accessed 25/4/2020.*

and Vallerin 1997: 410; Manguin 2009: 107).[5] In the post-war period, some 300 ancient gold objects were collected at Óc Eo sites in An Giang in the 1980s and 1990s, along with various types of artifacts in wood, sandstone, copper, precious stones and glass. All were transferred to AGM (Lê Xuân Diệm et al. 1995: 341). There were five Óc Eo sites where gold artifacts were found **[Fig. 1]**.

Óc Eo site

The Óc Eo site excavated by Louis Malleret in 1944 (Malleret 1951; Cœdès 1947) had by 1979 been damaged by farming and looting. Between 1979 and 1983, excavation uncovered a large brick structure with many square cells laid out like a giant chessboard. They contained artifacts such as beads, elephant teeth, turtle shells, copper slag and ceramics (Lê Xuân Diệm et al. 1995: 18-24).

Gò Cây Thị site

In 1944 Malleret found a 29.4 cm standing Chinese-style Buddha (BTLS.1586) in bronze at a shallow depth on a slope of the Gò Cây Thị (Cây Thị mound) also known in Khmer as 'Tûol Dơm Tonleap' (1951: 77-78). He estimated the date of the Buddha statue as mid-5th century CE (1960, II: 205-06).

In 1979, a second 31 cm high bronze Buddha (BTAG.2175/KL) was found by Vietnamese archaeologists on the west side of this mound that was dated to the first half of 5th century. It is on display at AGM (Lê Xuân Diệm et al. 1995: 284) **[Fig. 2]**.

Although many issues need to be clarified, the two bronze Buddha statues in Chinese style clearly indicate international Buddhist activity along the maritime route during the Funan period.

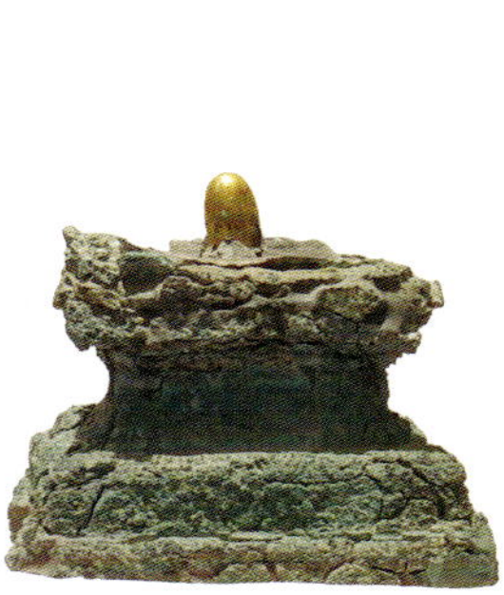

Fig. 3 *A miniature* liṅga-yoni *found at the Đá Nổi site, on display at An Giang Museum. (Photo by Nguyễn Hoàng Bách Linh)*

Ba Thê site

Ba Thê excavations uncovered artifacts in gold and bronze and an inscription plate (Malleret 1951: 85). In 1979 and 1984, Vietnamese archaeologists opened seven test pits in the precincts of the Linh Sơn temple and further pits in 1993 disclosed traces of damaged brickwork some 16 metres higher up the slope of the Ba Thê mountain (Lê Xuân Diệm et al. 1995: 27-29). This was judged to be a collapsed religious structure and gold objects there might have been offered with prayers at this site. Linh Sơn temple is now Buddhist and contains a well-known large stone statue of Viṣṇu Anantasayana in the

Phnom Da style (Malleret 1959, I: 79-89; Porte 2016: 141-58), which has been turned vertically and re-worked as a seated Buddha.

Đá Nổi site

Reports of gold looting led to the excavation of the Đá Nổi site in 1984 over an area of more than 2,000 square metres. It is considered by archaeologists as the most important monument of the Óc Eo culture because of its large scale (Lê Xuân Diệm et al. 1995: 32). The site has yielded 331 objects in gold, the most yet encountered in the region. Of these, many included human figures or the attributes held by Hindu and Buddhist deities. Several metal plates bearing Sanskrit inscriptions were found as well as a broken stone inscription. The most impressive find is a miniature *liṅga-yoni* **[Fig. 3]** made of gold and bronze which was recognized as a national treasure in 2018.

Nền Chùa/Ta Kev site

At Nền Chùa, or Ta Kev, a platform was found nearly one metre above the surrounding rice paddies, which was thought to be part of the 'port' of Óc Eo (Malleret 1959, I: 125-27; Lê Xuân Diệm et al. 1995: 43-44; Manguin and Vallerin 1997: 409-10). During the 1990s, excavations revealed a foundation of stone and brick measuring 30 m x 20 m, the largest stone structure uncovered at the Óc Eo architectural sites in this decade (Lê Xuân Diệm et al. 1995: 46). A further 19 small units in square or hopper shape were unearthed to the south of the main structure and distributed over an area 1500 m x 500 m. Some 33 artifacts were collected from these structures including 28 objects in gold from the small units. The finds included seals, coins, rings and beads found in the 'Lung Lớn' canal, which connects with Óc Eo and its linked gullies. The finds are in the Kiên Giang museum (Lê Xuân Diệm et al. 1995: 47-48).

Gold collection of An Giang Museum

One of the most striking among the 300 gold objects uncovered in the post-war period 1977-90 are the miniature *liṅga-yoni* **[Fig. 3]**, earrings, beads, and gold foils with embossed human figures (Lê Xuân Diệm et al. 1995: 32, 338-65). Although small in scale, the metallic *liṅga-yoni* is assumed to have been housed in a sanctuary for ritual performance (Barfoed 2018: 111-17).

Jewelry pieces recorded in Đá Nổi include four flower pendants with six to ten petals and an inlaid semi-precious stone at the center **[Fig. 4]**. There are three finger rings without decoration (Lê Xuân Diệm et al. 1995: 39; Phạm Thị Ngọc Thảo 2009: 35).

Numerous gold foils in varying shapes and sizes were found, some 39 with embossed human figures (Lê Xuân Diệm et al. 1995: 340-41). There are two embossed standing figures with both hands held before the chest that

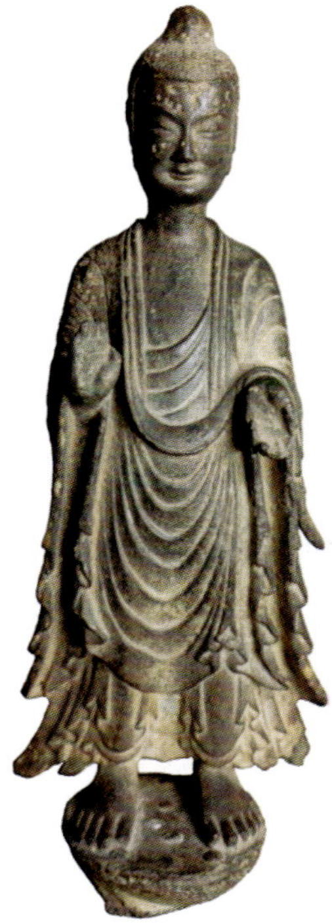

Fig. 2 *Standing bronze Buddha in Northern Wei style of the early 5th or 6th century on display at the An Giang Museum. (Photo by Nguyễn Hoàng Bách Linh)*

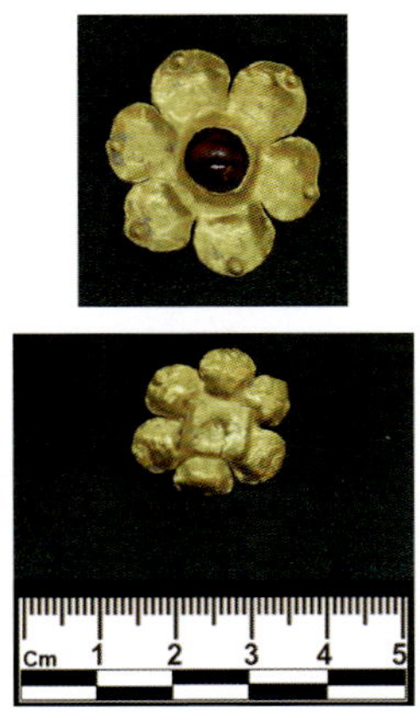

Fig. 4 *The front and back of a floral pendant with semi-precious stone. (Photo by Nguyễn Hoàng Bách Linh)*

may represent Sūrya. **[Fig. 5]** They await further study (Lê Xuân Diệm et al. 1995: 342).

Malleret (1966: 116-20) noted that pre-Angkorian epigraphy offers little about Sūrya cults being practised in the Mekong Delta. There are, however, five stone sculptures displayed in the Museum in Hồ Chí Minh that have been identified as Sūrya. They were found close to the Óc Eo site and also 120 km to the east in the inland wetland known as Đồng Tháp Mười (Plain of Reeds).

Two other gold foils have been identified with standing Viṣṇus, because of his *cakra* and conch attributes. Two other foils are tentatively identified as showing seated Buddhas on lotus thrones (Lê Xuân Diệm et al 1995: 341-42). There are 19 other fragments with standing human figures that are not yet identified.

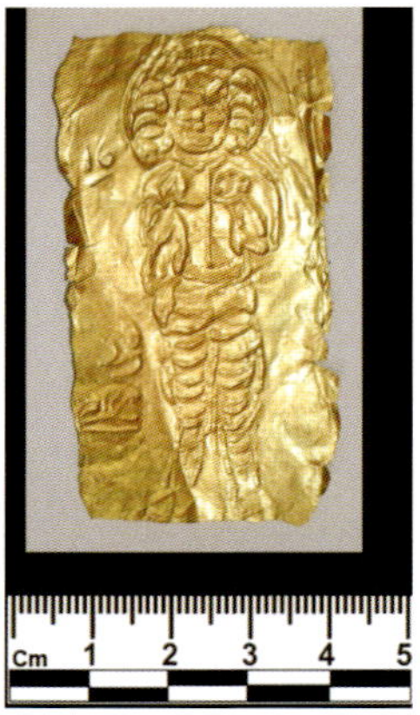

Fig. 5 *A gold foil with a standing figure assumed to be Sūrya. (Photo by Nguyễn Hoàng Bách Linh)*

Lajja Gauri (?)

Two gold foils were found at Đá Nổi and Nền Chùa sites depicting female figures (Lê Xuân Diệm et al. 1995: 245). One foil has a naked woman sitting in a yoga-squat position with her head elevated. The right hand is bent upwards holding a lotus-bud with an elongated stem at the level of the head. The left hand is obscured. **[Fig. 6 right]** The curved lines around the head of the other foil may show the blossoming lotus of the Indic fertility symbol Lajja Gauri (see Carol Bolon 1992: 11; Brown 1990: 1-16; Revire 2016: 119-21). The figure is in a squatting position (possibly in *uttanapad*, childbirth) with legs open and two arms reaching down **[Fig. 6 left]** These two foils are shown in drawings because they are now lost from the gold collection of AGM.

'Form Three' Lajja Gauri figures date from the 4th to 10th centuries in India and was once dominant in Madhya Pradesh and Gujarat. It appears in Andhra and Karnataka during the early Chalukya period of the 7th century (Bolon 1992: 12-13). In some examples of the Lajja Gauri image the sacred vase *purna-kumbha* is employed to represent the female body without breasts, arms or head and only the pot's mouth holding up a lotus flower (Bolon 1992: 11). These iconographical features may be depicted on a gold foil found at the Đá Nổi site and now numbered 85ĐN.M2 **[Fig. 7]**.

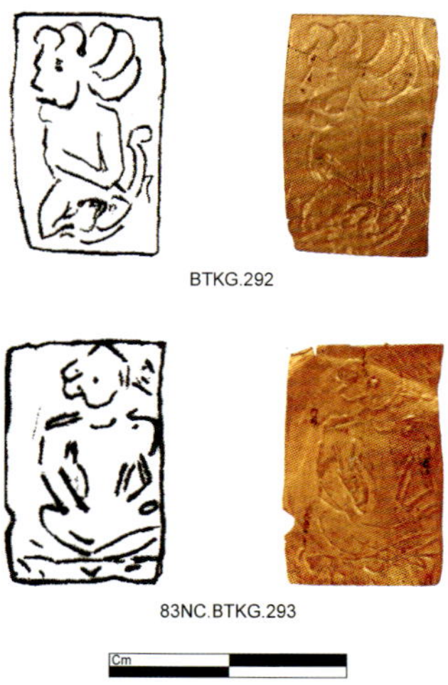

Fig. 6 *The two gold foils possibly depicting the Indic fertility symbol Lajja Gauri, a figure sometimes shown with a lotus-head (left), and (right) in a squatting (giving birth?) position. Illustrations from Lê Xuân Diệm et al. 1995: 246.*

The ancient Vedic *purna-kumbha* pot motif symbolizes wellbeing, fertility and the power of water as the source of life (Bolon 1992: 54-57). These symbols date back to the 2nd century CE and gained popularity in South India from the 3rd century before disappearing (ibid). An anthropomorphic female with thighs open found at the Gò Tháp site has been interpreted as a possible 'Goddess of Fertility' (Lê Thị Liên 2005: 151). The Gò Tháp gold foil may be compared with a female figure embossed in a squatting position at pit Gò 2A at the Cát Tiên site of Lâm Đồng province (Lê Thị Liên 2011: 421). She too holds a lotus flower in her left hand.

It has been suggested that the 'shield-shape' *Śrīvatsa* symbols on two gold foils found at the Đá Nổi site and now displayed at AGM, may also project the *uttanapad* pose of Lajja Gauri (Lê Xuân Diệm et al. 1995: 364) **[Fig. 8]**.

The gold foil could represent stylized curved limbs, according to Bolon (1992: 56), though they are more commonly identified as *Śrīvatsa* auspicious signs, which occur on coins/medallions. In recent decades, a few images which are similar to the *Śrīvatsa* symbols have been found at the Cát Tiên site northeast of Hồ Chí Minh. *Śrīvatsa*s are housed at the British Museum, London, in Sri Lanka and at the Patna Museum, Bihar. The dates of two *Śrīvatsa* images have been proposed as the 1st millenium BCE (Bolon 1992: 57) **[Fig. 9]** However, Michael Willis and Tsering Gonkatsang (2017: 347), making a comparison to seated Buddhas from Anuradhapura, have recently suggested bringing this *Śrīvatsa* forward to the 8th century CE.

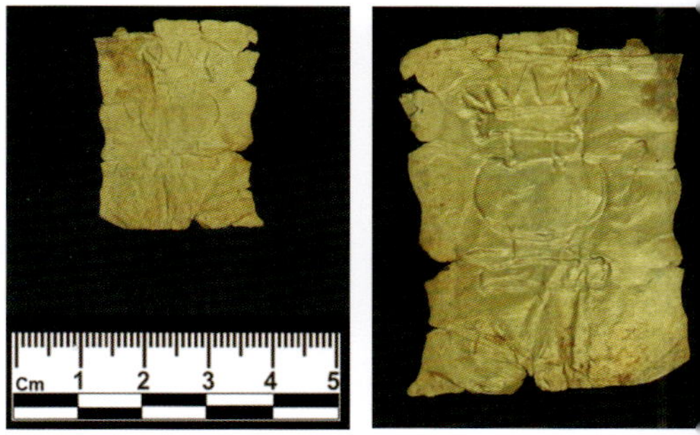

Fig. 7 *The gold foil (front and rear) depicting a pot motif found from the Đá Nổi site, An Giang Museum. (Photo by Nguyễn Hoàng Bách Linh)*

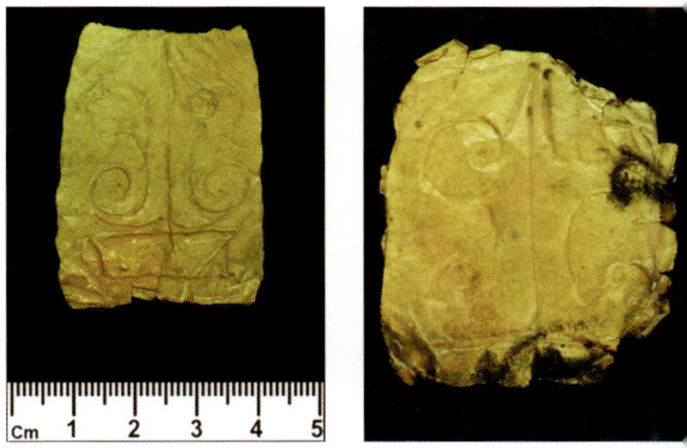

Fig. 8 *The two gold foils depicting the ancient auspicious* Śrīvatsa *sign in a 'shield-shape', found at the Đá Nổi site, which may also be a Lajja Gauri image. (Photo by Nguyễn Hoàng Bách Linh)*

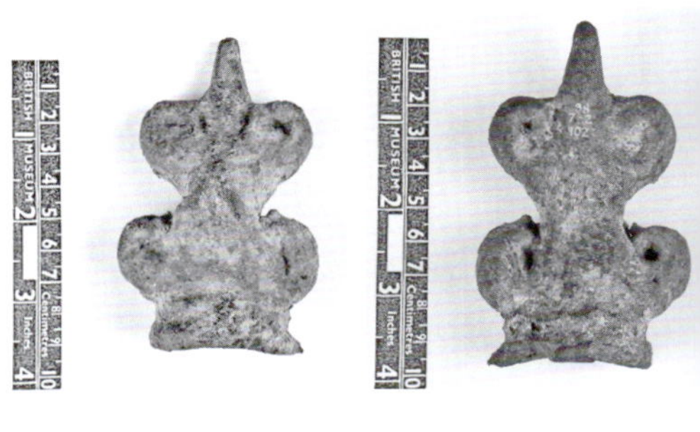

Fig. 9 *The auspicious emblem* Śrīvatsa, *also known as* Talisman, *with cross straps across the face; solid cast in a copper alloy; corroded from burial. Museum number 1898,0702.102. British Museum. Source: https://www.britishmuseum.org/collection/object/A_1898-0702-102. Accessed on 9/6/2020*

Óc Eo gold at the Museum of Vietnamese History Hồ Chí Minh City

In 1962 Malleret recorded 1,311 objects and noted that a few gold beads had been lost due to the explosion of fireworks next to the Museum on 8 April 1946 (1962, III: 2-3). In 1984 however, two former Directors recalculated the gold collection at 498 objects (Lê Trung and Trịnh 1984: 168; Phạm Thị Ngọc Thảo 2009: 2-3, 28). The jewelry can be divided into four categories: finger rings, earrings, gold beads and gold foils in different shapes and sizes. There is also an ornament imitating a Roman gold coin (BTLS.2182), a hair brooch and three sewing needles. A noted earring (BTLS.2166) was found at the Óc Eo site and transferred to the Museum by Malleret as object MBB.3181 (Malleret 1962, III: 73-74, pl. XIV: 3162 & 3700). It may be compared with the earrings of Roman gold found at the burial site of Pangkung Paruk in Bali that was published in 2020 (Calo et al. 2020: 116-18). The date of the Pangkung Paruk site is estimated as 2nd-4th century CE from charcoal associated with the pottery at the site. This chronology may be a guide to dating the Óc Eo earrings. The ribbed ring found at the Óc Eo site is similar in design and is among the earliest ear ornaments in Southeast Asia (Tjoa-Bonatz and Lockhoff 2019: 29) **[Fig. 10]**.

Finely made 12-sided dodecahedral geometric

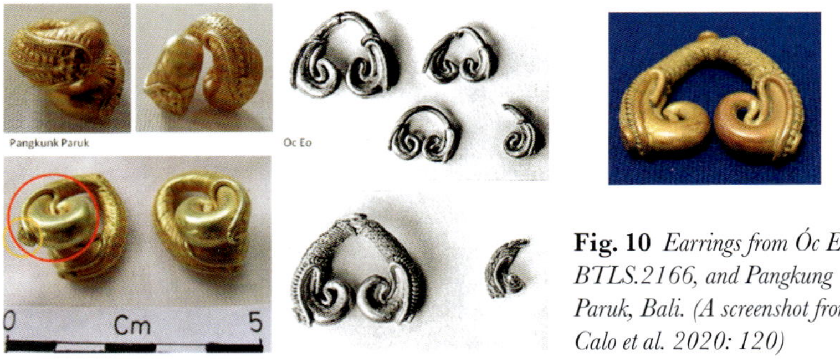

Fig. 10 *Earrings from Óc Eo BTLS.2166, and Pangkung Paruk, Bali. (A screenshot from Calo et al. 2020: 120)*

gold beads have been found at Óc Eo sites and many other sites in Maritime Asia **[Figs. 11a, b]**. This structure was first studied by Greek Pythagoreans in the 5th century BCE. Malleret saw them as local products in emulation of Roman samples (Malleret 1962, III: 73-74, pl. XIV; Demandt 2015: 313-14). Polyhedral beads have been recorded in many sites in Hòa Diêm in central Vietnam; Śrīkestra and Beinnaka in Myanmar; Air Sugihan in Sumatra; Batujaya in Java; Khao Sam Kaeo, Phu Khao Thong and Tha Chana in Peninsular Thailand, where they have been dated to the late 1st millennium BCE (Pryce et al. 2006: 310-11, fig. 17; Bennett 2009; Manguin and Indradjaya 2011; Nguyễn Kim Dung 2017: 326-27; Calo et al. 2020: ibid.).

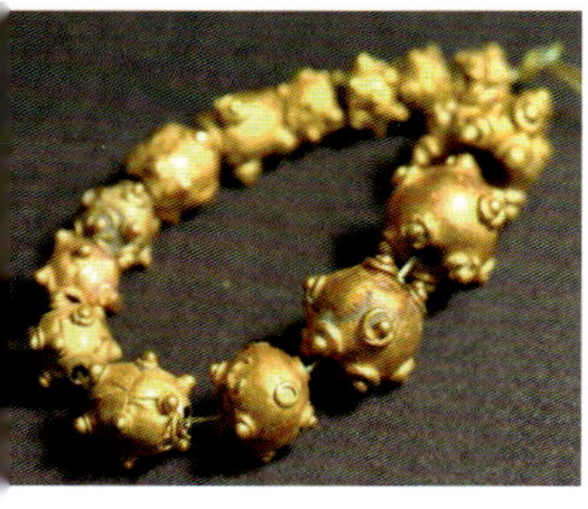

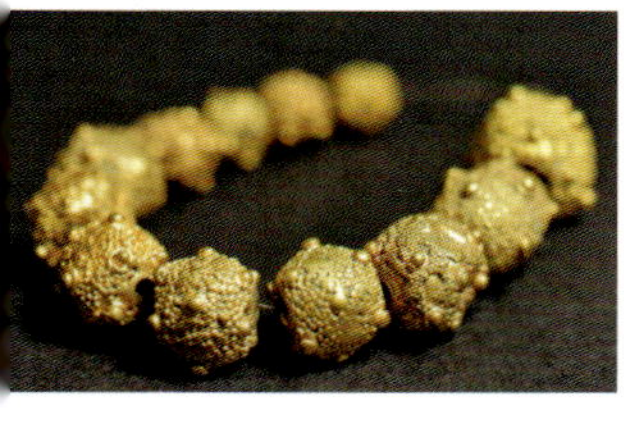

Figs. 11 a, b *Types of geometric 12-sided (dodecahedron) gold beads on display at Museum of Vietnamese History Museum Hồ Chí Minh City. (Photo courtesy of Museum of Vietnamese History Museum Hồ Chí Minh City)*

Michèle Demandt (2015: 321) notes that: 'Many gold ornaments from the early historical period have been found at sites that participated in long-distance trade and produced their own set of prestige goods such as beads. Examples of this are Óc Eo in Vietnam; U-Thong, Phu Khao Thong, Khao Sam Kaeo, and Khlong Thom in Thailand; possibly Hebu in China'.

The Óc Eo goldsmiths successfully adopted techniques from abroad as can be seen in bivalve casting moulds (BTLS.1896), droplets of gold, workshop tools and unfinished foils and gold objects found at the Óc Eo site (Malleret 1948: 275, pl. I; Malleret 1961, II: 349; Bennett 2009: 103; Demandt 2015). Paul Pelliot (1903: 254, 261) noted that the 6th century Chinese Southern *Qishu* and 7th century *Jinshu* (see 'Funan' and 'Zhenla' in Chinese annals' in this volume) record Óc Eo habitants as paying taxes in gold, silver, pearls and perfumes. However, the Óc Eo gold was not necessarily of local origin and the jewelry may have been melted multiple times and recast as Calo et al. have suggested (2020: 14): 'Geological sources for gold are difficult to identify due to possible multiple melting and recasting events and to gaps in our geological knowledge. Our comparative compositional study of gold excavated across Southeast Asia, however, is providing critical data to support or disprove stylistic and technological analyses concerning the origins of imported gold'.

From his work at the Bit Maes and Prohear sites in southern Cambodia,

Andreas Reinecke (2009: 114-56) expressed doubt that the gold resources of the Mekong Delta were sufficient to produce jewelry on the scale found at the Óc Eo cultural sites. Anna Bennett (2009: 100) examined damaged gold items and thought that all had been recycled by goldsmiths to satisfy domestic consumption. Reinecke also suggests that settlements were preferred by product craftsmen rather than proximity to raw material sources.

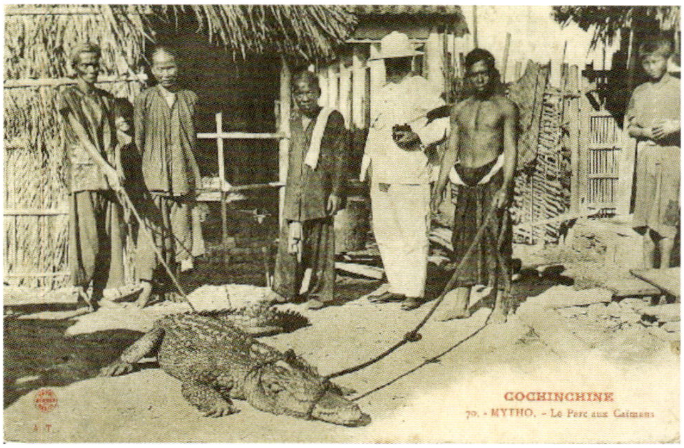

Fig. 12 *Cochinchine Vietnam, 'Le parc aux Caïmans, dans la province de My-Tho'. Collection de Cartes postales 1928. https://www.delcampe.net/en_GB/collectables/postcards/vietnam/vietnam-indochine-mytho-le-parc-aux-caimans-928429168.html. Accessed on 25/7/2020*

> 'Gold working need not take place near gold mining, but rather near potential consumers, who can order and pay in exchange for the products.
>
> Craftsmen could travel large distances on routes that are not necessarily identical to the gold and silver trade routes. They could also settle with their workshops in trade centers like those at Angkor Borei or Óc Eo in later times. (2015: 158)'

It may also explain why goldsmiths appear to have moved freely from market to market (Tjoa-Bonatz and Lockhoff 2019: 50). Reinecke suggests that local products could have been exchanged to import gold for jewelry. Forest products such as elephant tusks, rhinoceros horns, rosewood, kingfisher feathers, cardamom, gamboge saffron gum resin, lac and chaulmoogra tree oil were exchanged for Chinese gold or silver (Reinecke et al. 2009: 114-56). Caiman crocodiles were also traded and were still photographed in the Delta during the French colonial period in the early 20th century **[Fig. 12]**.

Honey and beeswax were also traded. Malleret noted that the Khmer term *Kramwn Sa* ('white-wax market'), used by Chinese residents in Hà Tiên of Kiên Giang province under the 17th-century Mạc dynasty, could derive from the name of an ancient location in Rạch-giá close to Óc Eo (Malleret 1959, I: 20-21). Honey and wax producers were, for example, exempted from other obligations to the court in an 11th-century inscription K. 913 (Cœdès 1937-1966, V: 270) found by Malleret in Tham-mo in the Plain of Reeds.

Further study is needed to compare the gold products in the Óc Eo culture with those dated to the 8th-10th century unearthed at the Cát Tiên archaeological sites in Lâm Đồng province, some 150 km northeast of Hồ Chí Minh City (Lê Xuân Diệm et al. 1995: 144-47). The Cát Tiên religious architectural complex, located at the watershed of the Đồng Nai river, may be identified as a hinterland of the Óc Eo culture.

Bibliography

Bailey, D. W. 2005. *Prehistoric figurines: Representation and corporeality in the Neolithic.* London: Routledge.

Barfoed, S. 2018. '*The use of miniature pottery in Archaic-Hellenistic Greek sanctuaries*', *Opuscula* 11: 111-126. Stockholm: Stockholm University.

Bennett, A. T. N. 2009. 'Gold in Early Southeast Asia', *ArchaeoSciences/Revue d'Archéométrie* 33: 99-107.

Bennett, A. T. N. 2015. 'Ancient Gold and Modern Fakes in Southeast Asia', *Gold in Early Southeast Asia* (eds. R. Barnes, E. N. Stein and B. Diebold): 183-236. New Haven: Yale Southeast Asia Studies.

Bolon, Carol R. 1992. *Forms of the Goddess Lajjā Gaurī in Indian Art.* Pennsylvania: Pennsylvania State University Press.

Brown, Robert L. 1990. 'A Lajja Gauri in a Buddhist context at Aurangabad', *The Journal of the International association of Buddhist studies*, Vol.13, No. 2: 1-16. Switzerland: Lausanne University.

Bunker, Emma C. 1993. 'Gold in the ancient Chinese world: A cultural puzzle', *Artibus Asiae*, Vol. 53, No. 1/2: 27-50.

Calo, A., P. Bellwood, J. Lankton, A. Reinecke, R. Bawono and B. Prasetyo. 2020. 'Trans-Asiatic exchange of glass, gold and bronze: analysis of finds from the late prehistoric Pangkung Paruk site, Bali', *Antiquity*, Vol. 94, Issue 373: 110-126. Cambridge: Cambridge University Press.

Cœdès, George. 1937-1966. *Inscriptions du Cambodge* (8 volumes). Editées et traduites par G. Cœdès. Hanoi and Paris: Imp. École française d'Extrême-Orient.

Cœdès, George. 1947. 'Fouilles en Cochinchine: Le Site de Go Oc Eo, Ancien Port du Royaume de Fou-nan', *Artibus Asiae*, Vol. 10, No. 3: 193-199.

Demandt, Michèle H. S. (2015), 'Early gold ornaments of Southeast Asia: Production, Trade, and Consumption', *Asian Perspectives*, Vol. 54, No. 2: 305-330.

Dube, R. K. 2003. 'Suvarnahumi, Suvarnadvipa: Origin, Identity and its Richness in Gold in Ancient and Medieval Times', *Bulletin of the Metals Museum* 36: 3-23.

Lavy, Paul A. 2003. 'As in Heaven, so on Earth: The Politics of Viṣṇu, Śiva and Harihara Images in Preangkorian Khmer Civilisation', *Journal of Southeast Asian Studies*, Vol. 34, No. 1: 21-39.

Lê Thị Liên. 2005. 'Gold plaques and their cultural contexts in the Oc Eo culture', *Bulletin of the Indo-Pacific Prehistory Association*, Vol. 25: 145-154. Source: https://journals.lib.washington.edu/index.php/BIPPA/article/view/11930. Accessed on 01/06/2020.

Lê Thị Liên. 2011. 'Hindu deities in southern Vietnam: Images on small archaeology artefacts', *Early Interactions Between South and Southeast Asia: Reflections on Cross-cultural exchange* (eds. Manguin, Pierre-Yves, A. Mani and G. Wade): 407-432. Singapore: Institute of Southeast Asia Studies.

Lê Trung and Trịnh Thị Hòa. 1984. 'Những hiện vật văn hóa Óc Eo tàng trữ tại Bảo tàng Lịch sử Thành phố Hồ Chí Minh', *Văn hóa Óc Eo và các văn hóa cổ ở Đồng bằng Cửu Long* ['The Óc Eo objects are being stored at the History Museum in Ho Chi Minh City', *The Óc Eo culture and other ancient cultures in the Mekong Delta*]: 166-176. An Giang: Published by Sở Văn hóa và Thông tin An Giang [Department of Culture and Information of An Giang province].

Lê Xuân Diệm, Đào Linh Côn and Võ Sĩ Khải. 1995. *Văn hóa Óc Eo những khám phá mới.* [*The Óc Eo culture: Recent discoveries*]. Hà Nội: Khoa học Xã hội Publishers.

Malleret, Louis. 1951. 'IV. Les fouilles d'Oc-èo (1944) – Rapport préliminaire', *Bulletin de l'Ecole française d'Extrême-Orient,* Tome 45, No. 1: 75-88.

Malleret, Louis. 1959-1963. *L'archéologie du Delta du Mekong* (4 volumes). Paris: École française d'Extrême Orient.

Malleret, Louis. 1961. 'Les dodécaèdres d'or du site d'Oc-èo', *Artibus Asiae*, Vol. 24, No. 3/4: 343-350.

Malleret, Louis. 1966. 'Une nouvelle statue préangkorienne de Sūrya dans le Bas-Mékong', *Artibus Asiae*, Vol. 23: 109-120 [Supplementum] (Essays Offered to G. H. Luce by His Colleagues and Friends in Honour of His Seventy-Fifth Birthday. Volume 2: Papers on Asian Art and Archaeology)

Manguin, Pierre-Yves and Michèle Vallerin. 1997. 'La mission «Archéologie du delta du Mékong»', *Bulletin de l'École française d'Extrême-Orient*, Vol. 84 (1997): 408-414.

Manguin, Pierre-Yves and A. Indradjaya. 2011. 'The Batujaya site: new evidence of early Indian influence in west Java', *Early interactions between South and Southeast Asia: reflections on cross-cultural exchange* (eds. P.-Y. Manguin, A. Mani and G. Wade): 113-136. Singapore: ISEAS.

Manguin, Pierre-Yves. 2009. 'The Archaeology of Funan in the Mekong River Delta: The Oc Eo Culture of Vietnam', *Arts of Ancient Vietnam: From River plain to Open Sea* (ed. Nancy Tingley): 100-118. Houston: Asian Society Museum of Fine Arts.

Nguyen, Kim Dung. 2017. 'The Sa Huynh Culture in ancient regional trade networks: a comparative study of ornaments', *New perspectives in Southeast Asian and Pacific prehistory* (eds. P. J. Piper, H. Matsumura and D. Bulbeck): 311-332. Canberra: Australian National University. (Terra Australis 45)

Phạm Thị Ngọc Thảo. 2009. *Hiện vật vàng trong văn hóa Óc Eo ở miền tây Nam bộ* [*Gold objects of Oc Eo culture found in the southwestern region of Vietnam*]. Dissertation submitted to fulfill the requirement for the Master of Arts degree in Department of Archaeology of School of Social Sciences and Humanities, The National University in Ho Chi Minh City.

Porte, Bertrand. 2016. 'Sculptures transformées, du Phnom Da au Núi Ba Thê', *Arts asiatiques*, tome 71: 141-158.

Reinecke, Andreas. 2015. 'Ancient gold and silver jewelry and the beginnings of gold working in mainland

Southeast Asia', *Gold in Early Southeast Asia: Selected papers from the symposium Gold in Southeast Asia* (eds. Ruth Barnes, Emma Natalya Stein and Benjamin Diebold): 126-166. New Haven: Yale Southeast Asia Studies. (Monograph 64)

Reinecke, Andreas, Laychour Vin and Sonetra Seng. 2009. *The First Golden Age of Cambodia: Excavation at Prohear*. Germany: Deutschen Nationalbibliografie.

Revire, Nicolas. 2016. *The Enthroned Buddha in Majesty: An Iconological Study,* Thèse de Doctorat Langues et civilisations orientales, Volume 1, Université Sorbonne Nouvelle, Paris 3.

Saint-Michel, Léonard. 1951. 'Situation des dodécaèdres celto-romains dans la tradition symbolique pythagoricienne', *Bulletin de l'Association Guillaume Budé: Lettres d'humanité,* No. 10: 92-116.

Stark, Miriam. 2015. 'Inscribing Legitimacy and Building Power in the Mekong Delta', *Social Theory in Archaeology and Ancient History: The Present and Future of Counternarratives* (ed. G. Emberling): 75-106. Cambridge: Cambridge University Press.

Tjoa-Bonatz, Mai Lin and Nicole Lockhoff. 2019. 'Java: Arts and representations. Art historical and Archaeometric Analyses of Ancient Jewellery (7th-16th century): The Prillwitz Collection of Javanese Gold', *Archipel*, No. 97: 19-68. Paris: Études interdisciplinaires sur le monde insulindien.

Pryce, T. O., Bellina-Pryce Bérénice and T. N. A. Bennett. 2006. 'The development of metal technologies in the upper Thai-Malay peninsula: initial interpretation of the archaeometallurgical evidence from Khao Sam Kaeo', *Bulletin de l'Ecole française d'Extrême-Orient*, Tome 93: 295-315.

Pelliot, Paul. 1903. 'Le Fou-nan', *Bulletin de l'Ecole Française d'Extrême-Orient*, Tome 3: 248-303.

Willis, Michael and Tsering Gonkatsang. 2017. 'Armlet of the pinnacle of the noble victory banner: Locating traces of imperial Tibet in a Dharani in the British Museum', *Locating Religions: Contact, Diversity, and Translocality* (eds. Reinhold F. Glei and Nikolas Jaspert): 345-366. Leiden: Brill.

Endnotes

1 Former Director of An Giang Museum

2 SOAS Alumna, University of Social Sciences and Humanities, National University in HCMC

3 Southern Institute of Social Sciences (SISS), Vietnam Academy of Social Sciences (VASS), in HCMC

4 Now called the History Museum-Hồ Chí Minh City.

5 Manguin (2009: 107) notes that '… an intensive fieldwork was conducted at the Óc Eo sites under the auspices of a Franco-Vietnamese cooperation program, including the Institute of Social Sciences in Hồ Chí Minh City and the École française d'Extrême-Orient from 1997 to 2002.'

10 | Cakras in the Mekong Delta

Pinna Indorf

The stone wheel fragment found at Óc Eo (**Fig. 1**), which measures about 24 cm along its extant diameter, may not at first glance seem impressive. However, look again, at the surface finish, the carefully executed ornament, the modeling (thicker at the centre, tapered to the edge), and its symbolism as well as its historic context and it proves to be quite significant. *Cakras* are among the older Hindu and Buddhist symbols found across South and Southeast Asia. The symbol seems to have originated (between the ninth and sixth centuries BCE as a weaponized chariot wheel (the hub sharpened and/or fitted with spear-like elements), which was associated with Viṣṇu as an attribute in his role as a warrior-god (Maxwell 1997: 78-79, 232). The *Rig Veda* likens Viṣṇu to a charioteer and his weapon, the *cakra*, is also able to act on his behalf (ibid: 232). The *cakra* was more than a weapon; it was also a symbol of divinity, royalty and continuity (ibid: 79). The charioteer was not just a warrior. Viṣṇu is also the Hindu God of preservation, a concept represented by the turning of the Wheel of Existence, *Bhāvacakra*, in the cycles or rounds of *samsāra* and linked to the cycles of the seasons. The wheel symbol, raised upon a pillar, was employed in Vedic tradition as a symbol of the sun (**Fig. 2.a**) (Maxwell 1997: 79) and Viṣṇu as the charioteer with ninety horses (representing ninety days in a season of the year) was thus also associated with the sun (Maxwell 1997: 73). The *cakra,* as one of the *cakravartin*'s treasures, also referred to in Buddhist Texts as a Celestial Wheel (a *Brahmacakra*) (**Fig. 2.b**), is said by Rhys Davids (1977 PTS edition of *Digha Nikāya II*, p. 202 fn.3) to be the disk of the sun. The symbolism of the chariot of the sun was, in time, transferred to Sūrya, a Hindu god whose image is also found in the Mekong Delta (Malleret 1959: 319, 412; Pl. LXXXVII, no. 135) and at Dvāravatī sites (Indorf 2014: 273, 294; Gallon 2014: 338) as well as Si Thep (Lavy 2014: 160-161; Malleret 1959: 413). This led one scholar to interpret a Dvāravatī *cakra* with a small image of Sūrya at its base as a rising sun (Lyons 1979: 358), a motif found on numerous early coins in the region, including the Mekong Delta.

It has been suggested by Kenneth Hall (1985: 60) that Funan's (i.e., the Óc Eo culture's) transition into the Pre-Angkor Khmer kingdom was a catalyst for the development of Dvāravatī. This could have occurred in several ways due to the transfer of power from one elite family or cultural group to another (cf. Vickery 1998), including the movement of some displaced elites to new and distant places in hopes of regaining a profitable foothold in the new trade or economic contexts of the time. It is possible the similarities between some Óc Eo *cakras* and early Dvāravatī *cakras* is not a coincidence;

after all, it has been widely reported that Óc Eo artifacts have been found at sites in Thailand. While the Óc Eo *cakras* seem to have been more or less plain with eight spokes and quite probably Vaiṣṇava, those of Thailand became embellished with ornament, had various number of spokes (Brown 1996; Indorf 2014), and were associated with sites considered Buddhist, even though some (e.g., Khao Si Wichai monument 6) also contained Hindu artifacts. It must also be mentioned that the Óc Eo *cakra* has carved-out or cut spokes, while only a few found in Thailand had cut spokes while most had *bas relief* spokes (Indorf 2014: 295-297). One possible explanation for the more embellished *cakras* in Thailand could be rooted in the socio-political context – being more stable in earlier Óc Eo, more dynamic and competitive in emerging states of Dvāravatī.

Given the legendary connections attributed to the early rulers and elite of Óc Eo or Funan with Peninsular Thailand's population (cf. Wheatley 1980: 14-17, 47-48), more people of Óc Eo culture may have shifted to Thailand (perhaps joining others already there for trade reasons) during the upheavals of the transition to Khmer dominance. This could account for the plain *cakras* at sites along the western coast of the Gulf of Thailand and western edge of the swampy area at the centre of Chao Phraya Delta, viz: Pattani/Yarang, Khao Si Wichai, Nakhon Si Thammarat, Nakhon Pathom and Sing Buri.[1] There is one more such *cakra*, with a plain felly and carved base, of unknown origin (Indorf 2014: Table 1, FII.C), which may belong to this group of sites, from some place also along the coast or edge of the floodplain. It is a small *cakra* (diameter 20 cm, with the No. T.B. 2337 on it; Dhanit Yupon 2533: fig. 13), with twelve *bas relief* spokes and what looks like a *bas relief* bent arm at the base, which could make it an *Indrakhila* (Indorf 2014: Table 1, FII.C, p. 279). In these new contexts, the *cakras* may have represented the elite or royal power of a group of related settlements/ peoples. Once the *cakra*s became associated with a specific socio-political power or royal family, so also the embellishments of the Dvāravatī artifacts may align them with specific kings or royal families (cf. Indorf 2014). It is thus possible that these coastal sites were the first homes in exile to some of the more successful refugees who fled upheavals during the transition from Óc Eo to Khmer control in the Mekong Delta. Perhaps they introduced this custom of eight- or twelve-spoke *cakra*s at religious or ceremonial sites, which (given the inclinations of the local population) were or became Buddhist or mixed Hindu and Buddhist sites. Larger, embellished *cakras* emerged as the custom spread inland to areas with more indigenous and even Khmer-influenced people.

Another hint of Óc Eo's culture as a catalyst for Dvāravatī may perhaps be found in the evidence of multi-deity practice reflected on Dvāravatī plaques with five depressions, most with Gaja-Lakṣmī (e.g., National Museum Bangkok artifact no K.133/134; **(Fig. 5.e**), which give prominence to a female spirit. Their connection to Óc Eo influences being the multi-deity practices represented by the stone plaques with circular depressions found at Óc Eo (see Malleret 1960: nos. 303-317; **Fig. 5.b**) and the enduring presence of the Mother Goddess cult in early Óc Eo (Lê Thị Liên 2006: 242). In Dvāravatī, the stone *cakra*s became identified with Buddhism and flourished for a time, while their use in the Khmer culture, which emerged from Óc Eo culture, faded, probably due to the rise in Śaiva cults and rituals, which eclipsed Vaiṣṇava deities as seen at the Cát Tiên site (Lê Thị Liên 2011: 428). This is, however, a theoretical scenario, which needs to be tested by carefully examining many small artifacts, as well as larger remains, and all inscriptions. There is, thus, much work to be done on the historic and archaeological contexts of these wheels and other small artifacts before the full historic contexts might be known. Nonetheless, the abundant remains, fragmentary as they are, still reveal a sophisticated and complex culture, originating or centered at Óc Eo, and integrated in a broad inter-regional community.

The number eight is associated with Viṣṇu and his embodiment of universal order (Maxwell 1997: 73), and is perhaps also a reference to the four cardinal plus four sub-cardinal directions of this earth of our existence, often referred to in ancient texts as the "world of four directions". Viṣṇu's *cakra* is, furthermore, associated with the beginning of a new era, initiated by the cosmic act of Viṣṇu or Indra (also known as Śakra [Skt.] or Sakka [Pāli]) in a creation myth (Irwin 1990: 14). The number twelve is also associated with Viṣṇu as the number of months in a year and thus the Rulers of the Months and also the twelve Lords of Wisdom, which figure in the five-*vyūha* concept of Viṣṇu related to multi-deity practices (e.g., *pañcāyatana* or five-shrine temples found at Cham sites in Vietnam and Khmer sites in Cambodia and Thailand; cf. Maxwell 1997: 82-83).

Over time, the significance of the *cakra* became more complex and variations were known as a *Bhāvacakra* or *Sangsāracakra* (Wheel of Life) as well as a *Brahmacakra* (Divine Wheel or Celestial Wheel) in its role as one of the treasures of the *Cakravartin* (universal monarch) (**Fig. 2.b**). These symbolic associations also became part of Buddhist tradition (cf. Brown 1996: 101-102). In Buddhism, the *cakra* became a symbol of the Buddha's First Sermon (delivered in the Sarnath Deer Park) and, as such, is known as a *Dharmacakra* symbolizing the *Paticcasamuppāda* (chain of causation, the topic of that first sermon with twelve spokes) or his enlightenment (with sixteen spokes). The *Dharmacakra* is often depicted with one or two small deer, a reference to the First Sermon (Indorf 2014: 285-286). The distinctions between the different types or roles of particular *cakra*s depend on the ornament, number of spokes, inscriptions and its associated motifs and context (ibid). Likewise, these small artifacts should be viewed in the context of archaeological finds in surrounding sites and the region.

In the grave pits of Gò Tháp, dated between 400-600 CE, small gold foil plaques were found incised or embossed with motifs, some being *cakras*. One of the *cakras* is shown on a pedestal, about the same height as the diameter of the *cakra*, composed of two volutes (Dao Linh Côn 1996: 114, Fig. 7, left). These deposit plaques with *cakras* were found in contexts indicating a royal connection, e.g., in what may be royal graves. (Dao Lin Côn 1994: 114; Fig. 7; Higham 2014: 282) This is not surprising as Viṣṇu is also the prototype of the Hindu ideal of kingship, taking over relevant attributes earlier attributed to Indra. The eight-spoke *cakra* supported by a *bhadrapīṭha* (splendid base/throne) style pedestal on a gold foil plaque clearly indicates that *cakra*s were deemed sacred, worthy of respect or worship and thus may have been set up in a sacred environment on a pedestal or perhaps a column, i.e., as *cakrastambha*, such as found in India, e.g., at Liṅgarajupalem (ca. 4th century, ASI 1960: Pl. LVII.C) and at Bodh Gaya (**Fig. 3**). It furthermore shows the practice of *cakras* on pedestals, and perhaps columns may date to the 5th century.

The artifacts found at Gò Tháp[2] (Tháp Mười Mound of Gò Tháp) also yielded Viṣṇu images (see Higham 2014: 277). Malleret (1959: Pl. LXXXIII.a) compared an image of Viṣṇu (MBB no. 3080, ht. 1.37 m) from Vatt Krapau Brik, northeast of Phnom Bathe to sixth century Dvāravatī images (ibid: 396). However, the sites were not exclusively Vaiṣṇava, nor even exclusively Hindu. Artifacts from Gò Tháp graves included many with lotuses, perhaps a symbol of Lakṣmī, one Viṣṇu's consorts, but it is a multivalent symbol. One plaque depicted a female figure with a lotus in place of a head (Lê Thị Liên 2006: 242). This figure appears in *trimurti* plaques of Andhra Pradesh, India and is known as Lajja-Gauri (Nagaswamy 2003; Sarma 1983, 1994) and in some places in Tamil Nadu as Cakra-rajani or Cakrayi. These lotus motifs are seen as related to the Mother Goddess cult, which has strong local roots evidenced from the second and third centuries CE (Lê Thị Liên 2006: 242). In addition the lotus is widely seen as a symbol of purity and the birthplace of purity (cf. Dehejia 1997). Wooden Buddha images have also been found at the Gò Tháp site (BTLS 1615). In fact, the range of artifacts has been interpreted as reflecting local beliefs along with Hindu Vaiṣṇavism and perhaps with Śaiva cults in a secondary position (Lê Thị Liên 2006: 242). And these co-existed with Buddhism. In a later study Lê Thị Liên (2011) focused on small artifacts from three sites: Gò Tháp, Da Noi and Cát Tiên. That study seems to point to an early focus on Vaiṣṇava deities and symbols at Gò Tháp (dated fifth or fourth century BCE to fifth century CE; Lê Thị Liên 2011: 427) and Da Noi (dated 4th-6th CE; Lê Thị Liên 2011: 428), with a shift at Cát Tiên to more complicated ritual, thus the later rituals in the period dated fourth to eighth or ninth century CE (Lê Thị Liên 2011: 428). The later rituals of that period included the multi-deity practices such as the *pañcāyatana* rituals (cf. Maxwell 1997). Evidence of multi-deity practices in the Mekong Delta is confirmed in the numerous small stone ritual plaques with three or more circular depressions (e.g., Malleret 1960: nos. 303 to 317; **Fig. 5.b**).

This particular *cakra* from Óc Eo (artifact no. 1749) (**Figs. 1.a-f**) had eight spokes, a lotus on its hub and incised lines near the inner edge of its felly. Given the range of motif specifically Hindu or related to Viṣṇu, it seems likely the Óc Eo stone *cakra* might represent Viṣṇu. If so, it might be questioned as to why, as the disk weapon, it has a lotus on the hub. The lotus, as a symbol of purity, is said to represent not mere presence nor static states, but dynamic forces (Sarma 1994: 89-90). Likewise, in the Buddhist tradition, purity is understood as playing a role in the destruction of ignorance and evil and is the root of good deeds and thus *puṇya*, an essential facet of good kingship. Between the fifth and thirteenth centuries in India, an important aspect of kingship, dating back to the second century BCE (Dehejia 1997: 305), was that only when a righteous king reigned, could prosperity and *dharmic* order be attained, i.e., it required the dynamic force of purity (Kinsley 1986: 26-27, 70). In that sense, the lotus represents a weapon against poverty and *adharmic* order or chaos.

After describing the *cakra* (artifact no. 1749 or MBB no. 3931, Malleret's no. 129) found between Gò Cây Trom and the mound Giong-cát at a depth of 50 cm (cf. Malleret 1959: 401, Pl. LXXXIVb), Malleret then mentions another fragment of a small *cakra* (given his no. 130 and the MBB no. 4346) found at a depth of 70 cm beside Monument B near the central canal of Óc Eo, in segment V (ibid: 401, not illustrated). Monument B appears to have been a 9.5 m square platform edged with brick revetment or retaining wall (Malleret 1959: Pl. XXV). The centre seems to have been hollowed out over time (plundered for gold artifacts?) but could have originally held a *cakra* on a pedestal or column (a *cakrastambha*) at its centre. The Óc Eo Stone *cakras* might be the oldest found in Southeast Asia, if they are from the fifth or the early sixth century, but they are not the only ones.

There are also pre-Angkor sites in Cambodia where traces of *cakrastambha*s or other honorific *stambhas* were used. The remains of a late sixth- or mid-seventh-century monument at Hanchey, Kompong Cham, a sacred site on top of a hill, has traces of *bas relief* on the tympanum of an arched niche, which includes *cakrastambha*s flanking a shrine (Indorf 2014: 274-275). In Indian and Indian-influenced traditions, honorific *stambhas* crowned with sculpted symbolic forms, have been used in both Hindu and Buddhist contexts, for example at Vidiśā (Besnagar, Madhya Pradesh; Huntington 1985; 57, Fig. 5.1), Sarnath (ibid: 46-47) and Bodh Gaya (**Fig. 3**) add identity, indicate royal association and give specific characteristics to a structure or site. At Sambor Prei Kuk N1, in Cambodia, the tympanum *bas relief* over the west door shows *stambhas* with carved figures on top flanking a shrine (cf. Indorf 2014: 275) and there are actual, large square stone base slabs, which could have held such *stambhas*, flanking gates into the inner court of that site (cf. Tranet 1997).

Cakrastambhas were also known in Arakan in Myanmar (sixth century, Gutman 1986: Pl. 2a), and nearby in Thailand, at sites known as Dvāravatī (generally, but not always specifically, dated sixth to ninth century; Brown 1996; Phasook Indrawooth 2009; Indorf 2014). A plain *cakra*, with many spokes or 'rays' was found in Arakan (dated ca. sixth century; Gutman 1986: Pl. 2a). Being also adorned with a figure and supported on a column, it was identified as an "*Indrakhila*" (Indra-*stambha*), a feature, which became a part of Buddhist monasteries in Myanmar and the region even into the fourteenth century in Sukhothai (Gosling 1996: 135). In these Burmese and Thai monasteries, the *Indrakhila* is said to serve as a reference to Indra's thunderbolt (*vajra*) representing the unshakable nature of the mind at enlightenment (ibid). This explanation appears to align its significance with Buddhist doctrine, but it could also carry the significance of the creation myth of Indra or Viṣṇu mentioned above. A pre-Angkorian *trimurti* stele (**Fig. 2.a**) from the easternmost sanctuary in Laos, at Ban Tatkum (thus close to Campā on the coast of Vietnam), represents the three deities with symbolic forms, including a *cakra*, being presented as a *cakrastambha*, for Viṣṇu (Lorrillard 2014: 192-193).

A few early *cakras* of a plain type, quite similar to the Óc Eo *cakra*, have been found in Thailand (**Fig. 6**) at sites dated between the sixth to the ninth or eleventh century, considered to be from the Dvāravatī period, a name derived from inscribed votive medals found in central Thailand (Revire 2016: 400-402, Fig. 2.2) and Chinese records, which located Dvāravatī west of Īśanapura (Smith 1979: 450; cf. Wheatley 1980: 56-59). Some scholars have even argued that Dvāravatī of the seventh century extended as far south as the Kra Isthmus.[3] Artifacts, including stone *cakras* (some highly ornamented), with similar characteristics to those associated with core Dvāravatī sites, have been found over a vast area, which, however, is unlikely to have been a single state in spite of their shared or similar aesthetic traditions and history.

At least three, possibly four plain stone *cakras* similar to the Óc Eo *cakra* (no. 1749, **Fig. 1**) have been found in Peninsular Thailand. One very similar *cakra* (**Fig. 6.b**) was found at Nakhon Si Thammarat (Phanuwat Ueasaman 2019: 52). Its spokes and felly show similar modeling and it has a lotus on the hub like the Óc Eo *cakra* (no. 1749) but lacks the incised lines on the felly and has twelve (a Vaiṣṇava reference to time), rather than eight (a Vaiṣṇava reference to space) spokes. A *cakra* found at Yarang, Pattani with only eight spokes, and supported by a sphere and a prism[4] (**Fig. 6.a**; cf. Indorf 2014: 279; Phanuwat Ueasaman 2019: 52, and Siriporn Sanghiran 2019: 64), also shows striking similarity in the modeling of the hub, spokes and felly, in being thicker at the hub and tapering to the felly edge. The Yarang site was found to have 44 mounds and the four excavated were identified as brick *stūpas*, based on the discovery of Buddhist aphorisms on bricks, votive *stūpas* and tablets, as well as bronze statuettes of the Bodhisattva Avalokiteśvara. But a stone *śivaliṅga*, a bronze Śūrya image and fragments of *candraśālās* or *kudus*, as well as other architectural elements such as doorframes (not necessarily part of a *stūpa*) were also found (Siriporn Sanghiran 2019: 63). Phanuwat Ueasaman (2019: 39, 43, 49, 52) refers to two stone *cakras* from Khao Si Wichai (sixth to tenth century hill sites), one from Monument No. 6 (a sixth to ninth century site)[5], which was also the find-site of a Viṣṇu image as well as a *śivaliṅga* and one from Monument No. 12 (a seventh to ninth century site) at the foot of the hill, identified as a Buddhist monastery (**Fig. 6.c**). The illustrated *cakra* (ibid: 52) had twelve plain cut-spokes and a plain felly, but the base seems to have been cut (sawed) out and may have had a carved element.[6] Monument No. 12 was also the find-site of a bronze *cakra* with four cut-spokes, which have ornamental motifs at the base and top of each spoke, like the ornamented Dvāravatī *cakras*, and may have a faintly modeled lotus motif with a depressed centre as the hub (Phanuwat Ueasaman 2019: 52 centre left). This may be compared with a similar carved motif held in the hand of the goddess on Candi Mendut in Java, dated to the late eighth century (ibid: 52 centre right). Three more plain stone *cakras* were found in Thailand, two of these in the core area of Dvāravatī culture: one at Sing Buri, with twelve cut-spokes (**Fig. 6.d**), and one at Nakhon Pathom, with eight *bas relief* spokes (**Plate 6.e**), but the find-site of the third, with twelve *bas relief* spokes and a carved basal element (**Fig. 6.f**), is unknown (Indorf 2014: 279). Although not all have been found in their original context, the Dvāravatī *cakras* have been generally assumed to be Buddhist (thus labeled "*Dharmacakras*"), and to have also been linked to kingship (cf. Dhida Saraya 1999; Phasook Indrawooth 1999, 2008). In some cases (e.g., Brown's [1996] *cakra* No. 5, which has Buddhist texts inscribed on its spokes), the term is justified. Also some of these *cakras* were supported on tall pillars (e.g., at U Thong site 11; Phasook Indrawooth 2008: 154) and are associated with small stone deer as a reference to the First Sermon at the Deer Park, Sarnath. However, more and more artifacts are being found related to Hinduism or specifically related to Kṛṣṇa and Viṣṇu at sites considered part of a Buddhist state known as Dvāravatī (Revire 2016). As noted above, even one of the *cakras* from Peninsular Thailand was found at a site (Khao Si Wichai, Monument 6) with a substantial Viṣṇu statue (Phanuwat Ueasaman 2019: 52). These customary assumptions should be re-examined in the context of a wider range of artifacts from the various sites in Thailand and across Southeast Asia. Lacking the definitive inscriptions and major works to clearly define developments in the past, it is the multitude of small artifacts, which must be examined carefully.

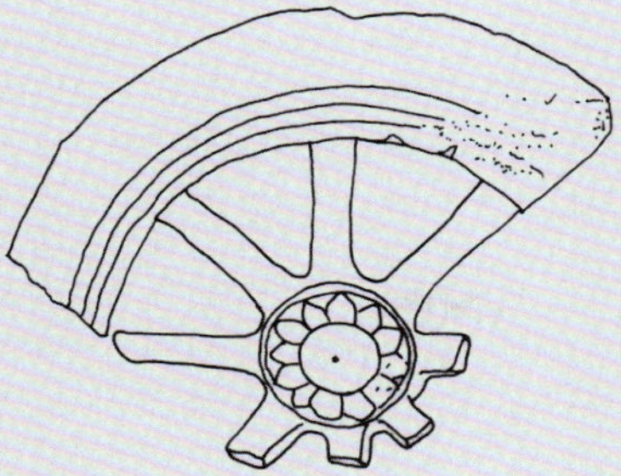

1a) Stone *cakra* from Óc Eo, Malleret's no 130, (1959: 401), also MBB no. 3931 and now with the (BTLS HCMC) no. 1749, date perhaps late 5th/early 6th? According to Malleret (1959: 401), found at a depth of 50 cm, (Drawn by Pinna Indorf 2011, after Malleret 1959: Pl. LXXXIVb) "MalleretLXXXIVbDrw" / "P1010727")[7]

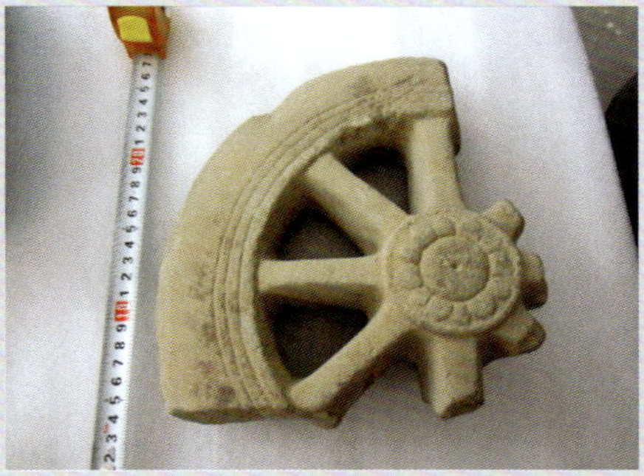

1b) Stone *cakra*, artifact 1749, originally with eight cut-spokes, had an overall diameter of approximately 30 cm and ornamentation comprising incised lines on the felly and a twelve-petal lotus on the hub. (Photo: Trần Kỳ Phương 2019?; 'KY_IMG_9568')

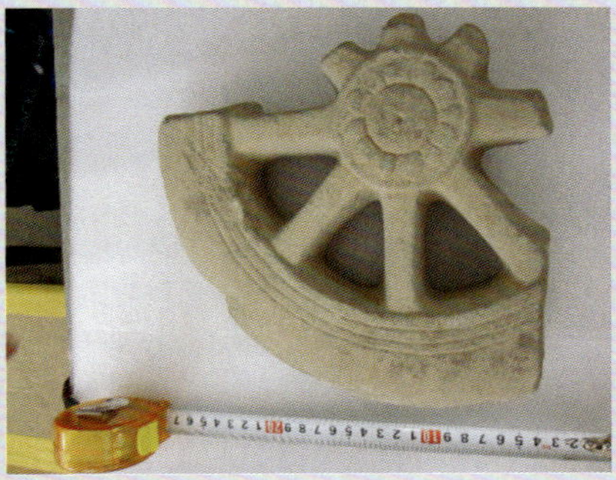

1c) Stone *cakra* artifact 1749, approximately 24 cm along remains of diameter (along approximately horizontal spoke). (Photo: Trần Kỳ Phương 2019?; KY_IMG_9569)

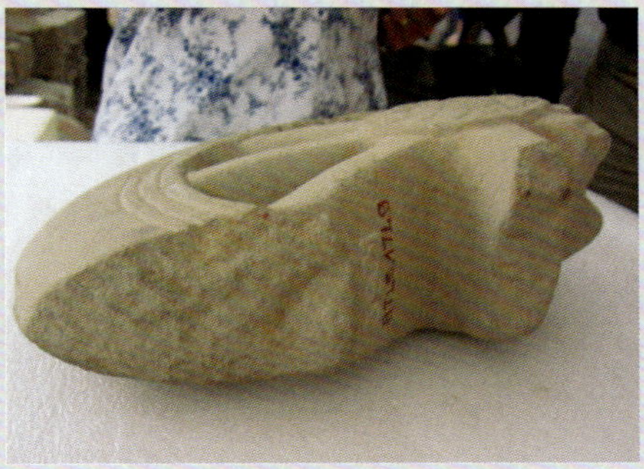

1d) Stone *cakra*, artifact 1749, approximately 8 cm thick at the centre of the hub. (Photo: Trần Kỳ Phương 2019?; 'KY_IMG_9567')

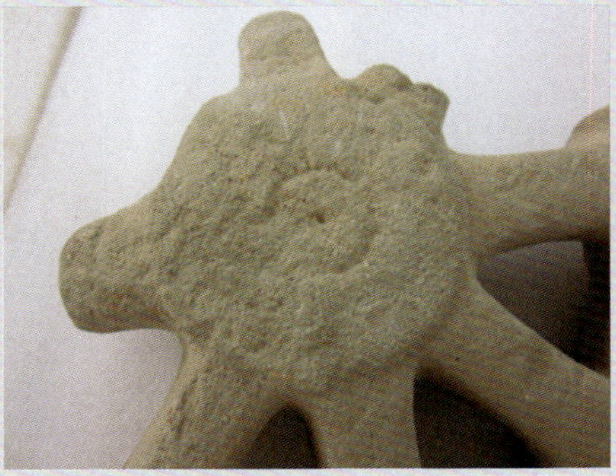

1e) Stone *cakra*, artifact 1749, detail of the hub, reverse side, which shows a badly damaged or unfinished lotus motif. (Photo: Trần Kỳ Phương 2019 "KY_IMG_9562")

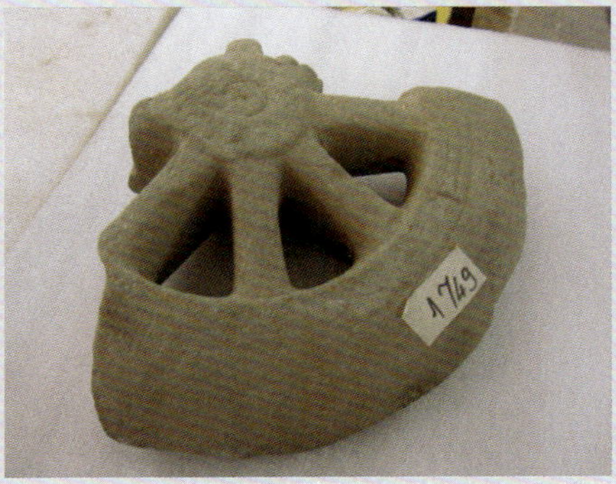

1f) Stone *cakra*, artifact 1749, seen from the back, where the lotus of the hub and incised lines on the felly show damage. (Photo: Trần Kỳ Phương 2019? 'KY_IMG_9561')

Fig. 1 *Fragment of a stone* cakra *from Óc Eo*

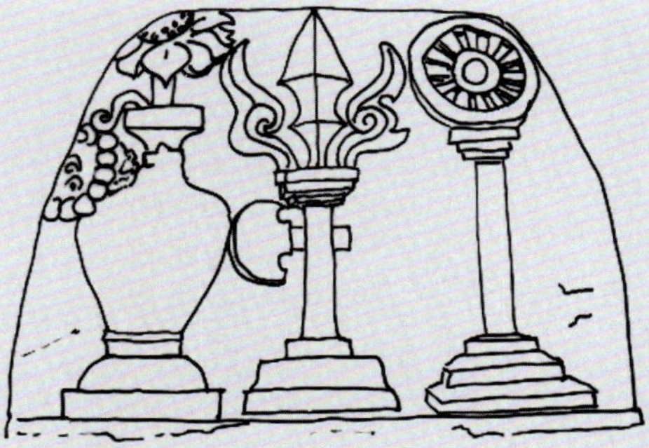

2a) Pre-Angkorian *Trimurti* stele from Ban Tatkum in Attapeu Province, Laos, which depicts Śiva (centre) with a *triśula*, Brahmā (left) with a *pūrnaghata* and Viṣṇu (right) with a *cakrastambha*. Below is perhaps a turtle supporting the earth (Lorrillard 2014: 192-193). This *cakra* on a pillar has twelve spokes as the symbol of the sun, to represent measured time, which is also associated with Viṣṇu. (Drawing by Pinna Indorf 2015 after Lorrillard 2014: Fig. 2; "JSS PL. 03.G._72"[drawing] & photo: RCSD-Published-Report-TKP-2013-39.psd / "RCSD-TKP-stele.jpg" photo by Trần Kỳ Phương 2013)

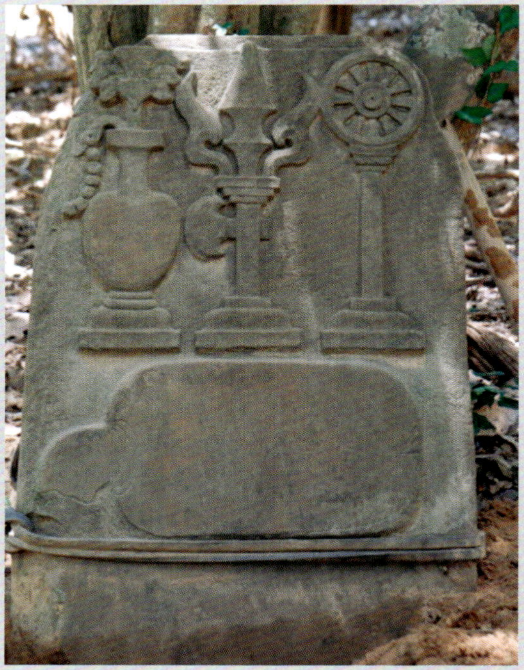

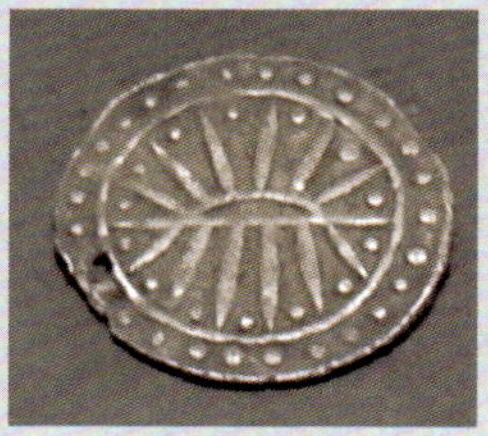

2c) Rising sun coins such as this one from Óc Eo, [BTLS.1882]. are found across mainland Southeast Asia. Although cut in half by the horizon out at sea, the motif is a disc with twelve spoke-like rays, (Pinna Indorf 2015 [DSC_0249, DSC_0249crop1/ risingSunCoin])

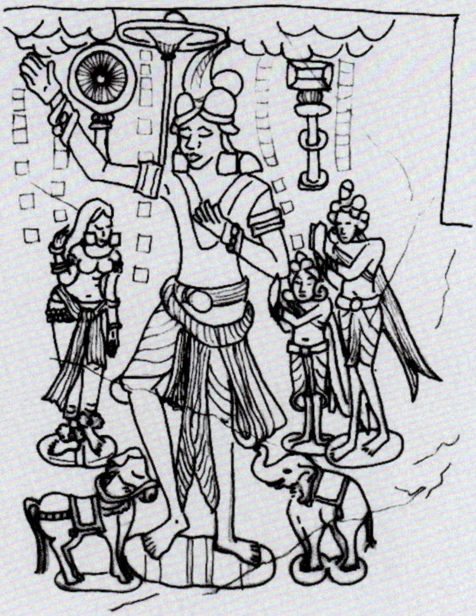

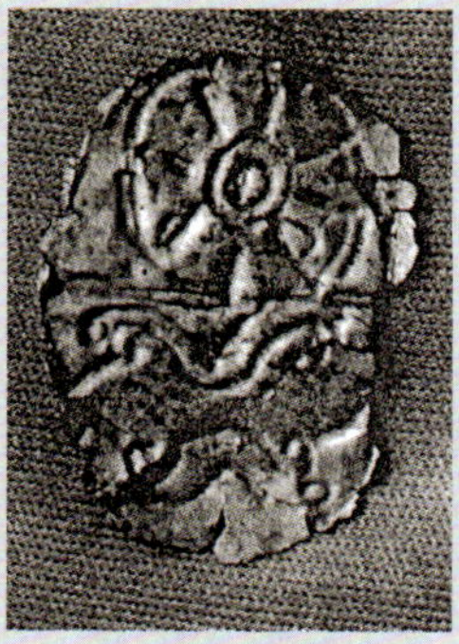

2b) *Cakravatin* plaque from the Buddhist *stūpa* at Jaggayyapeta, Andhra Pradesh (3rd-4th century CE; Zimmer 1986). The wheel treasure, a celestial wheel or *Brahmacakra*, is in the upper left corner with many spokes. (Drawn by Pinna Indorf 2011, after Zimmer 1986; "cakravartin02drw")

2d) A deposit plaque with a *cakra* mounted on a pedestal found at Go Thap, Vietnam. The pedestal mounting, as would a column, clearly shows the *cakra* was revered or added significance to a site.

Fig. 2 *Cakras found in different contexts*

Fig. 3 *Cakrastambha depicted on the vedika pillars around the Mahābodhi shrine, Bodh Gaya*
(3rd BCE-1st century CE, Barau 1975; Photos by Pinna Indorf 1990)

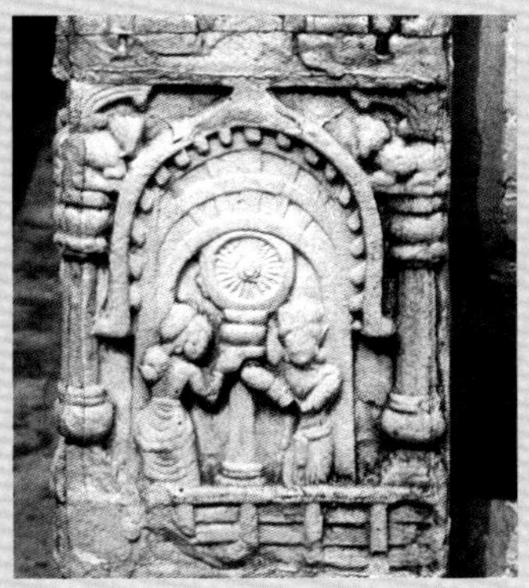

3a) Two devotees pay respect to a *cakrastambha* housed in a *chaitya* or shrine, which is flanked by two honorific, elephant crowned *stambhas*, and is surrounded by a *vedika*. The *cakra* has many spokes and could be a *Brahmacakra* (celestial wheel) or a *Bhāvacakra* (wheel of life) or, because of its context, a *Dharmacakra*. [BodhGayaWheel4dt"/ "BodhGayaWheel4dtH" OM203-03 51 BodhGaya 3B2]

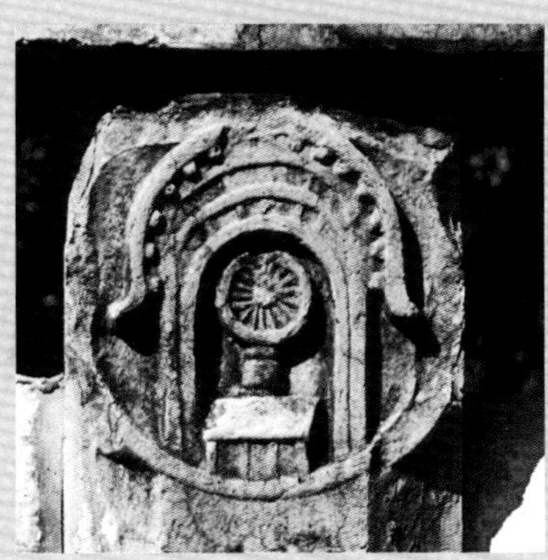

3b) The empty throne in front of the wheel with sixteen spokes suggests this wheel, on a short column or pedestal in a shrine, is a *Dharmacakra*, representing enlightenment (Indorf 2014: 286). "BodhGayaWheel3dt" = OM202-36 (51 BodhGaya 3A4))

Fig. 4 *Lajja-Gauri motifs*

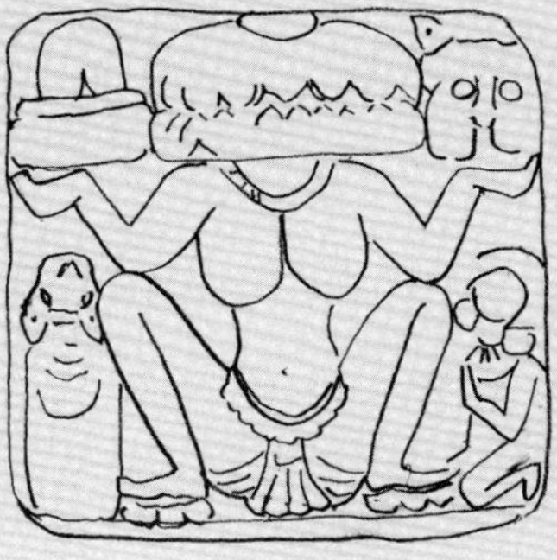

4a) Lajja-Gauri or Sri plaque with quincunx arrangement of elements from Keesaragutta, Andhra Pradesh, 9 cm sq. (Sarma 1994: 98). The central figure here is the form of Sri known as Lajja-Gauri. (dated 4th century CE, Metropolitan Museum of Art NY artifact acc. no. 2000.284.13; MoA website 6-8 Dec 2015) (Drawn by Pinna Indorf 2008 after Sarma 1994, PL. 101; cf IAR 1978-79, pl. XXXVIII.B, p. 63-64; "sriPlaqueQXDrw")

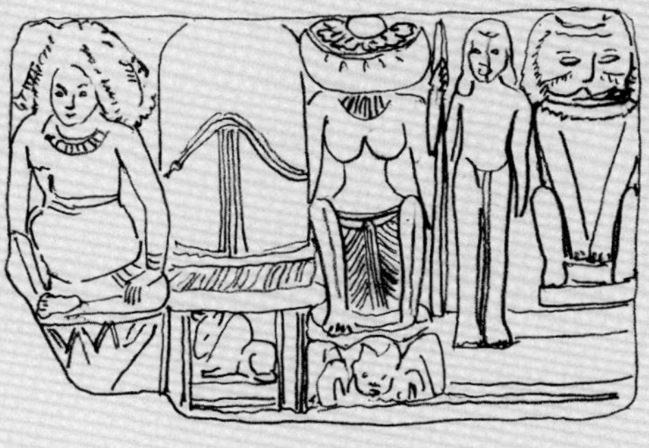

4b) Trimurti plaque with five figures from Kunidene, Andhra Pradesh, with a row of five motifs, dated 5th century (Sarma 1994: Pl. 91). It shows Lakshmi at the centre with lotiform head (as Lajja-Gauri) then Śiva (first flanking pair of motifs) and Viṣṇu and Narasiṃha (second flanking pair of motifs) at the edges of the plaque, i.e., the motifs are arranged in paired symmetry, reflected around the central figure. Thus on each side there is a form of both Śiva and Viṣṇu; the third deity is Sri as Lajja-Gauri. (Drawn by Pinna Indorf 2008 after Sarma 1994, Pl. 91A; "Trimurti5Drw")

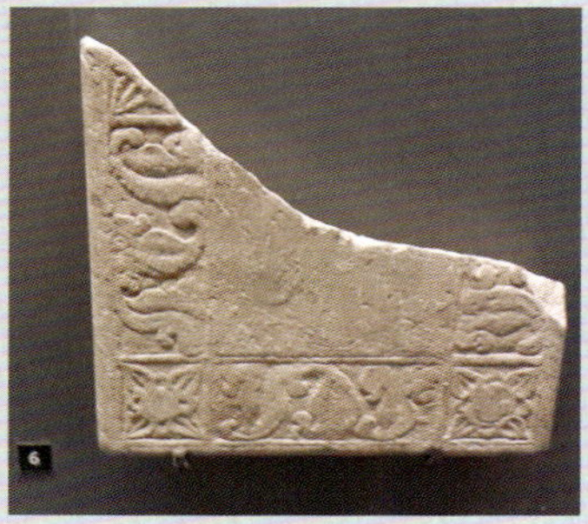

5a) Remains of a flat, rectangular plaque found at Óc Eo (Malleret 1959: no 304; BTLS no. 1742), similar to those in India labeled "*ayagapattha*", serving as an offering or to present an offering during a *pūja* and found at sites from Taxila to Borneo. (Photo by Pinna Indorf 2015; "MD304")

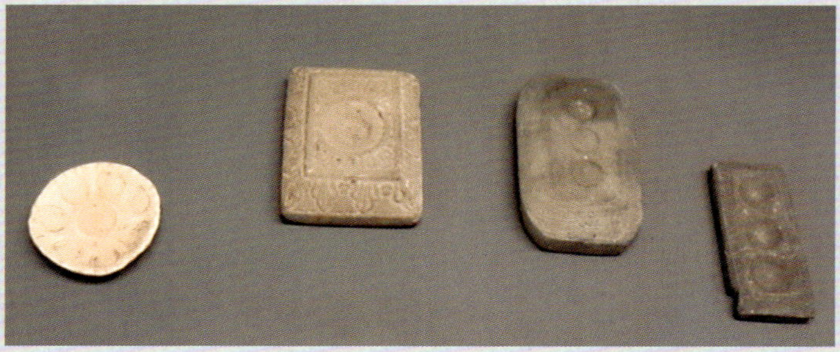

5b) Small offering plaques or *pūja* trays from Óc Eo / the Mekong Delta, with cupped depressions, left to right: i) circular dish with one central depression and seven around it; Malleret's (1959) numbers: ii) no. 321, with only one depression and a carved surface, iii) no. 318 (?) and iv) no. 314, both with three depressions each (artifact group no BTLS 1668). Those with several depressions are suitable for multi-deity *pūjas,* one depression for each deity. (Photo by Pinna Indorf 2015; "MDplaques")

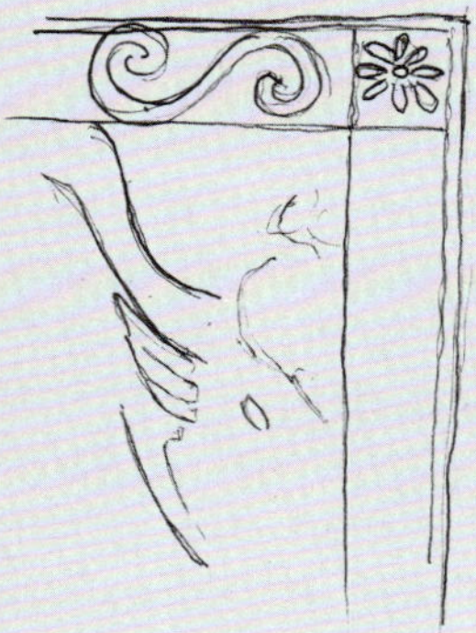

5c) Fragment of a terracotta plaque or *ayagapattha* from Santubong, Sarawak in the Sarawak Museum, Kuching, Malaysia, W. Borneo on display in 1987. The elephant head and trunk could be the remains of a motif known as Gaja-Lakṣmī or Lakṣmī-*abhisheka.* (Field sketch, Pinna Indorf 1987; "SantubongPQ"/ "SantubongPQH")

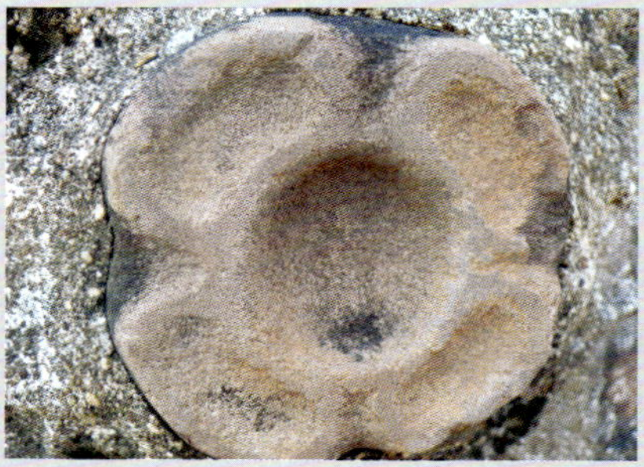

5d) A small ritual tray with five depressions, which thus may have been used in a pañcāyatana ritual, found at Wat Phra Pathon, Nakhon Pathom, Thailand and which now decorates a new landscape feature there. (Photo by G. Swati Reddy 2007; NP507ppcm384)

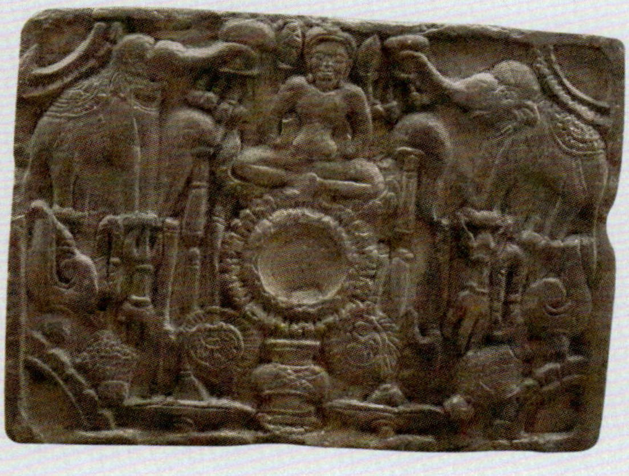

5e) A rectangular, 15 x 21 cm, stone, ritual tray found in Nakhon Pathom, Thailand, now in the National Museum Bangkok (artifact K.133/4). and dated to the 6th-8th century. The entire surface is covered with carved motifs including a Gaja-Lakshmī motif on one half and a *pūrnaghata* flanked by other auspicious or royal motifs on the other. It has five depressions (edged with lotus petals) in a quincunx arrangement, one in the centre and one in each corner, thus it is a multi-deity, *pañcāyatana* ritual tray.
(Photo by Pinna Indorf 2011; PQgajalakNMB1[8])

Fig. 5 *Ritual plaques or trays*

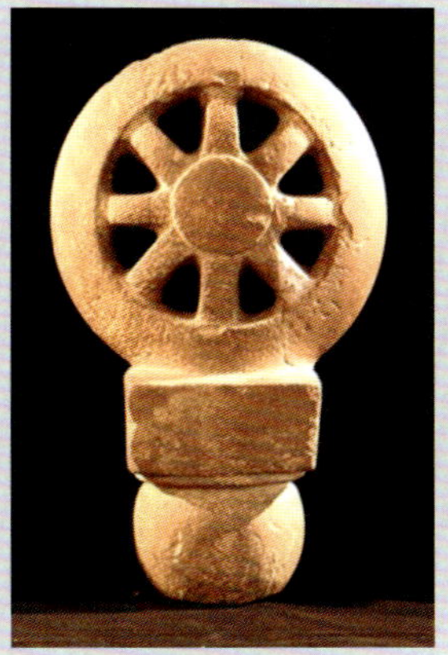

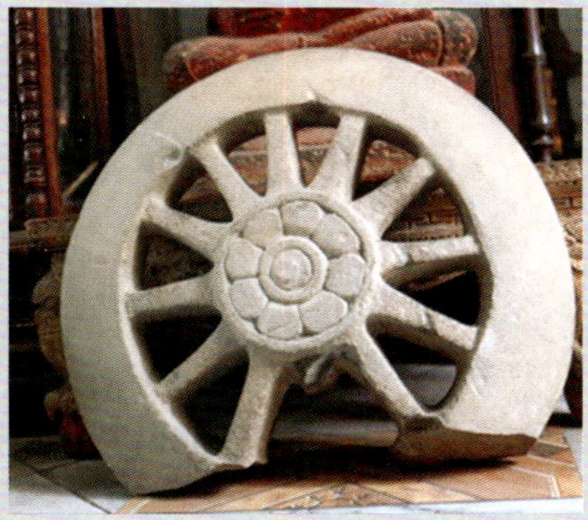

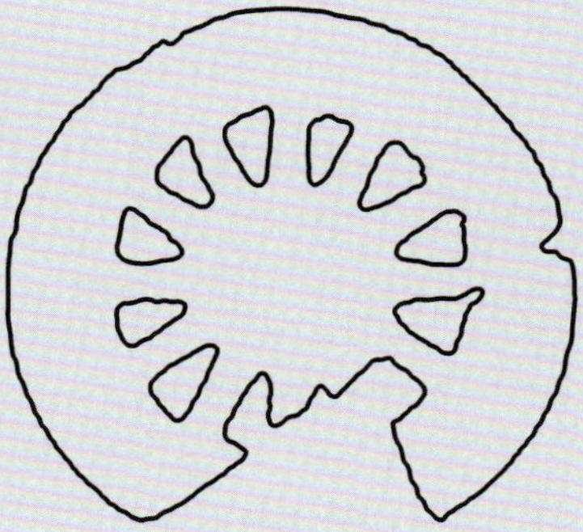

6a) This cut-spoke *Cakra* with eight spokes was found at the Yarang ancient city site (7th-8th century CE), Pattani in Peninsular Thailand, where 44 remains mounds were discovered. (Siriporn Sanghiran 2019: 58, 63) (Photo: Buncha Pongpanich 2019) ('Untitled-1a' or 'Y cakra' from Ky)

6b) A twelve cut-spokes stone *cakra* with an eight-petal lotus on its hub, said to be from Nakhon Si Thammarat, Peninsular Thailand, but of unknown provenance, now at Wat Phra Mahathat, Nakhon Si Thammarat, 6th-7th century. (Photo by Buncha Pong Panich, 2019? from Trần Kỳ Phương) ['Mekong Delta Like cakra 'Downloads/ 'untitled 1']; cf Phanuwat Ueasaman 2019: 52 top centre)

6c) A twelve cut-spokes stone *cakra* found at Khao Si Wichai in the remains of a 7th-9th century monastery, monument site 12, at the foot of a hill with a Hindu hill-top site dating back to the 6th century, where another *cakra* (not illustrated) was found. (Phanuwat Uaesaman 2019: 39, 43, 49, 52)

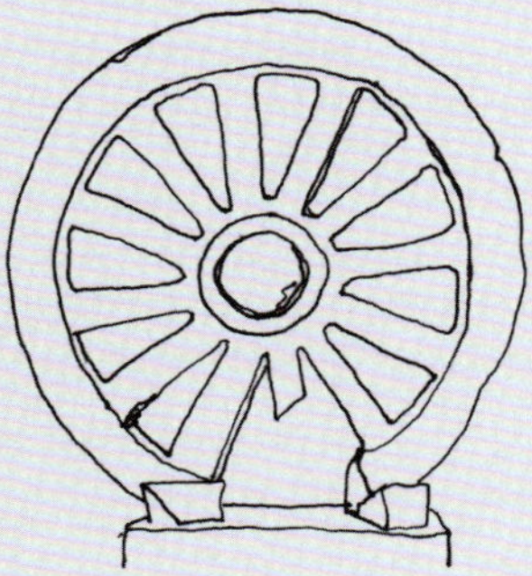

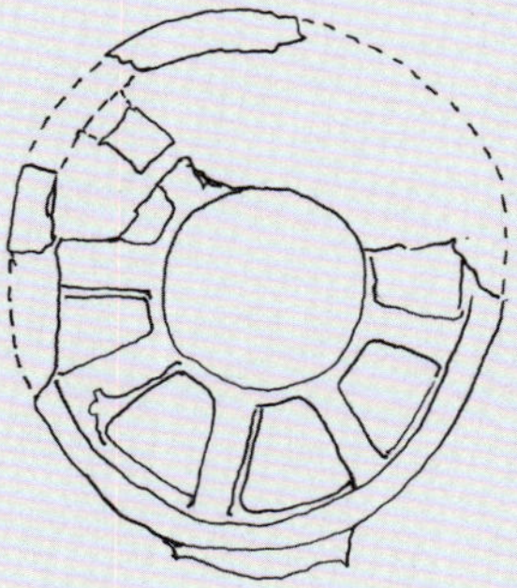

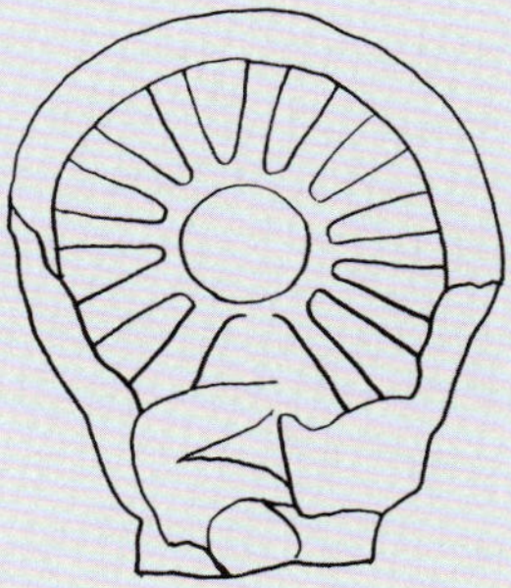

6d) *Cakra* from In Buri Kao, Sing Buri (near Lopburi), Thailand with twelve cut-spokes, perhaps late 6th-early 7th century. (Drawn by Pinna Indorf 2011, after Gosling 2004: 58; cf. Brown 1996: Pl. 39) ("FIIIA-B39"[72dpi] or "Scan110323-0023" [high res.])

6e) *Cakra* from Nakhon Pathom, Thailand, diameter 42 cm, height 50 cm (including part of the tenon remaining below) with eight *bas relief* spokes, perhaps of the late 6th-early 7th century. (Drawn by Pinna Indorf 2011, after Dhanit Yupho 2533: Fig. 12; cf. Brown 1996: Pl. 40) ("FIIIB-Y12" [72dpi] or "scan110323-0017"[high res.])

6f) *Cakra* of unknown provenance in Thailand, diameter 20 cm with plain felly and twelve *bas relief* spokes as well as a carved element at the base, which appears to be a bent arm, perhaps of Indra; dated perhaps 7th century. (Drawn by Pinna Indorf 2011, after Dhanit Yupho 2533: Fig. 13) ("FIIC-Y13-R")

Fig. 6 *Dvāravatī Period stone cakras with plain fellies found in Thailand, both from coastal sites not considered part of Dvāravatī and from Dvāravatī sites (d and e).*

References

Bauer, Christia. 1991a. *"Notes on Mon Epigraphy", The Journal of the Siam Society, Vol.79, pt.1, 1991*: 31-83.

Barau, Benimadhab. 1975. *Gaya and Buddha-Gaya, Vol. 11, Old Shrines at Bodh-Gaya*. Varanasi: Bhartiya Publishing House.

Braddell, Roland. 1950. *JMBRAS* vol. xxiii, pt. 1/1950, p. 27 cited by Wheatley 1980.

Briggs, Lawrence Palmer. 1950. *FEQ* vol. ix (1950) pp. 270-273 cited by Wheatley 1980.

Brown, Robert.1996. *The Dvāravatī Wheels of the Law and the Indianization of Southeast Asia.* Leiden: Brill.

Dao Linh Côn. 1996. "The Oc Eo Burial Group Recently excavated at Go Thap (Dong Thap Province, Viet Nam)," *Southeast Asian Archaeology 1994, Proceedings of the 5th International Conference of the European Association of Southeast Asian Achaeologists, Paris 24th-28th October 1994, Volume I.* Pierre-Yves Manguin, editor. Hull: Center for Southeast Asian Studies: 111-117.

De Casparis, J. G., 1956. "Selected Inscriptions from the 7th to the 9th centuries." *Prasasti Indonesia II.* Bandung: Masu Baru: 84-186.

Dehejia, Vidhya. 1997. *Discourse in Early Buddhist Art, Visual Narratives of India.* New Delhi: Munshiram Manoharlal.

Dhida Saraya. 1999. *(Sri) Dvaravati, the Initial Phase of Siam's History.* Translated by Abhassara Charubha. Bangkok: Muang Boran Publishing House.

Diffloth, Gerard. 1982 . Personal letter to Merritt Ruhlen cf. Ruhlen 1991.

Ehara et al. 1977. *The Path of Freedom (Vimuttimagga) of Arahant Upatissa; Translated into Chinese (Gedatsu Dô Ron) by Tipiṭaka Sanghapâla of Funan, translated from the Chinese by the Rev. N.R.M. Ehara, Soma Thera and Kheminda Thera.* Translated in 1936 by N.R.M. Ehara, Soma Thera and Kheminda Thera of Sri Lanka. Kandy (1961 by D. Roland D. Weerasuria): Buddhist Publication Society.

Gallon, Matthew D., 2014. "Monuments and Identity at the Dvāravatī Town of Kampaeng Saen" *Before Siam, Essays in Art and Archaeology.* Edited by Nicolas Revire & Stephen A. Murphy. Bangkok: River Books and The Siam Society: 330-351

Gosling, Betty (Elizabeth M. B.). 1996. *Old Luang Prabang.* Images of Asia Series. Kuala Lumpur: Oxford University Press.

Guillon, Emmanuel. 1991. The Ultimate Origin of the World, or the Mulā Muh", *The Journal of the Siam Society, Vol.79, pt.1, 1991: 22-30.*

Gutman, Pamela. 1986. "Symbolism of Kingship in Arakan," *Southeast Asia in the 9th to 14th Centuries.* Edited by David G. Marr and A.C. Milner, with an introduction by Wang Gungwu. Singapore: Research School of Pacific Studies, Australian National University and Institute of South East Asian Studies, Singapore: 279-288.

Hall, Kenneth. 1985. *Maritime Trade and State Development in Early Southeast Asia.* Honolulu: University of Hawai'i Press.

Halliday, R. 1955. *A Mon-English Dictionary.* Rangoon: The Mon Cultural Section, Ministry of Union Culture, Government of the Union of Burma.

Higham, Charles. 2004. *Encyclopedia of Ancient Asian Civilizations,* New York: Facts on File.

Higham, Charles. 2014. *Early Mainland Southeast Asia, From First Humans to Angkor.* Bangkok: River Books.

Huntington, Susan L., 1985. *The Art of Ancient India.* New York & Tokyo: Weatherhill.

Indorf, Pinna. 2014. "Dvāravatī *Cakras*: Questions of Their Significance," *Before Siam, Essays in Art and Archaeology.* Edited by Nicolas Revire & Stephen A. Murphy. Bangkok: River Books and The Siam Society: 272-309.

Irwin, John C., 1990. "Origins of Form and Structure in Monumental Art," *Symbols in Art and Religion, the Indian and the Comparative Perspectives.* Edited by Karel Werner. London: Curzon Press & the Riverdale Co.: 46-67.

Le Thi Lien, 2006 "Excavations at Minh Su Mound, Go Thap Site, Dong Thap Province, South Vietnam 2000-2003" *Uncovering Southeast Asia's Past; Selected Papers from the 10th International Conference of the European Association of Southeast Asian Archaeologists, The British Museum, London 14th-17th September 2004.* Edited by Elisabeth A. Bacus, Ian C. Glover & Vincent C. Pigott. Singapore: NUS Press: 298-309.

Le Thi Lien. 2011. "Hindu Deities in Southern Vietnam, Images on small Archeological Artefacts," *Early Interaction between South and Southeast Asia, Reflections on Cross Cultural Exchanges."* Edited by Pierre-Yves Manguin, A. Mani, and Geof Wade. Singapore: Institute of Southeast Asian Studies (ISEAS); India: Manoharlal: 407-431.

Lorrillard, Michel. 2014. "Pre-Angkorian Communities in the Middle Mekong Valley (Laos and Adjacent Areas)," in *Before Siam, Essays in Art and Archaeology.* Edited by Nicolas Revire & Stephen A. Murphy. Bangkok: River Books and the Siam Society: 186-215.

Luce. 1925. Luce in *JBRS* vol. xiv/ 1925: 188-189, cited by Wheatley 1980.

Lyons, Elizabeth, 1979 "Dvāravatī, a Consideration of its Formative Period," *Early South East Asia, Essays in Archaeology, History and Historical Geography.* R.B. Smith and W. Watson, Editors. Oxford/New York/London: Oxford University Press: 352-359.

Malleret, Louis. 1959. *L'archéologie du Delta du Mekong; Tome Premier L'Exploration Archéologique et les Fouilles d'Oc-Eo.* Paris: École Française D'Extreme-Orient.

Manguin, Pierre-Yves. 2009. "The Archaeology of Fu Nan in the Mekong River Delta: The Oc Eo Culture of Vietnam, "*Arts of Ancient Viet Nam from River Plains to Open Sea.* Edited by Nancy Tingley. Houston: Asia Society, The Museum of Fine Arts ; New Haven and London: Yale University Press: 103-118.

Maxwell, Thomas S., 1997. *The Gods of Asia, Image, Text and Meaning.* New Delhi: Oxford University Press.

Miksic, John N., 2003. "The Beginning of Trade in Ancient Southeast Asia: The Role of Oc Eo and the Lower Mekong River", *Art and archaeology of Fu Nan, Pre-Khmer Kingdom of the Lower Mekong Valley.* Edited by James C.M. Khoo. Singapore & Bangkok: Southeast Asian Ceramic Society & Orchid Press: 1-34.

Miksic, John N., 2010. *The A to Z of Ancient Southeast Asia.* The A to Z Guide Series, No. 141. Lanham, Toranto Plymothe, UK: The Scarecrow Press.

Moore, Elizabeth H. and San Win. 2014. "Sampanago: 'City of Serpents' and Muttama (Martaban)," *Before Siam; Essays in Art and Archaeology,* Edited by Nicolas Revire and Stephen A. Murphy, Bangkok: River Books and the Siam Society: 217-237

Nagaswamy. 2003. *Facets of South Indian Art and Architecture.* In two volumes. New Delhi: Aryan Books International.

Phanuwat Ueasaman. 2019. "Ancient Hill Temples and Holy Caves in Upper Southern Thailand and the Trans-peninsular Route Connection," *Ancient Maritime Cross-cultural Exchanges; Archaeological Research in Thailand.* Edited by Amara Srisuchat and Wilfried Giessleer. Bangkok: FAD Ministry of Culture: 37ff.

Phasook Indrawooth. 1999. *Dvāravati, a critical study based on archaeological evidence.* In Thai and English. Bangkok: Aksorn Samai.

Phasook Indrawooth. 2008. *Dvāravati Dharmacakras.* Bangkok: Sasopa Press.

Revire, Nicolas. 2016. "Dvāravatī and Zhenla in the seventh to eighth centuries: A transregional ritual complex," *Journal of Southeast Asian Studies, 47(3),* October 2016. Singapore: National University of Singapore: 393-417.

Rhys Davids. 1977. *Dhigha Nikāya II.* London: Pali Text Society.

Sarma. 1982. *The Development of Early Shaiva Art and Architecture (with special reference to Andhradesha).* Delhi: Sundeep Prakashan.

Siriporn Sanghiram. 2019. "Archaeological Sites and Findings on the Lower Peninsula of Thailand from the Seventh to Thirteenth Century Reflecting the Maritime Silk Road", *Ancient Maritime Cross-cultural Exchanges; Archaeological Research in Thailand.* Edited by Amara Srisuchat and Wilfried Giessleer. Bangkok: FAD Ministry of Culture: 57ff.

Smith, R.B., 1979. "Mainland Southeast Asia in the Seventh and Eighth Centuries", *Early South East Asia, Essays in Archaeology, History and Historical Geography.* R.B. Smith and W. Watson, Editors. Oxford/New York/London: Oxford University Press: 443-456.

Tongjai Hutangkura. 2014. "Reconsidering the Palaeo-shoreline in the Lower Central Plain of Thailand," *Before Siam, Essays in Art and Archaeology.* Edited by Nicolas Revire & Stephen A. Murphy. Bangkok: River Books and the Siam Society: 32-67.

Tranet, M., 1997. *Sambaur-Prei-Kuk, monuments d'Içanavarma I (615-628).* Two volumes (Vol. 1&2), record of work done 1995-1997. Phnom Penh: Travail d'inventaire finance par la fondation Toyota.

Vickery, Michael. 1986. "Some Remarks on Early State Formation in Cambodia", *Southeast Asia in the 9th to 14th Centuries.* Edited by David G. Marr and A.C. Milner, with an introduction by Wang Gungwu. Singapore: Research School of Pacific Studies, Australian National University and Institute of South East Asian Studies, Singapore: 95-116.

Vickery, Michael. 1998. *Society, Economics and Politics in Pre-Angkor Cambodia.* Tokyo: The Centre for East Asian Cultural Studies for UNESCO.

Vo Si Khai. 2003. The Kingdom Fun Nan and the Culture of Oc Eo", *Art and archaeology of Fu Nan, Pre-Khmer Kingdom of the Lower Mekong Valley.* Edited by James C.M. Khoo. Singapore & Bangkok: Southeast Asian Ceramic Society & Orchid Press: 35-86.

Waterson, Roxana. 1990. *The Living House, An Anthropology of Architecture in South-East Asia.* Singapore: Oxford University Press.

Wheatley, Paul. 1980. *The Golden Khersonese. Studies in the Historical Ggeography of the Malay Peninsula Before A.D. 1500.* Kuala Lumpur: Penerbit Universiti Malaya

Zimmer, Heinrich. 1984. *The Art of Indian Asia, Its Mythology and Transformations.* Delhi: Motilal Banarsidass.

Endnotes

1 Nakhon Pathom and Sing Buri (as well as Khu Bua, Kamphaeng Saen and U Thong), now far inland, were at the edge of swampy terrain, a floodplain (Trongjai Hutangkura 2014: 63) encompassing what are now the Tha Chin and the lower Mae Klong rivers (cf. Dhida Saraya 199: 63). Perhaps it was then very similar to the southern part of Tonle Sap today and accessible by boat for much, if not all, of the year. One of these sites, with an occupancy period of about two hundred years, could also have been Naravaranagara, the place of exile of the ancestors of the Śailendras, referred to in a Plaosan inscription of Java, as translated by de Casparis (1956: 184-186). However, many scholars now seem to accept Angkor Borei as the location of Naravaranagara, even though it seems internal to original Óc Eo culture. But perhaps there was more than one place of "exile."

2 The site was also known as Prasat Pram Loven (Lê Thị Liên 2006: 232; cf. Malleret 1959: no. 129, Pl. LXXXIV, p. 401).

3 Wheatley cites Luce JBRS vol. xiv/ 1925, pp. 188-189; Braddell, JMBRAS vol. xxiii, pt. 1/1950, p. 227 and Briggs FEQ vol. ix (1950) pp. 270-273).

4 According to Vedic symbolism, the sphere could be a reference to undifferentiated universals, the prism a reference to the universals particular to a/the manifest world/ earth.

5 It is listed in Table 2, 15.4, but is not described.

6 The base was perhaps a victim of looting and theft. The angle of the photo does not reveal the modeling (i.e., any variations in the thickness) and the size is not given.

7 Image file name or image address for reference only.

8 Alternative: Nicolas Revire also has an image of this artifact.

11 | Ancient Ornaments in Southern Vietnam

Nguyễn Kim Dung

This article briefly introduces the types of jewelry found in southern Vietnam, which presents a summary of statistics on the type of artifacts collected through archaeological excavations conducted by Vietnamese archaeologists, from 1975 until now. The article will present according to the chronology of the uncovered artifacts, including:

1. From the Neolithic to the late Bronze Age, equivalent from 4000 BP to 2500 BP. The artifacts of this period were mainly found at sites in the southwest region such as An Sơn, Rạch Núi (Long An province), bazalt stone bracelets are the main feature of the findings, having V-D cross-section; also small beads that come in many shapes, such as oval, spherical, or flattened cylinders; all those made of stone, bone and shellfish. Similar artifacts have also been discovered in the Southeast region of Vietnam, the sites are: Đồi Phòng Không, Suối Linh (Đồng Nai province), Bưng Bạc (Bà Rịa-Vũng Tàu province). In this area, the manufacturing method of bazalt bracelets with a V-D cross-section reflects a date of about 3000 BP to 2500 BP. The objects reflect the exchange of goods of the residents at sites called Dốc Chùa, Bình Đa.

2. Iron Age, from 2450 BP to 2000 BP: the artifacts were found in burial jars, located near the sea in Đồng Nai province, Hồ Chí Minh City, HCMC and Bà Rịa-Vũng Tàu province. They were also found at archaeological sites belonging to the early Óc Eo period, in the provinces of the Mekong Delta such as Đồng Tháp Mười, Long An, An Giang. Those artifacts may reflect the relationship with the ancient lands of Southeast Asia, and possibly evidence of commerce by sea and mainland.

Ancient jewelry in the Southeast Vietnam belongs to the earliest stages of the Óc Eo era

Before the Óc Eo period, a social model may have formed based on trade and commerce in the southern part of Vietnam. The variety of the jewelry reflects the difference between the Southeast and Southwest regions; for example, types of ornaments that were once popular in the Southeast such as jade stone, double-headed animal ornaments, and three-pointed earrings found at Giồng Cá Vồ (GCV) and Giồng Phệt (GP) sites, are completely absent from the Gò Hàng site.

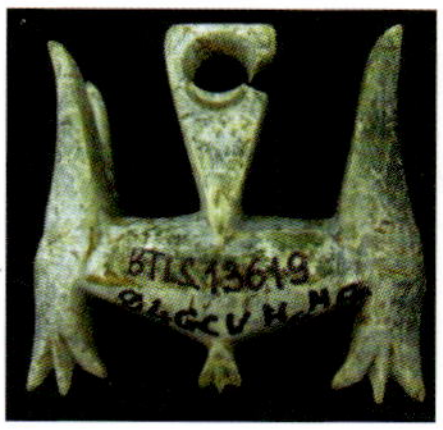

1. A double-headed animal ornament, jade stone, found at the Giồng Cá Vồ site.

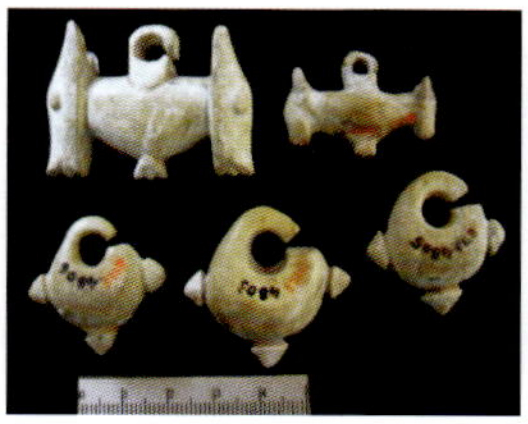

2. Ornaments in headed animal-shape, and, three-pointed earrings, jade stone, found from the Phú Hòa site.

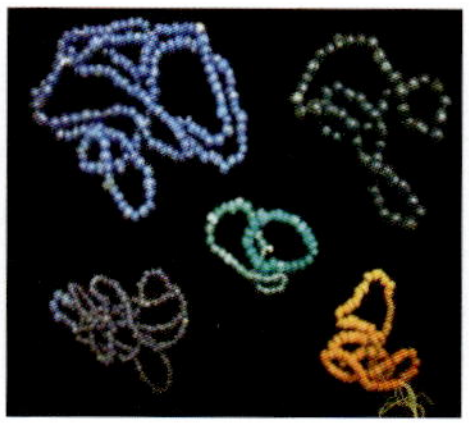

3. Glass-beads, possibly commecial products, found from the Giồng Lớn site.

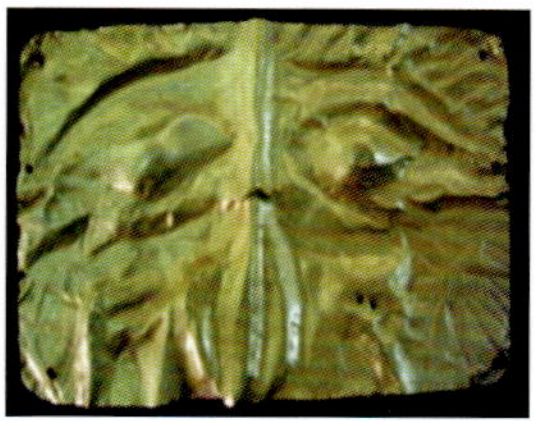

4. A golden mask, found from the Giồng Lớn site.

Fig. 1 *Ornaments from the pre-Óc Eo period in the southeast region of Southern Vietnam.*

Archaeological sites where ancient jewelry was found in the Southeast, include Phú Hòa, Dầu Giây, Hàng Gòn, Suối Chồn in Đồng Nai province; GCV, GP and Giồng Lớn sites in the coastal area of Cần Giờ district in HCMC; and Long Sơn site in Bà Rịa-Vũng Tàu province.

The dates recorded from the archaeological artifacts are: 1. the period 2450-2150 BP; 2. the period 400 BCE to about the 1st century CE; 3. about the 2nd to the 1st centuries BCE to the 2nd to the 3rd centuries CE.

The main materials are nephrite, agate, carnelian, garnet, amethyst, crystal, tectile, glass, metals (copper, iron, lead, tin, gold), ceramics and shells. The main shapes recorded are the double-headed animal ornaments, three-pointed earrings, turban-shaped earrings, bracelets with rectangular-section, beads and gemstones.

At the GCV site, the earliest traces of hand-crafted glass were recorded at several areas in this site. Analytical chemical composition includes manganese oxide or lead oxide, which confirms that the glass relics can be manipulated in situ by the casting method. Ornamental artifacts found in the burial jars of the Southeast region of Vietnam have also been found in the Philippines (Tabon, Mallunguh sites), Malaysia, Thailand, and Cambodia.

Nephrite is considered to originate from the mines in Fengtian, Southeast Taiwan; samples were found at sites such as the GCV site in HCMC and Khao Sam Kaeo (Thailand). This may demonstrate the exchange of jade stone from Taiwan to Southeast Asia; while other artifacts reflect trade relations with India, Thailand, and Myanmar, items including agate, crystal, garnet, glass, and gold beads.

The gold beads are shaped in an ellipse, polygonal shape similar to the gold beads found at the Vietnam sites of GCV, and Giồng Lớn; and Noen U-Lock site, Ban Don Ta Phet in Thailand; and parts of Myanmar, dating from the 3rd to the 4th century BCE.

The gold artifacts reflect a new development in the history of the local residents, in which an impressive number of objects were found at Giồng Lớn site, Bà Rịa-Vũng Tàu province: 178 gold beads, eight gold earrings, three

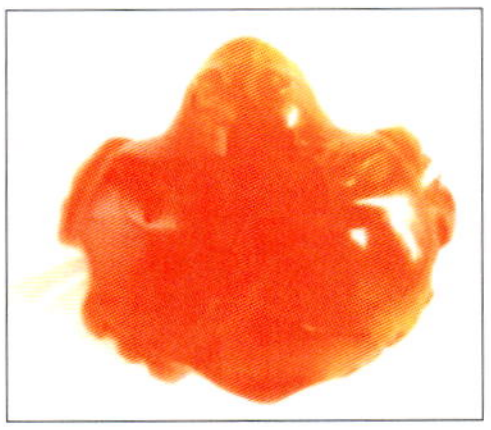

1. An ornament in the shape of a turtle, found at the Gò Hàng site.

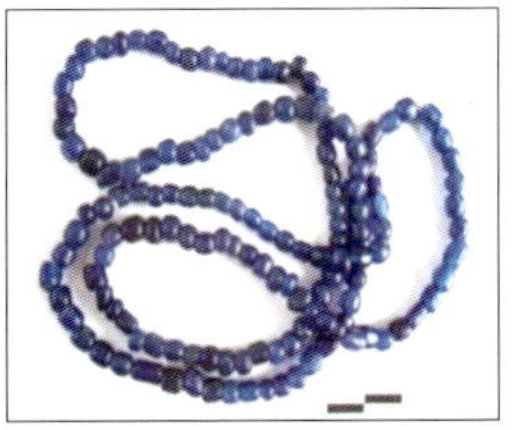

2. Glass-beads, possibly commecial products, found at the Gò Hàng site.

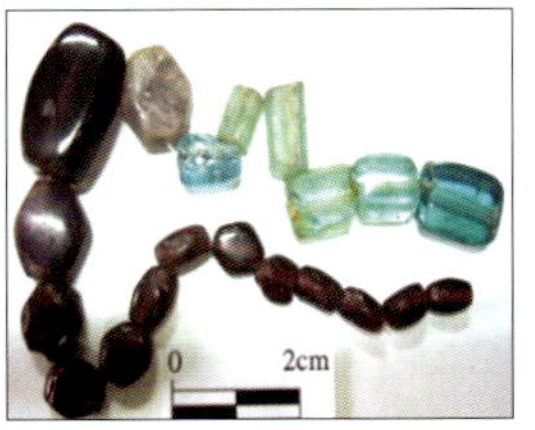

3. Glass-beads, possibly commecial products, found at the Gò Hàng site.

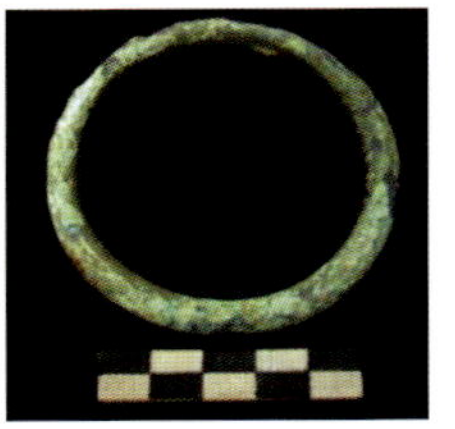

4. A golden mask, found at the Giồng Lớn site.

Fig. 2 *Ornaments from the period of pre-Óc Eo in the west region of Southern Vietnam.*

masks, one gold wire like a snake, and some metal ingots to craft gold (?). Earrings and masks are two types of gold items found in two graves identified as 03GLH4M1 and 05GLH1M1, which are similar to those found at Bit Meas and Prohear (Cambodia). Reineke proposes that there is a similarity in the shape of the two earrings of Giồng Lớn and some sites in Cambodia, so they may be imported products; and four of the remaining earrings may be local products.

The three golden masks of Giồng Lớn reflect the tradition of using golden masks to cover the face of the deceased as evidenced at sites in East India and Java in Indonesia. The gold ornaments reflect the commercial activities of the Giồng Lớn residents. Many argue that there were many 'early ports' distributed along the coasts of Central and South Vietnam, located on the trade route through the East Sea connecting Asia with the Western world (India, the Middle East and the Middle East, Roman) from about 300 BCE. Several 'early trading ports' may have played an important role along the coast of Vietnam, from the central region down to the Gulf of Thailand.

Ancient ornaments dating from before the Óc Eo period, in the Southwest Vietnam region

The archaeological sites will be divided into two groups:

The first group: These reflect indigenous elements, such as: the sites of Gò Ô Chùa and Gò Cao Su in Long An province; Long Bửu site in HCMC; Gò Cây Tung in Tịnh Biên district, An Giang province. Handcrafted pottery is characteristic of these monuments, ornaments are rarely found.

The appearance of ornaments confirms that the exchange of goods took place at these monuments. Finds include carnelian gemstone beads, crystal, agate, garnet or glass bracelets like products made in Vietnam.

These objects could have reached these sites via barter as is confirmed by evidence found in the layers of the late period of these sites, such as glass bracelets, others in carnelian, crystal, agate, garnet, including ornaments similar to those at the GCV site. Some products reflect the closeness to Thailand and Cambodia.

The second group: These reflect the workshops such as these of Gò Hàng, Gò Dung and Gò Đế, in the provinces Đồng Tháp Mười and Long An. Materials used are mainly gold, tin, precious stones, and glass. The metal consists of lead or tin (?), reflecting a continuation of the traditional shaping of the group of objects found in burial jars, dating before the Óc Eo period in the southeast region.

Metal was also used to craft bracelets, copper coins, and rattles; and the site includes many pieces of raw glass, glass slag, unshaped beads stuck together during the manufacturing process, broken beads, and small pieces of agate stone. The date is about 1970 +/- 50 BCE obtained from a coal sample in the lower layer identified by the Radiocarbon dating C14 method from the Gò Hàng site.

The once dominant marine trade economy is confirmed by the richness and diversity of ornaments found in the South, dating to earlier than the Óc Eo period. This factor probably created the incentive for the iron age culture to form in the southern coastal plain, and develop into the Óc Eo culture. It opened the potential for the economy to develop through exchanges between Óc Eo residents and foreigners.

Ancient ornaments in the Southern Vietnam during the Óc Eo period

Ornaments provide remarkable physical evidence of the Óc Eo period. In Óc Eo sites, although there were many bead types, the richness of types and materials mark the difference from the previous period. Items include gemstones, glass beads, and necklaces of gold and silver.

The very specific types that could be imported from Arikamedu (India) are not only raw materials such as carnelian, agate, amethyst, crystal, but also agate beads, acid etched agate beads, crystal beads, melon-beads, and so on.

A typical example of imported beads at the Gò Hàng site, is an onyx bead, 6.2 cm long, 1.8 cm in diameter, engraved with a floral pattern, which some argue represents the interconnected *swastikas*, meaning the 'Tree of Life and Eternal Life from the Tree of Knowledge'. These artifacts indicate that the upper Go Hang site has revealed typical examples of the Óc Eo cultural period, in the 3rd to the 4th century CE.

Although some types of earrings have been found at sites of the Óc Eo era, they are not found in earlier sites, which had blue glass serrated twisted earrings, whose shape resembles the twisted gold earrings found in Giồng Lớn. They have also been crafted showing evidence of copper, lead tin or gold metal as found at Gò Hàng and Gò Trâm Qùy sites in Long An province.

Some other glass ornaments were found at the Óc Eo sites, with light green or blue colors, round or slightly rounded D-section with small size; they have not been found in the early sites in the Óc Eo area, and also in the Đồng Tháp province.

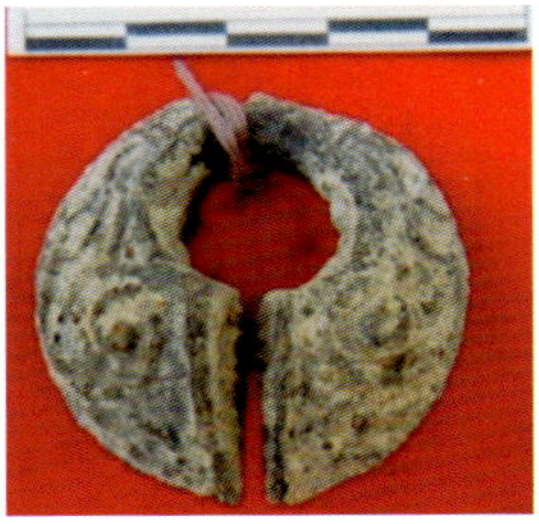

1. An earring, lead-tin alloy, found at the Cạnh Đền site.

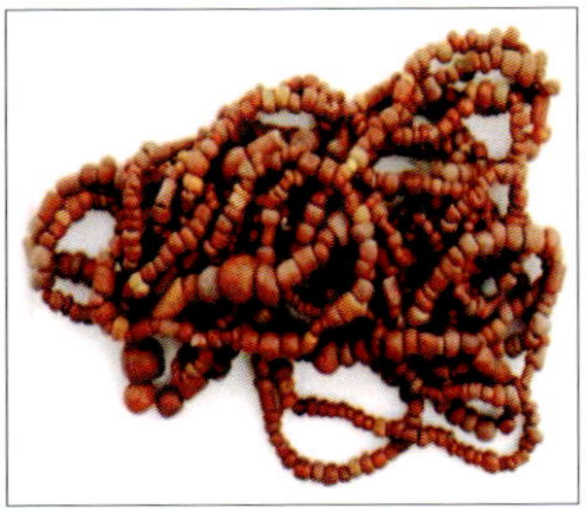

2. Glass-beads, possibly commecial products, found at an Óc Eo site.

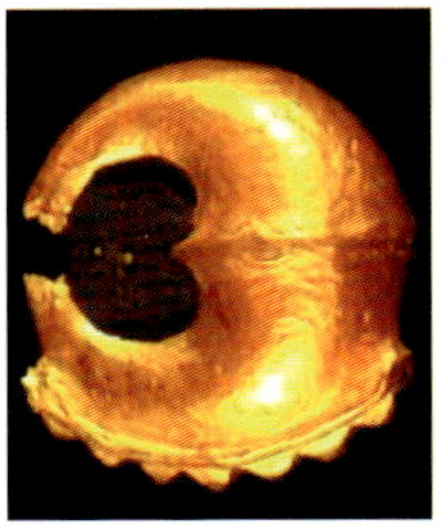

3. A gold earring, found at an Óc Eo site.

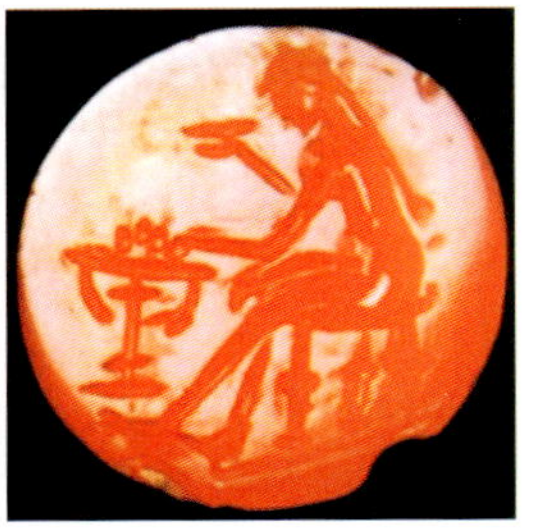

4. An intaglio with a human figure, found at an Óc Eo site.

Fig. 3 *Ornaments during the main period of Óc Eo culture in Southern Vietnam. (Photos by Nguyễn Kim Dung)*

Although metal ornaments are abundant, there are few types of earrings and rings. The moulds found reflect the integration of many jewelry patterns in one piece sandstone mold unearthed in the sites such as Nhơn Thành in Cần Thơ province; Gò Tháp in Đồng Tháp province; Óc Eo, Đá Nổi, Nền Chùa in An Giang province and Kiên Giang province.

The archaeological excavations carried out in 2018-2019, have produced 117 artifacts of lead-tin alloy, 16 gold and gilded items, nine pieces of glass and stone; some artifacts are similar to those found in the sites of Khlong Thom and U Thong, in Thailand. A gold earring of this type found by L. Malleret at the Óc Eo site has been dated to the 2nd to the 5th centuries CE, originating from Java, Indonesia. These types of gold earrings have also been found at U Thong in Thailand, and in Myanmar.

At the History Museum, HCMC, a finger ring is decorated with high protruding dots similar to those found at sites such as U Thong, Khuan Luk Pad, Bang Ro, and Bang Kluay in Thailand. This type of jewelry was also found in Java during the Early Classic period, and in many parts of Southeast Asia.

Through the survey, many have suggested that all these types of ornaments from Óc Eo sites could be imported products, demonstrating the trade of local residents in the Óc Eo era. Examples include a gold finger ring engraved with Sanskrit dating to the 1st to the 2nd century CE; a gold medallion in the Roman style, and a gold ring with a Nandin figure.

Glass finds may be local products, as evidenced by the bracelets and earrings found from the Gò Hàng site; such glass products can serve export demand, mainly Indo-Pacific beads have been found in large quantity, specifically at the Óc Eo site.

Nearly 200,000 monochromatic glass beads were found at the Lung Lớn site during archaeological excavation conducted by the Archaeological Center in 2018-19. 147,678 of beads with a diameter of less than 3 mm account for 87%; 81,507 red opaque beads found in area A of Lung Lớn site accounted for 44.86% of the total.

In addition, a popular pattern was red, black and white striped beads which were manufactured on site. Multi-striped beads have been found in several locations in Southeast Asia, such as Óc Eo, Angkor Borei (Cambodia), Kuala Selingsing (Malaysia), eastern Java Indonesia, and Khlong Thom (Thailand). The Indo-Pacific beads imitating the color of garnets are widely present in the Óc Eo sites, where there were also handcrafted glass beads. This leads to the assumption that the Óc Eo sites were a place of manufacture for all kinds of beads to meet demand in Southeast Asia and East Asia. It can be assumed that beads with a brick red color was crafted to satisfy the tastes of the nobility in East Asia and China, and striped beads and purple garnet beads may have been very popular in island Southeast Asia.

It can be assumed that there was a trade route with Rome, whereby Middle Eastern merchants reached the southern region of the Andaman Sea, continued across the Gulf of Thailand to Óc Eo, with goods of various types from the Mediterranean region and the Middle East. This hypothesis is based on the glass ornaments found by Malleret, and another piece of a glass ornament found in Lung Lớn from the archaeological excavation conducted in 2018 by the Center for Archeology of the Southern Institute of Social Sciences. High quality stone beads also reached the Óc Eo sites thanks to the maritime trade system, including products from Rome, Greece, India or Central Asian countries; typical materials include carnelian, agate, crystal, garnet, amethyst and polychromatic eye beads.

Conclusion

Ancient ornaments may have reached a peak in southern Vietnam, specifically in the periods before the Óc Eo times and during the Óc Eo era. The southern region of Vietnam has proved to be an important area in connecting sea/land trade routes in the previous centuries and the first millennium BCE, as attested by ancient ornaments.

The ancient coins, corresponding to phase I, demonstrate the process of international trade integration between the Óc Eo sites in southern Vietnam, with ancient states in India, the Middle East, and the Mediterranean. Phase II, corresponding to a period of 500-600 years, saw the formation and development of the Óc Eo-Funan culture, when trade relations with the Roman world became outstanding.

References

Bennett, A. 2017. *The Ancient history of U Thong, city of gold.* Bangkok: River Books.

Bérénice, Bellina 2003. 'Social change and interaction between India and Southeast Asia'. *ANTIQUITY,* Vol. 77, No. 296: 285-295.

Bùi Chí Hoàng (ed.). 2018. *Khảo cổ học Nam Bộ thời sơ sử.* Hà Nội: Nxb. Khoa học Xã hội.

Bùi Chí Hoàng 2020. 'Khu di tích Óc Eo-Ba Thê, Nền Chùa: Khai quật, nghiên cứu, bảo tồn và phát huy giá trị'. *Khảo cổ học,* số 1 (2020): 4-12.

Đặng Văn Thắng, Vũ Quốc Hiền, Nguyễn Thị Hậu, Ngô Thế Phong, Nguyễn Kim Dung và Nguyễn Lân Cường 1998. *Khảo cổ học tiền sử và sơ sử Thành phố Hồ Chí Minh.* TP Hồ Chí Minh: Nxb. Trẻ.

Fontaine, H. 1972. 'Note sur la découverte de perles au site de Dau Giay'. *BSEI,* XIVIII. No. 4: 619-620. Sài Gòn 1972.

Francis, P. 2002. *Asia's Maritime bead trade 300BC to the present.* Honolulu: University of Hawai'i Press.

Glover, I. C. 1996. 'The Southern Silk Road between India and Southeast Asia'. *Ancient trades and cultural contacts in Southeast Asia* (ed. The office of the National Culture Commission): 57-94. Bangkok.

Glover, I. C. and Bellina Bérénice 2001. 'Alkaline Etched Beads East of India in the late Prehistoric and Early Historic Periods'. *BEFEO* 88: 191-215.

Glover, I. C. and Bellina Bérénice 2003. 'Alkaline etched beads and Southeast Asia'. *Ornaments from the past: Bead studies after Beck* (eds. I. C. Glover and Helen Hughes Broek). London and Bangkok: The Bead Study Trust.

Hung, Hsiao-Chun, Yoshiyuki Iizuka, Peter Bellwood, Kim Dung Nguyen, Berenice Bellina, Praon Silapanth, Eusebio Dizon, Rey Santiago and Ipoi Datan 2007. *Ancient jades map 3000 years of prehistoric exchange in SEA.*

Miksic, John N. 2003. 'The Beginning of trade in ancient Southeast Asia: The role of Óc Eo and the lower Mekong river'. *Art and Archaeology of Funan-Pre Khmer Kingdom of the lower Mekong valley* (ed. James C.M. Khoo): 1-33. Bangkok: The Southeast Asian Ceramic Society, Bangkok.

Miksic, John N. 2011. *Old Javanese Gold: The Hunter Thompson Collection at Yale University Art Gallery.* New Haven: Yale University Press.

Nguyễn Kim Dung 1998. 'Ancient Jade-manufacturing tradition in Vietnam'. *East Asian Jade: Symbol of Excellence* (ed. C. Tang), Vol. 2: Hong Kong: The Chinese University of Hong Kong.

Nguyễn Kim Dung 2001. 'Jewelry from late prehistoric sites recently excavated in Southern Viet Nam'. *Bulletin of Indo Pacific Prehistoric Association 21.* Vol. 5: 107-113.

Nguyen Kim Dung 2014. 'Sa Huynh Jade Ornaments-Evidence of Early Trading Contact in Southeast Asia' 『東南アジア考古学』34号 (2014). *Journal of Southeast Asian Archaeology* 34 (2014): 15-31. Tokyo, Japan. (English and Japanese)

Nguyen Kim Dung 2015. 'The Sa Huynh Culture, In Ancient Regional Trade network: A comparative study of ornaments'. *New Perspectives in Southeast Asian and Oceanian prehistory* (eds. Phillip Piper, Hirofumi Matsumura and David Bulbeck): 317-344. Tera Australis XX. The Australian National University E-press.

Saurin, E. 1966. 'Un site archaeologique à Dau Giay, province de Long Khanh (Sud Vietnam)'. *The Archaeological Research Institute,* No 4: 90-104. Sai Gon.

Trần Anh Dũng, Bùi Văn Liêm và Nguyễn Đăng Cường 2001. 'Khai quật di chỉ Gò Cao Su lần thứ nhất (Long An)'. *Khảo cổ học,* số 4: 70-93.

Vũ Quốc Hiền, Trương Đắc Chiến và Lê Văn Chiến 2008. 'Di tích Giồng Lớn (Bà Rịa-Vũng Tàu) qua 2 lần khai quật'. *Khảo cổ học,* số 5: 33-48.

Vương Thu Hồng 2005. 'Sưu tập hạt chuỗi bằng đá ngọc ở Đồng Tháp Mười, tỉnh Long An. Trong'. *Một thế kỷ khảo cổ học Việt Nam* (eds. Viện Khảo cổ học), Vol. II: 814-834. Hà Nội: Nxb. Khoa học Xã hội.

Vương Thu Hồng và Nguyễn Đức Điệng 1997. 'Phát hiện về đồ trang sức bằng đá quý và thủy tinh tại di chỉ Gò Ô Chùa (Vĩnh Hưng-Long An)'. *Những phát hiện mới về Khảo cổ học năm 1997* (eds. Viện Khảo cổ học): 259-261. Hà Nội: Nxb. Khoa học Xã hội.

12 | Art of the Nguyễn Dynasty

Director Hoàng Anh Tuấn

The Nguyễn dynasty was established in 1802 when Nguyễn Phúc Anh came to the throne with the title of Emperor Gia Long after defeating the army of the Tây Sơn dynasty. By 1884, the French colonialists took complete control of the entire territory of the Nguyễn dynasty, and Vietnam became a semi-feudal colony. The last Emperor Bảo Đại abdicated and handed over the royal seal and sword of the Nguyễn Dynasty to the representatives of Democratic Republic of Vietnam in 1945. Artifacts representative of the rich cultural achievements of the Nguyễn period have been collected and displayed at the Museum of Blanchard de la Brosse and the Saigon National Museum since before 1975. The collections have been constantly enriched over 50 years in the renamed History Museum-Hồ Chí Minh (Bảo tàng Lịch sử – Thành phố Hồ Chí Minh).

This paper is designed as an introduction to the typical artifacts displayed at the HM-HCMC for scholars interested in the Nguyễn era. The royal king's robe will first be presented as a symbol of power of the Nguyễn kings. A group of bronze cannons will next be presented as a symbol of one of the military and technical achievements after many years of civil war with the Tây Sơn period, when the army was equipped and organized in the Western style under the reign of Gia Long. In addition, other artifacts are selected to illustrate the unique cultural life of this period such as religious statues and objects made of ceramic, wood and textiles.

1. Collection of the King's robes

There are five royal robes collected by the Saigon National Museum before 1975 (the Archives of NMS 1957-1974), and one was purchased after 2012, including the robes for kings and princes. Literary references to kings' robes occur in the ancient text compiled under the Minh Mạng reign entitled Đại Nam điển lệ toát yếu 大南典例撮要 ('Veritable records of Đại Nam era: Summary of Institution of Đại Nam period'). The yellow silk royal robes are considered as the most precious fabrics of the period (Nguyễn Sĩ Giác 1962: 319-321). The dragon symbolizes the emperor and combined with the sun, moon and mountains, showcases imperial power.

Three main motifs embroidered on the royal robe are: 1. A Sino script embroidered on the dragon's lower jaw positioned in the center of the robe and called 'Long Hàm Thọ' in Vietnamese; 2. An image of two dragons flanking the sun called 'Lưỡng long chầu nhật' in Vietnamese; 3. The motif of a dragon hidden in clouds called 'Long ẩn vân' in Vietnamese.

Those images are symbols of feudal kingship selected to decorate the

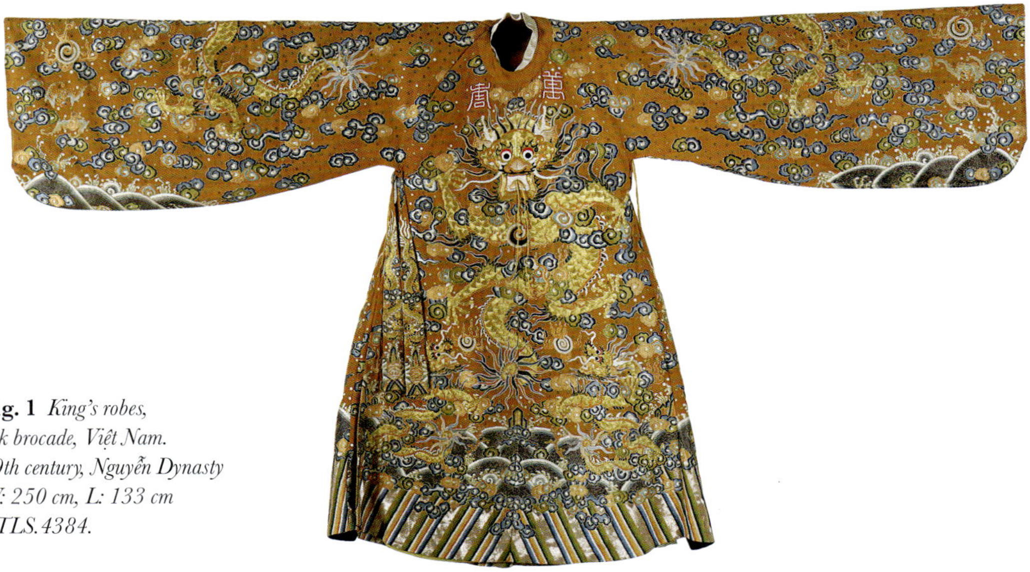

Fig. 1 *King's robes, silk brocade, Việt Nam. 19th century, Nguyễn Dynasty W: 250 cm, L: 133 cm BTLS.4384.*

costumes of the Nguyễn dynasty, based on folklore traditions. For instance, symbols of the desire for a favorable environment for farmers and agriculture, which are common in traditional agricultural countries. It may also indicate the impact of Confucian thought on all aspects of social life in Vietnam, not only the ruling class but also the artisans/craftsmen. The principle of symmetry in decorative patterns is strictly adhered to, but is not monotonous. It is a harmonious combination of shades with flexible postures of the images helping to reduce the constraint of the composition.

There is a wide-sleeved robe used in court meetings (Acc.no. BTLS 4384) (Fig. 1), which is the finest gown in the royal robe collection being stored at the HM-HCMC. It was made with exquisite embroidery, meeting the criteria of the royal robes. Especially, a line of Sino scripts in red ink are '同慶御覽' translated as 'Đồng Khánh ngự lãm' in Vietnamese, which may be known as 'The gown was noticed by the Emperor Đồng Khánh'. Those characters written inside the outer gown made of silk also announces that it may have been one of the King's robes (Hoàng Anh Tuấn 1992: 206).

The next two royal robes both have narrow sleeves. The costumes are assumed to be only for the 'Tịch Điền 籍田' ceremony, which is known as 'The Royal ploughing ceremony', an ancient royal rite in agricultural nations mentioned in the ancient scriptures (Nguyễn Sĩ Giác 1962: 319-321).

The other two royal garments are both embroidered dragons with four claws on a red silk fabric, which are presumed to be the prince's robes. The robe in Acc.no. BTLS.4382 features some Sino scripts written on the inner layer of this robe, which are translated into Vietnamese as 'Đặc tứ hoàng tử công long bào – Tiềm để cựu dụng – Đồng Khánh ngự phê', and in English as 'Specially bestowed on the Fourth Prince a robe that the Emperor had worn – Approved by the Emperor Đồng Khánh himself' (Trịnh Thị Hòa 1995: 242). This content may confirm that King Đồng Khánh gave the robe to Prince Khải Định at that time.

The decorations on the costume collection can be considered as unique works of art of the Nguyễn dynasty. They can be seen as a demonstration of the creative talent of Vietnamese artisans, and may also reflect aesthetic conceptions in Vietnamese royal art (Hoàng Anh Tuấn 1992: 216-217).

Compared to other museums in Vietnam, the dragon robes belonging to the Nguyễn dynasty, which are perhaps the complete collection so far, are being kept at the HM-HCMC. Their decorative details illustrate the Vietnamese royal style, such as the subtlety in the stitches, and the skillful embroidery. Those details may indicate the difference in imperial robes of the Nguyễn dynasty in Vietnam and other neighboring countries at the same time, such as China[1].

2. Collection of antique bronzes

Countless bronze antiques were cast under the Nguyễn dynasty including 'Cửu Đỉnh' or 'The Nine Royal Urns', 'Cửu vị Thần công' or 'Nine Holy Cannons', and so on; all the artifacts were made during the reigns of Gia Long, Minh Mạng and others. Although some antiques were unfortunately lost during the Vietnam War, others were fortunately distributed and kept in museums in Vietnam. Today a collection of cannons, bronze weapons, enameled bronzes, and so on, all that are being stored at HCMC History Museum. These are remarkable antiquities because they were probably crafted in imperial workshops; their rarity in quantity and style indicate that they may have been used by the royal family only.

Collection of cannons

There are 10 items made under the Gia Long's reign, and one item identified as being made in Minh Mạng's reign (Fig. 2); of these, the most special are possibly the cannons built in the 16th year of King Gia Long's reign (Đinh Sửu/The year of the Ox in 1817).

Generally, cannons of the Nguyễn dynasty are formed of a truncated cone with a swell in the muzzle part; the reinforced part is frequently divided into a first reinforcement and a second reinforcement; the cascabel part with a knob that is a subassembly of a muzzle-loading cannon with Sino scripts engraved on it regarding how to use and record the size of cannonballs. The trunnions and rimbase are both erected at the second reinforce part of the cannon, which is used to support and mount the cannon on its carriage. A thin tube is located near the breech of the cannon connecting the explosive charge inside with an ignition source outside. A flat circular space called the

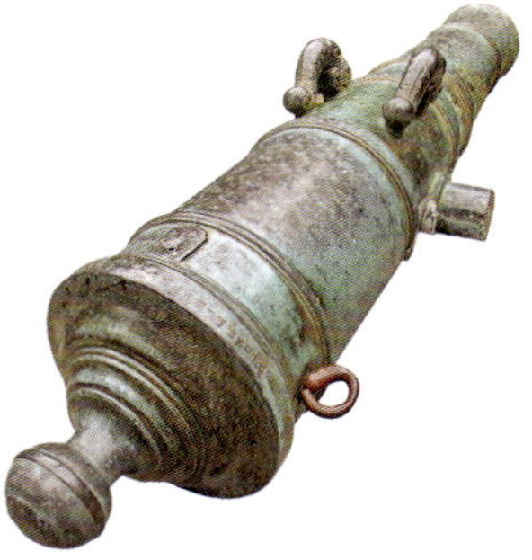

Fig. 2 *Canon, bronze, Việt Nam. 1817 L: 152 cm*

vent field is located on the top of the vent on the outside of the cannon which is engraved with two rows of Sino scripts detailing the cannon's name, serial number and the year of manufacture.

The conferment of titles for cannons was a special characteristic of Gia Long's reign, compared with the previous period; it is noted in the historical sources by the royal historians which can be seen from the bronze cannons as well (Institute of History 1993, XV: 29).

Collection of royal utensils.

There are thirteen surviving artifacts in a set of 33 bronzes, mainly sacrificial vessels that were ordered by King Minh Mạng in the year of the Pig (1839) (Fig. 3). Minh Mạng wrote that 'I made these items because I want to leave them for the generations to come; due to the fact that most of the artifacts are already antiques since the period of the Three Kingdoms; these bronzes will probably be antiques for thousands of years; Just like I thought.' (A Principal Records in the Second Dynasty of Minh Mệnh reign, 1963: 257). These artifacts were modeled after the Shang, Zhou, and Han dynasties of China, but the designs, patterns and measurements are all different.

Technically, the artifacts were cast solid and thickly, the decorative patterns reflecting the bronze casting skills of the royal workshops at that time.

Inscriptions in Sino-language carved on the objects are clear according to the standards of royal utensils.

From a cultural perspective, the content of the inscriptions reflect the king's anxiety about managing the country, and heartache at the turbulent times of King Minh Mạng (Phạm and Trịnh 1995: 218).

Fig. 3 *Bronze wares made under King Minh Mạng of the Nguyễn Dynasty, (1839).*

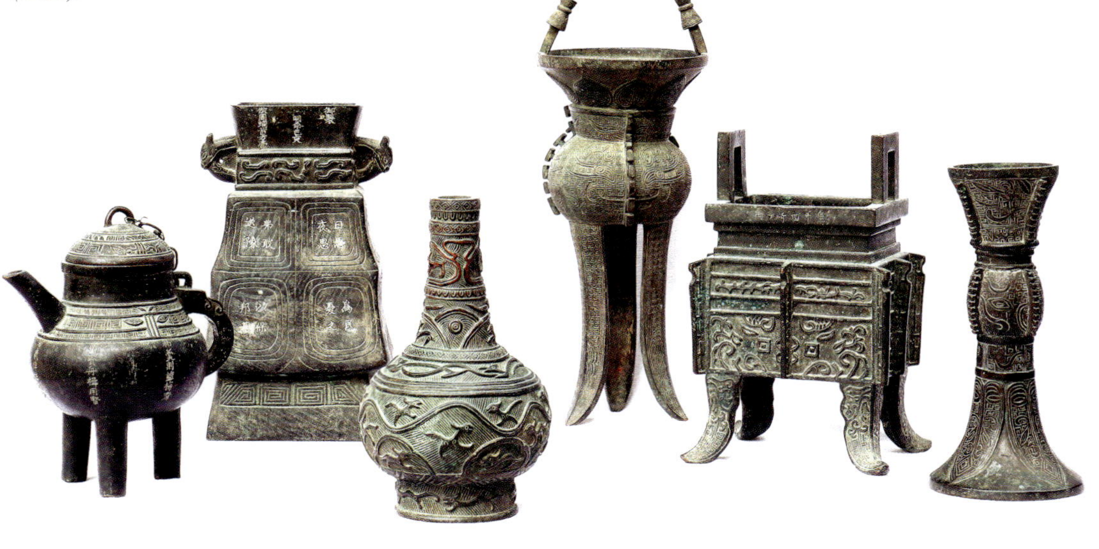

Collection of copper coins

The collection stands out for the presentation coins made of gold, silver or copper; those are also a special object of the Nguyễn dynasty. Those coins were first minted in the 11th year of King Minh Mạng's reign (The year of the Tiger, 1830).

The 'Annals of Đại Nam 大南寔錄' (2006: 64), an important historical source regarding the Nguyễn dynasty, notes the 'Minting of the presentation coins with the title of 'Minh Mệnh Thông Bảo' and a value equivalent to a 1,000 coins'. The minting of presentation coins continued in the next reigns such as King Thiệu Trị and Tự Đức. According to classification, there are two groups of presentation coins: Group 1 with eight characters engraved, and Group 2 has four characters engraved; in which Group 1 has 20 types, Group 2 has 11 types. The front of the coin represents the king's date, congratulatory message, or a poem written in Sino characters according to Confucianism on the back (including groups One and Two). There are also decorations showing dragons, clouds, sun and moon, stars and so on. The presentation coins are crafted with good materials, skillful technique and harmonious decoration.

These coins were made to reward those who had contributed to the court rather than for market consumption; they therefore have spiritual significance rather than monetary value. There are coins that are perforated and strapped as a commemoration of merit, or a kind of talisman that brings happiness and wealth to the owner.

Although appearing at the same time, there are differences between the presentation coins under the Nguyễn dynasty in Vietnam, and those coins produced in the Qing dynasty in China, such as the manufacturing method and its contents (HM-HCMC 2013: 27).

Some of the presentation coins that can be considered unique include the coin called 'Minh Mạng thông bảo – Phi long' made of silver (Acc.no. BTLS 35146 (Fig. 4ab)), a presentation coin 'Thiệu Trị thông bảo – Vạn thế vĩnh lại 紹治通寶萬世永賴' known as 'Thousand generations will have perpetual confidence', incised with a five-character four-line curtailed verse.

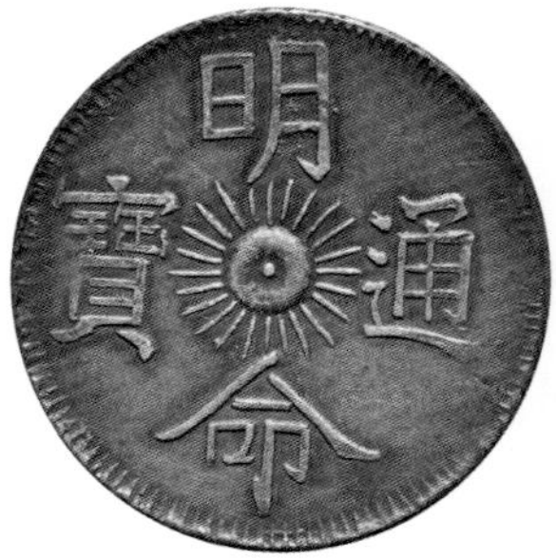

Fig. 4a *Coins of King Minh Mạng of the Nguyễn Dynasty, (1833) Việt Nam. Silver, Dia: 3.1 cm BTLS.35146 (frontside).*

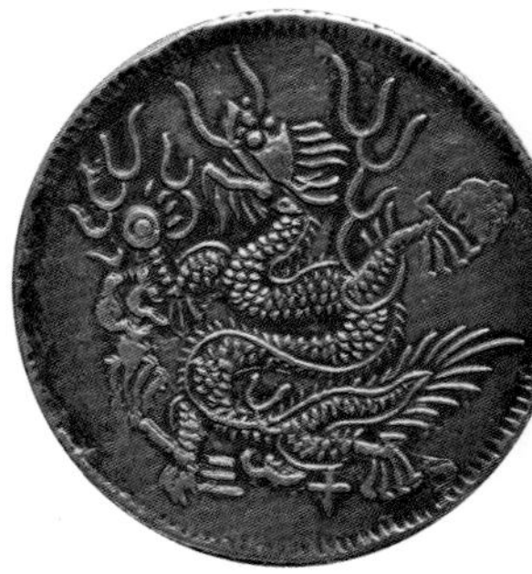

Fig. 4b *Coins of King Minh Mạng of the Nguyễn Dynasty, (backside).*

Collection of enameled bronze objects

This collection can be considered as a part of the Nguyễn dynasty treasures. The three objects include an oval enameled bronze basin (Acc.no. BTLS 201), an oval enameled bronze table screen (Acc.no. BTLS 1376) with a poem written by King Minh Mạng himself, a rectangular enameled bronze table screen inlaid with gold and silver (Acc.no. BTLS 35148). There are two artifacts ordered by Minh Mang based on their decorations such as the motif of 'a coiled dragon', 'two dragons flanking the sun', and 'dragons and clouds' (Fig. 5). These dragon images have four claws, some have five claws, in the style of the Nguyễn dynasty. It remains unclear whether the enameled bronzes

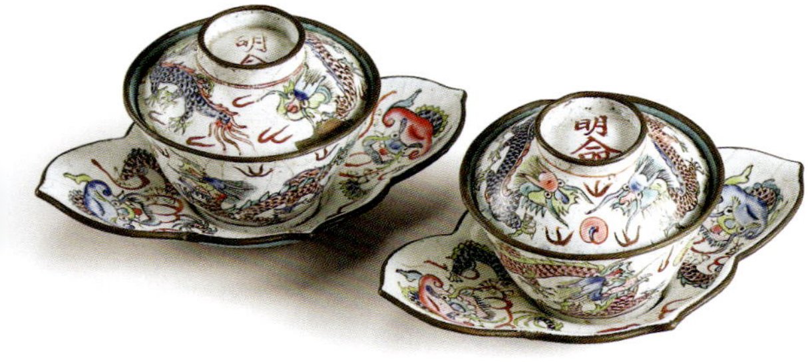

Fig. 5 *Enamel bronze wares of the reign of King Minh Mạng, (1820-1840). H: 6.0 cm BTLS.3047.*

were made in the royal workshops, or ordered from abroad (?). They can be confirmed as items for the royal family based on their decoration, and their inscriptions.

3. Collection of ceramics

The Vietnamese blue-and-white porcelain were found in Huế province, central Vietnam, and are known as 'bleu de Huế'. It is one of the important groups in the Nguyễn dynasty's antiquities, currently on display at the HM-HCMC (Fig. 6). These porcelains were ordered by the court from the Jingdezhen kilns (Jiangxi, China) with high quality commercial materials: ceramics made of fine kaolin, white and smooth, and bright enamel and blue cobalt. They are rich in types including all kinds of artifacts: bowls, cups, plates, bowls, vases, standings, so on. The differences include the decorative patterns, inscriptions and the king's reign written on the artifacts, which may also indicate that they were 'ordered products' by the courts. Such products are called by the term 'Đồ sứ ký kiểu' or 'Commissioned Patterned Porcelains' (Trần Đức Anh Sơn 1997: 154-155).

In terms of chronology, the 'Đồ sứ ký kiểu' are mainly in white enamel with blue patterns which dating from the reigns of King Minh Mạng (1802-1940), Thiệu Trị (1841-1847), Tự Đức (1848-1883), all of which were made in pottery kilns in China.

Later multicolored ceramics began to appear under Khải Định's reign (1916-1925). The decorative themes include images only for royal items such as the motif of 'a coiled dragon', a dragon hidden in clouds, two dragons playing with a pearl, chasing dragons, the three immortals or the three wise men, the Four Seasons, pheasants and chrysanthemums, mandarin duck, lotus, and so on.

Although the dragon image is shown on most of the ceramics ordered in China, there is only one vase, marked Acc. no. BTLS 6448 depicting a dragon that resembles image of the Qing Dynasty with Sino scripts saying 'Minh Mạng niên chế 明命年製', known as 'crafted under the Minh Mạng's reign'. From the Thiệu Trị period onwards, ceramics are depicted with dragon images in the style of the Nguyễn dynasty, with the following characteristics: dragon with thin mane, horn with a small barb, sparse dorsal fin, or a spiral tail (Cadière and Gres 1919: 86).

For further information, only one group of pottery was made in Bát Tràng, in north of Vietnam, marked with Gia Long's reign, dating to the early 19th century; this group is currently on display at the Hanoi National History Museum. It can be considered the only ceramic collection made in a Vietnamese kiln during the Nguyễn dynasty (?) (Nguyễn Đình Chiến 1995: 211).

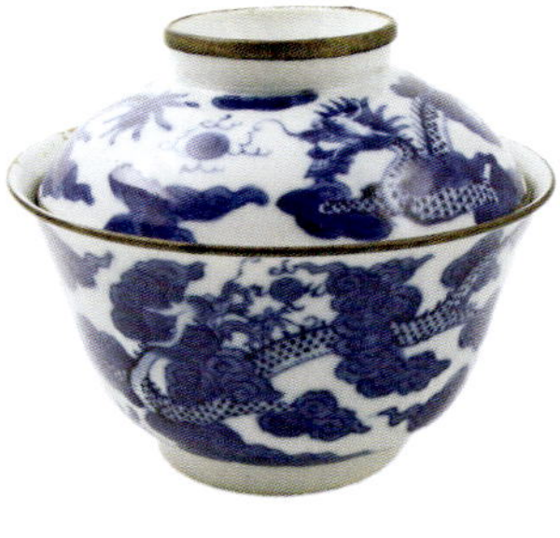

Fig. 6 *Covered bowl depicting dragons amidst clouds with inscriptions "嗣德年造" (Tự Đức niên tạo) ordered in China. 1848-1883 H: 3.8 cm, D: 26.5 cm BTLS.9363.*

Collection of wooden furniture

This collection showcases the style and skills of the carpenters in Huế, and represents a significant number of objects from the Nguyễn dynasty. Typical objects are religious statues, worship cabinets, decorative wooden furniture, utensils, and so on.

Compared to wood products manufactured abroad, Vietnamese wooden furniture has outstanding details such as: using intaglio and cameo woodcarving techniques combined with mother-of-pearl or bone, in which the most prominent is carved latticework (Trần Lâm Biền 1979: 47; Đặng Văn Thắng and Hoàng Anh Tuấn 1992: 71).

The latticework, which is also called 'Roman lattice', was a popular technique in decorative wood carving in Huế under the Nguyễn dynasty. Latticework may be functional or purely decorative, or some combination of the two, as can be seen in the wooden interiors on display at the HM-HCMC. Examples include a wooden cabinet (Acc.no. BTLS 33451), an altar/ shrine wooden cabinet (Acc.no. BTLS 13311), and a wooden screen (Acc.no. BTLS 4377).

The use of latticework technique employs regular repetition based on the principle of contrast, while still maintaining a visually delicate rhythm. (Nguyễn Hữu Thông 2019: 157).

The craftsmen in Huế were extremely skilled using the latticework technique in woodworking. It may be the major characteristic that the craftsmen aimed for, in order to create their own style of wood carving art in Đàng Trong region (Central Vietnam) under the Nguyễn dynasty (Nguyễn Hữu Thông 2019: 156).

On the subject of decoration, the craftsmen demonstrated royal themes such as: 'The Four Sacred Animals' as can be seen on the screen of Acc.no. BTLS.4377; a stylized dragon of a 'flower transformed into a dragon', or stylized floral patterns combined with geometric motifs that can be seen on wooden cabinets, and the altar/shrine cabinet marked at Acc.no. cabinet, Acc.no. BTLS 33451, and Acc.no. BTLS 13311 (Fig. 7).

Fig. 7 *Shrine wooden cabinet carved in the Nguyễn Dynasty, H: 97 cm, W: 85 cm BTLS.13311.*

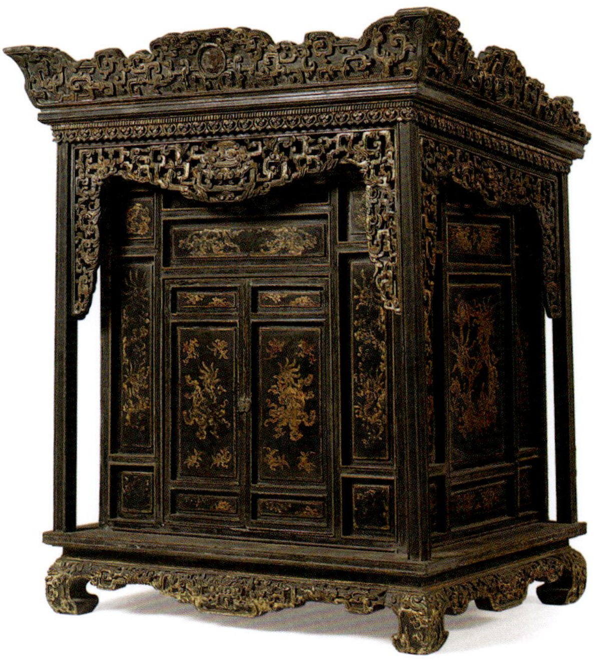

These decorations are not only typical of Eastern styles, they are also cultural and aesthetic symbols of Confucian thought. Images of trees and fruits such as the peach, pomegranate, Buddha's hand, melon, so on, reflect the artist's view of nature in daily life, and they also include symbolic meanings such as animals, or inscriptions (Cadière 1919: 75-79).

5. Collection of Buddhist statues

This is also an extensive collection made from many different materials under the Nguyễn dynasty, on display at the HM-HCMC. There are three main Buddhist figures depicted in this group.

Firstly, the wooden seated Buddha statue Acc.no. BTLS.1557 found at Khải Tường Buddhist temple which was probably commissioned by King Minh Mạng in 1832-1833. The Buddha is in meditation posture with legs crossed, the two hands rest in his lap, the right hand is placed above the left with both palms facing upwards performing the *dhyana mudra*, the tips of the thumbs touching. His face has a benevolent expression with a downward gaze. The flesh of his face is soft flanked by long earlobes. His hair is arranged in tight curls with a domed *ushnisha*. The Buddha image was probably gilded by gold leaf, whose traces remain as a way of honoring the Buddha's teachings, and a path to transfer good merits. The outer monk's robe covers both shoulders, while the inner garment wrapped around the body is open at the chest and tied at the midriff. There is the Buddhist swastika (卐) imprinted on the chest of the Buddha, it being an aniconic symbol for the Buddha in Oriental culture (Trần Lâm Biền 1997: 250-251). The Buddha statue is positioned on a lotus pedestal but the crafting style and wood are of the modern era.

Secondly, a wooden sculpture (Acc.no. BTLS. 9770) represents the Bodhisattva Avalokiteśvara holding a baby, which is also called 'Child-giving Guanyin'. She has a full round face with a downward gaze and no fancy jewelry, wearing a long robe knotted at the chest, simple and un-patterned, and a veil over her head. The folds of her costume create an extremely elegant feel, perhaps a sign of the crown. The goddess is sitting on a rugged rock with two legs pendant, a baby sitting on her lap.

The goddess may be the embodiment of a female figure named Thị Kính in a Vietnamese folk tale, a woman who apparently originated from rural northern Vietnam. The statue has been painted yellow, or maybe was covered with gold leaf traces of which still remain as a sign of luxurious decoration. The style of this statue is a continuation of the artistic style of the 17th-18th centuries.

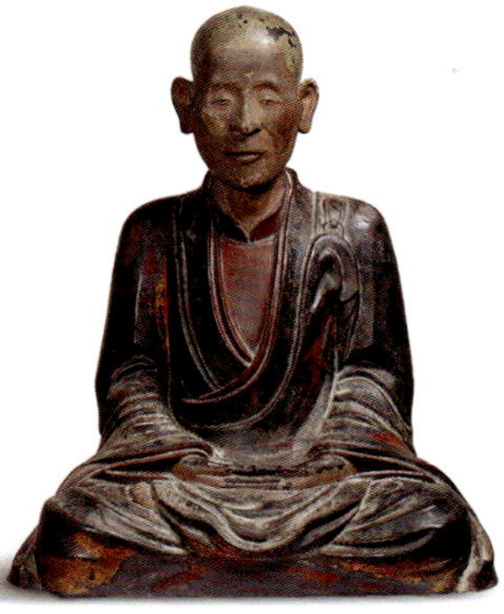

Fig. 8 *Carved wooden worshipping statue with lacquer, Nguyễn Dynasty, 18th century H: 63 cm W: 55 cm, L: 40 cm BTLS.13117.*

Thirdly, a wooden portrait of a Great Master (Buddhist monk) (Acc.no. BTLS.13117) (Fig. 8), in a meditation posture, the right hand resting on the upturned palm of the other with the thumbs slightly folded over the palms, performing the *dhyana mudra*. The shaved head is represented in dark grey, the half-closed eyes have a downward gaze, the straight nose has a strong line. He is wearing a long-sleeve costume, the outer dark green collar is open revealing the inner brown garment clearly visible up to the neck. The layers of clothing can be distinguished by the paint which is preserved in relatively good condition. The large folds of the robe cover the lower body as if the robe were woven from coarse fabric. The artistic styles is assumed to have prevailed around the 18th-19th centuries in Vietnam, and the statue may be a portrait of the head monk of a Vietnamese pagoda at that time (?). The figure's face has the quiet elegance that is often employed in Buddhist sculpture (Trần Lâm Biền 1997: 255-256).

Conclusion

The surviving collections introduced above are a small part of the cultural heritage of the Nguyễn dynasty that are on display at the HM-HCMC. They indicate the continuation and inheritance of previous artistic achievements, characteristic of Vietnamese art (Nguyễn Hữu Thông 2019: 157). The antiquities demonstrate the artistic heights achieved under the Nguyễn dynasty, with their particular distinctive style. They are the priceless artifacts of the museum waiting to be explored in the future.

Endnotes

1 MET Museum: *Imperial Court Robe 17th century*. Available at: https://www.metmuseum.org/art/collection/search/50487. Accessed on 8/6/2021

References

Bảo tàng Thành phố Hồ Chí Minh. 2013. *Sưu tập tiền Minh Mệnh trong Bảo tàng Thành phố Hồ Chí Minh*, Nxb. Hải Phòng

Cadière, Michel Léopold, and Edmond Gras. 1919. *L'Art à Hué*. Bulletin des Amis du vieux Hué, 6, no. 1. Hanoi: Impr. d'Extrême-Orient.

Đặng Văn Thắng and Hoàng Anh Tuấn. 1992. '*Đôi* nét về *Văn* hóa nghệ thuật Nguyễn'. Trong *Những vấn đề về văn hóa xã hội thời Nguyễn*, Nxb. Khoa học Xã hội.

Hoàng Anh Tuấn. 1992. 'Về áo vua triều Nguyễn hiện trưng bày tại Bảo tàng Lịch sử Vietnam Thành phố Hồ Chí Minh'. Trong *Những vấn đề Văn hóa – Xã hội triều Nguyễn*, Nxb. Khoa học Xã hội.

Nguyễn Đình Chiến. 1995. 'Sưu tập gốm men có ghi niên hiệu Gia Long tàng trữ tại Viện Bảo tàng Lịch sử Vietnam'. Trong *Những vấn đề Văn hóa Xã hội triều Nguyễn*, Nxb. Khoa học Xã hội

Nguyễn Hữu Thông. 2019. *Mỹ thuật Nguyễn*, Nxb. Tổng hợp Thành phố Hồ Chí Minh.

Nguyễn Sĩ Giác (trans.) 1962. Quốc sử quán triều Nguyễn: Đại *Nam* Điển *lệ toát yếu* [Internal Affair of Nguyễn Dynasty: Veritable Records of Đại Nam kingdom]. Viện Đại học Sài Gòn: Trường Đại học Luật khoa [The University of Saigon: School of Law].

Phạm Hữu Công and Trịnh Thị Hòa. 1995. 'Mười ba hiện vật bằng *đồng đúc* năm Kỷ Hợi *đời* Minh Mạng (1839)'. Trong *Những vấn đề Văn hóa Xã hội triều Nguyễn*, [tr.212], NXB Khoa học Xã hội

The Archives of NMS: Sổ ghi chép Viện Bảo tàng Quốc Gia Sài gòn 1957-1974 [The Archives of the National Museum in Saigon, 1957-1974]

Trần Đức Anh Sơn. 1997. 'Tổng quan về đồ sứ ký kiểu thời *Lê* – Trịnh và thời Nguyễn'. Trong Đồ *sứ men lam Huế những trao* đổi *học thuật*, [149] NXB Thuận Hóa

Trần Lâm Biền. 1979. 'Huế, mỹ thuật Nguyễn những cái riêng'. Trong *Tạp chí Nghiên cứu nghệ thuật*, số 3. Hà Nội: NXB Văn hóa Thông tin

Trần Lâm Biền. 1997. *Chùa Việt*, Hà Nội: NXB Văn hóa Thông tin,

Trịnh Thị Hòa. 1995. 'Vài nét về sưu tập hiện vật thời Nguyễn tại Bảo tàng Lịch sử Thành phố Hồ Chí Minh'. Trong *Những vấn đề Văn hóa Xã hội thời Nguyễn*. NXB Khoa học Xã hội.

Viện Sử học (trans.) 1963. Quốc sử quán triều Nguyễn: Đại *Nam Thực lục Chính biên* đệ *nhị kỷ* [Institute of History, Internal Affair of Nguyễn Dynasty: Veritable Records of Đại Nam/ A Principal Records in the Second Dynasty of Minh Mệnh reign]. Hà Nội: Nxb. Khoa học Xã hội, 1963.

Viện Sử học (trans.) 2006. Quốc sử quán triều Nguyễn: Đại *Nam thực lục* [Institute of History, Internal Affair of Nguyễn Dynasty: Veritable Records of Đại Nam kingdom], Vol. III, Hà Nội: Nxb. Giáo dục, 2006.

Viện Sử học (trans.) 1993. Quốc sử quán triều Nguyễn: *Khâm* định Đại *Nam Hội* điển *Sự lệ* [Institute of History, Internal Affair of Nguyễn Dynasty: The Supreme Court Rule on Adoption was compiled carefully by the Cabinet of Nguyễn Dynasty], Vol. XV; Hà Nội: Nxb. Khoa học Xã hội.

Website MET Museum: *Imperial Court Robe 17th century*. Available at: https://www.metmuseum.org/art/collection/search/50487. Accessed on 8/6/2021.

13 | A vibrant, untrammelled tradition

John Stevenson

This paper considers the ceramics of the region centered on the Red River Valley and Hanoi over the last two thousand years. This was the historic heartland of the country's culture and of the Kinh people who constitute close to 90 percent of Vietnam's population, the area from which a thousand years ago the country began to expand southward down the coast. It does not include non-Kinh cultures represented in Vietnam, such as the Cam, the Khmer, and the ethnic minority mountain peoples.

In a tropical region where ancient artifacts tend not to survive – objects made, for example, of textile or wood or paper – ceramics are among the important physical manifestations of Vietnam's artistic traditions. The production of ceramics in northern Vietnam began many generations before the first millennium BCE, by which time the Đông Sơn culture was already creating sophisticated ceramic shapes. Legend tells how a Chinese potter established his first kiln in the Red River delta during the second century BCE, teaching his skills to a Vietnamese potter; they are both now worshipped in the area as minor deities. As a neighbour of China, Vietnam developed the most advanced ceramic tradition in Southeast Asia. Vietnam owes China significant cultural debts even as it maintains a fierce independence, yet Vietnamese ceramics should not be considered a provincial form of Chinese ceramics. They have their own unique traditions, with many characteristics that bear no relationship to China.

Northern Vietnam is fortunate to have deposits of very fine clays – smooth, homogeneous, grey-white – that occur in quantity in the valleys of the Red and Mã Rivers. Contrast with Vietnamese clays the gritty clays of Thailand and Cambodia that are not able to support light, thin-walled ceramics. Vietnam has no *kaolin* or porcelain stone, however, rich in secondary mica, and though fired to temperatures as high as or higher than those that produce porcelain, even Vietnam's most highly fired ceramics are technically stoneware, not porcelain. When Vietnam developed iron- and cobalt-underglaze painting techniques in the 14th and 15th centuries, a white slip was usually applied to an unfired vessel to provide a suitable painting surface. So smooth and light coloured was the clay that a slip was not always considered necessary, however, and designs were sometimes painted directly onto the surface of an unfired piece.

At least since Han times, two thousand years ago, the Red River Valley provided an overland trade route via Yunnan as important as the maritime route along the coast. As a conduit for the exotic products of the south, such as ivory, tortoiseshell, rhinoceros horn, bird feathers, pearls, and tree resins, the area was of considerable economic importance to China. It served as a natural channel for cultural intercourse as well as trade. Han dynasty censuses indicate the strategic significance of the Red River Valley: during the first century CE it was much more heavily populated than the Yue regions of southern China, with double the number of people in the areas of what are now the provinces of Guangdong and Guangxi. Under the Tang dynasty (618-906 CE), the area was ruled as a province that the Chinese rather optimistically called Annam, "pacified south." It was in constant revolt. The strength of the local culture is suggested by leaders with Chinese roots who identified with the local peoples and established regional powerbases independent of China. It was not until the end of Tang, when Chinese immigration into the Guangdong area had provided an adequate counterweight to the population of the Red River Valley, that China's apparent strategic need to dominate Vietnam became less pressing.

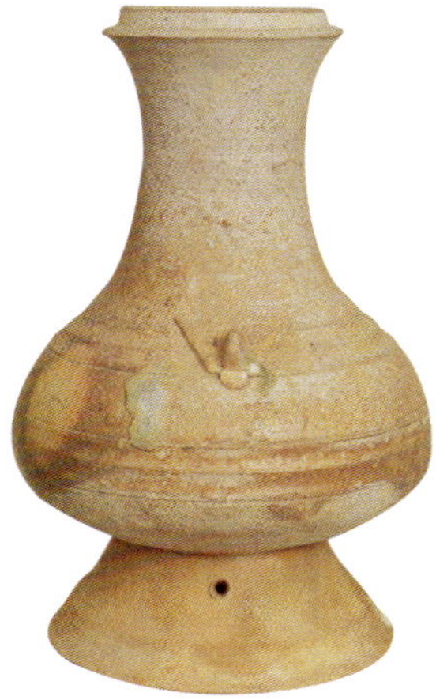

Fig. 1 *Han-Vietnamese* hu-*shaped funerary vessel with two stylized applied* taotie *1st-3rd century CE, height 28.5 cm. (Private collection)*

The Red River Valley was nominally incorporated into the Chinese Han empire in 111 BCE. The millennium of Chinese rule that followed was often tenuous and intermittent. During this time a distinct style of ceramics was not developed in Vietnam: most ceramics remained rather primitive, heavy and usually undecorated. Potters created Chinese shapes in Vietnamese clay. **Fig. 1** is a refined Vietnamese funerary vessel in the shape of a Chinese *hu* with stylised *taotie* decoration, more highly fired and much lighter than a contemporary Chinese green lead-glazed example of this shape would have been.

Throughout their occupation the Chinese never succeeded in Sinicizing the Vietnamese: whatever they did in Vietnam was conditioned by the filter of a different language, and thus of a different culture. At the same time, contact with the Khmer and Cam civilizations widened the perspectives of the Vietnamese and provided them with cultural and intellectual alternatives to China. Yet in early modern Western analysis of Vietnamese ceramics – for example, the writings of Goloubew and the excavation reports of Janse – they are described as provincial "Chinese."

After the Chinese were expelled from Vietnam in the 10th century, a member of the Lý clan, who was a Buddhist temple orphan, gained control of northern Vietnam in 1009 with the help of the Buddhist establishment. He made his capital at Thăng Long, "rising dragon," on the site of what is now Hanoi. This was a time of national self- exploration; after many generations of Chinese dominance, "Eleventh-century Vietnamese were genuinely engaged in discovering who they were," is the assessment of Keith Taylor (*Authority and Legitimacy in Eleventh Century Vietnam*, Singapore, 1986, p. 149). New ceramic styles blossomed. Distinctly Vietnamese shapes and designs were created, and during two native dynasties, the Lý (1009-1225) and the Trần (1225-1400), the skill and production of Vietnamese potters flourished and followed new directions. New production techniques were developed, the

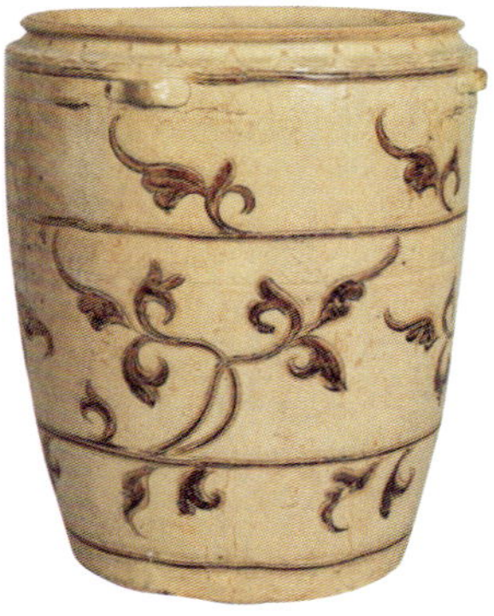

Fig. 2 *Ivory-glazed barrel-shaped jar with brown inlaid vegetal design 12th-14th century, height 32 cm. (Private collection)*

most original being a method of decoration in which an ivory-coloured glaze was applied overall to the body of a vessel and a design cut deeply through the glaze, into the clay. While the glaze was still viscous, the areas between the cuts were scraped clean and the now bare areas were inlaid with a dark brown iron-oxide. Designs included luxuriant vegetation, elephants, and tropical birds. This method of creating a design, a technique unique to Vietnam, was widely used for at least two hundred years. Its most characteristic shape was a barrel-shaped jar (**Fig. 2**), often with a frieze of Buddhist lotus petals around the shoulder. Perhaps the jars were used in Buddhist temples; perhaps the friezes were predominantly decorative.

The Chinese themselves valued fine Vietnamese ceramics. The *Yuanshi* (Yuan Dynastic History) records an edict of 1262 CE in which the Shizu emperor, Kublai Khan, defined the types of gifts he expected a Vietnamese prince to supply the following year (Song Lian et al. 1983, *Yuanshi*, Beijing: Zhonghua Shuqu, biographies section, chap. 96, *juan* 209, p. 4635). The usual tropical treasures were requested, plus *bai ci jian*, white stoneware bowls. Vietnamese potters did not copy Chinese models directly but would take elements such as vessel shapes, glazes, and decorative motifs and mix them in original ways. For example, the walls of Vietnamese covered celadon bowls were thinner than Chinese equivalents, their shapes elegantly broadened or inverted. A popular Song Chinese decorative motif suggests fertility by depicting male infants playing among flowers and is found on white and light-blue bowls, but when the Vietnamese used the motif it was almost always associated with dark brown or green glazes. A Vietnamese bowl with sinuous dragons molded in the cavetto may have a lotus blossom moulded into the well: Chinese potters followed conventions much more rigidly than Vietnamese and would have combined dragons with waves or clouds, never a flower.

Robust new forms were given to ewers for water, wine, or various kinds of tea. Some ewers were very finely potted, thin-walled, and as a result extremely light – the potting skills they demonstrate are most impressive (**Fig. 3**). Handles were inward-curling and non-functional, with spouts in the forms of dragons or *makara* (Indic sea-creatures resembling crocodiles). Dragons are associated with water and are especially loved by the Vietnamese, who in their creation myths consider themselves to be descended from dragons. The dragon of the Lý dynasty had a distinctive shape, more sinuous and snakelike than his Chinese cousin. It relates more closely to the *nāga* water-deities of India and Cambodia than to the *makara* of India or the dragons of China. A Lý architectural ornament shows a thin snakelike dragon within a *bodhi* leaf-shape, which represents the tree under which the Buddha attained enlightenment; the piece has echoes of the curly foliage typical of Khmer and Cham architectural decoration, and it was not until Trần, when Confucianism began to gain influence at the Vietnamese court at the expense of Buddhism, that the Vietnamese dragon began to take on Chinese characteristics. Early

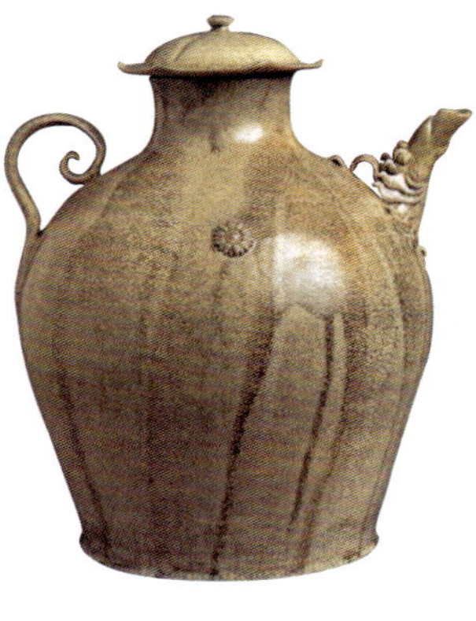

Fig. 3 *Large thin-walled ewer with* makara *spout, 12th-13th century, height 17.2 cm. (Private collection)*

representations of the mythical phoenix bird are also decidedly un-Chinese, with very long thick flowing tails. Rather than figures or geometric shapes, many forms were taken from the natural world – flowers, animals, birds, fish. The wide and inventive range of Vietnamese designs and shapes during Lý and Trần reflect great energy and observation; they suggest a happy freedom, almost an anarchy, of creativity.

For two or three hundred years from the late 13th century onward, the bases of many Vietnamese pieces were given a thin matte iron-oxide wash; this has become almost a hallmark of Vietnamese origin. The reason for the wash is not clear. Brown-washed bases have been explained as potters' marks, but the possible variety is too limited for this to be plausible. Citing no evidence, d'Argencé wondered whether "chocolate" bases implied temple use. Brown-washed bases are also (though rarely) found on some Chinese pieces of the period, especially Jun and some Longquan wares. This writer thinks that the reason for brown-washed bases was probably no more than aesthetic, a finishing touch given to complete a piece visually. A brown wash is a useful indicator of Vietnamese production, although the most decisive indicator is the clay from which the piece was made. The example of **Fig. 4** adds a painter's doodle to the brown wash in the sketchy form of a perky magpie-like *chích choè* bird.

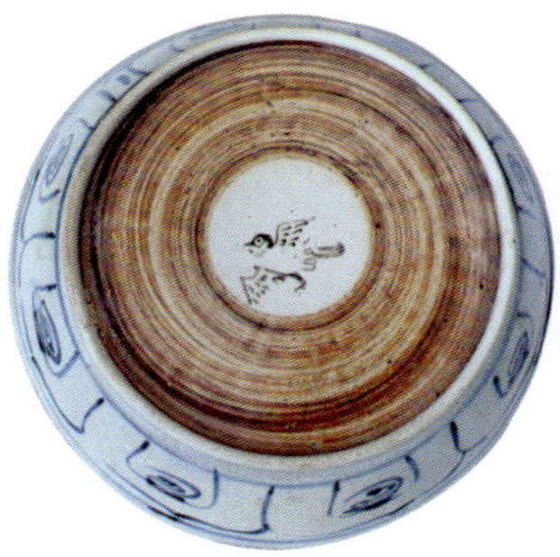

Fig. 4 *Small dish with painted cobalt-blue decoration, brown-washed base with informal sketch of magpie-like* chích choè *bird. 16th century CE, width 20.5 cm. (Private collection)*

During the Trần dynasty decoration began to be painted in the form of simple daubs of brown iron-oxide on white-slipped vessels, which were given a thin clear protective glaze, and fired. The underglaze decoration developed into vegetal swirls on the sides of a vessel or a cursory flower in the cavetto of a bowl with a scrolling band below the rim. These ceramics are a distinct and common Vietnamese type that has no obvious connections to any other culture, including its underglaze production. Sherds of a bowl with this loose floral painting and the hallmark Vietnamese brown-washed base have been found as far away as Japan in association with a wooden grave-marker bearing a date equivalent to 1330 CE. More elaborate flowers followed; ivory-glazed beakers with the same scrolling decoration are also common. Soon these motifs were being painted using a cobalt blue pigment more attractive than iron-oxide brown; sometimes the flower was painted in blue and its surrounding scrolling bands in brown. Cobalt blue was much more expensive than iron-oxide brown, but blue became the color of choice.

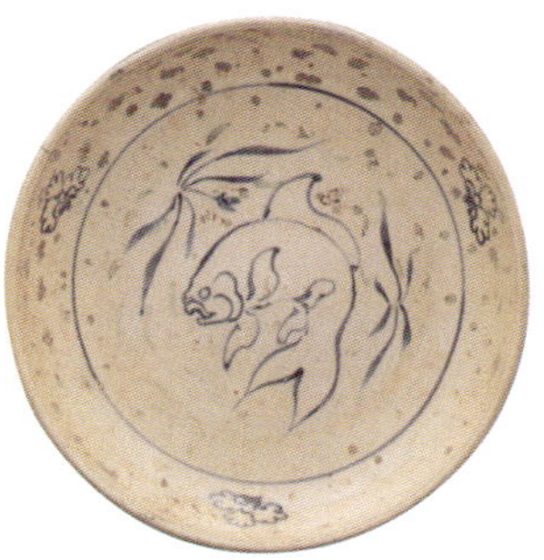

Fig. 5 *Large dish with fish among waterweeds painted in underglaze cobalt-blue and (much deteriorated) red and green overglaze enamels. Late 15th or 16th century CE, width 33.8 cm. (Private collection)*

As the 14th century unfolded, cobalt-painted underglaze wares became increasingly sophisticated and were developed into large serving dishes with complex designs of dragons, fish (**Fig. 5**), peonies, lotuses, and a multitude of other idiosyncratic designs for export largely to Muslim countries, from Turkey to Indonesia. Large serving dishes were well suited to Muslim communal eating traditions. The commercial success of these products during the 14th and 15th centuries was assisted by Ming China's isolationist trade policies as China withdrew from international trade, attempting for several decades

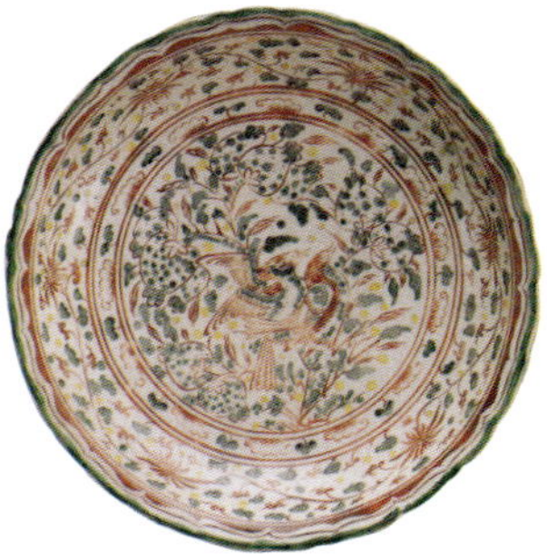

Fig. 6 *Large dish with mating birds and pomegranates painted in red, green, and yellow overglaze enamels. Late 15th or 16th century, width 36.8 cm. Formerly Menke Collection.*

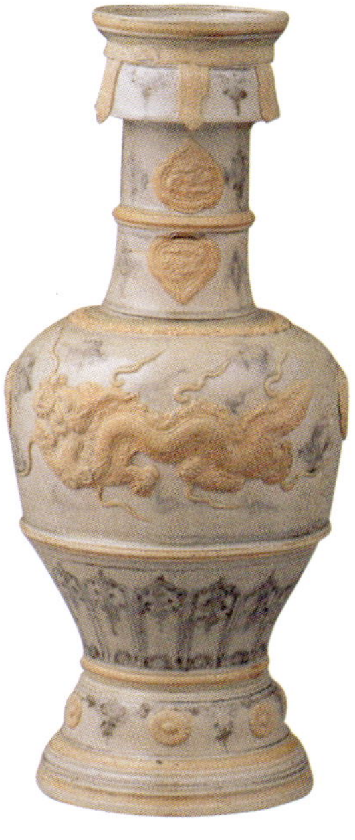

Fig. 7 *Candleholder in three sections, with dragons,* bodhi-*leaf panels, and rosettes in biscuit relief. Dated 1677, H: 60.5 cm. (Private collection)*

to safeguard itself from the activity of pirates by pulling populations inland away from its coastlines. Cobalt-blue painted Vietnamese wares were able to fill the gap left by China's commercial withdrawal, especially marked between the years 1436 to 1464 CE. The inscription on an extremely fine Vietnamese blue-and-white long-necked bottle, now in the Topkapi Sarai Museum in Istanbul, where it has resided for centuries, translates as, "Painted for pleasure by a lady artisan of the Bùi clan at Nam Sách in the eighth year of Thái Hoà [1450]". Its design motifs – peony blossoms – are obviously in the Chinese tradition, but the shape of this ceramic bottle is uniquely Vietnamese. Also, that it was decorated "for pleasure" by a lady reflects significantly different social attitudes in Vietnam and China, including a much higher status for women in Vietnam. The Topkapi Museum contains two other blue-and-white Vietnamese ceramics of the same period, an octagonal bottle and a *kendi*.

As the quantities of Vietnamese cobalt-painted production increased in the course of the 15th and 16th centuries, the quality of the painting declined. Locally mined cobalt was imported from Yunnan in southwestern China, which neighbours Vietnam; this ore contained far more impurities than the expensive cobalt pigments imported from the Middle East, resulting in a blacker, less intensely blue colour. Rather crudely cobalt-painted wares were exported from Vietnam to Southeast Asia in increasing numbers. The subjects painted, however, were extraordinarily varied and imaginative, far more wide-ranging than the more staid subject matter of China. Birds included phoenixes, parrots, peacocks, ducks, geese, *chích choè*, mynah birds, kingfishers, and a multitude of smaller birds that had caught a painter's attention. Animals encompassed dragons of all kinds, a lively form of lion, horses (magic and otherwise), deer, and *kỳ lân* (in Vietnamese) or *kylin/qilin* (in Chinese) (unicorns) to dragonflies and butterflies. Aquatic creatures ranged from fat *cá bống* and exotic carp to shrimp and turtles. Flowers focused on full-blossomed lotuses and peonies and included simple daisies and complex chrysanthemums. Colourful overglaze painted enamels – red, blue and occasionally yellow – were combined with the underglaze-blue of the designs of dishes, bowls, and jars. This required a second firing of a piece, at a lower temperature than the first firing that was required to fix the blue. Some of these polychrome creations were very elaborate. The red, green, and yellow painted dish in **Fig. 6** shows mating birds surrounded by pomegranates, fruits that contain many seeds; it was likely a marriage presentation gift, expressing the donor's hope that the union had many offspring. The theme of fertility could not have been more appropriately conveyed, yet such a motif was too *outré* for a Chinese product.

Significant ceramic creations of the 16th and 17th centuries included large and imposing items of altar furnishings, such as incense burners and candle stands, which were commissioned by Buddhist temples. Their shapes are baroque. A multiplicity of forms and glaze colors might be combined on a single piece – cloud motifs, rosettes, openwork, relief detailing, *bodhi* leaf panels, monster masks, biscuit appliqués (**Fig. 7**) and the purity of form of earlier wares was lost. Underglaze-cobalt painting was usually vigorous, but often watery and unrefined. The Chinese form of dragon became a primary ceramic motif, although it still exhibited some typically Vietnamese characteristics. Ceramic guardian figures in the shape of *nghê*, mythological doglike creatures, were popular. Besides the names of the temple benefactors who commissioned them and their date of fabrication, many large temple pieces were inscribed with the names of their makers. This suggests both a rising status for the potters, from anonymous craftsman to named artist, and the development of a market economy where it was worthwhile to sign one's creation. Several of the artisans named were women or husband-and-wife teams, another indication of the relatively high status of Vietnamese women.

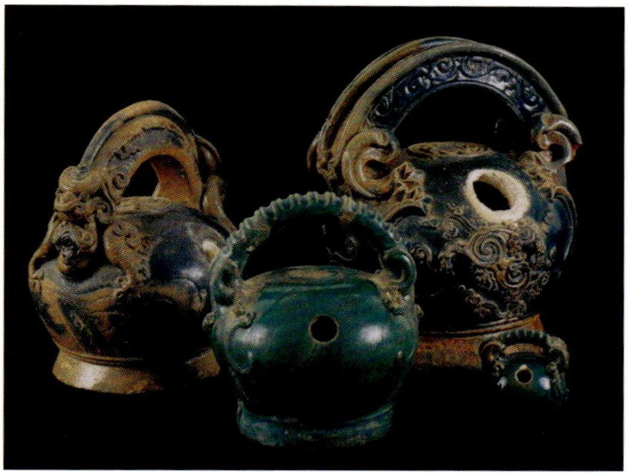

Fig. 8 *Lime-pots. 18th-19th century. H: 7.5 to 24.5 cm. (Private collections, France)*

Fanciful forms of the distinctive Vietnamese lime-pot, with bulbous body, small round opening, and high arched handle, were developed as accoutrements for the chewing of betel nut, which was a beloved and ubiquitous Vietnamese habit (**Fig. 8**). Lime-pots were used to store the powdered lime that was an ingredient of betel chewing. Although betel was used by other Southeast Asian societies besides Vietnam, the shape of the Vietnamese lime-pot is not found in the ceramic traditions of other countries, and exported examples have not been found.

From early in the 18th century the Vietnamese imperial court turned to China when it needed fine ceramics, commissioning porcelain with cobalt-blue painted designs from the imperial Chinese kilns at Jingdezhen and elsewhere in Jiangxi province. These wares are known in the West as *bleu de Huế* after the location of the Nguyễn dynasty capital. They were made to specific Vietnamese designs and can fairly be described as Vietnamese inspired. That ceramics used by the Vietnamese court were made in China symbolized the gulf that now yawned between a Sinicized elite in Vietnam and the masses of the population: sumptuary laws passed in 1720 CE specifically forbade the use of imported ceramics by commoners. The most technically advanced of later Vietnamese ceramics include vessels with a crackled ivory-colored glaze; these were made in Bát Tràng from the 17th to the early 19th century. They include archaisms: the potters and their customers of the later Lê dynasty (1428 to 1789 CE) were aware of their ceramic heritage. If ruling clans had been major patrons and supporters of fine ceramics during Lý and Trần, lower standards under later dynasties may be explained by the declining power and influence of the imperial courts and incessant rebellions and unrest.

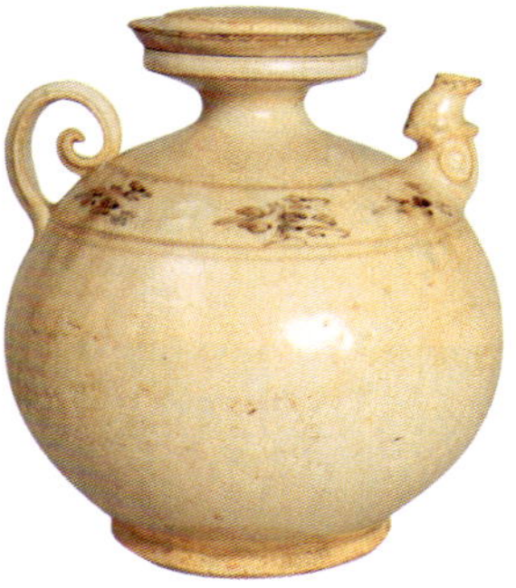

Fig. 9 *Bulbous ewer with dish-mouth and stylized dragon spout. Painted with underglaze-iron vegetal motifs, 13th-14th century CE. H: 17.2 cm. (Private collection)*

Along with the importance of ceramics for an understanding of Vietnamese history and culture comes a simple appreciation of their beauty. The best Vietnamese ceramics combine excellent clays with a lack of artistic restraint and great potting skills. They have an attractive informality, as Korean ceramics do. Yanagi Sōetsu, father of the Mingei movement in Japan, was awed by the beauty achieved so easily by Korean potters. They would casually set up their wheels and not care if the results were slightly out of true. Imperfections impart great vigor to such works, yet cannot be created deliberately without destroying their spontaneity. It is the interface between art and technology that gives ceramics their flavour. The Chinese potter aimed for perfect technique, characterized by the colossal and almost mechanistic production of the vast kiln complexes at Longquan and Jingdezhen. The Japanese potter responded to the beauty of kiln accidents, which were sometimes consciously orchestrated: a paradox. The Vietnamese ceramic tradition falls successfully somewhere in between.

Such a serendipitous combination of spontaneity with technical excellence makes Vietnamese ceramics very attractive. To hold the bulbous ivory-glazed ewer of **Fig. 9**, a distinctive Vietnamese ceramic type of the Trần dynasty, is a pleasure, the shape fitting beautifully in the hands, reminding us that ceramics are tactile objects besides being visual experiences. The ewer's distinctive shape, with round pregnant body, dish-mouth, narrow neck, and decorative handle, is pleasing, and the forming and luting together of the several elements is skillful. The piece would have been used for wine or water; the handle was non-functional, and both hands, one on each side of the body, would have been used when pouring. The application of slip and clear over-glaze is casual, and the very loose floral underglaze-iron decoration has been applied at speed, with abandon. Adding to the sense of informality is the natural melting of the glaze, which has collected in drips around the base. Again, the qualities achieved by such a relaxed approach cannot be controlled. Contrasting the perfection of Chinese products with the freedom and individuality of this sort of piece, a Vietnamese ceramics scholar from Huế commented: "Chinese ceramics are good for the eye; Vietnamese ceramics are good for the heart."

14 | Vietnamese ceramics 11th to 19th centuries

Phạm Ngọc Uyên

Vietnamese pottery has been an important part of the HM-HCMC collection since the Museum Blanchard de la Brosse opened in the former Saigon in 1929. This paper introduces selected artifacts dating from the 11th century to the early 20th century.

There was an explosion in the designs and volumes of Vietnamese pottery from the Lý dynasty (1009-1225 CE) to the Trần dynasty (1225-1400 CE) when Vietnam distanced itself from China. John Stevenson (2007: 3) says "it was the era when the Vietnamese…were fascinated and excited about establishing their own culture, and, freed from the threat culturally from China." Although Chinese ceramic had always been a great attraction during the Lý and Trần dynasties, Vietnamese craftsmen rarely copied directly from Chinese ceramics forms (Stevenson 2007: 3-4). They instead developed a variety of jars, pots and bowls with new shapes and new crafting techniques, and these indigenous features were combined with glazes and decorative motifs brought from abroad. Water and fuel for pottery kilns were abundant and convenient, as well as raw materials such as fine and bright clay (Stevenson 2007: 3-4).

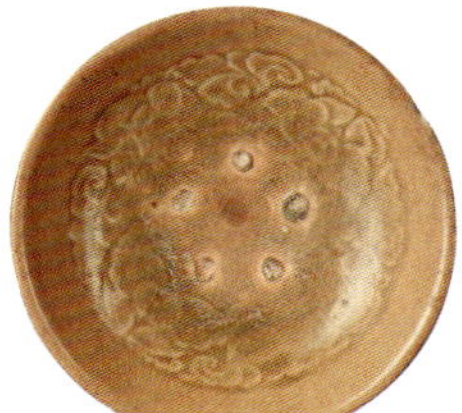

Fig. 1 *A Vietnamese celadon-glazed bowl from the Holbe collection, 12th-13th century. BTLS.3114. H: 3.5 cm, D: 17 cm.*

The Vietnamese pottery collected in 1929-1955

The collection of 2,106 objects of the former Navy pharmacist Victor Thomas Holbé was acquired by the 'Société des Études Indochinoises' in 1927. They were collected over nearly 40 years by Holbé himself (Thái Văn Kiểm, Trương Bá Phát 1974: 20; *see also* BTLS-HS.52[1]). The amount of Vietnamese celadon pottery in the museum was increased thanks to the former director of the 'Banque de l'Indochine' in Saigon, Paul Aimé-Hilaire Gannay, and some artifacts were imported from the Louis Finot Museum in Hà Nội during the period 1952-1954.

The term 'celadon pottery' was known since the Tang and Song dynasties, in China (Asian Art Museum of San Francisco/AAMuSF 2006: 51), 'celadon' is for artifacts whose enamel-color only uses 'celadon glaze'. The two bowls with olive-green glaze are also called straw-colored (Harrison-Hall 2002: 4). The enamel color levels are created by blending iron oxide (from 1-3%) with the enamel compound (AAMuSF 2006: 51); artifacts are then coated with this enamel and fired in a kiln. Iron oxide is an active ingredient in clay, which can change the colour and enamel with heat. It was used as the most common colorant in Chinese ceramics production until the 14th century (AAMuSF 2006: 51). Iron typically creates green of different levels, thus the most popular enamel glaze may have been coated with layers ranging from light green to dark green to mimic emerald green (**Figs 1-2**).

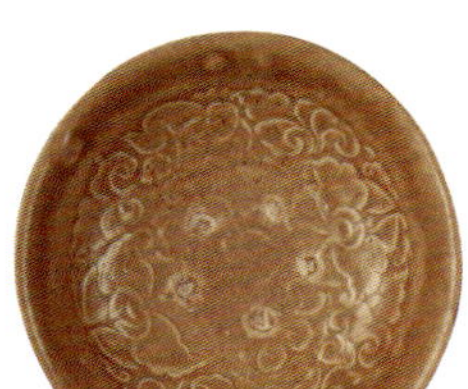

Fig. 2 *A Vietnamese celadon-glazed bowl from the Gannay collection, 13th-14th century. BTLS.3260. H: 4.7 cm, D: 6.7 cm.*

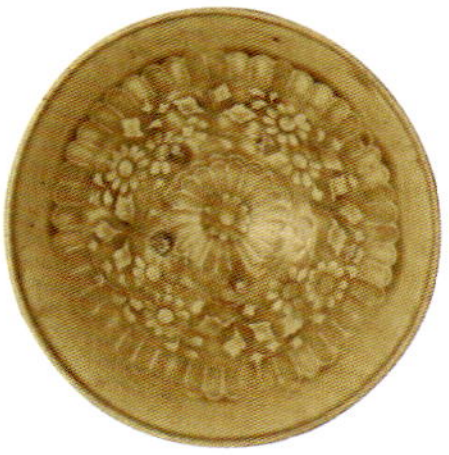

Fig. 3 *A bowl from the Gannay collection with Chrysanthemums pattern, Việt Nam, 12th-14th century. BTLS.1411. H: 6.5 cm, D: 17 cm.*

Vietnamese celadon is similar to that made in the Yaozhou region (Rastelli 2017: 6-8). The two bowls have five spur marks and the base is unglazed, showing the clay color as white. The bowls have floral decorations or an image a child playing with lotus flowers or peony flowers (Truong 2007: 53), motifs common during the Song dynasty. Iconographically, the decorations may suggest a pun on the Vietnamese word 'liên tử', which means successively giving birth to sons, also called lien-tzu/蓮子 in Chinese, related to the concept of male heirs in a traditional Chinese family. However, Vietnamese celadon with a baby figure is more realistically depicted with a body that is neither dressed nor adorned, in various poses such as swimming or sitting in the middle of a lotus, sometimes with a pomegranate flower. Truong (2007: 54) argues that Vietnamese craftsmen created different versions of the decoration as the result of artistic interaction between Vietnam and China around the late 13th century. Similar celadons are produced today in pottery kilns in Hống hamlet, Chí Linh town, Hải Dương province, Việt Nam.

Chrysanthemum bowls from moulds, with rims curved slightly inward, were popular under the Lý and Trần dynasties (**Fig. 3**). The chrysanthemum motif and spur/stilt marks are all found at the kilns in Tức Mặc, formerly Phủ Thiên Trường in Nam Định province, dating back to the Trần dynasty.

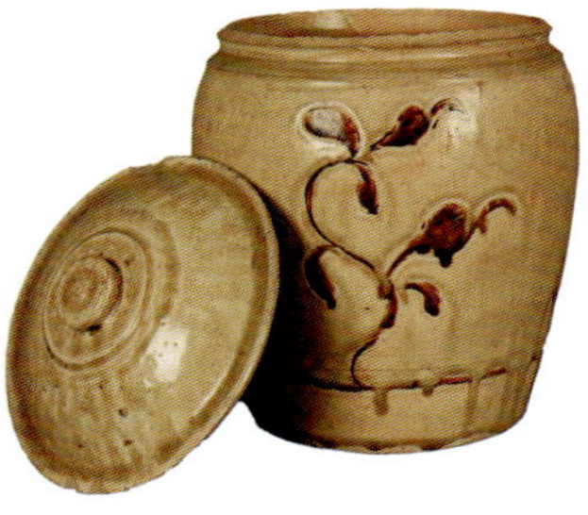

Fig. 4 *A Vietnamese creamy glazed stoneware, 13th-14th century. A lidded storage jar with incised brown enamel design. BTLS.1464. H: 25.5 cm, D: 20 cm.*

Pottery called 'gốm hoa nâu' in Vietnamese, is carved on its surface and brown or red enamel is inlaid into the design, before a translucent slip is added. This technique first appeared in the 11th-13th centuries. Similar pottery in Japan and China is called 'inlaid brown/iron brown' in the western world (Phạm Quốc Quân 2011: 13). For example, an ivory-glazed storage jar (**Fig. 4**) is a lidded-jar with a lotus petal design incised into the clay and highlighted with an iron wash underglaze. The jar was gifted to the Museum Blanchard de la Brosse in Saigon from the Museum Louis Finot in Hà Nội, in March 1934.

2. Vietnamese ceramics entering the Vietnam National Museum (Saigon) 1956-1975

The Vietnam National Museum in Saigon accepted donations from Olov Robert Thure Jansé in 1960-1962, and from Director Trương Bửu Lâm (*see* BTLS-HS.53/V). 150 artifacts were returned to the Museum by the Peabody Museum and Harvard-Yenching Institute. The lime pot BTLS.3331 is representative of these (**Fig. 5**). It is thickly potted with a spherical body on an unglazed flat bottom, with a small circle in the shoulder of the jar for filling and/or extracting lime. The heavy strap handle and shoulder decorations

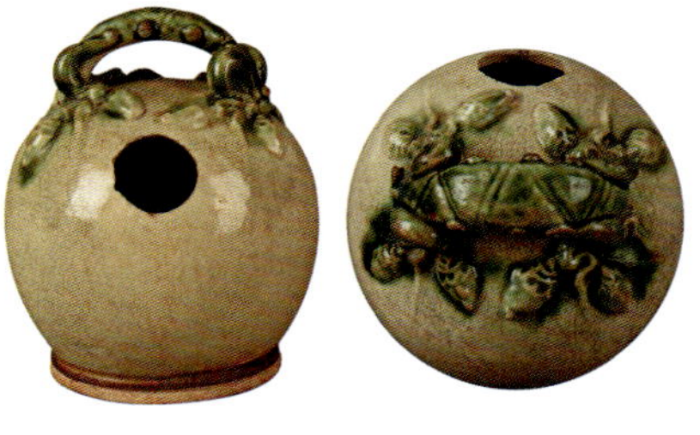

Fig. 5 *Lime pot from the Olov Jansé collection, its handle treated like an areca palm tree and betel nuts. BTLS.3331. Made of green-glazed stoneware, 15th-16th century. H: 14.2 cm, D: 12.2 cm.*

both evoke the betel nut palm tree. The lime pot is considered to be the one of the most original creations of Vietnamese potters (Nguyễn Xuân Hiên 2006: 507-8).

The shapes of these popular wares varied from the 14th-17th centuries (Truong 2007: 145). **Fig. 6** shows the skill of Vietnamese potters in reproducing natural forms (2007: 145, pl.113).

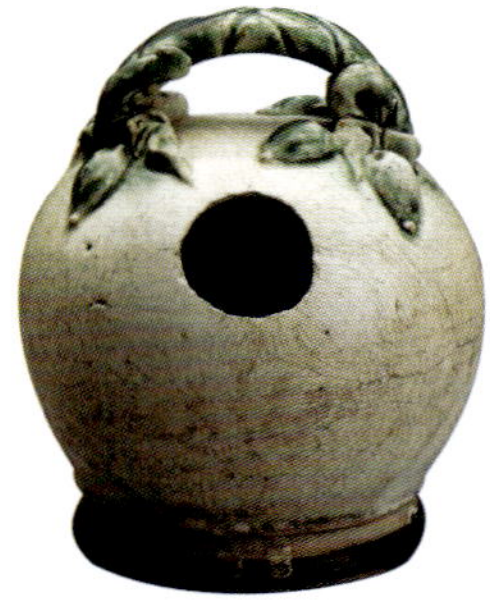

Fig. 6 *A lime pot, Bát Tràng pottery, 15th-17th century. A screenshot from* 'The Elephant and the Lotus – Vietnamese ceramics in the Museum of Fine Arts, Boston' *(Truong 2007: 145, pl.113).*

3. Vietnamese ceramics from 1975 to present

Vietnamese collector Vương Hồng Sển donated 849 artifacts to the HM-HCMC in 1996, including 'commissioned patterned porcelains' or 'Đồ sứ ký kiểu' Vietnamese designed porcelains manufactured in China (**Fig. 7-8**). The orders were made by people who served at court under the Lê-Trịnh dynasties (late 17th-late 18th centuries), under the Nguyễn dynasties (1691-1725), and under the Tây Sơn regime (Trần Đức Anh Sơn 2002: 15, 197). The term 'Đồ sứ ký kiểu' was coined by Vương Hồng Sển himself (Vương Hồng Sển 1960).

Such ceramics are classified as Vietnamese wares based on the following criteria: 1. The landscape decorations illustrate a specific location in Việt Nam; 2. It has adapted Chinese characters; 3. The objects bear the reign mark of the current Vietnamese emperor's title such as Hồng Đức, Gia Long, Minh Mạng, Thiệu Trị, Tự Đức, Khải Định; or, the reign mark coincides with the year when the Vietnamese envoys went to China; 4. Although the ware's decorations were made by Chinese artists, they are in Vietnamese style, using materials such as copper, fabric, paper… of sculpture, architecture and painting that dated from the Lê-Trịnh dynasty to the Nguyễn dynasty; 5. Porcelain products were exclusively for use by Vietnamese mandarins (Trần Đức Anh Sơn 2002: 198).

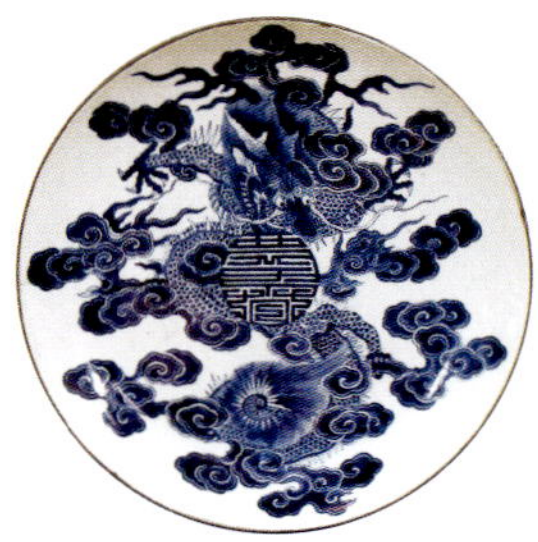

Fig. 7 *Plate depicting a dragon amidst clouds with inscriptions* "慶春侍左" (Khánh xuân thị tả), *blue and white porcelain, BTLS.15139, the Vương Hồng Sển collection.*

Vietnamese ceramics from the Hội An shipwreck

In 2000, the HM-HCMC received 4,362 ceramics excavated in 1997-99 on Chàm Island off Hội An town, Quảng Nam province. According to archeological excavation reports (Phạm Quốc Quân, Tống Trung Tín 2000: 94), the Thai ship was on its way back to Thailand from Vietnam, with Vietnamese pottery as the bulk cargo. These were mid-15th century trade wares, according to Scollard (1981: 93). The ceramics were in good shape and of high quality to meet export demand. Vietnamese and Thai ceramics dominated the 'Chinese' ceramic export market after the Ming court forbade the Chinese to export or go overseas in the 15th century. These shipwreck ceramics make up more than 50% of the Vietnamese ceramics in the HM-HCMC inventory and include blue and white, celadon, or a design like a lithophone instrument also known as 'hidden carved porcelain'. They were made in Chu Đậu, Mỹ Xá, Hải Dương province (Phạm Quốc Quân and Tống Trung Tín. 2000: 96).

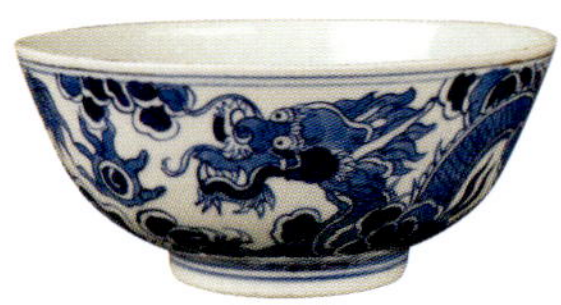

Fig. 8 *Bowl with inscriptions* "明命年製" (Minh Mạng niên chế), *blue and white porcelain, BTLS.14892, the Vương Hồng Sển collection.*

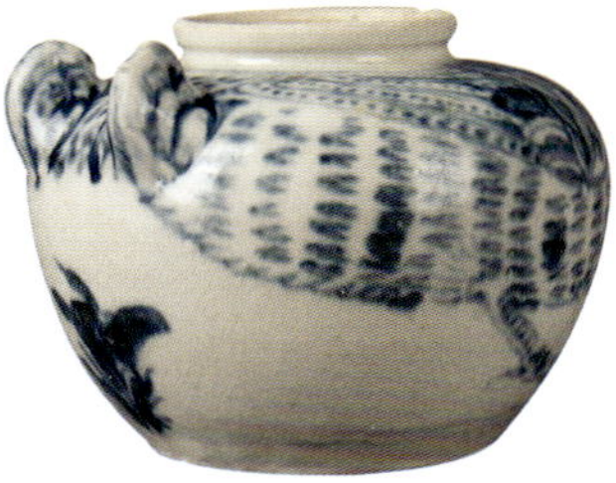

Fig. 9 *A water-dropper for calligraphy with the motif of a 'double mandarin duck' in a double phoenix shape, from the Cham island collection, BTLS.16894, 15th-16th century. H: 11 cm, D: 15 cm.*

Traces of the use of kiln furniture are found on some of these ceramics despite improvements in kiln technique in the early 15th century. For instance, Chu Đậu ceramics with five-prong spurs were introduced under the Trần dynasty and were replaced with new technology in the early Lê dynasty (Bùi Minh Trí and Kerry Nguyễn Long 2001: 19). Some products inlaid with gold have been found from this period (Phạm Quốc Quân 2011: 211).

A blue and white double mandarin duck jar

Philippe Truong (2007, 241) believed that Vietnamese potters may have produced their versions for export (the 'double phoenix') without ever seeing prototypes, which is why they were decorated with the phoenix shape instead of the duck design. This also inadvertently created unique and rich variations compared to the originals from China. Although that shown in **Fig. 9** is damaged, it is the only artifact representing this unique type of the Cham island group in the HM-HCMC.

Fig. 10 shows a similar shaped item in another collection (Truong 2007: 241, pl.193). It has a compressed spherical shape with an upright neck, and the shoulder is mounted with facing phoenix heads and tails, then colored with an underglaze blue outline forming the feathered bodies and feet separated by water grass. The slightly concave base is left unglazed. The phoenix heads and tails were applied after the compressed body was formed. The Hội An hoard jar had a hole in the beak of one phoenix head, so that they could function as a ewer or water dropper, following Chinese prototypes from the Ming dynasty (Bonhams 2017: 38). In the Lena Shoal shipwreck in the Philippines, many such jars were stacked in a special wooden box dating to the 15th-16th century (Truong 2007: 241). Philippe Truong proposes that the jar's shape imitated the brush washer used in oriental calligraphy under the Tuyên Đức reign of the Ming dynasty (1425-1435 CE). However, this jar was assumed to be used for ceremonial wine on special occasions like weddings (Adhyatman 1989: 6).

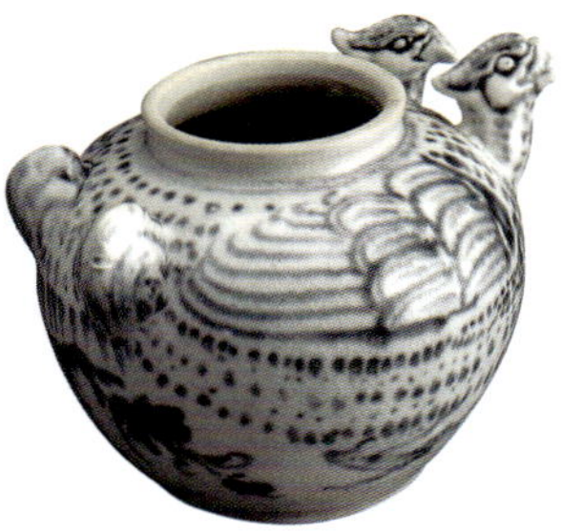

Fig. 10 *A water-dropper with two phoenix heads, 15th-16th century, a gift of Carol and Jeffrey Horvitz. A screenshot from* The Elephant and the Lotus – Vietnamese ceramics in the Museum of Fine Arts, Boston", *(Phillippe Truong 2007: 241, pl.193)*

The 'double mandarin ducks' were a popular motif in Chinese and Japanese art, symbolizing endurance and faithfulness (Snowdon 2016: 15). This suggests such pottery was exported to the markets of north and northeast Asia at that time. But the double mandarin duck motif was not favoured in the Persian market (Du 2020: 3). The great volume of pottery in the Hội An hoard, indicates that Đại Việt was engaged in international trade across Asia, in which glazed ceramics played a significant role during the 15th and early 16th centuries (Guy 2015: 107).

Vietnamese ceramic miniatures

There are many types, shapes and patterns, with under-glaze cobalt pattern and over-glaze enamel color, varying in size from 1.4 cm to 8 cm. These objects account for more than 50% of the total collection from Chàm Island, being stored at the HM-HCMC (**Fig. 11**).

They have been found in large numbers in Southeast Asia, especially in South Sulawesi, Indonesia. Such small-sized artifacts were presumably used for medicine or cosmetics, or as water-droppers for calligraphy (Beck 1989: 12). In Indonesia some are known as '*onroang pabora*', meaning medicine containers. Some had a similar function in the Philippines (Adhyatman 1989: 6). These small wares have been found in tombs and temple grounds, where a village or clan treasure was buried, or in burials as grave goods (Beck 1989: 10, 12).

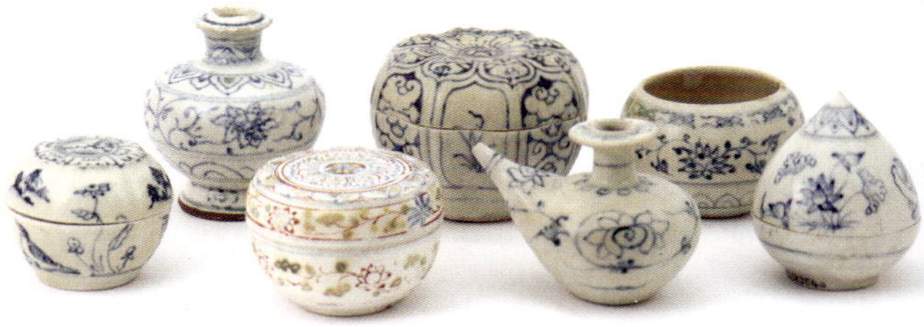

Fig. 11 *A variety of Chu Đậu miniatures.*

The Ming court banned the export of ceramics to foreign countries in the 15th century encouraging the kilns in Việt Nam and Thailand to ramp up exports to Indonesia, South Sulawesi and the Moluccas (Adhyatman 1989: 7). Vietnamese potters thus found new markets in this period. The presence of Chu Đậu ceramics with under-glaze cobalt patterns in Southeast Asian collections illustrates this expansion in cultural exchange.

Vietnamese ceramics in Shiwan style

Shiwan ceramics were for everyday use, such as kitchen pots. They had become everyday objects for the inhabitants in Guangdong province, at least since the Tang dynasty (Scollard 1981: 1). Scollard also notes that they remain an integral part of Southern Chinese cuisine to this day, with a presence in Hong Kong, Taiwan and Chinese communities across Southeast Asia. Notable are figurative ceramics representing historical, folkloric and religious figures (Scollard 1978: 105).

Shiwan is the name of a village in Guangzhou known for its pottery. The Guangzhou region maintained relatively stable under the Ming, though it was limited in trading abroad (Scollard 1981: 93). Guangzhou was allowed to trade goods with Yuenan (Vietnam), Xianlu (Siam) and some Western countries. Shiwan, partly due to its favorable geographical location, developed into a major ceramic production center providing for domestic and some foreign consumption (Scollard 1981: 94).

In Việt Nam, Cây-Mai was named after a fort in Saigon (fort de Cay-mai) at the end of the 19th century. The area includes the fort, the Chợ Lớn bus station and Cây Gõ area (Péralle 1895: 53-59; Huỳnh Ngọc Trảng and Nguyễn 1994: 13), all of them areas of Hồ Chí Minh City today. The term 'Cây-Mai ceramics', or 'poterie de Cay-mai', was used for pottery in the Shiwan-style produced in the Cây-Mai region of former Saigon, and notably ceramic statues (Péralle 1895: 53-59; Huỳnh and Nguyễn 1994: 26-27). By the early 20th century, many pottery craftsmen moved to settle in

Lái Thiêu town approximately 30 km far from the Cây-Mai region (Huỳnh and Nguyễn 1994: 40), which explains why Lái Thiêu pottery is considered as the later continuation of this artistic achievement (Trần Bạch Đằng 1991: 346; Nguyễn Thị Tú Anh 2014: 5-6).

The Cây-Mai pottery collection in the HM-HCMC

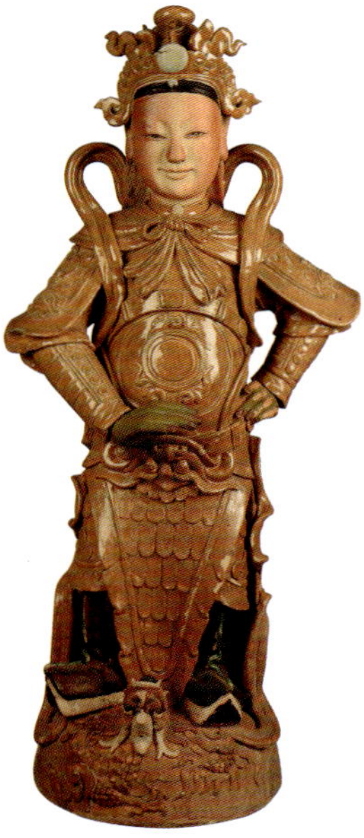

Fig. 12 *A Cây-Mai standing ceramic sculpture of the late 19th century, BTLS.30285. H: 95 cm, W: 25 cm, D: 17 cm.*

Aesthetically, Shiwan-style pottery looks everyday and heavy-handed compared with porcelain ware made of fine white clay, like Jingdezhen products (Scollard 1978: 101; Scollard 1981: 2). Shiwan-style ceramic products are rarely collected for display in museums. It differs from many other ceramics from the Qianlong dynasty, c.1790 (Scollard 1981: 110). The facial and flesh areas of figurines are always left unglazed, with only the garment enameled (**Fig. 12**). Scollard says it was to make flesh seem warmer (1978: 105).

A lidded, pottery ewer (**Fig. 13** BTLS.29181) with two handles, albeit slightly chipped, in Shiwan-style has these four incised characters '萬應藥酒', which suggests its function was as a container of herbal alcohol used for massage to improve circulation.

Péralle notes that Cây-Mai potteries were not moulded but were completely handmade, glazed, and dried by craftsmen (1895: 56-57). The weakness of Cây-Mai pottery was the colour that was used. Péralle (1895: 58) said enameled colour details tended to fade, peel or flake off after long use. Scollard (1981: 2) believes various types of Shiwan-style pots were exported to Việt Nam for use in religious buildings, such as the Tianhou temple (Miếu Thiên Hậu) in Hồ Chí Minh City that was constructed in 1760 (Corfield 2014: 13). The presence of Shiwan-style products from the Cây-Mai region before 1895 (see Péralle 1895: 55, Figs. 14-15) is supported by archaeological research in the 1990s. Péralle (1895: 57-58) notes that Cây-Mai pottery was not only well known in Cochinchine, but also abroad because the products were unique and affordable. Vietnamese Cây-Mai pottery awaits further study to confirm the role of ceramic production in Saigon in the late 19th and early 20th centuries.

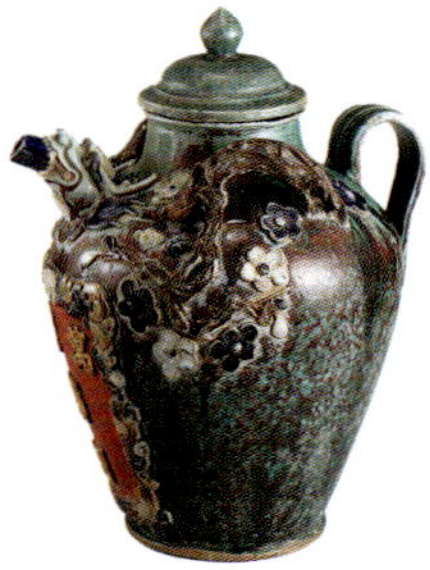

Fig. 13 *A lidded ewer in Shiwan style with incised characters '萬應藥酒' (Vạn ứng dược tửu), BTLS.29181 with prunus branch motifs and figural dragon head spout. 19th or 20th century. H: 50 cm, D: 40 cm.*

The Lái Thiêu pottery collection in the HM-HCMC

Lái Thiêu pottery, derived from the Cây-Mai pottery region (in Đề Ngạn/ the former Saigon-Chợ Lớn) migrated in the late 10th century to Lái Thiêu, Bình Dương province (Trần Bạch Đằng 1991: 346; Huỳnh Ngọc Trảng et al. 2009: 40). Lái Thiêu has three main style groups: Guangdong, Fujian, and Chaozhou (Huỳnh Ngọc Trảng et al. 2009). These were created by Chinese craftsmen who lived for generations in Saigon. Their products were used in home decór, architectural decór and kitchens. Although simple in design, the products vary widely in size and detail depending on when they

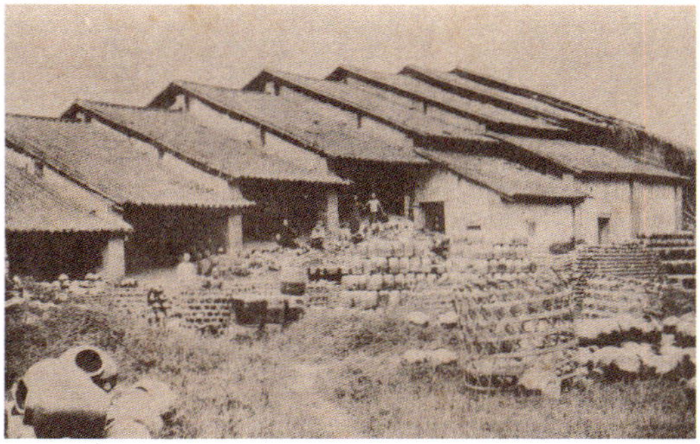

Fig. 14 *A pottery kiln in the Cây-Mai area. (A screenshot from Peralle (1895), "Industrie de la poterie en Cochinchine (Cay-Mai)". In* Bulletin de la Société des Etudes Indochinoises, *pp. 54, No.1.)*

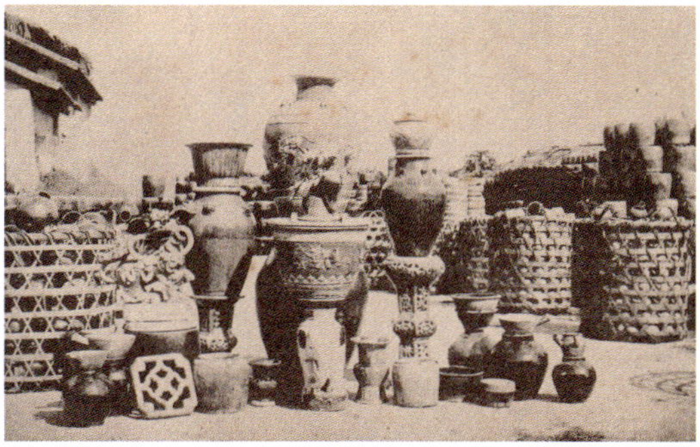

Fig. 15 *The products of a pottery kiln in the Cây-Mai area. (A screenshot from Peralle (1895), "Industrie de la poterie en Cochinchine (Cay-Mai)". In* Bulletin de la Société des Etudes Indochinoises, *pp. 59, No.1)*

were made (Nguyễn Minh Giao 2001: 37-41). A phoenix-shaped lampstand (BTLS.21357 **Fig. 16**) is one of 42 artifacts from the end of 19th to the early 20th century in the Lái Thiêu section of the museum (Nguyễn Thị Tú Anh 2014: appendix 1&6). The 30 cm lampstand is enameled in ivory color with a 3 cm crest-like cylindrical candle holder on the bird's head. The wings cling to the body and are decorated with green painted daubs. Such Shiwan-style pottery has almost disappeared in today's Vietnamese kilns.

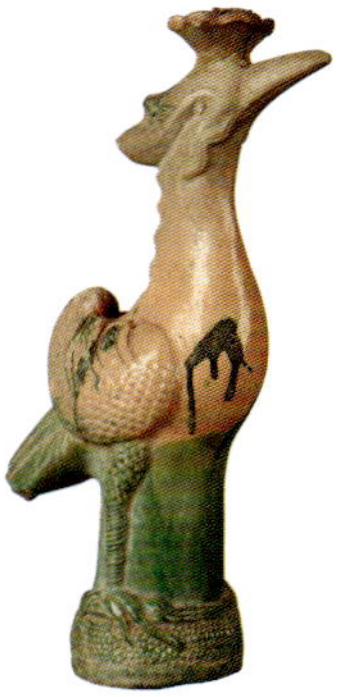

Fig. 16 *Lampstand, BTLS.21357. Lái Thiêu ceramics, 19th century. H: 30 cm.*

Conclusion

This paper introduces the Vietnamese ceramic collections stored at the History Museum-Hồ Chí Minh City. The objects selected represent sections dating from the 11th to the first half of the 20th century from different locations from the north to the south of Việt Nam today. Many of the ceramics mentioned have been little researched and await the attention of those who love them.

References

Adhyatman, Sumarah. 1989. 'Preface', *Vietnamese ceramics miniatures*, pp. 5-8. The Collection of Ulrich J. Beck. Switzerland.

Asian Art Museum of San Francisco. 2006. *China: The Glorious Tang and Song Dynasties*. Online Educational Units in Asian Art. Available at: <http://afemuseums.easia.columbia.edu/cgibin/museums/search.cgi/one_by_letter?letters=A-B;museum_id=2641;page=3>. Accessed on 20/2/2021.

Beck, Ulrich J. 1989. 'Introduction' [the Collection of Ulrich J. Beck], *Vietnamese ceramics miniatures*, pp. 9-15. Switzerland.

Bonhams. 2017. *Fine Asian Works of Art*. Principal auctioneer: Patrick Meade. Bonhams & Butterfields Auctioneers Corp. Available at: < https://images2.bonhams.com/original?src=Images/live/2017-12/07/S-24265-0-4.pdf >. Accessed 15/0/2021.

Bùi Minh Trí. 2017. 'Gốm vẽ nhiều màu Việt Nam' ['Vietnamese ceramics painted multicolor'], *Bulletin of Science*: 181-221. Hà Nội: Social Sciences Publications.

Bùi Minh Trí, and Kerry Nguyễn Long. 2001. *Gốm hoa lam Việt Nam* (Vietnamese Blue & White Ceramics). Hà Nội: Social Sciences Publication.

Colomban, P. H., H. Sagon, Nguyen, Q. Liem, Le, Q. H., L. Mazerolles. 2004. 'Vietnamese (15th century) blue-and-white, Tam thai and lustre porcelains/stonewares: Glaze composition and decoration techniques'. *Archaeometry* 46, 1. University of Oxford: 125-136.

Corfield, Justin. 2014. *Historical Dictionary of Ho Chi Minh City*. Anthem Press, Wimbledon Publishing Company.

Du, He Min. 2020. 'Cultural Creative Product Design from the Perspective of

Chinese Ancient Ware Modelling', *E3S Web of Conferences* 179, 02033. Available at <https://doi.org/10.1051/e3sconf/202017902033>. Accessed on 15/2/2021.

Harrison-Hall, Jessica. 2002. 'Vietnamese Ceramics in the British Museum', *Apollo:* 3-11. International Magazine of the Arts. London.

Huỳnh Ngọc Trảng and Nguyễn Đại Phúc. 1994. *Gốm Cây Mai Sài Gòn xưa* [Cây Mai pottery of Saigon in the ancient time]. HCMC: Nhà xuất bản Trẻ [Youth Publisher].

Huỳnh Ngọc Trảng, Trương Ngọc Tường and Nguyễn Đại Phúc. 2009. *Gốm Lái Thiêu – Chương 3. Khai thác và phối liệu*. Bảo tàng Mỹ Thuật. [*Lái Thiêu pottery – Chapter 3. Exploiting and auxiliary materials. Ho Chi Minh City Museum of Fine Arts*].

Källén, A and Hegardt, J. 2014. 'A Cosmopolitan History of Archaeology: The Olov Janse Case'. *Bulletin of the History of Archaeology*, 24: 7: 1-13.

Malleret, Louis. 1937-38 *Catalogue général des collections du Musée Blanchard de la Brosse*, (Deux Volumes). Hanoi: Imprimerie d'Extrême – Orient.

Morgan, Peter. 1991. 'New Thoughts on Old Hormuz: Chinese Ceramics in the Hormuz Region in the Thirteenth and Fourteenth Centuries'. *Iran*, Vol. 29. Taylor & Francis. London: 67-83

Nguyen Quang Liem, and Philippe Colomban. 2011. 'Applications of Modern Analysis Techniques in Searching back Ancient Art Ceramic Technologies', *Journal of Analytical Science & Technology*: A78-A83. Available at: http://jastmag.com/journal/view.php?Type=C&number=61. Accessed on 10/02/2021.

Nguyễn Thị Tú Anh. 2014. *Gốm Lái Thiêu (Qua các sưu tập ở thành phố Hồ Chí Minh).* [Lái Thiêu pottery through the collections in Hồ Chí Minh city]. A dissertation submitted to fulfill the requirement for the Master of Arts degree in Department of Archaeology of University of Social Sciences and Humanities, The National University in Ho Chi Minh City.

Nguyễn Xuân Hiên. 2006. 'Betel-Chewing in Vietnam. Its Past and Current Importance', *Anthropos.* Bd. 101, H. 2. Nomos Verlagsgesellschaft GmbH: 499-518.

Peralle, M. 1895. 'Industrie de la poterie en Cochinchine (Cay-Mai)', *Bulletin de la Societe dés etudes Indochinoises de Saigon,* No.1: 54-59.

Phạm Quốc Quân and Tống Trung Tín. 2000. Báo cáo khai quật khảo cổ học dưới nước tàu đắm cổ Cù Lao Chàm, Quảng Nam, 1997-1999 [Report on underwater archaeology of the ancient shipwreck of Cu Lao Cham, Quang Nam in 1997-1999]. Hà Nội: Ban khai quật tàu đắm cổ Cù Lao Chàm [Board of the excavation of the ancient shipwreck of Cu Lao Cham].

Rastelli, Sabrina. 2017. *The Yaozhou Kilns: A Re-evaluation.* A thesis submitted to the University of London in partial fulfilment of the requirements for the degree of Doctor of Philosophy. School of Oriental and African Studies (SOAS), University of London.

Scollard, Skinsnes Fredrikke. 1978. 'Shiwan Pottery Explored', *Journal of the Hong Kong Branch of the Royal Asiatic Society*, Vol. 18: 101-112.

Scollard, Skinsnes Fredrikke. 1981. *A study of Shiwan pottery*. A dissertation submitted in partial satisfaction of the requirements for the degree of Doctor of Philosophy at Department of Fine Arts. University of Hong Kong.

Snowdon, R. Lenore. 2016. *The Essence of Itō Jakuchū's Colorful Realm of Living Beings.* A thesis presented to the Department of the History of Art and Architecture and the Graduate school of the University of Oregon in partial fulfillment of the requirements for the degree of Master of Arts. University of Oregon Graduate School. Available at https://core.ac.uk/download/pdf/84755512.pdf. Accessed 10/2/2021

Stevenson, John. 2007. 'Ceramics as National Identity', *The Elephant and the Lotus – Vietnamese ceramics in the Museum of Fine Arts – Boston*. ed. Philippe Truong). Boston: MFA Publication: 1-9.

Trần Bạch Đằng (ed.). 1991. Địa chí Tỉnh Sông Bé [Chorography of Sông Bé (Bình Dương) province]. Sông Bé: Tổng Hợp Publication.

Trần Đức Anh Sơn. 2002. *Đồ sứ ký kiểu tại Trung Hoa từ 1804 đến 1924 hiện tàng trữ tại Bảo tàng Mỹ thuật Cung đình Huế.* [Commissioned Patterned Porcelains dating from 1804 to 1924 on displaying at the Museum of Royal Fine Arts in Huế]. A dissertation submitted in partial satisfaction of the requirements for the degree of Doctor of Philosophy in Archaeology at Department of History of the University of Social Sciences and Humanities, The National University in Hà Nội.

Trần Đức Anh Sơn. 2018. *Đồ sứ ký kiểu thời Nguyễn.* [Commissioned Patterned Porcelains in the Nguyễn Era]. Ho Chi Minh City General Publishing House.

Trần Khánh Chương. 2001. Gốm Việt Nam từ đất nung đến sứ [Vietnamese pottery: From terra-cotta to ceramics]. Hà Nội: Mỹ Thuật Publishers.

Truong Phillippe (ed.). 2007. *The Elephant and the Lotus: Vietnamese ceramics in the Museum of Fine Arts, Boston.* Boston: MFA Publication.

Vương Hồng Sển. 1944. 'Les Bleus de Hué à décor Mai hạc', *BSEI*, (1) Volume 19: 57-64.

Vương Hồng Sển. 1960. [reprinted 2004], Sài Gòn năm xưa [Saigon in the past]. Đồng Nai: General Publishing House.

Endnotes

1 The characters 'BTLS-HS' stands for Documentation of History Museum Hồ Chí Minh City, known as 'Hồ sơ lưu của BTLS' in Vietnamese.

15 | Campā kiln sites and ceramics

Bùi Minh Trí

Preamble

The first discovery of glazed ceramics collections at Gò Sành site in 1974 by the Saigon Institute of Archaeology in Sài Gòn marked a new chapter of Campā ceramics in Bình Định. After this discovery, Bình Định ceramics or Campā ceramics in Bình Định became known as Gò Sành ceramics. The term 'Gò Sành ceramics' was then used by Roxanna Brown in her publication *The Ceramics of Southeast Asia: Their dating and identification* in 1988. However, this term is confusing and vague because of the lack of archaeological materials at the ceramic centers in Bình Định.

Gò Sành is the name of one ceramic kiln complex among six ceramic production centers in Bình Định province. These kilns were located within the region of the Vijaya kingdom and were distributed along the banks of the Côn river (Map 1). The excavations in 1990-1994 at Gò Sành kilns showed that this was a huge production center of ceramics with the appearance of many kilns, specializing in producing many kinds of daily use ceramics, among them. These excavations at Gò Sành site had not found the clear evidence of the production of large brown-glazed jars with shoulder straps, and the body decorated with molded or engraved patterns similar to the Jars excavated from Hội An shipwreck (Vietnam) or Pandanan shipwreck (Philippines).

Fig. 1 *Studying the collection of Campā-Bình Định ceramics at Malaysia National Museum in 2018.*

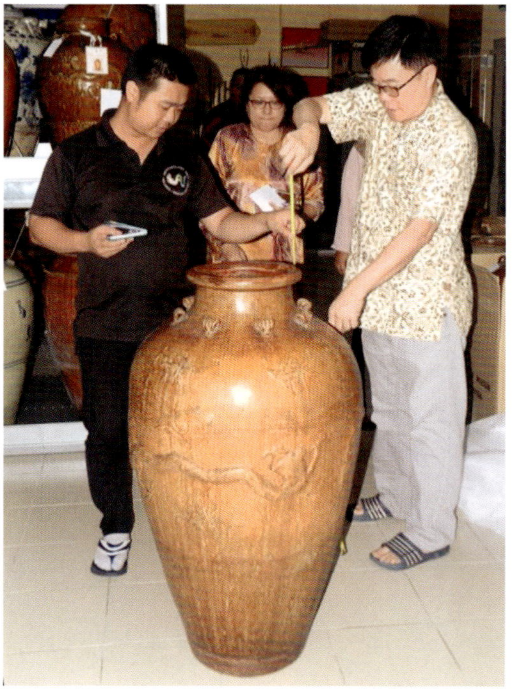

On the occasions of researching Vietnamese ceramics at museums or private collections in Southeast Asian countries, from Indonesia, Philippines, Malaysia and Singapore, I have found many Cam-Bình Định ceramics that were classified as Chinese ceramics dating from 12th to 16th centuries (**Fig. 1**). Among them there are many brown-glazed jars with straps on the shoulders, decorated with molded or engraved patterns that were called Martaban wares by Indonesian and Malaysian collectors. Martaban is the name of a port city located on the bay of Martaban in the Andaman sea, in the south of Myanmar. It is said that these jars were brought from the port of Martaban and their origin was probably China. Little was known about the dating, origin and function of these jars within the cultural and social life of contemporary societies. It was only known that these precious, expensive jars, were used as heirlooms among wealthy families.

In an attempt to discover the origin of precious jars found in the shipwrecks of Hội An, Pandanan or Thăng Long Imperial Citadels (Hanoi), from 2014 until now, we have conducted many archaeological investigations and excavations at Trường Cửu and Gò Cây Me kiln sites. The results were much new scientific data, contributing to understanding the ownership, dating and origin of various types of Bình Định ceramics. From this, vivid and clear evidence of the origin of the brown glazed jars for export has been revealed.

Based on archaeological and historical materials, and contemporary records, this paper introduces some new and important findings about Campā-Bình Định ceramics and examines them in the Asian commercial context in the 15th century.

I. Production Site and the Issue of Origin and Dating

1. Ceramic production site

Bình Định was known as the former Vijaya capital of the Campā kingdom, with a great history of development in ancient Southeast Asia. During the 11th-15th centuries, Vijaya served as the most important political, economic and cultural center of the Campā kingdom.

The Cam sites include the citadels like Cha citadel, Đồ Bàn citadel, Thị Nại citadel; the temples at Dương Long, Cánh Tiên, Hưng Thạnh tower, Bánh Ít tower as well as the ceramic production sites located along the banks of the Côn river (see Map 1).

Map 1 *Ceramic kilns in the Campā cultural heritage complex in Bình Định province.*

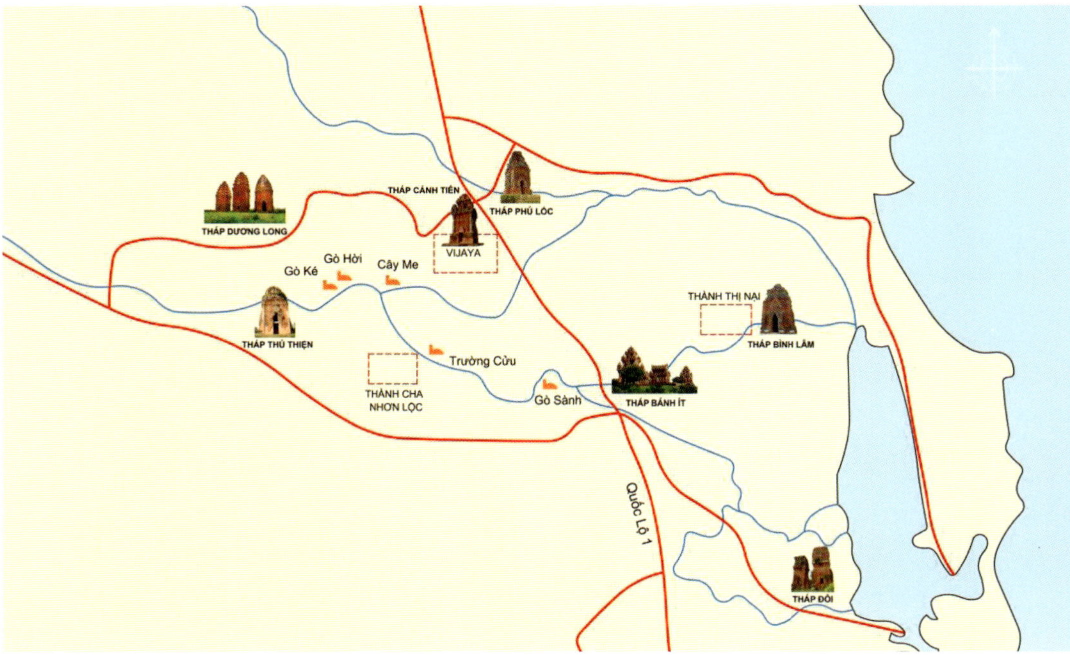

In the early 1990s, investigation work into Gò Sành ceramics began and many ceramic production sites were found. These were the sites of Gò Hời, Gò Ké, Gò Giang (Tây Vinh commune, Tây Sơn district), Trường Cửu (An Nhơn commune, An Nhơn district) and Gò Cây Me (Nhơn Mỹ commune, An Nhơn district). Of these six ceramic production centers, four sites have now been archaeologically excavated and researched. They were Gò Sành, Gò Hời, Trường Cửu and Gò Cây Me.

The Gò Sành site was excavated for the first time in 1990-1994 by Vietnamese archaeologists One was a joint excavation with Japanese archaeologists under the leadership of Prof Gakuji Hasabe and the late Professor Yogi Ayagi.

Eight years later, in 2002, the site was excavated by a joint program between the Bình Định Museum, the Institute of Archeology and the Royal Museums of Fine Arts in Belgium. In 2014, the site of Trường Cửu was excavated for the first time by the Research Center of Imperial Cities (now the Institute of Imperial Citadel Studies – IICS).

In 2017-2018, the Institute of Imperial Citadel Studies in collaboration with the Museum of Bình Định Province excavated the site of Gò Cây Me.

The results of these excavations at the above-mentioned ceramic sites have found many traces of ceramic kilns and many types of products, reflecting a developed history of ceramic production in Bình Định during the heyday of the Vijaya period.

1.1. Trường Cửu Kiln site

The excavation at Trường Cửu kiln site in 2014 found four traces of the kilns and many types of products, proving Trường Cửu was one of the large ceramic production centers in Bình Định, developed in the 14th and 15th centuries (Bùi Minh Trí, Đào Thế Tuấn, 2017: 119-147).

Although only the remains of the kiln floor were found, comparative studies with the kilns found at Gò Sành in 1991-1994 and Gò Hời in 2002 revealed that the ceramic kilns at Trường Cửu were of the tunnel kiln type. The furnace had a length of about 800 cm to 900 cm, and the body was about 300 cm wide. It is noteworthy that Trường Cửu kiln was built with pure soil (Vietnamese: *Trình tường*) and saggars.

Incandescent saggars were chosen to build the kiln wall by filling them with sandy clay and then compacting it. Each saggar was stacked together to form a very solid wall. Clay was used to bond between saggars, and after they were built, wet earth was used to cover the saggar to ensure the temperature inside the kiln. The dome arch of the kiln was lost, but based on traces among the debris, it is thought that they used bamboo to build the frame and embankment and to create the dome. This was a traditional technique that was popular in North Vietnam.

An important finding in the research on the history of ancient Bình Định ceramics was a 'door for transferring products' in the side body of the kiln, also called the oven door. At the excavation site of Gò Sành in 1994, although there were traces of doors for transferring products in the furnace in the north, the excavators did not recognize it as the oven door. At Trường Cửu, we not only found the oven door in the south, but also found the entrance to the oven door which was delineated by a funnel-shaped wall. This finding clarifies the technical tradition of the Bình Định ceramic kilns and decodes the technical similarities with the kilns in Gò Sành and Gò Hời.

Archaeologists have unearthed and discovered many sites of ancient ceramic kilns in the North of Vietnam, most of which were 'frog kilns', 'funnel gourd shaped ovens' and 'dragon ovens'. However, they did not find the type of 'tunnel oven' as in Trường Cửu or Gò Sành, Gò Cây Me. In 2014, at the Quả Cảm kiln (Bắc Ninh province), we found a terracotta kiln with a unique saggar-made wall construction technique. This type of 'long tunnel kiln' was similar in technology to the 'tunnel kiln' in Bình Định (Đặng Thị Khương, Cao Thị Huyền, Lê Viết Nga, 2015: 125-147).

Technological studies show that the oven door only appears in the type of furnace with a long body or with many rooms for firing such as the type of dragon kiln. Accordingly, the type of tunnel kiln in Trường Cửu, Gò Sành or Gò Cây Me is a type of kiln with a long body, which has a large and long firing Chamber, and so an additional door is made in the body to facilitate placing the products for firing and withdrawing the products after finishing firing. Types of frog kiln or funnel gourd shaped kiln often have a shorter body, so the additional doors in the side body were not made. The entrance door of this type of kiln was usually the front door, where there was a firing chamber. In other words, the door of the frog kiln or funnel gourd shaped kiln has a dual function, which is both the place of entry of products and the firing material (Nishimura Masanari and Bùi Minh Trí, 2004).

The above analysis shows that the type of tunnel kiln with additional doors in the body that was unearthed at the Trường Cửu and Gò Cây Me sites was a new and important discovery, not only contributing to clarifying the traditional pottery production technique in Bình Định but also being very significant in the study of ancient pottery kilns in Vietnam.

Although the excavated area was small, besides finding traces of four ceramic kiln foundations, the excavation at Trường Cửu uncovered a very large quantity of artifacts:18,237 including 11,998 ceramics, manufacturing tools, terracotta and architectural materials.

Trường Cửu ceramics are very rich and diverse with six ceramic lines, namely, celadon, white-glazed ceramics, brown-enameled ceramics, brown iron under glaze and brown-patterned ceramics. In these six ceramic lines, the most common were white glaze and blue glaze (or light blue) and brown glaze ceramics.

Trường Cửu kilns produced a great variety of bowls, plates, cups and large bowls, but they also produced large and small jars in a variety of sizes and designs. Vases and jars at the Trường Cửu kilns with brown glaze, have a shoulder strap attached and the body is normally slippery without decoration. The glaze on the body of jars from Trường Cửu is transparent and smooth with many different shades: dark brown or black brown, light brown, orange brown, yellow brown or green.

It is noteworthy that for the first time at Trường Cửu, we were fortunate to find wasters of brown patterned ceramics with very distinct characteristics of materials and glazes. They are large fragments of basins or jars, with thick, white glaze or light blue glaze, decorated with engraved patterns and floral motifs in brown. The shapes, decorative patterns, and the technique of sweeping glaze around the pattern all reflect the specific characteristics for making the brown, patterned ceramics of the Trần dynasty. This finding was important because brown patterned wares were hitherto considered unique to North Vietnam, the Lý dynasty (1010-1225) to the Trần dynasty (1225-1400) (Bùi Minh Trí, 2012: 69-74).

Along with the discovery of brown, patterned ceramics in the style of Đai Viet in the Trần dynasty, we also found glazed tiles and unglazed tiles (terracotta) and also architectural tiles for decorating the temples. The roof tiles are popular with rectangular tiles, including two main types, which are leaf-shaped and lotus-shaped. While the leaf-shaped tiles were popular tiles among the Cam, the lotus-shaped tiles are typical of Đại Việt. This type of roof tile was found on the roofs of palaces in Thăng Long royal palace during the Trần dynasty (Tống Trung Tin-Bùi Minh Trí, 2010; Bùi Minh Trí, 2016). According to Ma Doan, interpreter of Minh Emperor Zhengde who visited Vijaya in around 1413, the palatial roofs in the Campā citadels were covered by 'ellipse-shaped' small tiles – probably leaf tiles.

By studying the techniques and types of products, especially based on the brown iron underglaze ceramics, brown patterned ceramics, and lotus tiles, we have determined the dating of the Trường Cửu ceramic kilns. The ceramic kilns in Trường Cửu began to produce ceramics from the first half of the 14th century and lasted until the end of the 15th century (Bùi Minh Trí, Đào Anh Tuấn, 2017).

1.2. Gò Cây Me Kilns site

The excavation of Gò Cây Me in 2017-2018, uncovered eleven traces of ceramic kilns and 39,497 artifacts. Like the Gò Sành, Trường Cửu and Gò Hời kilns, we found mainly the tunnel kiln type, having a structure consisting of three parts: the oven, furnace body and the post furnace. It has a length of about 800 cm, a 300 cm wide body and the firing chamber of about 100 cm. The kiln wall was built from saggars full of soil. The tail sections are square in shape with baffles and a horizontal smoke outlet system. Above are the

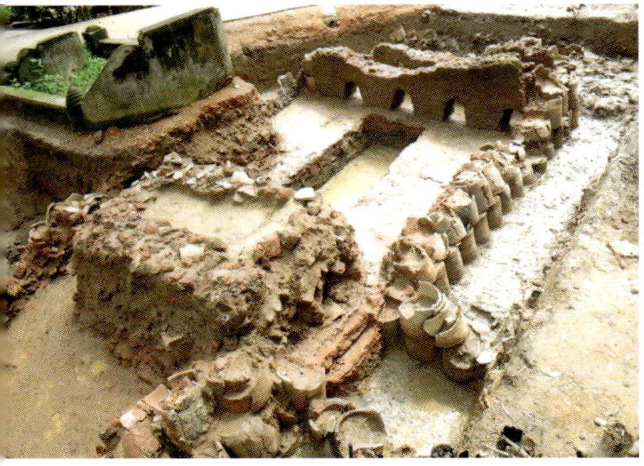

Fig. 2 *Vestige of kilns at Gò Cây Me site, excavated in 2017-2018. Source: Bùi Minh Trí*

chimney system, the middle of the furnace, and, to the left, an entrance door for transfering the products (**Fig. 2**).

The products of Gò Cây Me are very diverse, producing many kinds of products in one kiln, including ceramics, terracotta and architectural materials. Gò Cây Me ceramics have three main types of glaze: white glaze, brown glaze and brown iron under glaze, of which the most common are the brown glaze wares. At Gò Cây Me kilns, we have not found the typical celadon such as bowls, plates excavated at Gò Hời and Trường Cửu.

The jars at Gò Cây Me were mostly brown-glazed jars, with a funnel-shaped mouth, egg-shaped body, small base, flat bottom, and having four or six straps on the shoulder. The brown glaze covers from the mouth rim to the lower body, but not the base. The enamel is melted and uneven, and the surface has many tiny bubbles due to shrinkage when firing.

The excavations at Gò Cây Me site also unearthed four pieces of dragon-shaped molds and a variety of jars decorated with dragons (**Fig. 3**).

This showed that there was a group of professional and experienced potters in the Gò Cây Me kilns managing the production of large jars to serve the domestic markets as well as for export.

Surprisingly, the clay of Gò Cây Me jars and vases is often very thin, and they could be carried easily. In Đại Việt jars potters used molds to make separate decorative patterns, then applied these dried patterns on the body of the jars. The decorative patterns were applied after the jars were covered with enamel thus the patterns were usually left unglazed. This is a very distinctive difference in technique between Đại Việt and Campā ceramics.

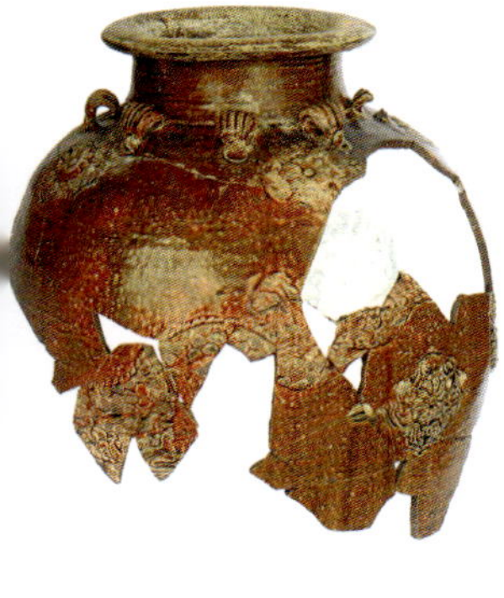

Fig. 3 *Brown-glazed jar with molded-dragon decoration, Gò Cây Me site, excavated in 2018. Source: Bùi Minh Trí*

Molded decorations on Campā jars are often enameled and applied before enameling. First, the molded decoration was attached to the jar after the clay dried. Secondly, the molds were used to create patterns directly on the body when the clay was still wet and soft. The potters pressed the molds on the body, one hand held the mold, the other hand used the fingers to push outward to the concave parts of the mold to create the decorative patterns on the jar body. For the molded pattern of flowers inside the lozenge-shaped frame, patterns were attached in symmetrical positions around the body, sometimes interlaced with other patterns on the shoulders. But creating the large dragon pattern with a long, winding body was more complicated. Many small patterns had to be made to form a dragon. Then, when making the decorative pattern the potters used each mold and pressed around the body until the entire image of the dragon was completed from head to tail.

Trường Cửu and Gò Cây Me potters attained a very high technical level in constructing the kilns and producing the ceramics. They were not only very skillful in making ceramics using the potter's wheel, decorating with molded patterns or using the ring setter technique when placing the product on the saggars and inside the kilns, but they were also very creative in constructing the tunnel kiln. This type of kiln was developed from the type of funnel gourd-shaped oven by making the kiln body longer, capable of firing more products. In particular, they cleverly used saggars to build the kiln walls, and at the same time were very scientific in organizing the system of chimneys as well as making the entrance door in the side body of the kiln. By making a thick kiln wall and putting soil inside the saggar they not only strengthened the kiln wall but also ensured that the temperature inside the kiln was stable and capable of firing at a high temperature. This clear evidence of the professionality and traditional experience of Trường Cửu and Gò Cây Me potters. The question now arises: who were these professional potters and where were they from?

2. Ownership and Dating

2.1. Ownership

The ownership of Bình Định kilns was debated extensively from the 1980s and 1990s after the excavation of the Gò Sành ceramic site. Three different theories formed about the ownership of Bình Định kilns: the owners could have been Chinese, Cam or Vietnamese.

Chinese ownership was quickly rejected because this did not fit into the historical context. Most researchers think that the owners of Bình Định ceramic kilns were Cam, though the issue is not fully resolved.

The ceramic centers in Bình Định were built, in the Cam Vijaya kingdom. Folk tales in the area call the areas of the ceramic kilns *Hời hamlet*, the old name of the land of the Cam. Second, despite similarities with Đại Việt glazed pottery, some of the pottery has distinct Cam characteristics such as the engraved ancient Cam characters and leaf-shaped tiles for decorating temples.

The ownership question arises because the production techniques in the Bình Định kilns were very different from the traditional ceramic production of the Cam people. Traditionally people only made pottery by hand and did not use firing kilns. We can still observe Cam pottery-making at the village of Bầu Trúc (Ninh Thuận province) today. They are unaware of the technique of making glazed ceramics using the potter's wheel, and they also didn't know how to use ring setters or place the products onto the saggars and fire them at a high temperature in solidly built kilns like those in Gò Sành, Gò Hời, Trường Cửu or Gò Cây Me. Accordingly, the discovery of a series of glazed ceramic production centers in Bình Định of high technical level and completely different from the traditional ceramic making tradition of Cam people poses research questions, especially regarding the issue of ownership.

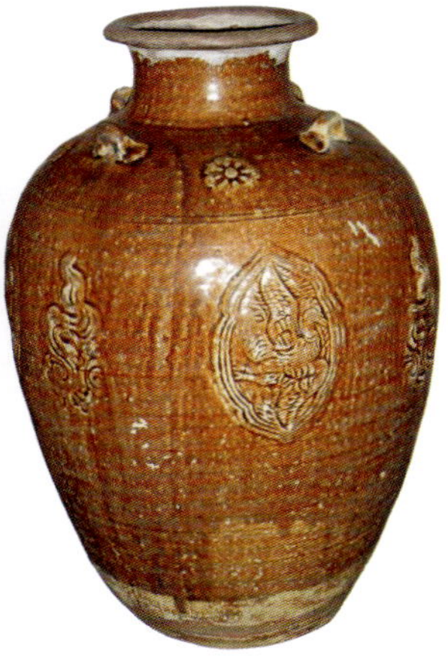

Fig. 4 *Brown-glazed jar with four handles, and molded swan pattern. Private collection in Bình Định province.*

In previous studies, we proved that ceramic making techniques at Trường Cửu kiln bore the technical characteristics of ceramic production of Đại Việt (Bùi Minh Trí, Đào Anh Tuấn, 2017: 119-45). It is noteworthy that in the 1980s, Roxanna Brown, from her first contact with fragments and saggars at Saigon National Museum collected by Hà Thúc Cần from the Gò Sành site noted that Gò Sành ceramics had many similarities in production techniques to those used in Northern Vietnam. She then suggested that 'the art of making glazed ceramics was introduced into Campā from Vietnam (Đại Việt) during the 13th-14th centuries' (Brown 1988: 36-9).

Based on the above analysis and on the new materials collected at Trường Cửu site, we have concluded that, during the historical formation and development of Trường Cửu ceramics, there might have been the participation of skillful potters from Đại Việt (Bùi Minh Trí, Đào Anh Tuấn, 2017: 119-45).

This analysis was based on the similarity of production techniques, typology, ceramic lines, and especially the finding of brown patterned ceramics, brown iron underglaze ceramics, ceramics with chocolate color on the bottom and types of tiles that bear Đại Việt cultural features. A new discovery of a type of brown yellowish jar decorated with half-moon-shaped patterns at Gò Cây Me site, as described below, is very interesting testimony to the profound influence of Đại Việt culture on Campā ceramics in Bình Định (**Fig. 4**).

The half-moon-shaped pattern on the ceramics of Thăng Long (Đại Việt) appeared on types of green-glazed, white-glazed and iron-white-glazed bowls. They were molded at the center while the iron brown bowls were decorated with such motifs on the inner body of the bowl. These motifs appeared on Thăng Long ceramics mainly in the 14th century. But it is interesting and unexpected that this motif also appeared on the brown-glazed ceramics at Gò Cây Me kilns in the first half to middle of the 15th century. On some types of huge dragon jars found in the Philippines and Malaysia, we also found the molded moon-shaped motifs in combination with Cam-style cloud and floral motifs. (**Fig. 1**).

Another type of carved pattern found, is related to Confucianism and the traditional culture of Viet people in the Red River delta, namely the "*Qui bối*" motif (turtle shell pattern). The implication of this motif is to convey the wish to live as long as the life of the turtle. In the culture of Cam people, we do not find this element. However, on many brown-glazed jars from Gò Cây Me site we do find this motif suggesting a profound influence from the art of Đại Việt ceramics.

In 1301 CE, King Trần Nhân Tông accepted an invitation from the Campā King to visit King Chế Mân (Jaya Sinhavarman III). Trần Nhân Tông stayed in the royal palace of Campā, from March to November. Trần Nhân Tông promised to marry his daughter to Chế Mân despite the fact that Chế Mân had a Queen named Tapasi from Java. In 1306 CE, Princess Huyền Trân became the third wife of Chế Mân. She was crowned as the second queen with the title Paramecvari and was considered as the most highly esteemed Queen. At the wedding ceremony, King Chế Mân brought many ceremonial objects, gold and silver, and including the territorial land of Ô and Lý prefectures (North of Quảng Trị and Thừa Thiên Huế nowadays) (Đại Việt sử ký toàn thư, 1998: 86, 90-1).

In such a historical context, it was possible that a group of Đại Việt potters migrated to Vijaya (Bình Định). They could find fine clay material in the lower Côn river and may have constructed ceramic kilns along the banks of that river.

We guess that a group of Đại Việt potters might have settled in Vijaya by the end of Tran period, in the 14th century. They could have constructed kilns specializing in making glazed ceramics close to the citadel in order to serve the needs of the Vijaya court, Cam communities as well as highlanders as far as Lâm Đồng plateau.

It is possible that there were groups of Cam people working there. Due to the size and the importance of these production centers in the commercial and economic development of Vijaya, we assume that they were put under the direct control of the Vijaya court. This is what happened at the official kilns in Thăng Long during the Lý, Trần and Lê period or the Jingdezhen kilns in China during the Song, Ming and Qing dynasties.

Even so, this does not mean that the owners of these kilns were Cam. For further research on Campā cultural history, I have proposed the name of Bình Định ceramics or Campā-Bình Định ceramics. This term is intended to separate the glazed ceramics of Bình Định kilns from the traditional earthenwares of the Cam people, commonly known as Cam pottery, and, at the same time, implies a separate type of glazed ceramics of Bình Định in the historical development of Vietnam's ancient ceramics.

2.2. Dating

Researchers basically agree that the ceramic kilns in Bình Định existed and developed mostly during the Vijaya period and ended in 1471 when the Đại Việt invaded. There are four major views on the dating of Bình Định ceramics.

- Vijaya period, from 13th to 15th centuries (Roxanna M. Brown, 1988; Le Dinh Phung, 1990, 1993; Dinh Ba Hoa, 2008, 2016 and others);
- 15th to 16th centuries (Bùi Chí Hoàng (chief editor), 2000);
- Vijaya period (11th to 15th centuries) and continued till 17th, 18th centuries (Kerry Nguyen Long, 1999);
- early 14th century till the end of the 15th century and ending by around 1471 (Bùi Minh Trí, Đào Anh Tuấn, 2017).

The third opinion of Kerry-Nguyen Long originated from the information that Japanese Hizen ceramics were found at ancient tombs in Đại Làng (Lâm Đồng province) along with many other Bình Định ceramics, which were defined by excavators as Gò Sành ceramics (Bùi Chí Hoàng, 2000). Kerry Nguyen Long assumed that 'the document from Đại Làng ancient tomb suggests production at a late stage of Bình Định ceramics, possibly in the late 17th or 18th centuries' (Kerry-Long, 1999: 105).

According to a report by Bùi Chí Hoàng, 20 Japanese Hizen ceramics were found in Đại Làng and Đạ Đường (Bùi Chí Hoàng, 2000: 62). Although, there were Bình Định monochrome ceramics found at these two sites they were not found together with the Hizen ceramics. There are many ancient graves in Đại Làng and Đạ Đường and the Hizen ceramics were found together with Chinese Ming ceramics rather than being found along with Bình Định and North Vietnam ceramics. Accordingly, the view of Bình Định ceramics existed till the 17th and 18th centuries is unreliable.

The view that Gò Sành or Bình Định ceramics date to the 15th to 16th centuries is based on the collections of North Vietnamese, Chinese, and Thai ceramics excavated at ancient graves in Lâm Đồng that were reported by Bùi Chí Hoàng. It is now clear that the ancient graves in Lâm Đồng province have the largest quantity of Bình Định ceramics, including very special ceramics as found in the shipwrecks of Hội An, Pandanan and at Thăng Long Imperial citadel.

Another issue to consider is the start date of Bình Định ceramic production centers. According to the first view mentioned above, Bình Định kilns were formed and developed from the 13th century. But when we examine carefully the excavation reports, it appears that those who proposed this point of view did not have convincing evidence of technical elements or distinctive art styles of Bình Định ceramics in the 13th century.

Studying the ceramics excavated at Gò Sành, Gò Hời and Gò Cây Me kilns, especially at the Trường Cửu kiln, we now have enough evidence to affirm that Bình Định kilns started in the 14th century, continued their activities in the 15th century and probably ended after the 1471 incursion.

The discoveries at Thăng Long citadel and at shipwreck sites mentioned in the next section will prove that there was a great development of Bình Định ceramics in the 15th century. A magnificent deity statue made of glazed ceramic found at the Yang Mum tower (Gia Lai province) is dated to the end of the 15th century, and this piece could be the last imprint of Bình Định kilns in history (**Fig. 5**).

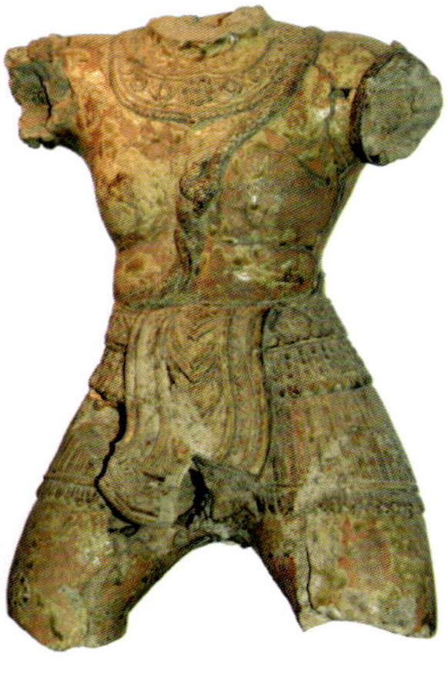

Fig. 5 *White-glazed statue of Siva, founded at Yang Mum site (Gia Lai province). Collection of Museum of History in Ho Chi Minh city. Source: Bùi Minh Trí*

II. Campā Ceramics in The Asian Maritime Trade Netwrok

As a coastal kingdom, Campā is often referred to by researchers as a "marine polity". Lying between the vast highland in the west and the ocean in the east, with a series of port cities Campā integrated well into the regional and international maritime trade networks, creating political, cultural and economic relations with major civilizations as China, India and also Southeast Asian countries.

Thị Nại was a major port and an economic and military centre. All the economic, political, religious and military power was located along the banks of the Côn river, creating an active region with favorable conditions for prosperous economic development.

Vestiges of the citadel, religious tower-temples, ceramic production centers and Thị Nại port are still visible nowadays in Bình Định and are evidence of Vijaya's prosperity during the period from 12th to 15th century (Map 1).

In the 15th century, the economy in Southeast Asia developed strongly, with the expansion of Sung dynasty trade. Accordingly, with many advantages in the natural resources, and with its huge ceramic production centres, Campā was very active in bringing unique local products to the international market.

The discovery of Campā-Bình Định ceramics together with North Vietnamese, Thai and Japanese ceramics at ancient graves in Đại Làng, Đại Lão, Đạ Đường in Lâm Đồng in the 1980s and 1990s, has shown that the vast mountain region in the west was a major market for Bình Định ceramics. Bình Định ceramics were found on the shipwrecks of Hội An, Sattahip (or Koh Khrom), Ko Si Chang (Thailand) and Pandanan (Philippines).

However, apart from the information regarding Campā ceramics found on the Pandanan shipwreck or at some archaeological sites in Bolino and Calatagan (the Philippines) or in Java, and Hội An (Đà Nẵng), there is relatively little information available on Cam ceramics.

From visits to collections in museums or private collections in Indonesia, the Philippines, Malaysia and Singapore, it appears that, Vietnamese ceramics are present in almost every island state in Southeast Asia, the largest collections being in Indonesia and the Philippines. However, it appears that Campā ceramics have been found together with North Vietnam ceramics at the sites but have been misidentified.

We know that, in 1971, the pioneering ceramicist William Willetts was unaware of Bình Định or Campā monochrome ceramics, and so identified the green glazed and brown glazed wares as Vietnamese.

The Pandanan shipwreck was excavated by the National Museum of the Philippines in 1995. Some 4,722 objects and fragments, mostly ceramics from Vietnam, China and Thailand were recovered. Vietnamese wares accounted for 70% with 3,288 bowls and dishes, 191 cups, dishes and jarlets. The ceramics collection from North Vietnam was small in number, mainly of blue and white ceramics, the rest was from central Vietnam. The light green-glazed bowls, dishes and brown-glazed cups, vases, and jars found on this shipwreck could all clearly be identified as Campā ceramics from the Bình Định kilns.

The most important discovery of Campā ceramics on this ship was 75 brown-glazed jars with a special shape and decoration. The jars include those decorated with molded patterns of chrysanthemum or apricot in a frame, intercropped with pillar-shaped or small daisy patterns, cloud patterns, a large jar decorated with a dragon on the body close to the straps on the shoulder and a fragment of a jar with a molded *Kāla* face typical of Campā.

The Chinese ceramics on the Pandanan shipwreck were dated to the reign of the Zhu Emperor Zhengtong (1436-49) and as most of the commodities originated from Vietnam, this ship could have set sail from Campā (Diem, 1988: 106-7).

In Brunei, there are no records of Campā ceramics found at archaeological sites, but in 1968 at the archaeological sites of Sungai Lumut and Kota Batu and Cam monochrome glazed bowls and dishes were found yet not identified.

Based on the dating of Chinese blue and white ceramics, the Brunei shipwreck was dated from late 15th to early 16th centuries, or during the Hongzhi period (1487-1505).

In addition, archaeological findings at Al Tur and Junfar indicate that Campā ceramics were exported to the Middle East together with Vietnamese blue-and-white ceramics and Chinese ceramics.

Al Tur was considered to be the richest Red Sea city in the 14th century. Since early 1985, Japanese archaeologists have excavated a collection of trade ceramics, including Vietnamese blue-and-white ceramics and Bình Định monochrome glazed wares.

In the Arabian Peninsula, north of Abu Dhabi, 15th century Vietnamese blue-and-white ceramics and green-glazed ceramics from Bình Định were also found at Junfar site. This was a busy trading port with the commercial exchange of ceramics from the 14th to the 16th century. Vietnamese ceramics, and Bình Định ceramics were found together with Chinese, Thai and 15th-century Persian ceramics. It's interesting to note that Campā-Bình Định ceramics and North Vietnamese ceramics were always shipped together to the markets in Southeast Asia and the Middle East.

Campā-Bình Định export ceramics were mainly monochrome glazed, while North Vietnamese export ceramics were mainly blue and white. The difference seems to have formed a great harmony in supplying the ceramic sources for diverse market needs in Southeast Asia and the Middle East. Besides daily-use ceramics, Bình Định kilns also produced and exported various types of large jars. An octagonal jar decorated with molded chrysanthemum flowers inside a frame, now kept at the National Museum of the Philippines is a typical example. Today we can observe countless rare Campā ceramics jars of perfect quality at museums or in private collections in Indonesia, the Philippines or Malaysia. However, they call Campā jars Chinese wares, or Martaban wares.

We know that the early Ming dynasty (1436-65 CE) ban on exports led to

Thailand, Burma, Đại Việt and Campā emerging as major export ceramic production centers.

The ceramic trade brought integration between Campā and the island world, with a creativity of cultures and rapid cultural integration facilitated by the maritime trade network.

It can be said that Islamic motifs inspired creativity in the Thăng Long and Vijaya potters.

The 15th century was the period that Vietnam engaged most actively in the ceramic export market with both Bình Định monochrome glazed ceramics and blue-and-white ceramics from the north (**Fig. 6**).

Vietnamese ceramics were exported to foreign markets mostly by foreign traders. The contemporary records indicate that Vietnamese traders – unlike the Cam – did not have much experience in seafaring. They did not take to the sea like the Cam did, but played a role as brokers and commodity collectors (Bùi Minh Trí, 2003: 49-74).

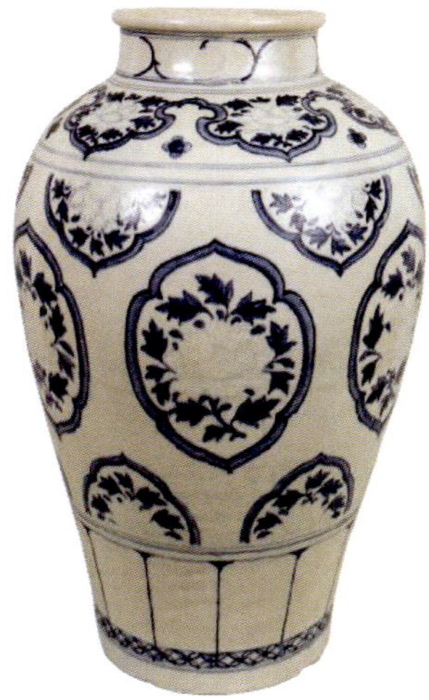

Fig. 6 *Blue-and-white jar in north Vietnam, 15th century. Source: Bùi Minh Trí*

III. Conclusion

Ceramic production centres in Bình Định were founded and developed during the heyday of the Vijaya polity. They produced glazed ceramics from the early 14th century till the second half of 15th century.

The participation in long distance trade of Bình Định ceramic not only proved the development at a very high level of Bình Định ceramics, but also reflected vividly the economic and cultural exchanges between Campā with Southeast Asian and West Asian countries. At the same time, given the strong relationship with Đại Việt, we believe that, ceramic kilns in Bình Định were put under the direct control of Vijaya court officials and enjoyed highly favourable conditions for integrating into the Asian maritime trade network.

References

Ann Degraeve, Miriam Lambrecht and Nguyen Tien Dong. 2006. 'The ancient kiln site of Gò Hời in Vietnam'. *Bulletin des Musées Royaux D'Art et D'Histoire Parc du Cinquantenaire Bruxelles*, Tome/Deel 77: 73-106.

Bùi Chí Hoàng (Chủ biên). 2000. *Những sưu tập gốm sứ ở Lâm Đồng*, Sở Văn hóa Thông tin Lâm Đồng, Đà Lạt – 2000.

Bùi Minh Trí, Lê Đình Phụng, Nguyễn Kim Thủy. 1993. 'Khu lò gốm Long Thọ (Thừa Thiên – Huế)' *Những phát hiện mới về khảo cổ học* : 222-223.

Bùi Minh Trí, Kerry-Nguyễn Long. 2001.*Gốm hoa lam Việt Nam – Vietnamese Blue & White Ceramics*, Nxb. Khoa học xã hội, Hà Nội.

Bùi Minh Trí. 2003. 'Tìm hiểu ngoại thương Việt Nam qua con đường gốm sứ trên biển' *Khảo cổ học*, số 5: 49-74.

Bùi Minh Trí. 2003. 'Gốm sứ cổ Việt Nam: Vấn đề niên đại và nguồn gốc', *Một thế kỷ Khảo cổ học Việt Nam*, Tập II, Nxb. Khoa học xã hội, Hà Nội: 390-407.

Bùi Minh Trí. 2012. Gốm Việt Nam thời Lý, *Khảo cổ học*, số 1: 69-74.

Bùi Minh Trí. 2015. 'Gốm Thăng Long thời Lê sơ và vai trò của nó trong đời sống Hoàng cung Thăng Long', *Thông báo Khoa học*, Trung tâm Nghiên cứu Kinh thành, Nxb. Khoa học xã hội, Hà Nội: 95-112.

Bùi Minh Trí. 2017. 'Gốm vẽ nhiều màu Việt Nam trong bối cảnh lịch sử – văn hóa châu Á', *Thông báo Khoa học 2017*, Trung tâm Nghiên cứu Kinh thành, Nxb. Khoa học xã hội, Hà Nội: 181-221.

Bùi Minh Trí – Đào Anh Tuấn. 2017. 'Di chỉ gốm Trường Cửu – Kết quả khai quật năm 2014', *Thông báo Khoa học 2017*, Trung tâm Nghiên cứu Kinh thành, Nxb. Khoa học xã hội, Hà Nội: 119-145.

Brown Roxanna M. 1988: *The ceramics of Southeast Asia: Their dating and Identification*, Oxford University Press, Singapore: 36-39.

Diệm Allison. 1988. 'Đồ gốm buôn bán bằng đường biển châu Á', *Khảo cổ học*, số 2: 106-107.

Diem Allison. 1998: Ceramics production in Central Vietnam (Vijaya)', *October 23-25*, Chicago.

Đại Nam thực lục chính biên. 1963. Tập IV, Đệ nhất kỷ tam, Nxb. Sử học, Hà Nội.

Đại Việt sử ký toàn thư, 1998, Tập II, Nxb. KHXH, Hà Nội.

Đặng Thị Khương, Cao Thị Huyền, Lê Viết Nga. 2015. 'Di chỉ gốm Quả Cảm: Nhận thức mới về đồ sành thời Lê sơ qua kết quả khai quật năm 2014', *Thông báo Khoa học*, Trung tâm Nghiên cứu Kinh thành, Nxb. Khoa học xã hội, Hà Nội: 125-147.

Đinh Bá Hòa. 1995. 'Di tích gốm Chăm trên đất Bình Định, *Nghiên cứu Đông Nam Á*, số 4: 97-100.

Đinh Bá Hòa. 1996. 'Hình rồng trên đồ gốm Gò Sành và hình rồng trên ché uống rượu của đồng bào Chăm ở Vân Canh', *Những phát hiện mới về khảo cổ học năm:* 626.

Đinh Bá Hòa, Trịnh Hồng Lan. 1991. 'Đào thám sát Gò Sành', *Những phát hiện mới về khảo cổ học năm 1991*: 195-197.

Đinh Bá Hòa, Võ Bá Thắng. 1997. "Gốm Campā những phát hiện và triển vọng nghiên cứu', *Những phát hiện mới về khảo cổ học năm 1997:* 655-658.

Đinh Bá Hòa. 2008. *Gốm cổ Campā Bình Định*, Nxb. KHXH, Hà Nội.

Đinh Bá Hòa. 2013. 'Về chủ nhân của gốm Chăm Bình Định', *Bình Định Online*, ngày 07/3/2013.

Đinh Bá Hòa 2016. 'Gốm cổ Campā Bình Định', *Xưa & Nay*, Hội Khoa học Lịch sử Việt Nam, số 467 tháng 1 năm 2016: 44-47.

Hanapi Haji Maidin. 2017. 'A preliminary study of Campā ceramics found in Brunei, Kỷ yếu Hội thảo quốc tế "Gốm cổ Bình Định – Vương quốc Vijaya và mối quan hệ với Thăng Long – Đại Việt, thế kỷ 11-15"', Viện Nghiên cứu Kinh thành, Hà Nội.

Kerry – Nguyen Long.1998. Decorative motifs on selection of Bình Định Wares, *Arts of Asia*: 84.

Kerry – Nguyễn Long. 1999. Di tích gốm cổ Bình Định, gốm và sản phẩm gốm liên quan, *Khảo cổ học*, số 3: 101-111.

Lại Văn Tới và cộng sự. 2015. *Báo cáo kết quả khai quật di tích thành Cha (Bình Định) lần thứ nhất, năm 2015*. Tư liệu Thư viện Viện Nghiên cứu Kinh thành.

Lê Đình Phụng 1990. 'Gốm Campā – một vài nhận xét', *Những phát hiện mới về khảo cổ học năm 1990*: 193-194.

Lê Đình Phụng. 1993. 'Các trung tâm sản xuất gốm Campā ở Bình Định', *Khảo cổ học*, số 3: 54-66.

Lê Đình Phụng – Đinh Bá Hòa. 1998. 'Khai quật Gò Sành lần thứ nhất', *Khảo cổ học*, số 2: 78-92.

Ngô Văn Doanh. 1994.*Văn hóa Campā*, Nxb. Văn hóa Thông tin, Hà Nội.

Nguyễn Bá Lăng. 1972. 'Gò Sành, một trung tâm sản xuất gốm cổ tại Bình Định', *Khảo cổ học tập san*, Sài Gòn: 36.

Nishimura Masanari and Bùi Minh Trí. 2004. Excavation of the Duong Xa site in Bắc Ninh Province, Vietnam', *Journal of Southeast Asia Archaeology*, Volume 24, Japan Society for Southeast Asian Archaeology: 91-131.

Tống Trung Tín – Bùi Minh Trí. 2010. *Thăng Long – Hà Nội: Lịch sử nghìn năm từ long đất*, Nxb. Khoa học xã hội, Hà Nội.

Trung tâm Nghiên cứu Kinh thành. 2015. *Báo cáo kết quả khai quật di chỉ gốm Trường Cửu (Bình Định) năm 2014*. Tư liệu Thư viện Trung tâm Nghiên cứu Kinh thành.

Viện Nghiên cứu Kinh thành. 2017. *Báo cáo kết quả khai quật di chỉ gốm Gò Cây Me (Bình Định) năm 2017*. Tư liệu Thư viện Viện Nghiên cứu Kinh thành.

William Willetts. 1971. *Ceramic art of Southeast Asia*, Singapore.

16 | Cam ritual objects

Anne-Valéry Schweyer

The Vietnamese Museum of History in Hồ Chí Minh, conserves magnificent examples of Cam metal ritual objects dating to the 10th-18th centuries. Some bear inscriptions that help us discern their ceremonial use in ritual practice. They include dishes, offering plates and vases, bowls and vases for libation, incense-burners, and betel boxes. We will study the circumstances of their discovery and their deposition in the Museum. A more detailed study will then focus on both the inscriptions on the objects and an ethnographic account of how the different forms that evolved for ceremonies.

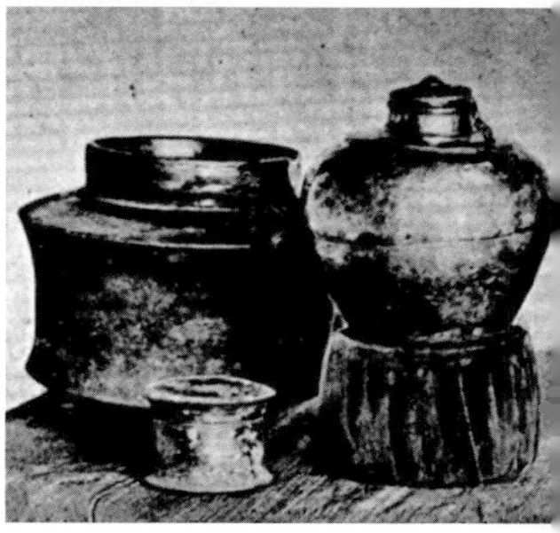

Fig. 1 *Vases found in Po Klong Garai sanctuary in 1901: upper left a* vatā, *upper right a* ghaṭa. *BEFEO 1901 fig. 72, p. 409. (Courtesy of the EFEO)*

Discovery and conservation of Cam ritual vessels

These objects emerged from multiple sources – hidden caches unearthed in excavations, a royal family collection, donations. Before the historical events that shook Việt Nam in the course of the 20th century, numerous objects had been unearthed that had been hidden during raids. Such caches are often called 'treasures'. They are difficult to date for the Cam country in central Việt Nam underwent many periods of conflict when precious objects were removed from the sanctuaries and hidden to await a more peaceful time. Such could have been the case for objects of the 'La Thọ treasure' apparently buried in the 11th century CE in Điện Bàn district, Quảng Nam province.[1] Similarly for the objects conserved by descendants of the royal family, as in the royal deposit of Tịnh Mỹ, conserved on the site of the former Cam capital of Bal Canar or Palei Canar on the Phan Rí plain. There are also objects without real provenance which were found by farmers and sold. Other 'treasures' have been identified, like that of La Thọ, or the one found in 1901[2] in the sanctuary of Po Klong Garai [Fig. 1], or the one found in sanctuary C at Mỹ Sơn, where a deity's jewellery was hidden beside silver bowls.[3]

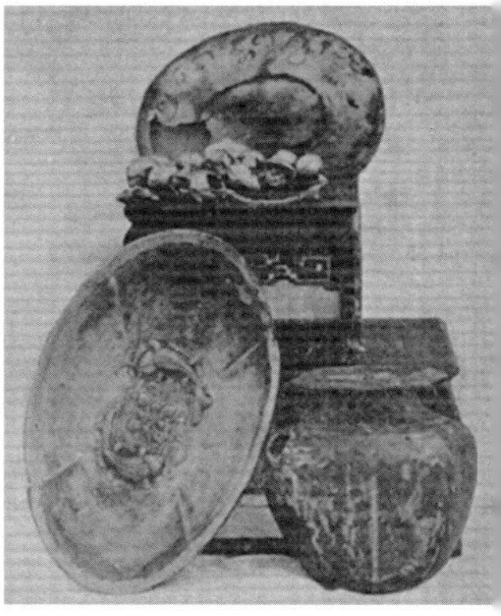

Fig. 2 *La Thọ silver objects found in 1911: top a plate or offering dish, below left a plate or* bhājana *and, below right a ewer or* kalaśa. BEFEO *1911 fig. 44, p. 473. (Courtesy of the EFEO)*

The La Thọ treasure was discovered under piles of bricks from a former sanctuary. It contained a necklace made with 12 golden beads, a gold ring with sapphire, a silver dish, a silver plate and a small silver ewer. The 1911 photograph in Fig. 2 shows the plate with two fish and the ewer.

Early in the 20th century, several deposits of precious objects were recorded in the provinces of Ninh Thuận and Bình Thuận, there where the Cam traditions still exist, or on the high plateau. In their 1905[4] publication, Henri Parmentier and Eugène-Marie Durand, inventoried eight deposits protected by the Cams or their allies at Tịnh Mỹ /Bal Canar, in Bình Thuận, at Phước Đông/Mblang Kacak, Hậu Sanh/Thuận et Hữu Đức/ Hamu Tanran in Ninh Thuận province and at Palei Cvah/Cuah, Lavang, Palei Praik/Praik Riyom and Kajong towards the plateau. Marcel Ner in

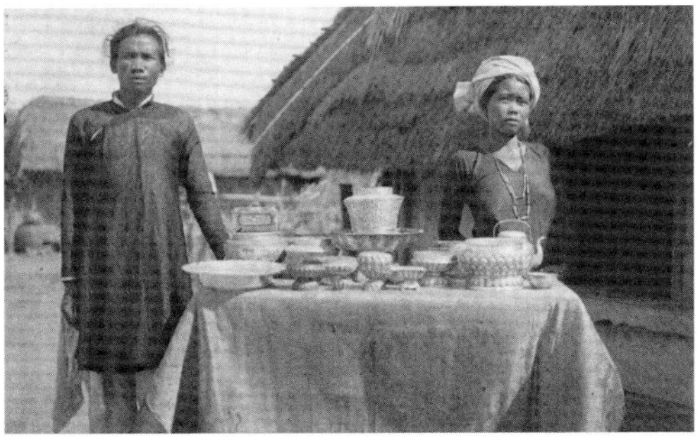

Fig. 3 *Silverware of the Tịnh Mỹ /Bal Canar royal deposit. At the centre is a* vatā, *placed on an offering stand and immediately in front an offerings vase. On the right of the table is an imposing betel vase. Photothèque EFEO no. 931.*

1930[5] and Nghiêm Thẩm in 1957-59[6] enriched the descriptions. However the wars of the 20th century decimated these former royal possessions; stolen or melted down, pieces in gold or silver are found only rarely today. The treasure said to be that of two kings Po Klauṅ Maḥ Nai and Po Klauṅ Gahul,[7] the royal deposit of Tịnh Mỹ, comprised 22 articles in gold (vases, cups in many forms, tiaras and diadems) and eight in silver. According to the 1902[8] inventory, this was considered to be the property of a Cam princess, descended from a branch of the royal family. A photograph kept in Paris [Fig. 3] shows the descendants of the royal family posing with the most beautiful pieces, of which only four are known today.

The Cam metal vessels underwent the turbulent history of Việt Nam and studying them is difficult. When archaeological excavations brought the precious objects to light, they were deposited in the Museum of History in Hanoi[9] in 1953. Thus pieces from the La Thọ treasure, the bowl and incense holder of Po Nagar in Nha Trang were conserved along with the three 'beautiful pieces' from the Tịnh Mỹ deposit, which were offered to the Museum 'in honour of the Cams' in 1928. It was Jean-Yves Claeys who placed these last in Hanoi with an illustration [Fig. 4], which enables us to identify them. Most of these objects were transferred to the Museum in Hồ Chí Minh City in 1954, where they may be seen today.

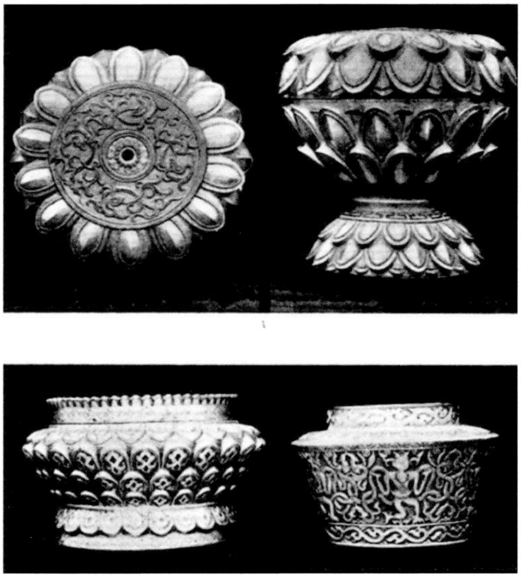

Fig. 4 *Top, a vase for presenting offerings, decorated with rows of lotus petals; bottom left, a vase for storing ingredients for betel quids with a flat top as a serving tray; bottom right, a decorated vase or batā.*

Cam ritual vessels

A. Inscriptions

Some of the objects in the Museum of History in Hồ Chí Minh bear inscriptions which offer information on both the deity honoured and the dedicator from the royal family. The texts usually take the form 'offered by X or Y to divinity Z', but sometimes there is only the name of the deity and the name of the king.

The inscriptions[10] are the only means for naming the form of a vessel from these times, because no ritual, oral or written, has survived to help clearly identify the vessels. Names from the modern era suggest that ritual use has been profoundly modified for there is little correspondence, except for the *batā/vatā* that will be discussed below. The semantic evolution may be explained by linguistic influence: in earlier centuries Sanskrit was predominant in the Cam inscriptions, through the adoption of the *brāhmī* script from India. In modern Eastern Cam there is no remnant of Sanskrit, which is replaced by Malay or Vietnamese influence, dependent on the period when the words fixed themselves in the vocabulary.[11] The short list of objects with inscriptions in Sanskrit or Old Cam is in Annex 1.

Among the La Thọ pieces, inscription C.143 [Fig. 5b] is inscribed on a dish [Cat. 38.a] which bears a motif of two fish in relief. [Fig. 5a]. The motif is typical Tang Chinese. The inscription under the dish has almost disappeared; only three syllables remain *ajñā po*, which are elements of a title of members of the royal family in the 10th century CE. One can therefore suggest the dish was offered to the divinity of a temple by one close to the king.

A silver dish, in poor condition at discovery, has now disappeared. It bore inscription C.144 [Fig. 6], with the deity name śrī Vanāntareśvara, the 'Lord of the interior of the forest'.

Sanskrit inscription C.145[12] is indited on a small jug or ewer [Fig. 7], whose spout is missing [Cat. 85]. It says: 'To this blessed Vanāntareśvara, who is famous everywhere, the king of Campāpura [gives] of his own faith this silver ewer'. A king of a 'kingdom of Campā' therefore offered it to the 'Lord of the interior of the forest'. The site where these three pieces of silverware were discovered has not been precisely identified[13] nor explored, but this enigmatic divinity could have been a local forest spirit erected for divine protection.

Three silverware objects published in 1999, but now lost, are remarkable. The group includes a ewer, an incense holder and a tray datable to the 9th century CE. Two of the pieces found in Đồng Dương were offered by a king named Rudravarman to a divinity named Rudrasvayambhuveśvara. The small ewer [Fig. 8] bears the Sanskrit inscription C.205[14], which says: 'This silver ewer was donated by śrī Rudravarmadeva to śrī Rudrasvayambhuveśvara'.

C.206[15] is inscribed on an object which resembles a perfume burner or an incense-holder [Fig. 9] and reads: 'śrī Rudravarmmadeva gave (…) with (its) holder'.

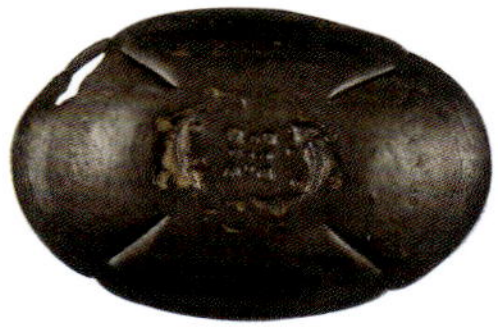

Fig. 5a *Dish with fish motif serving to make offerings for a divinity.*

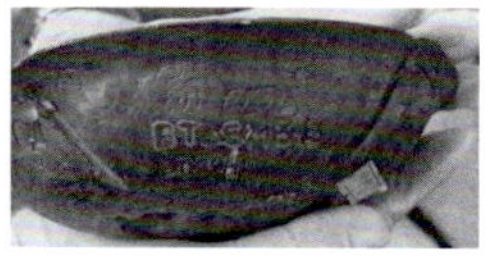

Fig. 5b *Inscription C.143 on the dish with fish.* BEFEO *2008: 476, fig. III. 7.2. (Courtesy of the EFEO)*

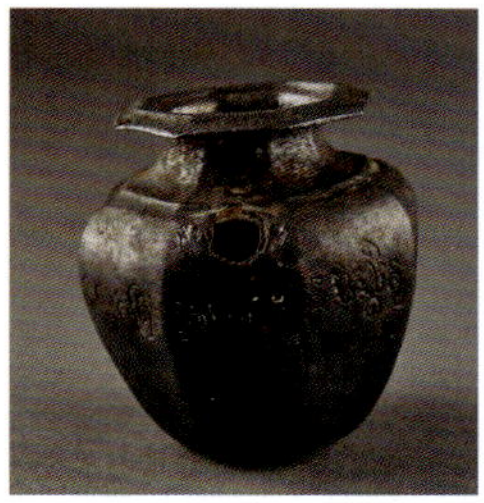

Fig. 7 *Ewer BTLS.1295 from the La Thọ treasure.*

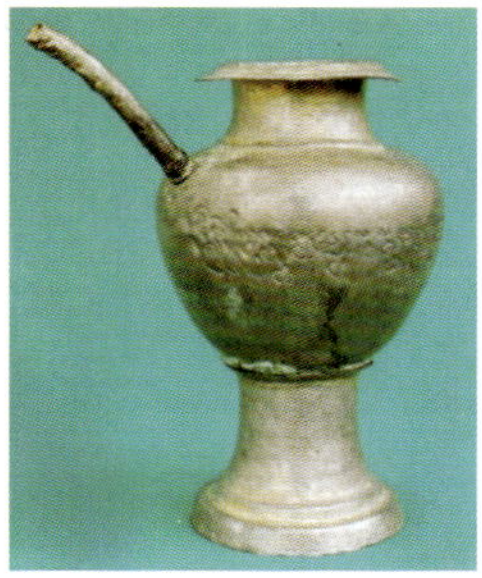

Fig. 8 *Silver ewer from Đồng Dương, Quảng Nam province, with inscription C.205. The foot and spout are modern. (Photo Vu Kim Loc 1998)*

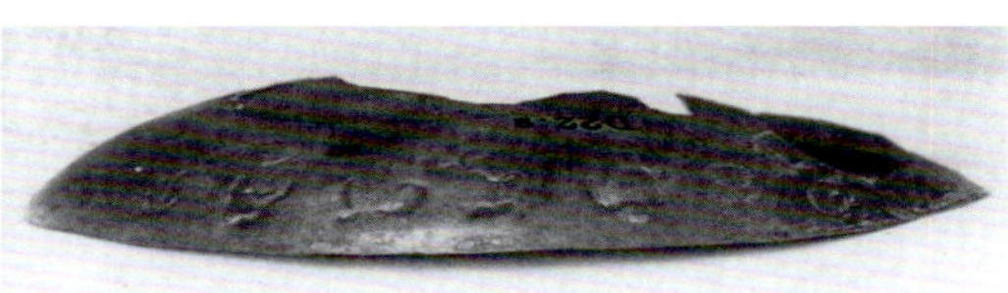

Fig. 6 *Silver dish from the La Thọ treasure bearing inscription C.144. Photothèque EFEO no. 01203.*

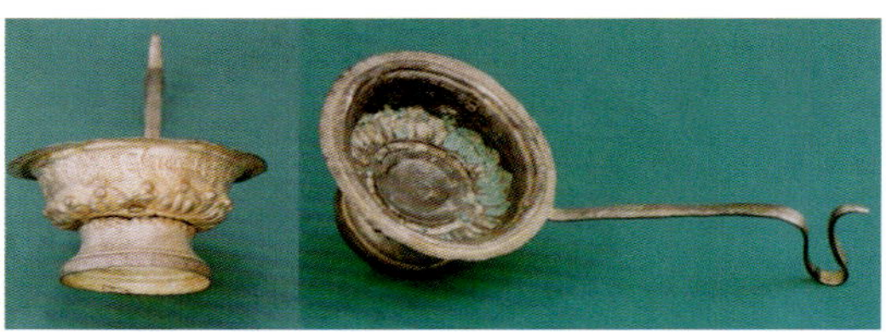

Fig.9 *Incense holder or offering presenter from Đồng Dương with inscription C.206. The handle is modern. (Photo Vu Kim Loc 1998)*

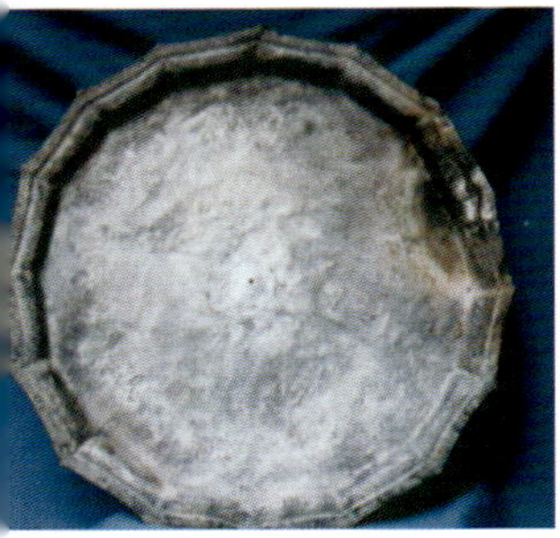

Fig. 10 *Silver tray from the district of Đại Lộc, north of the Thu Bồn river, in Quảng Nam province. It bears inscription C.207. (Photo Vu Kim Loc 1998)*

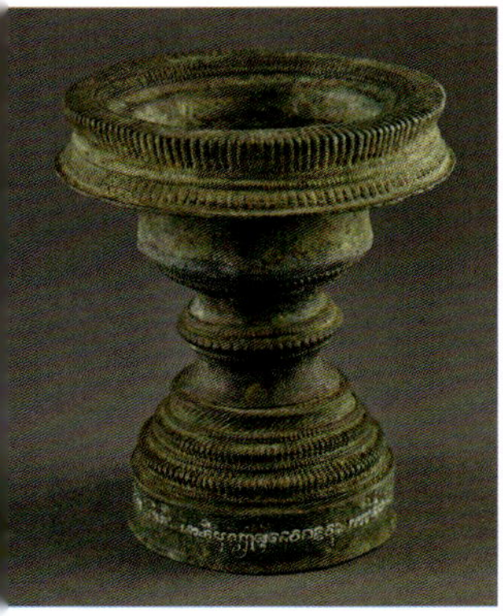

Fig. 11 *Incense-holder BTLS 24202 in bronze with a 12th century inscription.*

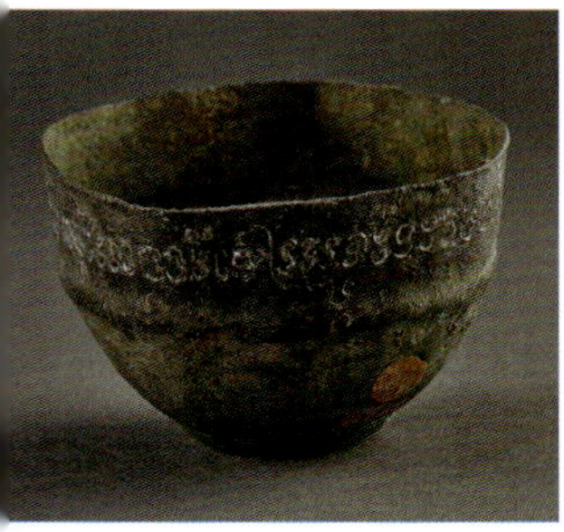

Fig. 12 *Small silver receptacle BTLS.1302 with inscription C.118 is dated to the late 12th century CE.*

The existence of these cult objects suggests that before the expansion of the Đồng Dương sanctuary, the grandfather of king Indravarman[16] had built a sanctuary to a divinity, a self-manifested form of Śiva/Rudra, to whose name he had added his own to show the link that united him to this protector god. The divinity[17], probably in the form of a stone *liṅga*, had apparently emerged from the earth to manifest his interest in Rudravarman.

The admirable silver tray [Fig. 10] has the Sanskrit inscription C.207[18] that proclaims: 'Happiness! To Blessed Śrī Bhadraliṅgeśvara, this son of Śrī Bhadravarman, kṣatriya, (noble) which bears a name of good omen, for the fame of the essence of Bhṛsu, gave this silver dish out of devotion to him'.

Two further objects from the 12th century CE dedicated to the goddess Po Nagar of Nha Trang were discovered when the sanctuary was excavated. A small bowl or lid [Fig. 12] carries the Old Cam inscription C.118[19] saying: 'The blessed king Śakrānta from Mandā-Vijaya gives (this) to the goddess Po Nagar in the year of the king of Śaka 1119 (1197 CE)'. It is an offering to the Po Nagar goddess from an otherwise unknown Cam king.

An incense-holder [Fig. 11] bears inscription C.208[20] which says: 'Majesty of majesties, the prince Pamṅ, Sir Dhiḥ, man of Rupaṅ, son of P. L. Śrī Devarāja, offered this incense-holder to the image of Parameśvarī [Durgā] in [the year] 1052 of the king of Śaka [1130 CE].' In this case a crown prince in the 12th century offers a perfume holder to a goddess (probably Po Nagar).

This small array of inscribed texts shows that ritual instruments were offered to divinities by kings or members of the court in exercising their cults. They also had a practical role. The inscription rendered visible to the god and the people the value of giving and the benefits for the donor: it played a social role proclaiming the glory of the divinity and its generous donor.

B. Types of vessels

Objects found include liquid containers for divinity libations, trays or plates for offerings and containers for burning incense. Their names are hardly known and have changed over time. In Old Cam we can recognise a great variety of ritual vessels in gold or in silver. They are categorised under the Sanskrit nouns *paribhoga* 'cult utensils' or *upabhoga* 'objects of use'. They form the largest object group made of precious metals. These include the badges of divinity or royalty – such as parasols, flywhisks, fans, palanquins, canes, swords with scabbard, *omkara*[21] – or cult vessels. The indications of weight or value of the vessels are often found in the Old Cam inscriptions but are very rare in the Sanskrit inscriptions where they appear only from the 11th century CE. But paradoxically most nouns recognised as distinguishing the forms of vessels are in Sanskrit.

It is thanks to the inscribed vessels now held in the museums that we can recognise certain types of vessels. The inscriptions in fact name numerous objects we can no longer identify today, because they have not been associated with any known forms. This absence strongly limits our knowledge of the old ritual vessels, for the utensils used today in Cam rituals appear less varied and have names one does not find in the inscriptions (with the notable exception of *batā/vatā*). It is however possible to distinguish water vases from trays or plates and censors (see Annex 2). A quick glance allows us to discern the ritual objects known in the inscriptions from the 8th-mid 13th centuries CE, essentially in Quảng Nam and on the Po Nagar site in Nha Trang (Annex 3). We cannot however limit the diffusion of these objects to these findspots, as we know only a minute fractions of the objects in precious metal that could have been made and which were mostly pillaged and/or melted down.

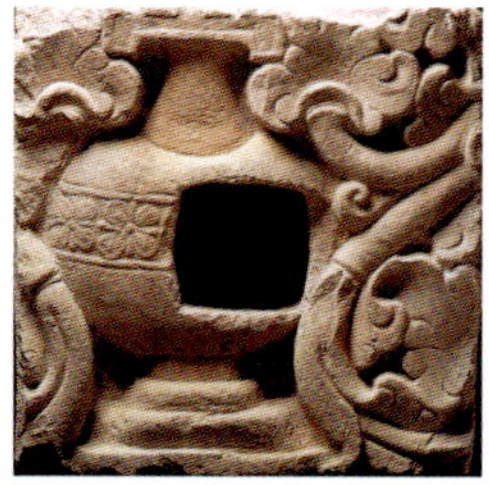

Fig. 13 *Sculpture representing a vase of abundance or* purnaghata *from Đa Nghi, in Quảng Trị. 7th century CE. Đà Nẵng Museum of Cam Sculpture.*

Water vases

The *kalaśa* is an ewer often mentioned in the inscriptions. In modern Cam it is called *kalaih.*[22] It is a water vase of small to medium size with or without a spout, which is still in use in India today, but which is not found in the later Cam treasures, even though they are mentioned in certain rituals.[23] It was used for pouring libation water into a larger receptacle. It was essential in the ceremonies. Whether the divinity honoured was a *liṅga* of Śiva, an anthropomorphic representation of the god or a simple sacred stone representing a local spirit, all the rituals included the ablution of the divinity with liquids drawn with an ewer from a larger receptacle. The ewer is often mentioned among the donations made to the gods by kings up to the 13th century CE.

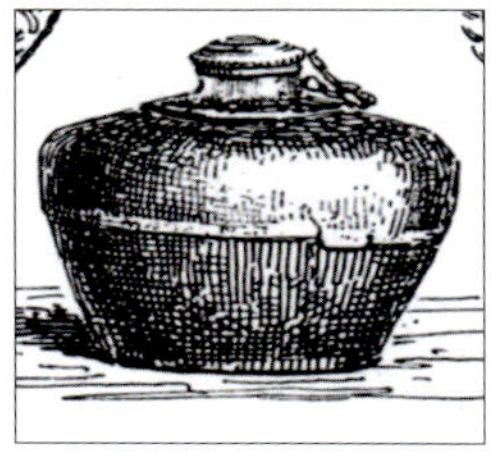

Fig. 14 *Po Klong Garai treasure: golden vase with lid and chain.* BEFEO *1901 fig. 73, p. 410. (Courtesy of the EFEO)*

Two ewers [Figs. 7 and 8] with inscriptions written in Sanskrit using Old Cam characters[24] are called *kalaśa*. A ewer is particularly precious because it is used to raise the libation liquid for pouring on the divine image. The *ghata* is a ewer of larger format. There is an image of one from the 7th century CE from the Đa Nghi site in Quảng Trị,[25] province that is like a symbol of fertility and abundance [Fig. 13].

One *ghata* was recovered in an early 20th century excavation[26] at the Po Klong Garai site in Ninh Thuận province [Fig. 14]. It is now lost.

The *kumbha* or *kuṇda* is another vessel for liquids. An 11th century inscription describes the *kumbha* as 'a golden water vase from the place where the goddess is installed'. The vase itself was honoured as a divinity, as can be found today in India during the important *Lakṣmīpūja.*[27]

The *bhṛṅgāra* appears to be a small ritual vessel. Although we have nothing to prove it, we may consider this form to be that of the small receptacle found in the Po Nagar sanctuary [Fig. 12] bearing an inscription in Old Cam. Bowls of this kind [Fig. 17] were in widespread ritual use from the 17th century CE.

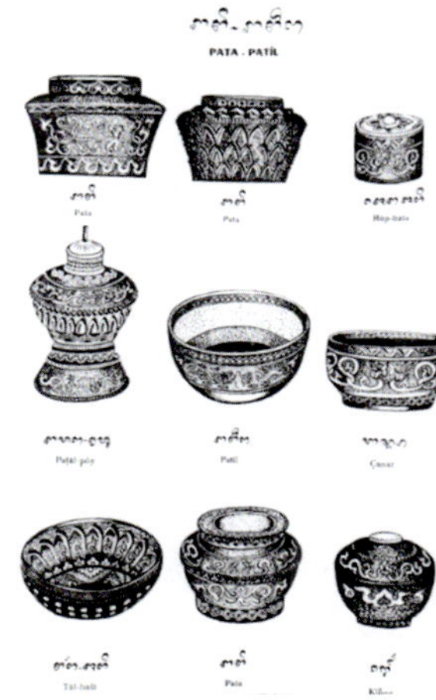

Fig. 15 *G. Moussay Dictionnaire Cam-Vietnamien-Français 1971 p. 269. Metal vases used in Phan Rang in the 20th century. (Author's photo)*

One form used later is taken to be a water vase, a *batā*[28] or *vatā*. This is found in two Cam inscriptions from the 11th and 12th centuries.[29] It is mentioned in the description of a coronation ceremony[30], where a cup of

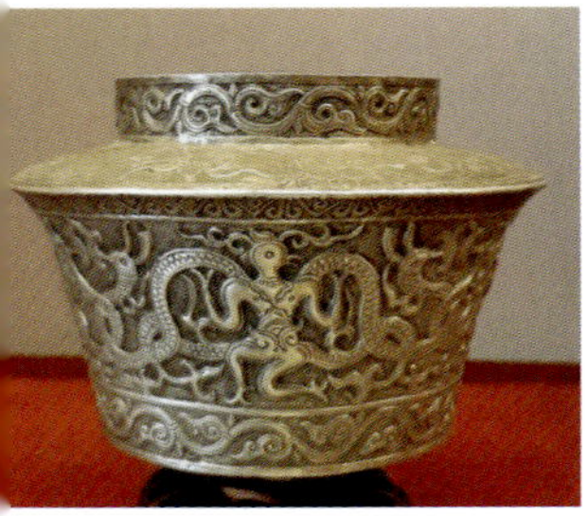

Fig. 16 *Batā in silver decorated with 'garuts' and 'inögarais'. Museum of Phan Thiết, Bình Thuận province. (Author's photo)*

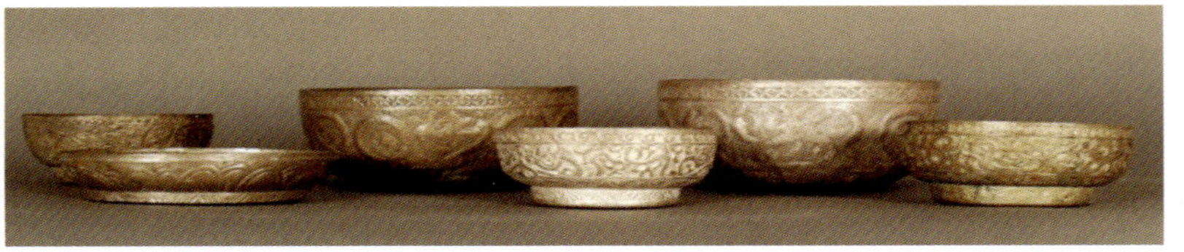

Fig. 17 *Silver offering bowls. 18th century. Private collection. (Author's photo)*

wine is poured into the silver *batā* by the priest. For G. Moussay[31], all forms of ritual vessel are *patil* 'metal bowls', most of them identified as *pata* [Fig. 15].

The *batā* in the BTLS collection is from a royal deposit[32] and may be dated to the 17th-18th centuries. It attests to the continuity of usage of an old form. Only few examples of silver *batā* are known, most of them are in museums. [Fig. 16].

Trays

The *bhājana*, often mentioned in inscriptions, is a large plate or tray for offerings. Some have specific functions, for example for betel use.[33] This is referred to in an inscription on an 18th century so-called 'elephant foot vase', which contained the necessary ingredients for making betel quids with a tray on top for offering them. Betel quids are important in hospitality. It served numerous moments in social life and also in court rituals, marriages and religious ceremonies. Archaeological sources, royal chronicles and oral histories attest to daily and ceremonial use. Three essential components are lime, areca nut and betel leaf and the necessary implements are scissors, a lime pot and spoon. The betel box had to be large enough to hold all this.

Other trays [Fig. 18] or plates [Fig. 5a] were used simply for placing offerings before the deity. Offering vessels with lids only came into use from the 17th century, perhaps from Vietnamese influence as perhaps indicated by the recurrent lotus bud and petal motifs.

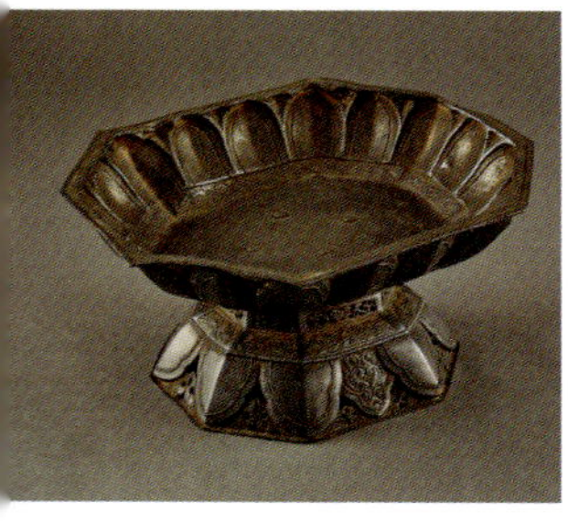

Fig. 18 *Silver tray for offerings [Cat. 79] dating probably to the 18th or 19th centuries.*

Perfume burners

Perfume burners or censors were long in use in Campā. The Cam kingdoms were known for their trading, their ports and the access they provided to the produce of the highlands. An exceptional product was eagle wood or aloe wood[34] which yielded a perfumed resin reserved for gods and kings which was burnt in incense-holders [Figs. 9 and 11].

In the Po Nagar inscription C.208,[35] the object offered is called *asaṅ*, '[incense] carrier', where, in the phrase *asaṅ dhūpa* , the word *dhūpa* for 'incense is taken as understood. The inscription C.206 of Đồng Dương[36] uses the term *dhūpādhāra* = *dhūpa-adhāra* for incense carrier. These Sanskrit terms have disappeared from the modern language.

Rituals in Cam society

Gold and silver vessels play important roles in Cam society. They are of historical as well as ethnographic interest because they permit the study of their roles in social groups, in political systems with kings, religious systems with gods and the rituals that honour them.

Prayers, chants and libations are offered to the divinity in such rituals, along with numerous offerings of food. There can be earthly dishes but also subtle and refined odours. Burning incense was a luxury reserved for gods and kings. Despite the disappearance of the Cam kingdom, the Cams conduct numerous rituals in their temples and in their houses such *Peh mbang yang* (the ceremony of opening doors in November of the Cam calendar, *Cuh yang yang apuei* (a fire sacrifice for the god in April), the *Katé* festival, *Cambur* (the ceremony for the goddess Po Ina Nagar) or *Raja Praong* (in honour of the ancestors).[37] Manuscripts set out clearly the sequence of actions for the priests to perform the rituals correctly. There are two orders of priests: the cult practitioners (*Paseh* or *Baśeh*) and those responsible for organisation (*tamnei* or *camanei*):

> The *Tchamenei*, priests of a lower rank than the *Bashêh*, are a kind of sexton or deacon charged with guarding the ornaments of the gods and the cult utensils: plates, bowls, cups, ewers, spittoons in bronze or silver. Their duty is to survey and maintain the temples. They hold the keys and open the doors when there are ceremonies. As officiants, they clothe and adorn the deities and make offerings after administering delicacies.[38]

After attending certain ceremonies more than a century ago, Etienne Aymonier recorded these ritual vessels in use: 'Metal ewers with spouts are placed on the *Baganratch*,[39] as well as vases and small metal cups for the ceremonial brandy. There are also perfume-burners…'[40]

Some ceremonies were performed for authorisation from the deity – for the right to consult the manuscripts, for example, or for the right to make copies of inscriptions engraved on the temple walls, or to take photos of the god. A special ritual was performed when Aymonier asked to make copies of the Po Klong Garai inscriptions:

> All the assistants murmured prayers asking for the blessing of the deities and their authorisation for making rubbings of their inscriptions. The *Tchamenei*, taking a ewer in one hand and a lit candle in the other began his performance. From time to time he poured water into a vase. Setting down the ewer, he took

Fig. 19 *Po Klong Garai temple ceremony in Cabaton 1901: 60. Author's photo.*

Before the god in the form of a liṅga, *are (7) small cups for alcohol* (cavan) *and, on supports, (8) the large metal vases* (batā) *holding the lustration water; in front a tray of offerings.*

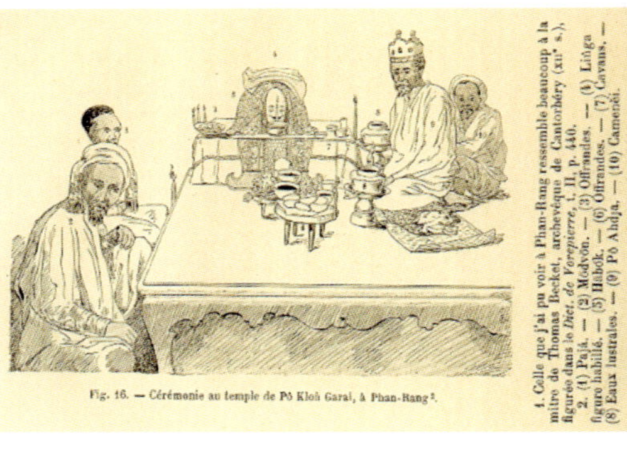

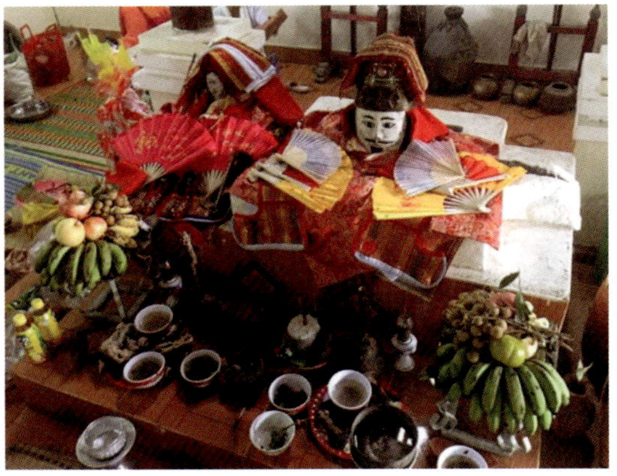

Fig. 20 *Po Klong Chan temple ceremony*[42] *in the village of Danaw Panrang (Bầu Trúc, Ninh Thuận). The god of Po Klong Chan, in the form of a* liṅga *with a face, inserted into a* yoni, *and beside him his consort. During the Katé feast, they are washed and dressed. Before the altar are the ritual bowls for making offerings. In the rear are the libation vases:* batā *and* ghata, *as well as an earthenware jar. (Image FB, accessed 28 July 2021)*

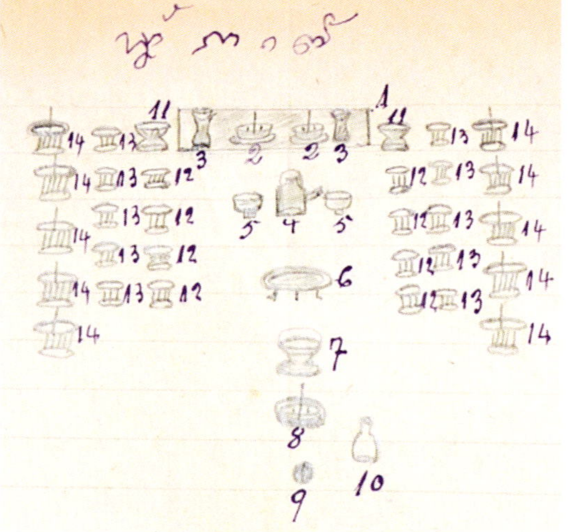

Fig. 21 *Extract from Cam manuscript 125 conserved at the EFEO. Offerings ritual for the Katé ceremony. Probably written by Paul Mus in 1932-34. (Courtesy of the EFEO)*

a small plate in the form of a flared cup containing areca and betel and moved the candle over the plate. Then he stuck the candle in a plate of rice beside a larger candle. He again began his movements, offering all kinds of food, pouring a little water each time into the vase. Taking a branch of leaves as a sprinkler, he dipped it into the cups of lustral water to sprinkle the ewer and the food. Finally, taking a little rice in the tips of his fingers, he rolled it between thumb and fingers and stepped down from the platform after throwing a piece of eagle wood into the perfume burner.[41]

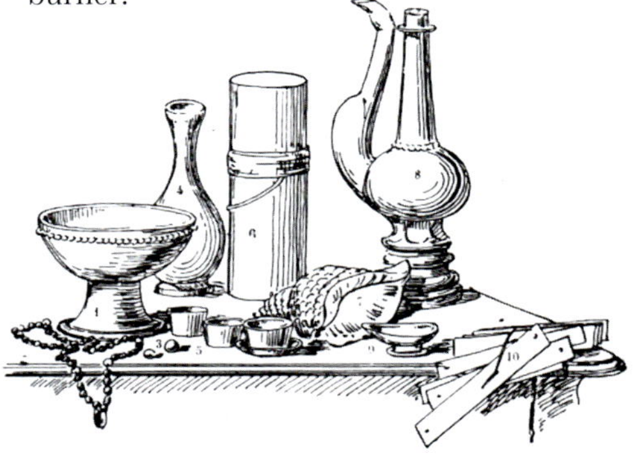

Fig. 22 *On this tray of ceremonial objects, along with the rosary, are the conch for summoning the divinity and the manuscripts on palm leaves (10), a footed bowl called* hābok *(1), ewers called* kalaiḥ *(4) and (8), small cups for alcohol* (cavan) *(5), plus a small cup for making libations* (bap) *(9), in Cabaton 1901: 57, fig. 10.*

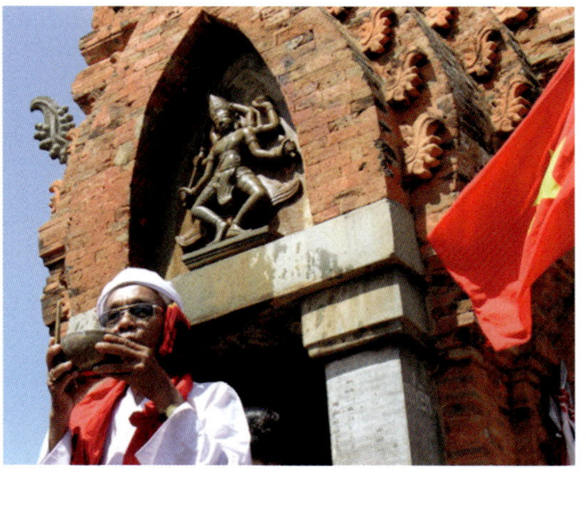

Fig. 23 *Po Klong Garay (Phan Rang, Ninh Thuận) Katé festival October 2005. The 11th century dancing Śiva is today called* ganuer matri *(chief guardian). He has been sprayed with water by the* camanei *(temple guardian). Such rituals persist across the centuries at such sites. (Photo: Agnès De Féo)*

Such ceremonies appear to have changed little over time.

Cam manuscript 125, conserved at the EFEO, which was probably written in Cam by Paul Mus during his stay in the Cam country from 1932-4, records the scheduling of offerings made during the two great Cam rituals of Katé and Cambur [fig. 21].

The Katé ritual as described in EFEO manuscript 125

As described in the manuscript, the ceremony takes place facing East and offerings are place on a mat facing North. There are two betel boxes (*ndvan hulā*[43]) with candles (1) and two stands (*kanvan*) (2) with two 'water bowls' (*patil*[44] *Ayā*). In front of them are (3) a teapot (*patil Ayā caiy*), (4) two bowls (*paṅin*[45] *mañuṃ Ayā*), (5) a tray (*śalav*), (6) a bowl of incense called 'bowl of fire' (*jhai Apvei*), (7) a box (*tuk hop*[46]) with two cups for alcohol (*cavan*) and (8) eight candles, (9) a jar of alcohol (*kalauk alak*), (10) preceded by the officiants executing the rites. To the right and left there are numerous plates with food: two boxes of cakes (*thố*),[47] (11) eight plates with cakes (*cambaḥ*) with plates with feet (*anaiḥ*[48] *maṅ takai*), (12) ten plates with bowls (*paṅin Ayā*) of chicken noodles and (13) ten plates with feet (*śalav takai*[49]) holding rice and meat.

The vocabulary has changed with the disappearance of Sanskrit and the inclusion of Malay and Vietnamese words, though it seems the ritual objects long remained unchanged. So when Cabaton, in 1901, described ceremonies he saw he noted the use of vases with water or betel, which he called *hābok* or *kuṇḍa*, with ewers he called *kalaiḥ* – noting the word comes from the Sanskrit *kalaśa*, or boxes he called *thoṅ*, 'for carrying offerings on its lid'. Today the word *kalaiḥ* no longer means a sprinkler or a cruet:[50] the lustration ritual has been preserved but the small ewer discovered in the archaeology, has disappeared in favour of a small cup.

The testimony of Paul Mus in 1932-34 shows how the cultural objects are retained even if their names have changed. The ewer is called a 'water bowl', the perfume burner a 'fire bowl', but boxes, bowls and trays are still used. In showing the diverse range of bowls (*pata, patil*) in 1971 [Fig. 15], Gérard Moussay suggested there were multiple uses, the importance of some being known only to priests, but their function endured.

Our ethnographic excursion has shown how traditional ceremonies are conserved. Ritual practices in the course of which divine figures are lustrated appears to always be based on old texts transmitted from generation to generation in priestly families (*baseh*). The importance of these rituals is permitting the Cam people to conserve the status of their great civilisation in the heart of modern Vietnam.

Annex 1: Inscriptions

Inscription	Object	Name	dedicated to	dedicated by	Findspot	Date
C.143	silver plate			ajñā po: a royal family member	La Thọ, Quang Nam	10th century
C.144	silver plate		śrī Vanāntareśvara		La Thọ, Quang Nam	10th century
C.145	silver ewer	kalaśa	śrī Vanāntareśvara	Campāpurapatī: a king	La Thọ, Quang Nam	10th century
C.118	silver bowl		yāṅ pu nagara	rāja oṅ śakrānta urāṅ mandāvijaya: a king	Po Nagar, Nha Trang	1197 CE
C.205	silver ewer	kalaśa	śrī Rudrasvayambhuveśvara	śrī Rudravarman: a king		mid-9th century
C.206	silver incense burner	dhūpādhāra		śrī Rudravarman: un roi		mid-9th century
C.207	silver plate	bhājana	śrī Bhadraliṅgeśvara	son of śrī Bhadravarman: royal family member		mid-9th century
C.208	silver incense holder	asaṅ	yā parameśvarī	ciy pāṅ pu dhiḥ urāṅ rupaṅ: royal family member	Po Nagar, Nha Trang	1130 CE

Annex 2: Table of ritual objects identified in inscriptions with names and dates

Objet	name	gold	silver	unknown material
ewer	kalaśa	C.38 of 784 EC; C.90 C of 1080 EC; C.82 of 1114 EC; C.92 A of 1165 EC; C.30 A3 of 1167 EC.	C.61 of 892 CE; C.145 end of 9th c.; C.205 end of 9th c.; C.142 B of 908 CE; C.30 B3 of 1050 CE; C.90 of 1080 CE	
large ewer	ghaṭa	C.38 B of 784 CE; C.30 B3 of 1050 CE		
pot, vase	kumbha		C.24 B of 801 CE	
	batā, vatā, vat	C.30 A1 of 1084 CE	C.30 A3 of 1183 CE.	
	bhṛṅgāra	C.38 B of 784 CE	C.61 of 892 CE; C.142 B of 908 CE; C.30B3 of 1050 CE; C.31 A2 of 1064 CE.	
plate	bhājana	C.31 A2 of 1064 CE; C.30 B3 of 1050 CE; C.92 A of 1165 CE	C.24 B of 801 CE; C.207 end of 9th century; C.142 B of 898 CE and 908 CE; C.31 A2 of 1064 CE; C.30 A3 of 1183 CE.	C.31 A2 of 1064 CE; C.92 A of 1165 CE
tray	suvauk, suvok	C.6.1 of 1244 CE		
incense burner	asaṅ (dhūpa) dhūpādhāra	C.31 A2 of 1064 CE	C.206 end of 9th c.; C.30 A1 of 1084 CE; C.208 of 1130 CE	

ANNEX 3: TABLE OF RITUAL OBJECTS CLASSED BY DATE AND PROVENANCE

Date	Inscription	site	province
late 9th c.	C.205	Đồng Dương	Quảng Nam
late 9th c.	C.206	Đồng Dương	Quảng Nam
late 9th c.	C.207	?	Quảng Nam
late 9th c.	C.145	La Thọ	Quảng Nam
1050 CE	C.30 B3	Po Nagar, Nha Trang	Khánh Hòa
1064 CE	C.31 A2	Po Nagar, Nha Trang	Khánh Hòa
1080 CE	C.90 C	Mỹ Sơn	Quảng Nam
1084 CE	C.30 A1	Po Nagar, Nha Trang	Khánh Hòa
1114 CE	C.82	Mỹ Sơn	Quảng Nam
1130 CE	C.208	Po Nagar, Nha Trang	Khánh Hòa
1165 CE	C.92 A	Mỹ Sơn	Quảng Nam
1167 CE	C.30 A3	Po Nagar, Nha Trang	Khánh Hòa
1183 CE	C.31 A2	Po Nagar, Nha Trang	Khánh Hòa
1183 CE	C.30 A3	Po Nagar, Nha Trang	Khánh Hòa
1197 CE	C.118	Po Nagar, Nha Trang	Khánh Hòa
1244 CE	C.6.1	Phan Rang	Ninh Thuận

BIBLIOGRAPHY

Anonymous. 1911:'Chronique'. *BEFEO* 11: 471-2.

Aymonier, Étienne, 'Légendes historiques des Chame', *Excursions et Reconnaissances* XIV n°32 (1890): 145-206.

________________, *Les Tchames et leurs religions*, Paris, 1891.

Aymonier, Étienne & Cabaton, Antoine, *Dictionnaire Cam-Français*, Paris, Leroux éd., 1906.

Cabaton, Antoine, *Nouvelles recherches sur les Chams*, Publications de l'École française d'Extrême-Orient, Paris, 1901.

Claeys, Jean-Yves, 'Chronique. G. Binh-thuan. Phan-ly cham', *BEFEO* 28 N°3(1928): 608-610.

Cœdès, George, et Parmentier, Henri, *Listes générales des inscriptions et des monuments du Champa et du Cambodge*, 1923, Hanoi, Imprimerie d'Extrême-Orient.

Cœdès, George, *Inscriptions du Cambodge*, vol. 1, Hanoi, 1937.

Durand, Eugène-Marie. 'Notes sur les Chams. IX. L'Abhisheka cham', *BEFEO* VII 1907: 345-351.

Filliozat, Jean, 'Çivaisme et bouddhisme au Cambodge', *BEFEO* LXX, 1981: 95.

Griffiths, Arlo, Lepoutre, Amandine, Southworth, William & Than Phan, 'Études du corpus des inscriptions du Campā III. Épigraphie du Campā 2009-2010: prospection sur le terrain, production d'estampages, supplément à l'inventaire', *BEFEO* 95-96 (2008-2009): 435-97.

Lafont P.-B., Po Dharma & Nara Vija, *Catalogue des manuscrits cam des bibliothèques françaises*, Publications de l'École française d'Extrême-Orient Volume CXIV, 1977, Paris.

Moussay, Gérard, *Dictionnaire Cam-Vietnamien-Français*, Centre culturel Cham, Phanrang, 1971.

Ner, Marcel, 'Chronique', *BEFEO* 30(1930): 552-76.

Nghiêm Tham, 'Sơ-lược về các kho-tàng chứa bảo vật vua Chàm' (Report on the Cham treasures », Việt-nam Khảo-cổ tập san (Bulletin on the Historical Research Institut of Viêt Nam), 1(1957-59) : 151-163.

Parmentier, Henri, 'Chronique', *BEFEO* I, fasc. 4, 1901, p. 409-411.

Parmentier, Henri, 'Découverte de bijoux anciens à Mi-son', *BEFEO* 1903 : 664-5.

Parmentier Henri et Durand Eugène-Marie, 'Le trésor des rois chams', *BEFEO* 5(1905) : 1-46.

Phạm Hữu Mý & Vương Hải Yến 'Collection of Champa artefacts in the Museum of History of Viet Nam – Ho Chi Minh City' in *Sưu tập hiện vật Champa tại Bảo tàng Lịch sử Việt Nam Thành phố Hồ Chí Minh* (Champa collection Viet Nam Historical Museum Ho Chi Minh City), and in T. P. Hồ Chí Minh, Bảo tàng Lịch sử Việt Nam,1994.

Rougier, Virgile, in 'Nouvelles découvertes cames au Quang-Nam' *Bulletin de la Commission archéologique de l'Indochine*, 1912 : 211-212.

Sakaya (Truong Van Mon), 'Relationships between Champa and the Malay Word through Raja Praong and Mak Yong Rituals', International Champa Conference, Paris 2012 (oral presentation).

Sanderson, Alexis, 'The Śaiva Religion among the Khmers', *BEFEO* 90/91 (2003-4): 349-462.

Schweyer, Anne-Valérie, 'La vaisselle en argent de la dynastie d'Indrapura (Quảng Nam, Việt Nam) Études d'épigraphie cam – II', *BEFEO* 86(1999) : 345-355.

__________________, 'N°80' and 'N°81' in *Trésors d'art du Vietnam. La sculpture du Champa Ve-XVe siècles*, P. Baptiste & T. Zéphir (eds) 2005, Paris, Réunion des musées nationaux et Musée Guimet, p. 297-8.

__________________, 'Po Nagar de Nha Trang. Seconde partie : Le dossier épigraphique', *Aséanie* 15, juin 2005 : 87-120.

Stock, Emiko, 'Parce que Champa et Cambodge ne faisaient qu'un… Lorsque les esprits s'emmêlent pour tisser la trame d'une histoire passée sur le métier d'une 'intégration présente', *Udaya* 8, 2007 : 258-270 http://www.yosothor.org/uploads/images/Udaya/UDAYA_ISSUES/Udaya_08/06_Emiko%20Stock_UDAYA08.pdf

Zéphir, Thierry, 'n°3', in *Trésors d'art du Vietnam. La sculpture du Champa Ve-XVe siècles*, P. Baptiste & T. Zéphir (eds) 2005, Paris, Réunion des musées nationaux et Musée Guimet.

Endnotes

1 'Chronique' *BEFEO* 1911: 471-2.

2 Parmentier *BEFEO* 1901: 409-10: 'This deposit held 18 metal pieces: a silver dish, 14 vases of the same kind, two gilt silver vases and one in gold.'

3 Parmentier *BEFEO* 1903: 664-5.

4 Parmentier and Durand *BEFEO* 1905: 1-46.

5 *BEFEO* 1930: 552-76.

6 Việt-nam Khảo-cổ tập san: 151-63.

7 The first is identified as Po Maḥ Taha who, according to the royal Chronicle, reigned from 1622-27; the second, better known under the name Po Romé, was the son-in-law of the first. See Aymonier 1890: 151-152.

8 The original inventory of the Tịnh Mỹ deposit is conserved in the archives of the EFEO in Paris (Parmentier et al. 19 April 1902).

9 Formerly the Musée Louis-Finot.

10 All inscriptions are inventoried as follows: the letter C refers to the corpus of Cam inscriptions. This letter is followed by a number of the inscriptions listed either by Cœdès & Parmentier in 1923 for numbers C.1 to C.170, or in Cœdès 1937 for C.171 to C.200, or in Griffiths-Lepoutre 2008-9: 488-91 for C.201 to C.233.

11 For example, among the ritual vessels, the word *kalaśa* for designating an ewer disappeared and was replaced by the word *halong*, see Moussay 1971: Index p.2, or *halauṅ* Aymonier-Cabaton 1906: 520. Cabaton in 1901 and Aymonier-Cabaton in 1906 still indexed the use of the word *kalaih* (Cabaton 1901: 57; Aymonier-Cabaton : 68), but Moussay does not mention it in 1971; for dish or plate, *bhājana* was replaced by *thong hala*, *cabah* or *salaw*, idem, ibid., p.31.

12 C.144 *vanāntareśvarāyāsmai śrīmate diśakīrttaye campāpurapatī raupyam kalaśam śraddhayātmanah* | | Schweyer 2005: 297.

13 The information given in *BEFEO* 1911: 471-2 are too summary for finding a sanctuary dedicated to this god.

14 C.205 *śrīrudrasvayambhuveśvarāya rajatakalaśo yaṃ śrīrudravarmmadevena datta iti*: Schweyer 1999: 348-9.

15 C.206 *tam imă ca dhūpādhāraṃ śrīrudravarmmadevo dattavān iti* | |: Schweyer 1999: 349 and Griffiths et alii 2008-9: 479.

16 On the dynasty of Indrapura, cf. Schweyer 1999: 345-355.

17 On the god Śiva *svayambhu*, see Sanderson 2003-4: 410-421.

18 C.207 *svasti // śrībhadraliṅgeśvarāya bhagavate śrībhadravarmmāṅgajo yaṃ bhaṭanāmadheyo yah kṣatriyo rajatabhājanam idam asmai bhṛsvātmakirttaye tadbhaktyā dattavān iti* // Schweyer 1999: 349-50.

19 C.118 *poṅ yāṅ pu rāja bhagavanta oṅ śakrānta urāṅ mandāvijaya vuh pak yāṅ pu nagara śakarāja* 1119: Schweyer, 2005: 297-8.

20 C.208 | | yāṅ po ku di yāṅ ciy pāṅ pu dhiḥ urāṅ rupaṅ anāk pu lyaṅ śrī devarāja vuḥ asaṅ nī pak yāṅ parameśvarī rūpan kāla śākarāja 1052: Griffiths et alii 2008-9: 477-8.

21 This is an object with the shape of the sacred syllable Oṃ, used principally for coronations.

22 Cabaton 1901: 57.

23 Durand *BEFEO* 1907: 349: 'during the royal ritual *mamun*, the high priest wears a kind of mitre called a *kanôm*. He takes in his left hand a small ewer with a wader bird's neck called *kalaiç* …'. On the *mamun* ritual practised by the Cams in Cambodia, cf. Stock *Udaya* 2007: 258-70.

24 See inscriptions C.145 and C.205 above.

25 Zéphir 2005: 179.

26 It can be seen in the EFEO photographic archives under number 23037. The reference card says 'a gold vase from Po Klaun Garai' was deposited in the Louis Finot Museum as D.22.43. Now disappeared.

27 On the symbolic representation of Śiva and Parvatī by 'pots of scented

water, surrounded by a number of varied pots representing their escort gods (*parivāra*[*deva*])', cf. Filliozat 1981: 95.

28 The noun *batā* is found in Parmentier-Durand 1905, section 'III. Vases' p. 14-28.

29 Po Nagar inscriptions: C.30 A 1 from 1084 CE. Princess Garbhalakśmī gave to the goddess a gold *vatā* of 56 thil (more than 2 kg). C.30 A 3 the *mānśiai grāmapuravijaya* gave a silver *vatā* of 10 thei, (c. 380 gr.) Schweyer 2005: 88-91 and 93-4.

30 Durand 1907: 348.

31 Moussay 1971: 269-70.

32 Parmentier – Durand 1905: 20-22.

33 A betel nut tray (*thong hala*) is mentioned in the Raja Praong ritual, see Sakaya 2012.

34 Eagle wood has various names which distinguish its fragrances: calambac, aloe wood, eagle wood, or in English *gharu wood* or *agarwood*. It was a luxury product sought for cosmetic or pharmacopoeia use, or as incense. It was called aloe wood or eagle wood dependent on whether it flowed or not (the best quality flowed completely).

35 See Fig. 11.

36 See Fig. 9.

37 On the rituals, see Sakaya 2012.

38 Aymonier 1891: 44.

39 A box containing ritual objects whose lid served as a plate. Cabaton 1901: 56.

40 Aymonier 1891: 51.

41 Aymonier 1891: 54.

42 For the cult of Po Klong Chan, see Aymonier 1891: 56-7: 'Numerous minor deities are celebrated in villages around. Po-Klong-Tchan is a recent example of how minor gods may figure in Cam cults. In 1868, two men from Panrang, were digging a canal near their village when they uncovered a carved stone. The villagers placed the rock under a shelter and made homage to it. Soon a woman declaring herself to be Padjao and the god speaking through her, told the people it was the king of Po-Klong-Tchan. A villager became the Kadhar of the new divinity and one of the gods who discovered it, his Tchamenei. These three priests or servants venerate the deity periodically at annual feasts. They also venerate the deity on behalf of people who fall ill.'

43 *hulā* = *halā 'betel'*.

44 Aymonier-Cabaton: 259 metal bowl.

45 Aymonier-Cabaton : 255, 259 et 299. These are probably small ceramic bowls rather than *patil*, which are larger and often in metal.

46 The expression is formed from two words *tuk* forth plate and *hop* for the box. It could be a vase with feet (*tal takai lamân*) [Cat. *37.b*] which served both as both a box and a plate for presenting the offering.

47 The word is borrowed from Vietnamese.

48 Aymonier-Cabaton: 13.

49 *śalav takai* may be translated as 'tray with feet'.

50 Aymonier-Cabaton: 68.

17 | The South and Nagara Campā

John Whitmore

The basic fact of the south of the land we call Nagara Campā is that the territory is very arid, with cactus, "one of the driest areas of Vietnam" (Southworth 2012: 66), an area with "the lowest rainfall in Southeast Asia' [having] [s]trong winds, little precipitation, and dusty soils". Phan Rang's total annual rainfall is half that of Nha Trang's, which in turn is half that of Hue (Southworth 2012: 66; following Momoki 1999: 35).

As the very dry territory on the southern fringe of what became the Cam world, the question remains, how did this southern territory come to be part of Nagara Campā? I propose, following the work of Anne-Valerie Schweyer, that the consolidation of Nagara Campā evolved in five stages, during the sixth, seventh, ninth-tenth, eleventh, and thirteenth centuries. In accord with Andrew Hardy (2019: 221-52), the consolidation of this *nagara* through these centuries

> involved the mobility of the king, his court, and his army [physically and/or ritually] ... the foundation of religious Institutions and the institutions of traditions of worship ... [and] the commissioning of sacred iconography and memorial inscriptions ... The foundations were then handsomely endowed to become centres of economic activity and human settlement, contributing to the region's development.

By pursuing the history of this southern region in this manner, I address what Arlo Griffiths, Andrew Hardy, and Geoff Wade ask in their volume *Champa: Territories and Networks of a Southeast Asian Kingdom:* 'How these territories held together to form the kingdom of Campā?' In doing so, this work is based on the splendid research of Schweyer, Griffiths, Southworth, Amandine Lepoutre, and their fellows. I hope that I do their work justice.

The first millennium CE saw the rise of 'Funan' in the Mekong Delta and the spread of its influence into different parts of the Southeast Asian mainland. On the eastern seaboard of the mainland, this Indic cultural input appears to have generally moved past the undeveloped territory that would become Pāṇḍuraṅga to impact better endowed regions up the coast as far as the Thu Bồn valley. The Võ Cạnh inscription of the late fourth century CE shows this in the Nha Trang area, and later sculptures appeared there and in other localities to the north, including 'Xitu' south of the Hải Vân Pass. Meanwhile the Katuic 'Linyi' north of this pass prospered until the mid-fifth century when Chinese forces conquered it. At this point, in the fifth and sixth centuries, 'Xitu,' influenced by 'Funan,' came to dominate the central coast and to take the name 'Linyi' for itself.

Simultaneously, the maritime shipping pattern that had led 'Funan' to such wealth and power changed. Instead of following the old coastal route, with transshipment across the Malay Peninsula at the Kra Isthmus, the maritime route came directly across the sea from the Sumatra/Java region, bypassing 'Funan' on its way more directly to the Chinese ports. This meant that the central coast of the eastern seaboard became a prime stopover point for the maritime shipping and traders. 'Xitu' in the Thu Bồn valley became that point. This was a region occupied by people calling themselves Cam with their sacred centre in the Mỹ Sơn valley just off the Thu Bồn valley. There they began to construct their temples and compose Sanskrit inscriptions. In the seventh century, as their wealth and power grew, these people adopted the Indic name Campā for their realm, while retaining 'Linyi' in their dealings with China. Thus, the sense of being Cam ethnically and of creating Nagara Campā began in the Thu Bồn valley with its sacred centre of Mỹ Sơn before spreading up and down this central coast in later centuries.

While Campā moved north into the old 'Linyi' territory, its lords showed no sign of interest in the south, the areas that would be Kauṭhāra and Pāṇḍuraṅga. Surviving a Chinese attack in 605 CE, the new Campā prospered from trade and agriculture, building its capital and its religious structures, through the seventh and the first half of the eighth centuries.

In the mid-eighth century, this all changed. Where Campā in the centre (the Thu Bồn valley) had been building temples and producing inscriptions since the sixth century, these activities now ceased. And the Tang dynasty in China changed its name for the land from 'Linyi' to 'Huanwang.' The latter means Circle of Kings/Princes, and I take this to indicate a number of relatively equal local lords, none of whom was able to dominate the others and develop the wealth and power needed to produce new temples and inscriptions. As a consequence, I feel, maritime trade moved south to the harbor of Kauṭhāra (Nha Trang), with a strong orientation to the sea. Here a new regime developed through the middle of the century that built the great temple to its local Goddess (Kauthareśvarī, Lady Lord of Kauṭhāra) and left inscriptions. This region also seems to have taken a Sanskrit version of their own name (in Sanskrit it simply means axe). In Kauṭhāra, a good stopover point, the heavy flow of maritime shipping and trade to and from the great cosmopolitan Tang empire of China brought wealth and power to the local lord. Through the second half of the eighth century, we see such wealth and power develop here, particularly in the shrine of the local Goddess (Kauthareśvarī). Besides Sanskrit, they, like those in Campā, also used their Austronesian language in an Indic script (which we call Cam).

This development became so strong that the regime felt constrained by the limits of its own territory and (with little water) of the region they called Pāṇḍuraṅga. Under the ruler Satyavarman, the main records of their activities lay farther south, in this territory of Pāṇḍuraṅga. Here the king and his forces took over and established it as part of their domain through building temples, setting up *liṅgas*, and composing inscriptions, especially at Po Dam, Phú Hài on the south, and finally Hòa Lai on the north – in a distinctive and unique local style, as Michael Vickery (2011, 47) stated, "different and independent" from that established in the Thu Bồn valley. In the process, Satyavarman recapped local *liṅga*s by adding metal covers (*kośa*) in his own name for them, thus bringing them and their localities within his own domain.

In this time the temple of the Goddess of Kauṭhāra (burned in a Java attack) became a fully established brick construction. There the region celebrated, in the local matrilineal Austronesian fashion, their powerful Goddess with their wealth. They replaced the burnt wooden structure with a large brick temple to what was most likely an indigenous cult, protecting the region. In time, a subsidiary Śaiva shrine appeared, placing the temple more strictly within the Hindu domain, thus blending the indigenous with the Indic. In addition, there was a temple to Gaṇeśa, the elephant son of Śiva and Bhagavatī (the Goddess), reflecting the strong association of the local society with elephant training and use. Hence, a local line, now with wealth and power, became a royal lineage with their cult in its wooden building becoming a major shrine. Satyavarman and his successors built up Kauṭhāra, developed the temple of the Goddess, and pushed south into the territory they named Pāṇḍuraṅga. All this was separate from the growth of Campā in the centre. The people of Kauṭhāra, I believe, were not Cams, and Kauṭhāra was not part of Nagara Campā at that time.

The inscriptions, often carved by the same hand in both Kauṭhāra and Pāṇḍuraṅga, were in both Sanskrit and the Austronesian language with distinctive local features. At their centre stood the temple of the Goddess. These inscriptions established the region of Kauṭhāra and its lord Satyavarman as dominant both here and in Pāṇḍuraṅga. Satyavarman, as ruler of Kauṭhāra, set up his personal *liṅga*s in Pāṇḍuraṅga to establish his authority and legitimacy therein. His inscriptions proclaimed his glories being victorious over this territory – as master of this land (as Śiva was lord over Viṣṇu and Brahmā), Satyavarman dominated Pāṇḍuraṅga. Backed by the Lady Lord of Kauṭhāra, this king brought Śiva to this land as he established the Realm of the Three Worlds (Trailokyanagara) there. The might of this Śiva, "all powerful in every direction, ... protects the lands of the region of Pāṇḍuraṅga." (Griffiths & Southworth 2011: 28-32).

Satyavarman placed Pāṇḍuraṅga under the command of his nephew. This land was not an independent realm (*nagara*) but a domain (*viṣaya*) (for the Chinese, a *zhou* rather than a *guo*), run by lords of Kauṭhāra, not by the kings themselves. Here in this very dry region, as William Southworth (2012) explains, it seems that the initial/further construction of the local irrigation system proceeded with the building of the temples. The temples and the inscriptions reflect the pattern of a local distribution of water that advanced the region's agriculture. Managing the flow in this way aided the growth of the local population and thus the wealth and power of the realm of Kauṭhāra. Indeed, where the inscriptions recorded donations of water buffaloes, rice fields, and the grain produced, the action probably described the development of local lands in a fashion similar to other inland Southeast Asian realms of these centuries, all protected by appropriate curses. This development continued for about a hundred years into the middle of the ninth century.

As the wealth and power of the realm of Kauṭhāra, together with the domain of Pāṇḍuraṅga, grew rapidly from the mid-eighth century, they became part of the flourishing maritime scene. The eighth century witnessed not only the rise of Kauṭhāra (and with it Pāṇḍuraṅga), but also that of Mataram in central Java and its link with the maritime empire of Śrīvijaya on Sumatra and the Malay Peninsula. Their aggressive maritime forces struck the eastern seaboard of the mainland over at least two decades from 767-787 CE, attacking Kauṭhāra and the Tang Protectorate of Annam (now northern Vietnam). Striking at centres of wealth and power, the invaders burned the wooden temple of the Goddess in Kauṭhāra and its adjacent Śaiva shrine. Satyavarman pursued and defeated the attackers at sea but lost the cult items seized. Rebuilding, Kauṭhāra and Pāṇḍuraṅga used Javanese and Khmer elements in their reconstruction. Located on the southern edge of the Austronesian coast, Kauṭhāra and Pāṇḍuraṅga interacted with the Khmer in the Mekong valley as well as with the maritime networks, especially Mataram at its height. While a part of this Austronesian world (witness the language on the inscriptions and the use of the *kośa*), the Kauṭhāra/Pāṇḍuraṅga regime was creating its own tradition around the Goddess (female/esoteric) with its strong Śaiva (male/exoteric) ritual, as seen in its temples and its inscriptions. Culturally and textually, this southern Austronesian coastal region defined itself separately from the Cam region of the Thu Bồn valley, mainly Śaiva in its expression.

Despite operating in the dynamic flow of Mahāyāna/Tantric Buddhism of the age, Kauṭhāra remained staunchly local and Śaiva in its own way. But the mid-ninth century led to the Thu Bồn valley utilizing this Buddhist connection, especially the Bodhisattva Avalokiteśvara, to regain the major maritime port on this coast. A new regime rose in Indrapura, possibly one of the earlier 'Circle of Kings/Princes' with no connection to the prior lord of Nagara Campā. Developing a genealogy back to Bhrgu and Uroja that legitimized them, they claimed to rise to power on their own merits. Stepping into the concept of Nagara Campā and the Mỹ Sơn Śaiva cult, probably being Cam themselves, they built a magnificent Buddhist polity and pushed being Cam north into the old 'Linyi' territory, proclaiming themselves Great King of Kings (*Mahārājādhirāja*) over a greater Nagara Campā.

Indrapura paralleled Angkor in its development from the second half of the ninth century through the middle of the tenth and competed with it. But the south was not part of this. Temple building and inscriptions ceased there, and Pāṇḍuraṅga was not mentioned elsewhere. Reaching out to Kauṭhāra and the Goddess in the south, Indrapura acted to bring them ritually into the new Campā that it was forming through the tenth century. Its ruler, Jaya Indravarman, presented donations to the shrine of Bhumiśvarī (Lady Lord of the Land, i.e., the Goddess), partnering her and Bhadreśvara (the Śiva cult of Nagara Campā in Mỹ Sơn). Speaking of "the entire land clothed by the water of the ocean," in 918 CE the king "devoted to the protection of Nagara Campā, … desired the renaming of this land in the world." Then, following a Khmer attack on Kauṭhāra in 965 CE, the king re-established the Goddess in a stone image.

Thus, it would appear that Indrapura sought to bring the entire Austronesian coast into its newly defined and expanding network. Seeing the Goddess as Bhagavatī enabled Indrapura to link her as the spouse of Śiva to the cult of Bhadreśvara at Mỹ Sơn. In both north and south, this new regime in the centre utilized ritual to consolidate these ethnic realms. But before this could happen to any significant degree, Campā's push north collided with the developing Việt realm, and the warfare between the two in the 980s CE brought Indrapura's growth to an end. Earlier Angkor had sacked Kauṭhāra. Thus, Nagara Campā's effort to develop their classic Southeast Asian realm (akin to those of Angkor, Bagan, and Thăng Long) was disrupted. This disruption via the competition between the Cam and the Việt would last about a hundred years, into the second half of the eleventh century.

During these decades, there was little development of wealth and power, as the varied river valleys sustained themselves with little temple construction or inscription composition. In the meantime, a new dynasty, the Song (r. 960-1279 CE) unified China, and maritime trade grew. Pāṇḍuraṅga emerged in the south and, on its own, in 997 CE together with Arabs sent an embassy to the Song court. Thus, Pāṇḍuraṅga seized the opportunity for political fragmentation and commercial growth to take its place on the maritime sea route. In addition, beginning in the mid-tenth century, the warmer and wetter climate, the Medieval Climate Anomaly, would have brought better agricultural conditions to these dry areas. Utilizing the irrigation system from earlier centuries, it seems that Pāṇḍuraṅga, like other realms across the mainland, flourished. Quite possibly, these years saw, as Lieberman & Buckley (2012: 17) have stated, "ideal conditions for agriculture and political expansion, especially in these 'rain-shadow' dry zones, … climactic amelioration between 950 CE and 1030 CE contributed significantly, even critically, to early charter vitality across the mainland."

With the north and the centre of the coast wrecked by the Cam-Việt conflict, the south (Kauṭhāra and Pāṇḍuraṅga), while damaged by the Khmer, was able to develop agriculturally and commercially through the first half of the eleventh century and to build its wealth and power. Chinese sources indicate Pāṇḍuraṅga as a separate realm at the time, though associated with Nagara Campā. In 1016 CE, the Chinese noted Pāṇḍuraṅga as a stopover point on the maritime trade route.

In mid-century, with the Cam-Việt conflict continuing, the south saw signs of this growth and power. Suddenly, in 1050 CE, renewed temple donations and the inscriptions recording them appeared. The prospering Parameśvara, lord of Kauṭhāra (I believe), made a strong and impassioned personal appeal for victory (in Sanskrit) to his Goddess along with significant contributions to her cult and sent two nephews to lead forces against Nagara Pāṇḍuraṅga and its wealth. Victorious, the two set up *liṅga*s (as well as victory memorials) on the hilltop of Po Klong Garai, establishing Kauṭhāra's sovereignty again over the territory. The wealth they captured came back to equip the Goddess and her worship. In the process, writing in, they marked off and inspired the locals (once more) in Kauṭhāra's presence in Pāṇḍuraṅga, with *liṅga*s located on Po Klong Garai, facing east, to the south of Po Klong Garai, to the west, and to the north. Claiming to be Protector of Nagara Campā, Parameśvara displaced the lord of Pāṇḍuraṅga. In the mid-1050s looking north, he made donations in the Thu Bồn valley, including at the central shrine of Nagara Campā at Mỹ Sơn, providing aid in the wrecked centre of the land, as well as in his home territory where he restored a shrine for an eighth century lord, and then south in the Pāṇḍuraṅga plain he endowed a Buddhist site. In the latter, Parameśvara claimed a link to Uroja (and hence to Indrapura a century earlier) and to be a *cakravartin rājā* of Nagara Campā. He sent his victorious forces into Kambujadesa. In the process, Parameśvara proclaimed the Goddess for the first time to be not only Bhagavatī, spouse of Śiva, but also Yang Pu Nagara, Lady Lord of the Realm.

This lord (I believe of Kauṭhāra) thus defined in Pāṇḍuraṅga, the scene of his victories, through descent from the Indrapura regime his status as lord of Nagara Campā, a Campā brought into existence by that prior regime, taking the ethnonym Cam for the entire Austronesian-speaking coast. Yet, over the next three decades, his successors found it difficult to carry out Parameśvara's claims. The armed forces (of Kauṭhāra?) were quite active, especially to the south and the west. In 1064 CE, Rudravarman, one of the 1050 CE nephews, renovated the temples and donated to the Goddess, including wealth from Kambujadesa. He spoke of kings, each in his own territory (of greater, lesser, or medium strength) and claimed, being from a distinguished family, to outshine them all, being singular among them. Two decades later, Paramabodhisattva (the other nephew of 1050 CE) described events in Nagara Campā of those past years for the Goddess in the local Austronesian language (or was he actually using Cam?). As this power of the Austronesian world worked toward the restoration of the land following the Việt-Cam conflicts, Paramabodhisattva recounted how the preceding sixteen years had brought him to the throne. Rudravarman had attacked a stretch of Campā. As a result, ten competing kings had sprung up. Bloody fighting then brought Paramabodhisattva to reunite Nagara Campā with his capital of Siṅhapura in the Thu Bồn valley. Finally, over ten years, only the realm of Pāṇḍuraṅga stood against him. Having taken Pāṇḍuraṅga, Paramabodhisattva, with the help of the Goddess, became "the king with the single parasol [over Nagara Campā], engaging royal power." (C.30 A1)

The Goddess now officially became Yang Pu Nagara, Lady Lord of the Realm, fully equipped with Paramabodhisattva's rich donations, including an elephant. In addition, there was the Little Goddess (Malada/Lamada Kauṭhāra) in a shrine next to that of the Goddess, sheltering Kauṭhāra as the Goddess herself now sheltered all Nagara Campā. In Anne-Valerie Schweyer's words (2004, 131), '... from the mid-eleventh century, the Goddess of Kauṭhāra was becoming the "Goddess of the Country"'.

Over the final third of the eleventh century, the house of Parameśvara from Kauṭhāra and the temple of the Goddess defeated Pāṇḍuraṅga (first and last) and moved against nine other claimants to Nagara Campā in the midst of the wreckage following the devastating 1069 CE attack by Đại Việt. Then the Vietnamese, distracted by the threat of Song China, ceased to be a problem for the Cams, and the house of Parameśvara moved north to reunite and reform greater Campā, establishing itself in the Thu Bồn valley (Amaravati) as the new Siṅhapura regime. Thus began the second effort to establish the classical Nagara Campā, following that of Indrapura two centuries earlier. Indrapura had moved out of Campā and the Thu Bồn valley, bringing in the north (the former 'Linyi') and reaching out to Kauṭhāra in the south. Now the north had become a Cam/Việt battle zone, and the south (Kauṭhāra + the defeated Pāṇḍuraṅga) had taken over the north, I believe, finally binding the centre and the south into the new Nagara Campā.

Siṅhapura rose as the new capital of this restored and reformed Nagara Campā and for the next one hundred years ruled the land. The gods of the house of Parameśvara, now the Siṅhapura regime, moved out of Kauṭhāra and the south to embrace all Nagara Campā, north, centre, and south. The rulers of the new realm acknowledged the many earlier faults of their realm, sought to correct these faults, and acted to restore Nagara Campā as good as it had once been (that is, the earlier regime of Indrapura). Its rulers saw themselves as *cakravartin* and the ultimate protectors of Nagara Campā as a whole. Now as Cams ruling Nagara Campā, they restored the devastated central Cam Śaiva cult of Bhadresvara at Mỹ Sơn with a golden *kośa* and joined it to that of Yang Pu Nagara, the Goddess, in the south – Śiva as the cosmic lord, the Goddess as the earthly (Bhūmiśvarī) power of the realm, no longer just of Kauṭhāra and the south.

This grand restoration led to "the return of Nagara Campā to its ancient glory." (C.93). After the civil war and the Vietnamese destruction, Siṅhapura rose, "beautiful and flourishing as before." (C.99B). Inscriptions from 1080 CE to 1114 CE attested to this. Utilizing elements from contemporary Karṇāṭaka in west India in their reconstruction, the new regime built a number of temples in a coherent style across the original Cam territory (C.94), including Chánh Lộ, Bằng An, Chiên Đàn, and Mỹ Sơn itself, consolidating their position in this central region. Thus a force outside Nagara Campā (I believe from Kauṭhāra) reconstructed and rebuilt the original Nagara Campā in the Thu Bồn valley, now as Siṅhapura, as it made the second effort at a Cam classical realm. Yet the twelfth century brought another disruption to this effort, this time by Angkor.

The reason for this latest disruption was the surge of private Chinese shipping and trade from the later eleventh century, making contact with numerous coastal sites within Southeast Asia. This drew Angkor east to gain access to the new flourishing local trade pattern. After futile diplomatic and warfare efforts from the 1110s CE into the 1130s, during the 1140s, Sūryavarman II of Angkor moved into what are now the Central Highlands of Vietnam to create a nagara there, then down into the lowlands to join local Cams in Vijaya, the south central region of Nagara Campā (now the Quy Nhơn region). There the Khmer-Cam regime established their port (Śrī Banoy/Thị Nại, the New Territory of the Chinese, as opposed to the Old Territory of the Thu Bồn valley), making contact with the new trade pattern. This Khmer effort split Nagara Campā under the Siṅhapura regime, creating a wedge between its capital in the centre (the Thu Bồn valley) and its original base in the south (Kauṭhāra/Pāṇḍuraṅga). This Khmer/Cam faction of Vijaya fought to retain its foothold on the coast at the same time that it became heavily involved in the succession politics of Angkor following Sūryavarman II's death in 1149.

The new ruler, a much younger brother of Sūryavarman's, Tribhuvanādityavarman, initially was involved in maintaining his brother's empire, while basing his regime in Tantric Buddhism. It seems that in doing so he may have sent out a magnificent nāga-enthroned Buddha to Vijaya. Yet the new ruler quickly became disillusioned with the effort and sought to retreat from empire and his brother's efforts. As a result, on the one hand, the Siṅhapura regime took advantage of the situation to attempt to regain control over its entire territory, and, on the other, the Khmer/Cam faction of Vijaya felt left bare by the new ruler and sought to depose and replace him, in the process restoring Angkor's empire as before. The entire second half of the twelfth century would see the struggle for Nagara Campā play out.

Meanwhile, the house of Parameśvara in Siṅhapura had undergone changes. Through the 1130s, a seemingly smooth transition occurred in the ruling family as Jaya Indravarman (1139-43? CE) took the throne there. Reaching back into the past, this new ruler linked himself to Uroja, claimed as ancestor by Indrapura in the ninth century, to Bhadreśvava of the original

Cam realm in the sixth century, and to Jaya Siṅhavarman of the Siṅhapura line, as well as to the founding ancestor of the Kauṭhāra regime, also of the ninth century. Through all this, Jaya Indravarman, besides establishing his own authority and legitimacy, was remaking and consolidating Nagara Campā, creating thereby the new 'imagined community' of the Cams. This he carried out physically as he acted in both the centre and the south, placing similar inscriptions in Nha Trang and Mỹ Sơn, as well as donations to other temples. The new ruler thus certified himself and his line throughout his territory, in the meantime defining his regime and Nagara Campā in this way. He also broke with Sūryavarman II and Angkor. Where preceding rulers of Siṅhapura had joined the Khmer ruler in his diplomatic and martial efforts in dealing with the Song court in China and with Đại Việt, this partnership now ceased.

So, in the mid-1140s CE, the Khmer intrusion into Vijaya badly disrupted the Siṅhapura regime. Jaya Indravarman disappeared, and his nephew and heir Jaya Harivarman (r. 1145-62 CE) fled the country. He reappeared in the domain of his father (Jaya Indravarman's brother or brother-in-law?) in Pāṇḍuraṅga. From there, he and his forces emerged to defeat the Angkorian and Vijayan forces in the lowlands, followed by victory in the highlands over local forces allied with the Khmer. Then the king had to overcome a Cam noble allied with Vietnamese. Through the 1150s, Jaya Harivarman regained control of Nagara Campā for Siṅhapura, including more fighting in Pāṇḍuraṅga. By 1160, he declared victory over the Khmer and the Vietnamese, in the centre, the south-centre, the west (in the Central Highlands), and the south, that is, the entire realm of Nagara Campā. He thereupon donated to the Lady Lord of the Land (Yang Pu Nagara) and proceeded to set up inscriptions to Bhadreśvara at Mỹ Sơn, to the Goddess as the Lady Lord of the Land in Kauṭhāra, and in Pāṇḍuraṅga. Newly the King of Kings, Jaya Harivarman, just as his uncle had done, linked himself to prior kings of the land, of differing places and times, adding Paramabodhisattva of the late eleventh century, one of the founders of Siṅhapura. In addition, he made a major addition to the great Cam shrine of Bhadreśvara, first restoring existing temples, then constructing Group G, a distinctive section of the shrine ("built on the basis of no preconceived model" [Zolese 2009: 234]). Khmer, Sinic, and highland elements all mingled with Cam. As Jaya Harivarman built this temple to himself in the central shrine of the Cam people, he also worked on that of the Goddess (with some similar elements), stating that he enjoyed success "over the land extending to the ocean on which the gods depended." (C130 A2; Schweyer 2005: 92)

Yet Vijaya, with its Khmer/Cam faction, it appears, remained autonomous, more allied with Siṅhapura than conquered by it. I conjecture that 1) Jaya Indravarman of Siṅhapura pressured Tribhuvanādityavarman to leave Nagara Campā, and 2) the Khmer/Cam faction of Vijaya led by a Khmer prince rejected Angkor's new retreat from empire. In the process, these two, Siṅhapura and Vijaya, joined forces to oppose Tribhuvanādityavarman.

Once Jaya Harivarman passed on in the 1160s, another Jaya Indravarman succeeded him who felt he was unable to spread his beneficence over all the Ten Regions of Nagara Campā. It seems that he joined his Siṅhapura forces with those of the Khmer/Cam faction of Vijaya, led by the Khmer prince, to attack and displace Tribhuvanādityavarman at Angkor. Jaya Indravarman first approached the Goddess (Kauthareśvarī) in 1167 CE and then, sixteen years later, announced victory over Kambujadesa and, with five royal women and a son, bestowed captured wealth on the shrine. The Khmer prince of Vijaya became Jayavarman VII at Angkor who, after establishing his rule over Kambujadesa, in the 1190s turned back to Campā. There he took Siṅhapura, brought Jaya Indravarman (or a successor) back to Angkor, and destroyed the *liṅga*s of Nagara Campā. Having removed Campā's royalty and displaced its capital of Siṅhapura, Jayavarman sought to consolidate Campā's place within his empire.

Thus Jaya Indravarman ruled Nagara Campā from the 1160s into the 1180s. In Siṅhapura, he kept the south, Kauṭhāra and Pāṇḍuraṅga, within Nagara Campā, while dealing with Vijaya. He and his house celebrated the Goddess as Lady Lord of Kauṭhāra. In Amandine Lepoutre's view (2013), Nagara Campā lasted through an extended (three decade) period of 'troubles' from 1169 to 1201 CE, as later inscriptions recorded in both the centre and the south. This was the view from Siṅhapura – not so much a direct conflict between Kambujadeśa and Nagara Campā as a fractured time in which elements of each joined each other to oppose other joint factions. It was the internal civil strife aggravated by the Khmer presence, especially in the 1190s, that brought the "troubles' to a Siṅhapura trying to hold the realm together. Regions of this territory fought each other (with or without Khmer help), now not for local power, but to rule Nagara Campā itself, as elements of the old Siṅhapura sought to maintain control.

Jayavarman VII, having removed Siṅhapura, aligned himself with one claimant to the throne of Nagara Campā, but the latter took the name Sūryavarman and set himself up in the south (Vijaya and Pāṇḍuraṅga, and most likely Kauṭhāra as well). After about a decade of chaos, Jayavarman in 1201 CE chose to work with a prince of the former ruling family of Siṅhapura, Ansaraja, a descendant of the rulers from the 1240s to the 1280s. In the same years Jayavarman also sent another Cam who claimed descent from Parameśvara, southern founder of the house of Siṅhapura, as well as receiving the favor of the ancient cult of Bhadreśvara at Mỹ Sơn. In the end it was the prince of Siṅhapura who gained (and served) Jayavarman's favour. This prince proceeded to act as Angkor's viceroy of Campā from the Khmer/Cam base of Vijaya and led troops in campaigns against Siamese, Baganese, Tavoyans, and Vietnamese in the west and north of Angkor's empire.

After almost two decades of such service for Jayavarman, the latter died and in 1220 CE the Khmer again retreated from empire, leaving the Cams finally to themselves. The prince of Siṅhapura, having built Angkor's (and his own) power in Campā, proceeded to re-establish Nagara Campā with Vijaya as its new capital and himself as king, taking the name Parameśvaravarman (following that of the founder of the Siṅhapura house). Holding his *abhiṣeka* (initiation/coronation) six years later, he re-sacralized the shrines of the land with their *liṅgas* and *kośa*s (in his own name, of course) and ruled the new Nagara Campā under his single umbrella, north to south as the inscriptions proclaimed. In this new age of Nagara Campā, the king "protect[ed] the Ten Regions [of Nagara Campā] from fear." In the process, the new regime built a new monumental style of temple, perched on hilltops overlooking the valleys, strongly influenced by the recent Angkorian style.

In this final formation of Nagara Campā, the king himself brought the centre (Siṅhapura) into the newly re-created realm, and he made Vijaya in the south-centre his new capital. In this new age of Nagara Campā, his main task was to consolidate the realm by bringing the south, Kauṭhāra and Pāṇḍuraṅga, into Nagara Campā and finally make it part of the Cam world, finishing what Indrapura had attempted to start and what Siṅhapura had worked to bring about. His name itself, I feel, demonstrated this. Emphasizing the continuity of space and time, he was showing the link between Vijaya and Siṅhapura. At one point explicitly denigrating the role of Angkor in Campā, Parameśvarvarman was returning Campā to the Cams. Now, as his donations and inscriptions reflected, the new king concentrated on regaining the south that had originally been brought into Nagara Campā by his namesake and the latter's successors. Ruled by the Cam claimant Sūryavarman for over a decade during the 1190s and early 1200s, this territory required a particular approach, as seen in the inscriptions (of the thirteen known from his reign, ten came from the south, Kauṭhāra three, Pāṇḍuraṅga seven). The approach first meant reintegrating the Goddess of Kauṭhāra into the realm as Lady Lord of the Land, with her ties as Bhagavatī to the Bhadreśvara cult of Mỹ Sơn, the original cult of the Cams. Parameśvaravarman gave a statue, paddy fields, and labour to the shrine there. This labor included Khmers, Cams, Lao (or probably Chinese), Siamese, and Baganese, many undoubtedly obtained by his forces during his campaigns for Jayavarman VII.

But it was distant Pāṇḍuraṅga that required the most effort by the king to consolidate Nagara Campā. There, it was the eighth century temple of Svayamutpanna where Parameśvaravarman and his house personally chose to establish his authority. This authority was embodied in his personal form of Śiva and his *liṅga.* The numerous donations included cult objects, precious gifts, paddy fields, and labor – the latter likewise being Khmer, Cam, Siamese, Lao (Chinese?), and Baganese, plus this time Javanese. The amount of these donations indicate the extent of Parameśvaravarman's effort to bring Pāṇḍuraṅga into Nagara Campā and make this distant territory a firm part of his realm. As Andrew Hardy has noted, such ritual and economic activity brought peripheral territories firmly within Nagara Campā.

The status of Svayamutpanna, as Parameśvarvarman's main and personal temple in Pāṇḍuraṅga, may be seen by comparing its donations to those at the main Cam temple at Mỹ Sơn and the Goddess in Nha Trang. With its Śiva cult being re-established, Svayamutpanna received its Śaiva image and more cult objects than the other two sites (mainly in silver, with less gold than for Bhadreśvara, but more than for the already established cult of the Goddess). On the other hand, being on the fringe of Nagara Campā and a lesser territory, Svayamutpanna also received less labor and much less paddy fields than the Goddess whose cult was already firmly established and of greater importance in the south. Hence Jaya Parameśvara was bringing the south firmly within Nagara Campā through both ritual and economic means, generally with more ritual and less economic aid for the fringe Pāṇḍuraṅga, but with less ritual and more economic aid for the more important Goddess, Lady Lord of the Realm.

Vijaya proceeded with its consolidation of Nagara Campā through the second half of the thirteenth century, continuing its focus on the south. Jaya Parameśvaravarman's younger brother, Jaya Indravarman, made donations of paddy fields and goods not only to the Goddess (Kauthareśvarī), but also to his own Śaiva *liṅga* cult, plus an image for the Small Goddess. As this king turned more toward Śaivism, a daughter of his in the 1250s and 1260s CE gave donations to the Lady Lord of the Realm as well as to Matrilingeśvarī (Lady Lord of the *Liṅga* and the Mother). These donations included fields in Pāṇḍuraṅga.

Then the Mongols struck in the 1280s and the Vijaya court took refuge in the highlands. During this catastrophe, there is no sign of other regions, especially the south, splitting off from Nagara Campā and joining the invaders (unlike in Đại Việt). Thereafter, the new Vijayan king Jaya Siṅhavarman, "of the lands from north to south," made an even greater effort at consolidating his realm. He established royal temple estates on the fringes, in the north, up in the highlands to the west, and down south in Pāṇḍuraṅga. This approach was more one of local economic development than cultic. We see this particularly in Pāṇḍuraṅga. Here on the site of eleventh century inscriptions, the king constructed a Vijayan temple, Po Klong Garai, on the crest of a hill overlooking the valley. Herein, as in the north and the west, he placed his *liṅga*, bringing these border areas firmly within Nagara Campā. It appears that, in this post-Mongol era, Jaya Siṅhavarman was creating a network of royal temple estates, at least on the edges of his realm. Here at Po Klong Garai, in a unique situation he recorded an extensive territory of paddy fields comprising the domain of the temple, linked to the newly reconstructed irrigation system, which yielded 'paddy fields of the realm'. Following undoubted damage through the middle and late twelfth century and more recently the ending of the Medieval Climate Anomaly (leading to the dryer and cooler Little Ice Age), Jaya Siṅhavarman's active royal development programme brought not only stronger political control, but also needed local economic development.

By 1300 CE, Nagara Campā under the Vijayan kings ruled the Austronesian coast of the mainland's eastern seaboard. Though contesting its north with the Vietnamese, they controlled the centre, the west, and the south. While factionalism might occur at the royal court, hereafter there appears to have been no further inter-regional conflict along this coast. Thus, I would argue that instead of the dichotomy of one vs. many realms of this land, there was instead a thousand year process (say 300-1300 CE) in which the numerous river valley communities of this coast formed their own realms and then finally, after several efforts, merged into the one realm of Nagara Campā, becoming Cams in the process. The Cams of the Thu Bồn valley emerged as a community, then brought about the realm of Nagara Campā. Indrapura moving north in the ninth and tenth centuries created a greater Campā. Siṅhapura in the eleventh and twelfth centuries merged south and north. Vijaya in the thirteenth century completed this effort. In the south, Kauṭhāra dominated Pāṇḍuraṅga and brought both into Nagara Campā. Nevertheless, it took Vijaya's ritual and economic efforts to ensure that the south was Cam and came under Nagara Campā's one umbrella.

References

Griffiths, Arlo and Southworth, William. 2011. 'Étude du corpus des inscriptions du Campà-II. La stèle d'installations de Sri Ādidevesvara: Une nouvelle inscription de Satyavarman trouvée dans le temple de Hoà Lai et son importance pour l'histoire du Panduranga'. *Journal Asiatique*, No. 299.1(2011) : 271-317.

Griffiths, Arlo, Hardy, Andrew Geoff Wade, Geoff. 2019. *Campā: Territories and Networks of a Southeast Asian Kingdom. Champa: Territories and Networks of a Southeast Asian Kingdom.* Paris: École française d'Extrême-Orient.

Hardy, And *etworks of a Southeast Asian Kingdom. Champa: Territories and Networks of a Southeast Asian Kingdom* (eds. Arlo Griffiths, A. Hardy and G. Wade) Paris: École française d'Extrême- Orient: 221-252.

Lieberman, V. & Buckley, B. 2012. 'The Impact of Climate on Southeast Asia, circa 950–1820: New Findings'. In *Modern Asian Studies*, Volume 46, Issue 5, September 2012: 1049-1096. DOI: https://doi.org/10.1017/S0026749X12000091

Lepoutre, Amandine. 2013. «Études du corpus des inscriptions du Campā, IV: Les inscriptions du temple de Svayamutpanna: contribution à l'histoire des relations entre les pouvoirs cam et khmer (de la fin du XIIe siècle au début du XIIIe siècle)». Journal Asiatique. 301 (1): 205-278. doi:10.2143/JA.301.1.2994464.

Momoki, Shiro. 1999. 'The Dry Areas in Southeast Asia: Harsh or Benign Environment?'. In *Final Report of a Cooperative Project under the Kyoto-Thammasal Core University*

Program, Fukui Hayao, Ed, (The Center for Southeast Asian Studies (CSEAS), Tokyo University, March 1999).

Schweyer, Anne-Valérie. 2004. 'Po Nagar de Nha Trang (1re partie)', Aséanie 14, December 2004: 109-140. DOI : 10.3406/asean.20034.1830

Schweyer, Anne-Valérie. 2005. 'Po Nagar de Nha Trang. Seconde partie : Le dossier épigraphique', Aséanie: <https://doi.org/10.3406/asean.2005.184710.3406/asean.2005.1847>

Southworth, William. 2012. 'Religious architecture and irrigation in the plain of Phan Rang'. In *Old myths and new approaches: Interpreting ancient religious sites in Southeast Asia* (ed. Alexandra Haendel). Australia: Monash University Publishing: 263-283.

Vickery, Michael .2011. 'Champa revised'. In *The Cham in Vietnam: History, Society and Art.* Eds Trần Kỳ Phương and Bruce M. Lockhart. Singapore: NUS Press: 363-420.

Zolese, Patrizia .2009. 'Results of the Archaeological Investigations at Mỹ Sơn G Group (1997-2007)'. In *Champa and the Archaeology of Mỹ Sơn (Vietnam)* (eds Andrew Hardy, M. Cucarzi and P. Zolese). Singapore: NUS Press: 197-237.

18 | Esoteric Buddhist goddesses of the Campā Vijaya state

Trần Kỳ Phương & Nguyễn Thị Tú Anh[1]

Based on the corpus of Cam inscriptions, scholars have asserted that Cam Buddhism was unable to reach the same powerful religious role as Brahmanism in Campā (Mus 1933: 369; Mabbett 1986: 294; Bronkhorst 2011: 52-3).[2] In this essay, we counter this by arguing that Buddhism expanded as successfully in the final centuries of the Campā state as Brahmanism had done earlier. The huge collapsed complex of the Lakṣmīndra-Lokeśvara *vihāra* in Đồng Dương, provides clear evidence for a surge in the role of Buddhism in Campā, particularly Cam forms of Esoteric Buddhism, from the 8th-9th centuries. Furthermore, new investigations of the visual arts of Bình Định province are revealing for the first time the presence of Esoteric Buddhist deities in the ensuing centuries who may be tentatively identified as the Esoteric Buddhist goddesses Pāṇḍaravāsinī and Vajratārā. A small stone icon of one of these goddesses can be found in the collection of the History Museum in Hồ Chí Minh City. This paper brings them to public attention for the first time.

Buddhism in the Campā kingdom since the 7th century

The strong growth in global trade that characterized the 7th century CE also shaped and developed the communities along the southern rim of Asia. Countless merchants were plying the seas between the eastern Indian coast to the ports of Tang China. Cultural exchanges intensified as shown by the numerous Buddhist monks who recorded their travels. The prominent Chinese monk Yijing (635-713 CE), left valuable information on his voyage from Guangzhou to the south in 673 CE on a Persian merchant's boat (Paine 2014: 37; Sen 2018: 348). Campā was one of Yijing's destinations, where an intensification of Buddhist activities was recorded at the end of 7th century "In this country [Linyi/Campā] Buddhists generally belong to the *Āryasammiti-nikāya*, and there are a few followers of the *Sarvāstivāda-nikāya.*" Yijing also recorded that the Hīnayāna was popularly practiced in coastal states (Mabbett 1986: 295-96; Sen 2018: 360). Some historians see a 7th century 'Buddhist cosmopolis' expanding across Asia (Paine 2014: 37-53; Sen 2018: 345-68).

Textual sources and archaeological evidence indicate that South India and Sri Lanka were key to the propagation of Esoteric Buddhist doctrines through the famous Esoteric Buddhist masters Vajrabodhi (671-741 CE) and Amoghavajra (705-774 CE). Early Tantric texts such as the *Mahāvairocanatantra* and the *Sarvatathāgatatattvasangraha* were translated and cultivated there in the 8th century (Sen 2014: 52-3; Acri 2016: 9; Sharrock and Bunker

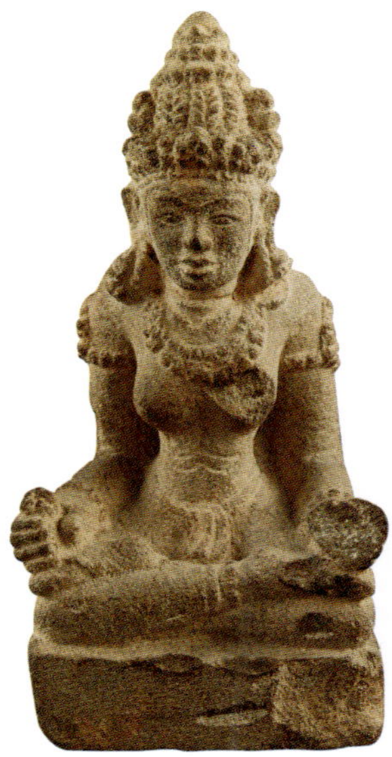

Fig. 1 *Pāṇḍaravāsinī (?), spiritual consort of Amitābha, (Quảng Nam province?), BTLS.614.*

2016: 237-52). The geographical location of Sri Lanka favoured it as a centre for the spread of Esoteric Buddhism to the Malay Peninsula, Sumatra, Java, Campā and on to East Asia. On their long journey to China, delayed by difficult monsoons, these Esoteric Buddhist masters brought Tantric Buddhism to the Buddhist communities along the sea lanes. On the extended maritime route connecting South and East Asia, the Cam coastal entrepôt network provided ideal stopovers to resupply food and fresh water (Chutiwongs 2005: 68-9; Acri, Blench and Landmann 2017: 1-37; Hall 2018: 19-30). From the 7th to 10th centuries, the maritime trade network built links among the Khmer kingdom, Campā, Java, the Malay peninsula, and China. In addition, it was Esoteric Buddhism that played an active role in political institutions and the establishing of political and commercial links between the locales in Southeast Asian states over many centuries during the medieval period (Acri 2016: 5-7).

The late 9th century Lakṣmīndra-Lokeśvara *vihāra* in Đồng Dương

The Đồng Dương monument was the most important centre of Esoteric Buddhist practice in Campā. This can be seen in the art and architecture of the Đồng Dương site, which was only excavated in the early 20th century and was unfortunately destroyed during the wars in Vietnam from the mid-20th century. We therefore rely heavily on the in-depth studies and scientific drawings of Henri Parmentier (1909; 1918).

The large Đồng Dương monument complex has been identified from its foundation inscription C.66 as a *vihāra* dedicated to the Bodhisattva Lakṣmīndra-Lokeśvara, which was constructed during the reign of Śrī Jaya Indravarman II in 875 CE (Majumdar 1985, III: 82-8; Golzio 2004: 60-73 [C.66]). The *vihāra* included a large number of tower-sanctuaries built in a complex 1,300 meters in length.

Parmentier named the three main compounds in the *vihāra* as Enclosure I, II and III. Enclosure I was the *karmamaṇḍala*, Enclosure II its *mandapa* and Enclosure III a meeting and lecture hall (*vihāra*). A *dhārani* was inscribed on what is now called the 'Xuân Sơn column' by a square lotus pond built on the east in front of the temple complex (Parmentier 1909: 281-2, 439-505) **(Fig. 2)**.

There are three large statues found at the Buddhist monastery including a bronze standing Buddha, a sandstone sitting Buddha with legs pendant, and a sitting Buddha making *bodhyangīmudrā* also made of sandstone. The An Thái stele offers information to identify the three sculptures.

The An Thái stele[3] is the only Cam inscription that provides information on the tantric disciplines, known as *sadhanās*, of contemporary Campā Buddhism, dating back to 902 CE (Golzio 2004: 89-92, C.138). It emphasizes a system of worshiping the three Buddhas in the Esoteric Buddhism of Campā, including *Śākyamuni*, Amitābha and Vairocana, who have blessed the three *jinālayaḥ* (victor realms) those are *Vajradhātu*, *Padmadhātu* and *Cakradhātu*

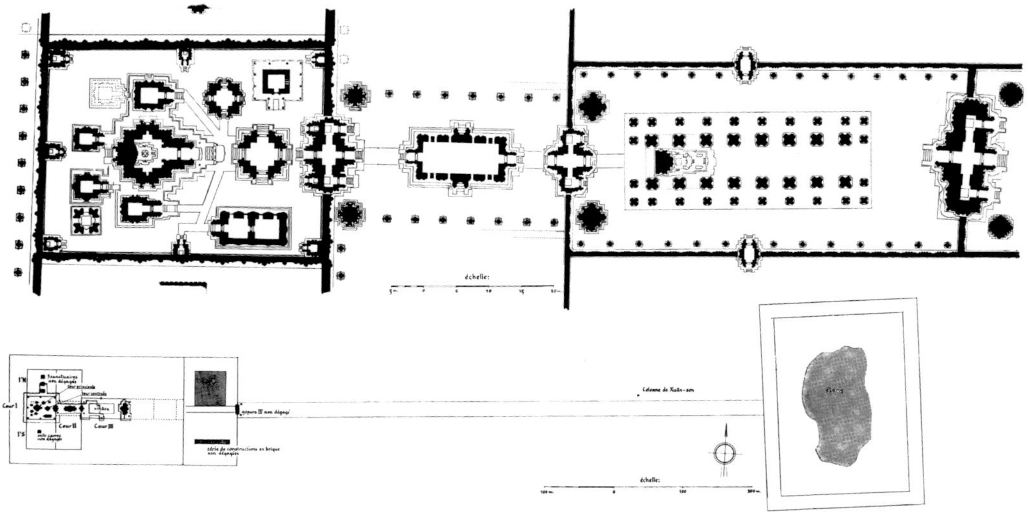

Fig. 2 *The ground plan of the Lakṣmīndra-Lokeśvara* vihāra *at* Đồng *Dương, Quảng Nam province, according to Parmentier's drawing in 1909.*

to manifest the *Śūnyatā* (Emptiness), *Mahaśūnyatā* (Great Emptiness), and *Śūnyatātīto* (Transcendental Emptiness) (Huber 1911: 272-82; Finot 1925: 232; Majumdar 1927: III, 105-09; Mabbett 1986: 301-02; Golzio 2004: 89-92; Chutiwongs 2005: 80-1).

It is possible to compare the three *jinālayaḥ* mentioned in the An Thái stele, with the *trikūla* of the Vajrayāna form of Tantric Buddhism, including *Vajrakūla* or *Vajradhātu* is associated with Śākyamuni; *Padmakūla* or *Padmadhātu* associated with Amitābha; and, *Buddhakūla* or *Cakradhātu* associated with Vairocana; that are the three families (*kūla*) in the Womb Realm, also known as the *Garbhadhātu-maṇḍala*, which appear in many tantric texts, especially in the *Mahavairocana-sutra* and the *Susiddhikara-sutra*.

There are two main mandala forms established in Vajrayāna for the practice of the initiation ritual (*abhiṣeka*), namely Womb Realm mandala, and the other is the Adamantine Realm which known as *Vajradhātu-maṇḍala*.

It is known that the Womb Realm followed a three-family format (*trikūla*) for classifying and arranging the deities, otherwise, the Adamantine Realm was replaced by a five-family format (*pañcakūla*) in which *Buddhakūla* or *Cakradhātu* associated with Vairocana; *Vajrakūla* associated with Akṣobhya; meanwhile *Ratnakūla, Padmakūla* and *Karmakūla* are associated with Ratnasambhava, Amitābha, Amoghasiddhi respectively (Giebel 2001; 2005).

The Womb Realm mandala represents Great Compassion, formed from the *Mahāvairocanābhisaṃbodhi-sūtra;* while the Adamantine mandala represents the Great Wisdom which formed from the *Sarvatathāgatatattvasamgraha-sūtra (STTS);* both of them symbolizing the nonduality of Mahayanist thought (Abé 1999: 44; Grotenhuis 1999: 36-38; Orzech 2011: 263-85; Faure 2016: 191-4).

Therefore, the titles of the three *Jinas* (Buddhas) are mentioned in sequence in the An Thái stele, which offers a hypothesis that the three large

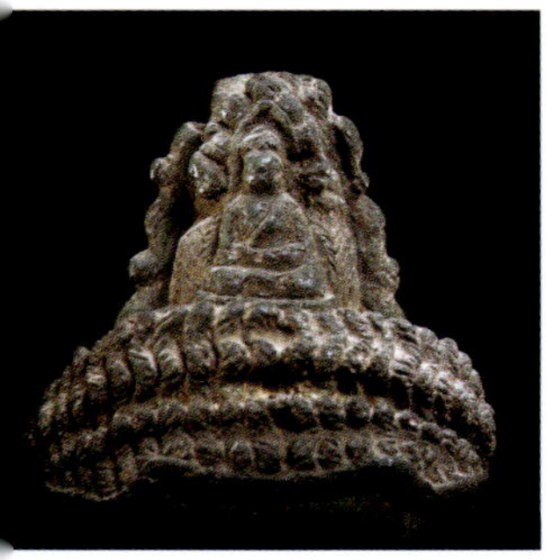

Fig. 3b *detail.*

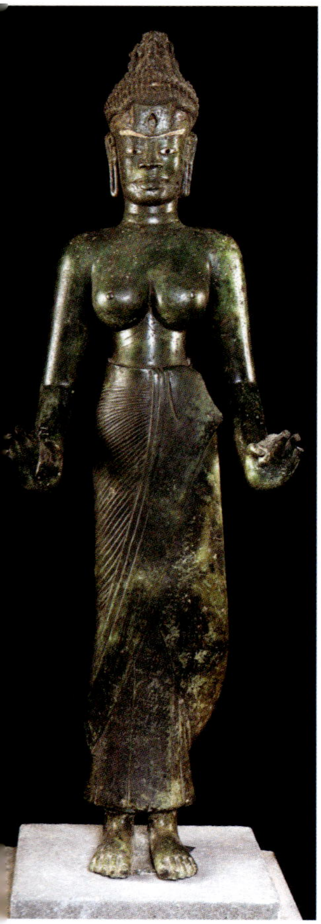

Fig. 3a *The bronze statue found at Đồng Dương. 114 cm high. Đà Nẵng Museum of Cam Sculpture. (Photo River Books)*

Buddha statues were discovered in the Đồng Dương site are Śākyamuni Tathāgata, Amitābha Tathāgata, and Mahavairocana Tathāgata respectively. The positions of the three statues can thus be assumed, as follows: The standing bronze Śākyamuni statue can be positioned on the main altar of the main Buddha hall (*tour principal*), performing the gesture of discussion (*vitarka-mudrā*) with his right hand (Parmentier 1909: 443-46)[4]. Next mentioned is a sitting sandstone Buddha with legs pendant and hands resting on knees, possibly Amitābha, who may be positioned in a four-door temple or '*tour central*' in front of the main Buddha hall, both belonging to Enclosure I (Parmentier 1909: 452-55; Woodward 2011: fig.1; Dhar 2014: 120; Baptiste 2019: 344-47)[5]. Finally, a sandstone sitting Buddha represented the figure of Mahavairocana, identified by his hands in *bodhyangīmudrā*, an esoteric gesture denoting the zenith of the universe. This statue was positioned in the four-door sanctuary (some of its walls still standing today) in Enclosure I (Parmentier 1909: 482, 502). It can be assumed that the sitting Buddha with both legs pendant represented the image of Amitābha, since he is associated with the Bodhisattva Laksmīndra-Lokeśvara, the main deity of the Đồng Dương *vihāra*, honored in the inscription by King Jaya Indravarman.

The content of the An Thái stele supports identifying the Buddha with pendant legs with Amitābha. (Dhar 2014: 120). Although it has been argued to the contrary that the seated Buddha with pendant legs also has his hands placed on his knees, a posture otherwise unknown in Cam icons. This position is however known in several large Chinese Buddhas and notably in the giant 71 m Maitreya Buddha carved into the cliff-face at Leshan in 803 CE, at the confluence of three rivers – the Minjiang, Dadu River and Qing Yijiang in southern Sichuan province (Tu 2018: 79-88)[6].

Therefore, it can be proposed that the design of the Đồng Dương *vihara* followed a Womb Realm mandala, based on the arrangement of the Three Buddha Family format of the Laksmīndra-Lokeśvara monastery. The Womb Realm mandala was also established in conjunction with the Adamantine Realm mandala, symbolizing the practice of the initiation ritual (*abhiṣeka*) in China and Japan in the 8th-9th centuries (Grotenhuis 1999: 33-77; Faure 2016: 210-8; Trần and Nguyễn 2025: 132-59). In contemporary ancient Southeast Asia, among the Vajrayānist monuments, all of them may represent the combination of the Womb Realm and the Adamantine Realm, in which the tantric temples in the Prambanan valley in central Java are examples (Tingley 2006/7: 65-80; Chandra 2009: 137-61; Kandahjaya 2009: 1-24; 2016: 67-112; Sharrock and Bunker 2016: 237-9; Chemburkar 2017: 197-22).

The Đồng Dương *vihāra* was most probably one of the most prominent Buddhist monasteries during the flourishing period of Esoteric Buddhism in Southeast Asia in the 10th century and demonstrates that Campā served as an essential link in contemporary trans-Asian Buddhist cultural exchanges.

Cam Buddhism from the 11th to the 13th century

It should be mentioned that, at the end of 10th century, many wars occurred between Đại Việt and the Song empire in China. The Song emperors tried to lure Campā allies into the wars against the Đại Việt from the southern borders, which seeded later conflicts between Đại Việt and Campā (Hoàng Xuân Hãn 1966: 234-63; Wade 2011: 152). In 981/2 CE, Lê Hoàn took the initiative to attack Campā to reduce war threats from the south and the Lakṣmīndra-Lokeśvara *vihāra* in Đồng Dương was badly damaged. Lê Hoàn's attack, along with an uprising of Campā residents against Lưu Kỳ Tông's usurpation in the following year, caused many Cam people to flee to Hainan island (Wade 2011: 143-5; Trần and Nguyễn 2021: 3-5).

Moreover, in the year 1000 CE, King Sri Yang Pu Ku Vijaya sent an envoy to the Chinese court to announce the relocation of the Cam capital to Vijaya. In 1044, 1047 and 1069 CE, the Lý dynasty of Đại Việt repeatedly attacked the north of the Campā kingdom, causing the kingdom to fall into crisis (Cœdès 1968: 125, 139-40). However, the southern Cam polity remained stable. King Jaya Parameśvaravarman in the southern Pāṇḍuraṅga region thus dedicated a Buddhist monastery called Rājākula in 1055 CE, in the present Phan Rang area in Ninh Thuận province. The king identified himself as a *cakravartin* (universal ruler), and also a devout Buddhist believer as the Phú Quý inscription C.122 indicated (Golzio 2004: 131). King Harivarman, who reigned from c.1074-81 CE, restored the kingdom after years of war. According to inscription C.90 A-C, D he ordered the reconstruction of the holy mountain shrine Śrīsanabhadreśvara, at Mỹ Sơn (Golzio 2004: 138-43). In around 1081 CE, Harivarman died leaving a young Prince Vāk as his successor. Prince Pãn, the younger brother of Harivarman, was assigned to rule the kingdom as regent. Prince Pãn took the title Śrī Paramabodhisattva and is called a Mahāyāna devotee and *rājācakravartin* in inscription C.89 (Golzio 2004: 147). Śrī Paramabodhisattva's regency should be construed as aligned with the matriarchal custom in Campā, rather than usurpation, as some scholars have argued (Maspero 1928: 147-8; Cœdès 1968: 154; Schweyer 2009: 324). In 1088-9 CE, Śrī Paramabodhisattva abdicated in favour of Prince Vāk who took the reign name Jaya Indravarman. Like his uncle, Jaya Indravarman was also a Buddhist. He ordered an inscription to be carved in praise of Paramabodhisattva and constructed a Buddhist monastery named Śrī Indralokeśvara in Tranul district, probably not far from Mỹ Sơn (Majumdar 1985, III: 172).[7]

Decades later, Paramabodhisattva's merit was again praised in the Mỹ Sơn inscription C.101 dated 1157 CE, which was erected by King Jaya Harivarman, who also claimed to be his descendant (Golzio 2004: 166-7). Jaya Harivarman was celebrated as a hero for defending Campā against a Khmer attack in 1150 CE. The inscription says the king was a native of *Bhūmiratnavijaya,* i.e. Vijaya state. It is understood from later Khmer inscriptions that a young Khmer prince served in his army who would later become the great Cambodian Buddhist King Jayavarman VII from ca.1182-1220 CE (Sharrock 2018: 116-8).

After Jayavarman VII took power in Angkor by driving out the remnant of a Cam force that had penetrated the Khmer capital and killed his predecessor Tribhuvanādityavarman (Sharrock 2018: 112), he fought to return Vijaya to the Khmer empire, but was held up for a decade by his former Cam protégé who defeated an invading Khmer army and proclaimed himself king Śrī Sūryavarmadeva of a briefly united Campā kingdom. King Sūrya celebrated his victory, according to his long and historical inscription C.92 B-C, by constructing in 1194 CE a temple to Esoteric Buddhist deity Śrī Heruka. Positioned next to the stone temple of presiding Mỹ Sơn god Śiva-Bhadreśvara, this was the first fully Esoteric Buddhist shrine built in Campā (Golzio 2004: 174-6; Chutiwongs 2005: 85; Schweyer 2018: 76). Heruka, the fierce emanation of the supreme Buddha Vajrasattva, was later adopted as the most powerful deity of the Vajrayāna by the courts of Angkor, Java, Sumatra and Mongol China in the 12th-14th centuries (Schnitger 1937: 26, fig. XXXIV; Sharrock 2009: 49-64; Bautze-Picron 2014: 107-28; Calo 2020: 1-20).

The political and military upheavals between the Cams and Khmers during the late 12th-early 13th centuries linked with the economic pull of the new deep-water port of Vijaya that was key to profiting from the burgeoning sea trade of the Song dynasty (Whitmore 2018: 31-6; Sharrock 2018: 111-9). This was reflected in the boom in art and architecture, most of it Esoteric Buddhist, in the two states. In Campā, this was vividly present in Mỹ Sơn and in the region around Vijaya. Esoteric Buddhism grew steadily in Campā in an economic boom from the Song trade in the 12th-15th centuries (Acri 2016: 19-22; Whitmore 2018: 31-6).

The flourishing of forms of royal Esoteric Buddhism in Khmer, Javanese and Sumatran courts during the 11th to 13th centuries (Bautze-Picron 2014: 107-28; Sharrock 2022: 126-159), now invites closer scrutiny of related forms in the visual arts of the Vijaya state.

The Pāṇḍaravāsinī (?) statue found at Xuân Mỹ, Bình Định province

Parmentier (1909: 155-7) noted that the statue was found in Xuân Mỹ village, Quảng Nghiệp district, Tri Phước district, Bình Định province, south of Bình Lâm temple.[8] The site currently belongs to Xuân Mỹ village, Phước Hiệp commune, Tuy Phước district, Bình Định province, some 10 km from Quy Nhơn city. There are three temple structures at Xuân Mỹ. The statue was found inside the principal temple and brought to the French Résidence de Quy Nhơn by a Father Salomez, before entering the Cam Museum in Đà Nẵng in 1918 (Parmentier 1919: 31-2). Two inscriptions were said to be buried inside the collapsed structures.

Jean Boisselier (1963: 343) saw the Xuân Mỹ statue as representing the goddess Śrī or Lakṣmī with her *kirīṭa-mukuṭa* hairdress replaced unusually by an ascetic's *jāṭa-mukuṭa* but with rows of pearls. He pointed to the lotus bud attributes and abdominal "trois plis de beauté" as well as a goose or *haṃsa* on the square pedestal. However, it should be noted that in Cam art the lines on the abdomen represent maternity and are never applied to the Hindu goddess. Swati Chemburkar (2018: 238) notes that the *haṃsa* could indicate Sarasvatī, the ancient Indic goddess of wisdom, but her usual attributes of rosary, water bottle, manuscript and musical instrument are absent.

The Xuân Mỹ statue was the principal icon worshipped in the main shrine or *kalan*. The goddess is represented in the round, sitting in *vajrāsana* posture on a square-shaped pedestal on which the upper part of a bird rises in a striking posture beneath her. (**Fig. 4**) What is the identity of this bird? We will suggest that the small, raised wings, the assertive stance and the head-crest suggest a peacock, which is usually associated with the tantric Buddhist protective goddesses Pāṇḍaravāsinī, consort of Jina Amitābha, or Mahāmāyūrī ('great peacock').[9] A *jāṭa-mukutā* with a string of pearls between each level, rises high on her head, her distended earlobes are adorned with round flat earrings, and her prominent thick eyebrows are joined above her eyes. Her body is adorned with rich jewelry including necklaces and bangles for her arms and wrists, and her hands rest on her knees, holding lotus buds.[10] Maternity lines show under her breasts and her heel-length sarong has woven patterns of rhombuses and zigzags lines. The designs are very similar to the woven patterns on the textiles of the various ethnic groups living in the central highlands of Vietnam today.

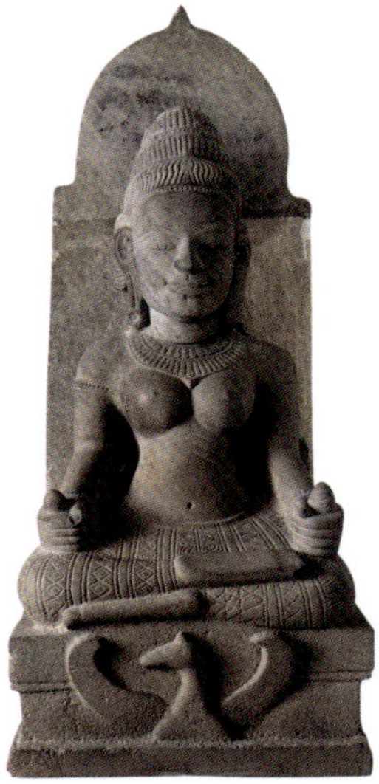

Fig. 4 *The 13th century statue of Pāṇḍaravāsinī at the Đà Nẵng Museum of Cam Scupture. Sandstone; 90 cm high, 40 cm wide; 30 cm thick (Acc. no. BTC 210/11.2). (Photo River Books)*

Boisselier dated the Xuân Mỹ statue to the 12th-13th centuries (1963: 343) because of the large necklace and rounded earrings, which he compared to the terracotta tympana representing the goddesses sitting in *vajrāsana* posture from the Mỹ Sơn G1 temple. The circular motif of the earrings indeed appears on the Mỹ Sơn G1 temple, which is associated with the inscription of Jaya Harivarman dating to ca.1157/8 CE. The Mỹ Sơn G1 inscription is key to setting a timeframe for the Bình Định or Tháp Mẫm style identified by Philippe Stern (1942: 105-7) and Boisselier (1963: 251-4). In this context, the Xuân Mỹ goddess can be dated to the late 12th century, before Jayavarman VII conquered central Campā in 1203 CE (Southworth and Trần 2019: 340-2). We would like to propose that the identity of the goddess in the contemporary context of Esoteric Buddhist development in the Campā Vijaya state, is Pāṇḍaravāsinī, based on her specific iconographical features as will be discussed below.

Iconographical features of Pāṇḍaravāsinī

In later Tibetan art, Pāṇḍaravāsinī, or Pāṇḍara is a *vidyārājñī* ('wisdom queen') sometimes regarded as the Mother of the Buddhas (Jinas). Pāṇḍaravāsinī is the consort of Jina Amitābha, in the western universe quadrant of the

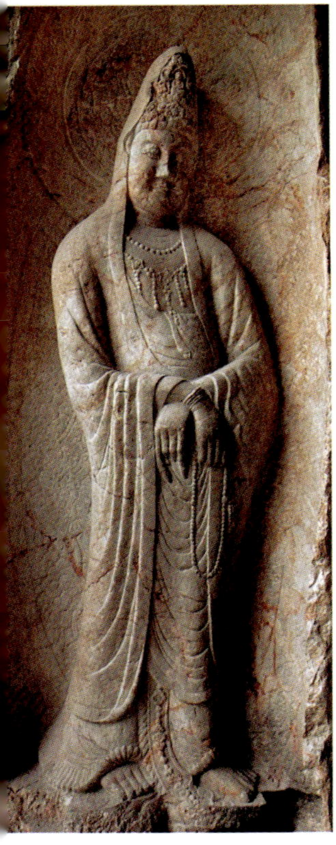

Fig. 5 *White-robed Guanyin at Yanxia cave, Hangzhou province. Circa the mid-10th to mid-11th centuries; marble; 185 cm high. (Broeskamp 2014: 120, fig. 2)*

Vajradhātu-maṇḍala; representing discriminated wisdom. Pāṇḍaravāsinī means 'the person in the white robe'. Her red body, ornamented with splendid jewelry, symbolizes the purity of compassion. She sits in *vajrāsana* and holds a white lotus (*utpala*). Her mount is a peacock like Amitābha's. (Battacharyya 1958: 50-1; Getty 1988: 139; Elizabeth 2002: 56; Vessantara 2004: 39-49).

According to the *Vairocanābhisaṃbodhi-sūtra*, Pāṇḍaravāsinī is 'positioned behind Avalokiteśvara and beside Tārā and has a high bun, and is dressed in a white silk, holding a lotus in hand'. Her mantra is *Namaḥ samanta buddhānāṃ, paṃ*! ('Homage to all Buddhas! Paṃ!') (Giebel 2005: 29, 65). In another important Vajrayāna *sūtra*, the *Advaya-vajra-sangraha-sūtra*, Pāṇḍaravāsinī is described thus, "[I]n the Vayu corner on the orb of the moon there is Pāṇḍaravāsinī originating from the (red) germ syllable Parh. She is red in color and has the *padma* (lotus) as her recognition symbol. She is the embodiment of the element of Fire. She belongs to the Lotus family and is full of attachment." (Bhattacharyya 1958: 50-1). Vessantara (2004: 39-49) describes Pāṇḍaravāsinī as sitting in the *vajrāsana* posture on a crystal throne, dressed in delicate attire adorned with precious things and with a top in pure white that covers her red body. She wears a five-jeweled crown covering a topknot though the rest of her long black hair flows over her shoulders. Her aura radiates around her head and body, her beauty becomes noble with an infinitely benevolent smile. These details fit the Xuân Mỹ statue quite well.[11]

Pāṇḍaravāsinī or White-robed Guanyin in Chinese art

In China, from the end of Tang dynasty, Pāṇḍaravāsinī was venerated as 'Pai-i Guanyin' or 'White-robed Avalokiteśvara', one of the 33 transformation bodies of Guanyin. Her Chinese image was locally stylized as a woman in white with a veil on her head, holding a *kamandalu* (pot or gourd) and willow branch in her hands. She belongs to the Lotus family of Amitābha in the court of Avalokiteśvara/Guanyin. All wear white, symbolizing the 'mothers' of Buddhas and Bodhisattvas (Stein 1986: 31-44; Yu 2001: 249-50).

In the art of the Tang dynasty, the image of White-robed Avalokiteśvara was portrayed interchangeably with male and female genders. Most of the Zen masters tended to create scroll paintings of a Water-moon Guanyin (White-robed Guanyin), however, with a more masculine than feminine look (Yu 2001: 247-8).

During the Song period, early in the 11th century, the cult of the White-robed Guanyin was widely developed; this bodhisattva was worshipped as a goddess of wealth and prosperity as well as fertility and was called 'Child-giving Guanyin' (Yu 2001: 52-6; Broeskamp 2014: 120). Art historians have claimed that the earliest images of the White-robed Guanyin appearing in female form were the two bodhisattva statues at the entrance to the Yanxia cave, Hangzhou province. These two high-reliefs of White-robed Guanyin, life size at 185 cm, were erected on either side of the door to the patio of

Yanxia cave. (**Fig. 5**) The Guanyin statues of Yanxia cave are believed to date from the mid-10th to mid-11th century (Howard 1985: 11-2; Yu 2001: 182; Broeskamp 2014: 117-20, figs. 2 and 4). Representing the teaching of sublime emptiness of the *Heart Sūtra* and symbolizing the serenity of Zen meditative states, the White-robed Guanyin has adorned the walls of monasteries in China and beyond in Korea and Japan (Yu 2001: 127; Lippit 2008: 192-232).

White-robed Guanyin, or Pāṇḍaravāsinī, was popular in China from the 10th century. The Pai-i Guanyin image protected seafarers '*tz'u-hang* 慈航' ('compassionate sailors') and offered them solace during long and stormy voyages (Yu 2001: 52-6, 247-50). Given the close maritime relationship between Campā and China, the Chinese cult of the White-robed Guanyin may well have influenced a cult of Pāṇḍaravāsinī in Campā.

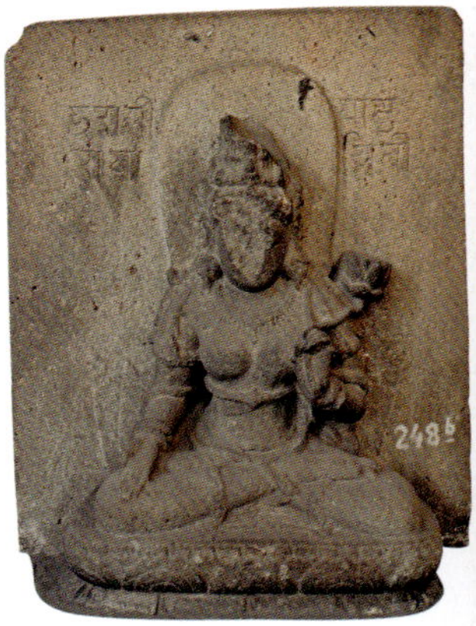

Fig. 6 *Pāṇḍaravāsinī at Candi Jago; 13th century; andesite stone; 28 cm high. National Museum in Jakarta. (Photo courtesy of Marijke Klokke)*

Pāṇḍaravāsinī in the Amoghapāśa-maṇḍala at Candi Jago, East Java

Candi Jago is a 13th century East Javanese Hindu-Buddhist temple complex with Tantric elements built under the Singhasari dynasty. Candi Jago faces west towards the Sukhāvatī paradise of Amitābha, and is dedicated to Amoghapāśa Avalokiteśvara, a key deity for merit transfer ceremonies for the dead. It was built by the powerful Buddhist-Śaiva king Kṛtanagara as a *shraddha* memorial sanctuary 12 years after the death of his father king Wishnuwardhana. In the top shrine of the stepped sanctuary, covered with reliefs, a large relief of a standing Amoghapāśa was surrounded by the four directional Jinas and their consorts (Kinney, Klokke, Kieven 2003: 95-8).

Pāṇḍarāvāsinī from Jago, here as consort of Jina Amitābha, sits on a double lotus throne with aureole on a high backslab with *Bharālī Pāṇḍurāvāsinī* written in Nagari script. Her hair is raised in a high *jāṭa-mukutā* and she is richly adorned with earrings, necklaces and armbands. Ornaments are also to be seen across her chest and on her wrists and ankles. Her right hand with palm upwards rests on her right knee in the boon-granting gesture or *varada-mudrā* (as usual with the Jina consorts). Her raised left hand holds a white lotus stem whose flower blooms above her left shoulder. The sashes of her dress float up the back-slab in typical of East Javanese sculptural fashion (Fontein 1990: 154). (**Fig. 6**)

Four other Candi Jago sculptures have been identified as the Jinas Akṣobhya and Ratnasambhava and their consorts Locanā and Māmakhī. The first three are now at the National Museum in Jakarta while the last is in the Raffles collection at the British Museum. The contemporary 13th century statue at Candi Jago lends some support to the tentative identification of the goddess at Xuân Mỹ in Campā, as these were two coastal polities in ongoing direct contact, which were focused on maritime trade and engaged in state protection Esoteric Buddhism.

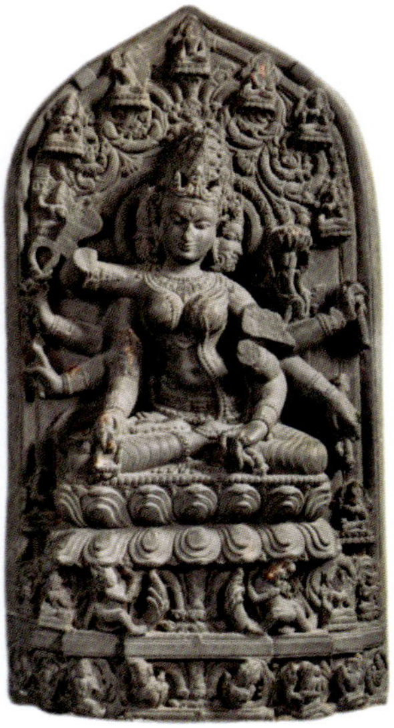

Fig. 7 *Stele of Vajratārā-maṇḍala, Pala style (1075-1200). Perhaps from Nālandā, Bihar state. Asian Art Museum of San Francisco. http://searchcollection.asianart.org/view/objects/asitem/60718/22/dateAdded-desc?t:state:flow=e4b9c11a-c270-4e37-bcad-cfecc9efdcb3*

Tympanum of Vajratārā of Châu Thành

According to the *Niṣpannayogāvalī*, the 11th-century Buddhist textbook on iconography from Vikramaśīla monastery, Vajratārā is an emanation of Jina Ratnasambhava as a yellow goddess with four heads of which "[...] the principal face is golden in colour, the right is white, the one behind is blue and the left red... she is graceful and resplendent with the auspicious marks of a virgin... she is effulgent in her blooming youth, has swaying earrings, sits on the double lotus, and radiates red-hued light [...]" (Bhattacharyya 1958: 240-1) She has eight arms holding a *vajra* (thunderbolt), a noose (*paśa*), arrow and conch in her four right hands; in her left hands she holds a yellow night lotus (*utpala*), a bow, a goad, and she raises her other hand in the threatening *tarjanī-mudrā*. The contemporary Esoteric Buddhist meditation manual *Sādhanamālā* describes Vajratārā as sitting on a double-lotus throne in the *vajraparyaṅka* position bearing the images of the five Jinas in her crown (Bhattacharyya 1958: 241); she holds in her right hands a *vajra*, a noose, conch and arrow; and in the left the *vajrāṅkuśa*, *utpala*, the bow and *tarjanī-mudrā*.

Donaldson (2001: 256-60) notes two 10th-11th-century images of Vajratārā, one from Ratnagiri, Odisha in Northeast India in which she is unattended and the other from Ayodhya where she is accompanied by four goddesses. The Ratnagiri Tārā has three visible heads and eight arms and sits in *vajraparyaṅka*; her right hand attributes are a noose, an arrow, a conch, and she performs the *tarjanī-mudrā* in front of her chest and the *varada-mudrā* in her lower hand; her left hands hold a bow, a goad and an *utpala* in the two lowered hands. The hair in *kiriṭa-mukuṭa* bears no Tathāgata figurine. Meanwhile, in the sanctum of Uttareśvara temple near Ayodhya, the Vajratārā figure is larger and more impressive with three visible faces illuminated by a soft smile. Each head wears a tiara adorned with lotus petals and bears a Buddha image with his hands in front of his chest. In her four right hands, she holds a *vajra*, a conch, an arrow and a noose; in her left hands a *vajrāṅkuśa*, a *nīlotpala*, a bow and the *tarjanī-mudrā*. There are four goddesses surrounding the Tārā figure, including Puṣpatārā on the east, Dhūpatārā on the south, Dīpatārā on the west and Gandhatārā on the north. They all sit in *vajraparyaṅka* on a *viśvapadma* with their attributes in both hands resting on their laps (Donaldson 2001: 260). **(Fig. 7)**

Sarvajñamitra is described as a follower of Tārā who lived in Kashmir in the 8th century, rhapsodizes the 'universal form' (*visva-rupa*) of Tārā in response to the needs of each being (Shaw 2006: 337; Willson 1992: 268-9). Vajratārā's appearance comes with multiple heads and arms in order to reach all sentient beings and for this was exceptionally popular in Esoteric Buddhism (Ghosh 1980: 81; Donaldson 2001: 257). These textual descriptions lend iconographical support to identifying a Cam sculpture now in the Bình Định provincical museum. **(Fig. 8)**

In 1988, a Cam sandstone tympanum goddess was found at the Châu Thành temple ruin in Châu Thành hamlet, Nhơn Thành village, An

Nhơn district, Bình Định province.[12] The site is now being excavated by archaeologists from the Bình Định provincial museum. The tympanum relief represents a goddess with three visible heads who sits in *vajraparyaṅka* on a lotus throne with a high plain petal-shaped back-slab. She has an idealized female form with narrow waist, broad hips, and high, rounded breasts; her three headdresses are shaped as *kiriṭa-mukuṭa* decorated with lotus petals, a new stylistic feature appearing in Cam art in the Vijaya period. Dangling earrings (*kundalas*) distend the earlobes of the principal face as her own specific characteristic (Ghosh 1980: 77). The three visible faces smile compassionately under elegant joined eyebrows above almond-shaped eyes without pupils. The upper body is bare but for a necklace and her elegant limbs are adorned with jewelry. Her lower limbs are covered by a gracefully draped Khmer-style *sampot* secured at the waist by a heavy girdle with pendant ornaments. The front fold falls in a kind of pleated corolla which is very similar to those of Khmer drapes of the end of 12th century or later (Trần 2018: 248-9, cat.76).

In the *Niṣpannayogāvalī* (Bhattacharyya 1958: 240), Vajratārā has eight arms but here she has four. In this Cam statue, the rear hands are raised and hold a rosary and a stalk of a lotus (*utpala*/night lotus). The principal hands are not elaborated but appear to be in a wrist-touching gesture; the upper hand may also be in *tarjanī-mudrā*. All in all, the Châu Thành tympanum has numerous Vajratārā iconographical features. In Cam temple architecture, the tympanum is an emanation of the principal divinity worshipped in the sanctum (Parmentier 1918: 427). In this case the temple which housed the tympanum Vajratārā Châu Thành would have been dedicated to the Jewel (Ratna) family of Ratnasambhava, in Pañcakūla of Vajradhātumaṇḍala, the Jina who emanates Vajratārā. The tympanum shares characteristics of the style of statuary from the Tháp Mẫm site of the early 13th century, during or shortly after the Khmer occupation of Vijaya (Southworth and Trần 2019: 340-2).

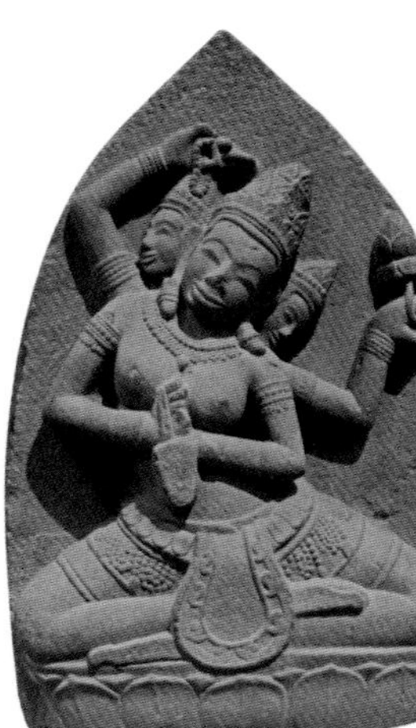

Fig. 8 *Vajratārā (?) tympanum of Châu Thành at the Bình Định provincial museum. 13th century; sandstone; 80 cm high, 50 cm wide, 35 cm deep. (Acc. no. BTBĐ 963/Đ.108). (Photo courtesy of Hoàng Như Khoa)*

Conclusion

This paper invites a reassessment of Esoteric Buddhist art in Campā, following the major spiritual and artistic breakthrough of the great Đồng Dương *vihāra*. It may prove that this Tantric sect was introduced to Campā from the early time. It also explores a wider horizon of linkages between the late Buddhist art of Campā, the Khmer kingdom and Java in the 13th century. Further research is now required into links with Odisha, China, Nepal and Tibet in this period after Islam destroyed the Ganges Valley monasteries and sent the Buddhist masters fleeing over the mountains and the seas.

Anne-Valerie Schweyer (2018: 77) and Peter Sharrock (2022: 126-64) have recently suggested some of the Buddhist images found in Campā Vijaya belonged to the Buddhist third 'Vajrayāna' wave, such as a tympanum of the huge Cam Dương Long temple depicting Cakrasaṃvara, a variant form of Heruka also found in the late 11th century in the western wing of the Khmer empire at Phimai (today northeast Thailand). Archaeological research continues apace in the former Cam territories and two sandstone statues of Tathāgatas have been uncovered in Vijaya and identified as Vairocana and Amoghasiddhi, dated to the 12th century (Trần and Nguyễn 2020b). **(Fig. 9)**[13]

An important bronze Avalokiteśvara was found at Hoài Nhơn, Bình Định province. Other statues from the Esoteric Buddhist Vijaya period are being identified in places of worship, like the unpublished eight-armed Avalokiteśvara in veneration at Phước Sa Buddhist temple in Quy Nhơn city. **(Fig. 10)**

Together with the figures of Pāṇḍaravāsinī and Vajratārā, the Esoteric Buddhist sculptural works found in the Campā Vijaya increasingly demonstrate Buddhism flourishing across the Cam polities from the 8th-13th centuries. Our understanding of the Buddhist overhaul of Brahmanism in late Campā can be expected to grow rapidly in the coming years.

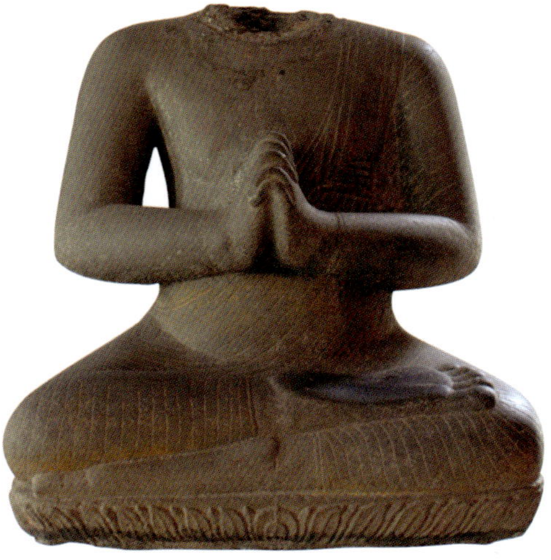

Fig. 9 *Vairocana statue dated to the 12th century found in Bình Định province; sandstone; 64 cm high. The Fine Arts Museum in Ho Chi Minh City. (Photo Tú Anh)*

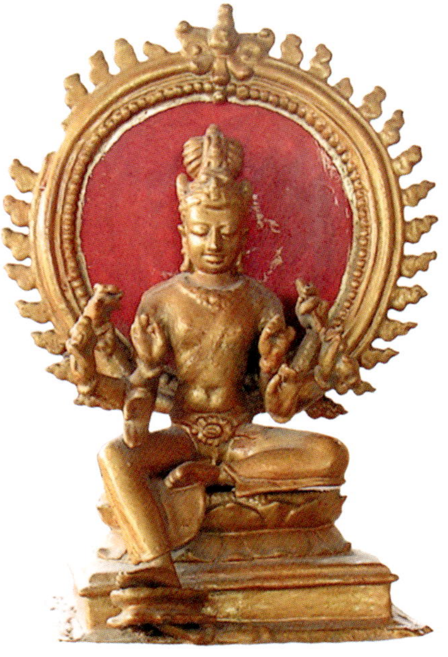

Fig. 10 *Eight armed Avalokiteśvara, probably of Srivijayan origin, bronze, 23 cm high. Venerated at the Phước Sa Buddhist temple in Quy Nhơn city. (Photo courtesy of Hoàng Như Khoa)*

Bibliography

Acri, Andrea (2016). 'Introduction', *Esoteric Buddhism in Mediaeval Maritime Asia: Networks of Masters, Texts, Icons* (eds. Andrea Acri), pp. 1-25. Singapore: ISEAS-Yusof Ishak Institute.

Acri, Andrea, Roger Blench and Alexandra Landmann (2017). *Spirits and Ships: Cultural transfers in early moonson Asia.* Singapore: ISEAS-Yusof Ishak Institute Publishing.

Baptiste, Pierre (2019). 'Đồng Dương Temple Iconography: Study of a Pedestal with Mara', *Campā: Territories and Networks of a Southeast Asian Kingdom* (eds. Arlo Griffiths, Andrew Hardy and Geoff Wade), pp. 341-353. Paris: École française d'Extrême-Orient.

Bautze-Picron, Claudine (2014). 'Buddhist Images from Padang Lawas region and the South Asian connection', *History of Padang Lawas, North Sumatra. II: Societies of Padang Lawas (Mid-Ninth – Thirteenth Century CE)* (ed. Daniel Perret), pp. 107-128. Paris: Cahiers d'Archipel, vol. 43.

Bhattacharyya, Benoytosh (1958). *The Indian Buddhist Iconography: Mainly Based on the Sādhanamālā and Cognate Tāntric Texts of Rituals.* India: Calcutta, Firma K. L. Mukhopadhyay.

Boisselier, Jean (1963). *La Statuaire du Champà: Recherches sur les cultes et l'iconograpghie.* Paris: Publications de l'Ecole française d'Extrême-Orient 54.

Broeskamp, Bernadette (2014). 'The Construction and Dissemination of a New Visual Idiom- The White-robed Guanyin and the Upper Tianzhu Monastery in Hangzhou', *Searching for the Dharma, Finding Salvation – Buddhist Pilgrimage in Time and Space* (eds. Christoph Cueppers and Max Deeg), pp. 109-262. Kathmandu: Lumbini International Research Institute.

Bronkhorst, Johannes (2011). *Buddhism in the Shadow of Brahmanism.* Leiden-Boston: Brill.

Calo, Ambra (2020). 'Durgā Mahiṣāsuramardinī in Likely Tantric Buddhist Context from the Northern Indian Subcontinent to 11th-Century Bali', *Pratu* (Volume 1, 2020, Article 3), pp. 1-20. <https://pratujournal.org> ISSN 2634-176X. Accessed on 08 October 2020.

Chandra, Lokesh (2009). 'The Hidden Base in the Cosmosophy of the Borobudur', *Uncovering the Meaning of the Hidden Base of Candi Borobudur* (eds. Dr. Endang Sri Hardiati et al.), pp. 137-161. Jakarta: The National Research and Development Centre of Archaeology.

Chemburkar, Swati (2017). 'Visualising the Buddhist *Mandala*: Kesariya, Borobudur and Tabo', *India and Southeast Asia: Cultural Discourses* (eds. Anna L. Dallapiccola and Anila Verghese), pp. 197-222. Mumbai: The K R Cama Oriental Institute.

Chemburkar, Swati (2018). 'Catalogue 67', *Vibrancy in Stone: Masterpieces from the Danang Musuem of Cham Sculpture* (eds. Trần Kỳ Phương, Võ V. Thắng and Peter D. Sharrock), p. 238. Bangkok: River Books.

Chiao-Hui Tu, Grace (2018). 'Sinitic transfers into Cham art', *Vibrancy in Stone: Masterpieces from the Danang Musuem of Cham Sculpture* (eds. Trần Kỳ Phương, Võ V. Thắng and Peter D. Sharrock), pp. 79-88. Bangkok: River Books.

Chutiwongs, Nandana (2005). 'Le Bouddhisme du Campā', *Trésors d'art du Vietnam: La sculpture du Campā, V-XV siècles* (eds. Piere Baptiste and Thierry Zéphir), pp. 65-87. Paris: Musée Guimet.

Chutiwongs, Nandana (2011). 'Buddhism in Campā: Narrative reliefs on the two image pedestals at Dong-duong', *Lettre de la Société des Amis du Campā Ancien* (SACHA) No. 14 (2011), pp. 12-27.

Cœdès, G. (1968). *The Indianized States of Southeast Asia* (trans. Susan Brown Cowing, ed. Walter F. Vella). Honolulu: University of Hawai'i Press.

Dhar, Parul Pandya (2014). 'Buddhism, Art, and Ritual Practice Đồng Dương at the Intersection of Asian Cultures', *Asian Encounters: Exploring Connected Histories* (eds. Upinder Singh and Parul Pandya Dhar), pp. 111-136. New Delhi: Oxford University Press.

Donaldson, Thomas Eugene (2001). *Iconography of the Buddhist sculpture of Orissa* (text and illustrations in 2 vols.). India: Indira Gandhi National Centre for the Arts and Abhinav Publication.

English, Elizabeth (2002). *Vajrayogini: Her visualizations, rituals, & forms: a study of the cult of Vajrayogini in India.* Massachusetts: Wisdom Publications.

Fontein, Jan (1990). *The Sculpture of Indonesia.* Washington and New York: National Gallery of Art and Harry N. Abrams, Inc.

Frédéric, Louise (1995), *Buddhism: Flammarion Iconographic Guides.* Paris-New York: Flammarion.

Getty, Alice (1988/1928). *The Gods of Northern Buddhism: Their History and Iconography.* New York: Dover Publications.

Ghosh, Mallar (1980). *Development of Buddhist Iconography in Eastern India: A Study of Tara, Prajnas of Five Tathagatas and Bhrikutis.* New Delhi: Munshiram Manoharlal Publisher Prv. Ltd.

Giebel, Rolf W. (2005). *The Vaircanabhisambodhi-Sutra,* translated from the Chinese (Taishō Volume 18, Number 848). Berkeley: Numata Center for Buddhist Translation and Research.

Golzio, Karl-Heinz (ed.) (2004). *Inscriptions of Campa.* Achen: Shaker Verlag.

Hall, Kenneth (2018). 'Campā port-of-trade networking on the coastline c.300-1500 CE', *Vibrancy in Stone: Masterpieces from the Danang Musuem of Cham Sculpture* (eds. Trần Kỳ Phương, Võ V. Thắng and Peter D. Sharrock), pp. 19-31. Bangkok: River Books.

Hoàng Xuân Hãn (1966). *Lý Thường Kiệt: Lịch sử ngoại giao và tông giáo triều Lý.* Sài Gòn: Đại học Vạn Hạnh. [*Lý Thường Kiệt: History of Diplomacy and Religion of the Lý Dynasty.* Sài Gòn: Vạn Hạnh University.]

Howard, Angela F. (1985). 'Royal Patronage of Buddhist Art in Tenth Century Wu Yueh', *The Museum of Far Eastern Antiquities Bulletin,* No. 57, 1985, pp. 1-60.

Kandahjaya, Hudaya (2009). 'The Lord of All Virtues', *Pacific World: Journal of the Institute of Buddhist Studies*, Third Series, Number 11 (Fall 2009), pp. 1-24.

Kandahjaya, Hudaya (2016). 'Saṅ Hyaṅ Kamahāyānikan, Borobudur, and the Origins of Esoteric Buddhism in Indonesia', *Esoteric Buddhism in Mediaeval Maritime Asia: Networks of Masters, Texts, Icons* (ed. Andrea Acri), pp. 67-112. Singapore: ISEAS-Yusof Ishak Institute.

Kinney, Ann R., Marijke J. Klokke and Lydia Kieven (2003). *Worshiping Siva and Buddha: The Temple Art of East Java.* Honolulu: University of Hawai'i Press.

Krairiksh, Piriya (2012). *The Roots of Thai Art* (translated by Narisa Chakrabongse). Bangkok: River Books.

Lippit, Yukio (2008). 'Goryeo Buddhist Painting in an Interregional Context', *Ars Orientalis*, Vol. 35, pp. 192-232.

Mabbett, Ian (1986). 'Buddhism in Campā', *Southeast Asia in the 9th to 14th centuries* (eds. David G. Marr and A. C. Milner), pp. 289-313. Singapore: Institute of Southeast Asian Studies.

Majumdar, R. C. (1985/1927). *Campā: history and culture of an Indian colonial kingdom in the Far East 2th-16th centuries AD.* Dehli: Gian Publishing House.

Maspéro, George (1928). *Le Royaume de Campā.* Paris et Bruxelles: Librairie nationale d'art et d'histoire/ G. Vanoest Éditeur.

Missions archaéologiques françaises en Annam: les monuments du Campā. Paris: Les Indes Savants-Musée Guimet 2005.

Mus, Paul (1933). 'Cultes Indiens et Indigènes au Campā', *Bulletin de l'École française d'Extrême-Orient* (BEFEO) 33 (1933), pp. 367-410.

Ngô Văn Doanh and Lê Văn Dương (1989). 'Bức phù điêu mới phát hiện ở tháp Phú Lộc (Nghĩa Bình)', *Những phát hiện mới về khảo cổ học năm 1988* (ed. Viện Khảo cổ học), p. 193. Hà Nội: Nxb. Khoa học Xã hội.-

Pain, Lincohn (2014). 'The Indian Ocean in the seventh and eighth centuries', *Maritime Contacts of the Past: Deciphering Connections amongst Communities* (ed. Sila Tripati), pp. 37-53. New Delhi: Delta Book World.

Parmentier, H. (1902). *Journal des fouilles du Sanctuaire de Đồng Dương: Périod du 7 Septembre au 27 Novembre 1902.* Ho Chi Minh City: Handwriting report housed at Library of the History Museum of Ho Chi Minh City.

Parmentier, H. (1909). *Inventaire descriptif des monuments Cams de l'Annam: vol. I. Description des monuments.* Paris: Leroux (Publications de l'École française d'Extrême- Orient 11).

Parmentier, H. (1918). *Inventaire descriptif des monuments Cams de l'Annam: vol. II. Étude de l'art Cam.* Paris: Leroux (Publications de l'École française d'Extrême- Orient 11).

Parmentier, H. (1919). 'Catalogue du Musée Cam de Tourane', *Bulletin de l'École française d'Extrême-Orient* (BEFEO) 19 (1919), pp. 1-114.

Revire, Nilolas (2017). 'From Gandhara to Java? A Comparative Study of Bhadrasana Buddhas and their Related Bodhisattva Attendants in South and Southeast Asia', *India and Southeast Asia: Cultural Discourses* (edited by Anna L. Dallapiccola and Anila Verghese), pp. 279-304. Mumbai: K.R. Cama Oriental Institute.

Roberts, Peter Alan (trans.) (2013). *The Basket's Display Kāraṇḍavyūha.* Published by 84000: Translating the words of the Buddha. <http://read.84000.co/#!ReadingRoom/UT22084-051-004/0>

Samdarshi, Pranshu (2014). 'The Concept of Goddesses in Buddhist Tantra Traditions', *The Delhi University Journal of The Humanities & The Social Sciences*, Vol.1, pp. 87-113. University of Delhi.

Scheurleer, Pauline L. and Marijke J. Klokke (1988). *Ancient Indonesian Bronzes.* Leiden: E. J. Brill.

Schweyer, Anne-Valérie (2009). 'Buddhism in Campa', *Moussons* 13-14, 2009, pp. 309-337.

Schweyer, Anne-Valérie (2018). 'Buddhism in Campā', *Vibrancy in Stone: Masterpieces from the Danang Musuem of Cham Sculpture* (eds. Trần Kỳ Phương, Võ V. Thắng and Peter D. Sharrock), pp. 71-78. Bangkok: River Books.

Sen, Tansen (2014). 'Buddhism and the Maritime Crossings', *China and Beyond in the Mediaeval Period: Cultural Crossings and Inter-Regional Connections* (eds. Dorothy C. Wong and Gustav Heldt), pp. 39-62. Amherst and Delhi: Cambria Press and Monohar.

Sen, Tansen (2018). 'Yijing and the Buddhist Cosmopolis of the Seventh Century', *Texts and Transformations: Essays in Honor of the 75th Birthday of Victor H. Mair* (ed. Haun Saussy), pp. 345-368. Amherst: Cambria Press.

Sharrock, Peter D. (2009). 'Hevajra at Banteay Chmar', *The Journal of the Walters Art Museum*, Vol. 64/65 (issue year 2006/2007, published 2009), pp. 49-64.

Sharrock, Peter D. (2018). 'Cham-Khmer Interactions in 1113-1220 CE', *Vibrancy in Stone: Masterpieces from the Danang Musuem of Cham Sculpture* (eds. Trần Kỳ Phương, Võ V. Thắng and Peter D. Sharrock), pp. 111-119. Bangkok: River Books.

Sharrock, Peter D. (2022). 'Heruka-maṇḍalas across Maritime Asia', *The Creative South: Buddhist and Hindu Art in Medieval Maritime Asia* (eds. Andrea Arci and Peter Sharrock): 126-64. Singapore: ISEAS Publishing.

Sharrock, Peter D. and Emma C. Bunker (2016), 'Seeds of Vajrabodhi: Buddhist Rituals Bronzes from Java and Khorat', *Esoteric Buddhism in Mediaeval Maritime Asia: Networks of Masters, Texts, Icons* (eds. Andreas Acri), pp. 237-252. Singapore: ISEAS-Yusof Ishak Institute.

Shaw, Miranda Eberle (2006). *Buddhist Goddesses of India.* Princeton University Press.

Southworth, William and Ruth Prior (2010). 'History and Archaeology at Tra Kieu', *50 Years of Archaeology in Southeast Asia: Essays in Honour of Ian Glover* (eds. Bérénice Bellina, Elisabeth A. Bacus, Thomas Oliver Pryce and Jan Wisseman Christie), pp. 183-194. Bangkok: River Books.

Southworth, William and Trần Kỳ Phương (2019). 'The Discovery of Late Angkorian Khmer Sculpture at Campa Sites and the Overland Trade Routes between Campa and Cambodia', *Campā: Territories and Networks of a Southeast Asian Kingdom* (eds. Arlo Griffiths, Andrew Hardy and Geoff Wade), pp. 323-343. Paris: École française d'Extrême- Orient.

Stein, R. A. (1986). 'Avalokiteśvara/ Kouan-yin, un exemple de transformation d'un dieu en déesse', *Cahiers d'Extrême-Asie*, vol. 2, 1986, pp. 17-80.

Stern, Philippe (1942). L'art du Campā et son évolution. Paris: Publication du Musée Guimet.

Studholme, Alexander (2002). *The Origins of Om Manipadme Hūm: A study of the Kārandavyūha Sūtra.* Albany: State University of New York Press.

Tingley, Nancy (2006/2007). 'Avalokiteśvara in Javanese Context: Gaṇḍavyūha, Kūṭāgāra, and Amoghapāśa', *The Journal of the Walters Art Museum*, Vol. 64/65, A Curator's Choice: Essays in Honor of Hiram W. Woodward, Jr. (2006/2007), pp. 65-80.

Trần Kỳ Phương (2018). 'Trà Kiệu *apsaras*', 'Brahmā', *Vibrancy in Stone: Masterpieces from the Danang Museum of Cham Sculpture* (eds. Trần Kỳ Phương, Võ V. Thắng and Peter D. Sharrock), pp. 222-225, 248-249. Bangkok: River Books.

Trần Kỳ Phương and Nguyễn Thị Tú Anh (2020b). 'Nhận xét về hai pho tượng Phật thời kỳ Campā Vijaya trưng bày tại Bảo tàng Mỹ thuật TP. Hồ Chí Minh và Bảo tàng Điêu khắc Chăm Đà Nẵng', tham luận tại *Hội nghị Thông báo Khảo cổ học lần thứ 55*, ngày 29-30 tháng 9 năm 2020 tại Hải Phòng.

Trần Kỳ Phương and Nguyễn Thị Tú Anh (2021). 'A proposed relationship between Campā and Chola dynasties during the 11th and 13th centuries: A view from the historical sources and artistic evidences/Về mối quan hệ khả hữu giữa các vương triều Campā và Chola trong thế kỷ 11 đến 13: Nhìn nhận từ những cứ liệu lịch sử và nghệ thuật', *SPAFA Journal*, Vol 5 (2021), pp. 1-20. https://doi.org/10.26721/spafajournal.2021.v5.673

Trần Kỳ Phương and Nguyễn Thị Tú Anh (2025). 'The Ninth Century Lakṣmīndra-Lokeśvara Vihāra Đồng Dương Viewed as a Maṇḍala Architecture', Recentering Southeast Asia: Politics, Religion and Maritime Connections (ed. Himanshu Prabha Ray), pp. 132-159. London and New York: Routledge.

Trần Kỳ Phương, Im Sokrithy and Chutiwongs Nandana (2020). 'Vimayapura, Yashodharapura and Bhumi Vijaya: More visual evidence of artistic and iconographic affinities', *Liber Amicorum: Mélanges réunis en hommage à / in honor of Ang Chouléan* (eds. Grégory Mikaelian, Siyonn Sophearith and Ashley Thompson), pp. 239-266. Paris/ Phnom Penh: Péninsule / Association des Amis de Yosothor.

Vessantara (2004). *The Five Female Buddhas: A Commentary on their Sadhanas and Pujas.* Cambridge: Published by Dharmachari Vessantara.

Wade, G. (2011). 'The 'Account of Campā' in Song Hui Jigao', *The Cham of Vietnam: History, Society and Art (*eds. Trần Kỳ Phương and Bruce Lockhart), pp.138-168. Singapore: NUS Press.

Whitmore, John K. (2018). 'Nagara Campā and the Vijaya Turn', *Vibrancy in Stone: Masterpieces from the Danang Musuem of Cham Sculpture* (eds. Trần Kỳ Phương, Võ V. Thắng and Peter D. Sharrock), pp. 31-36. Bangkok: River Books.

Willson, Martin (1992). *In Praise of Tārā: Songs to the Savioures*s. Wisdom Publications: Subsequent Edition.

Woodward, Hiram (2004). 'Esoteric Buddhism in Southeast Asia in the Light of Recent Scholarship: A Review Article', *Journal of Southeast Asian Studies* 35, no. 2 (2004), pp. 329-354.

Woodward, Hiram (2011). 'The Temple of Dong Duong and the *Kārandaravyūha-Sūtra*', *Beyond the Eastern Horizon: Essays in Honour of Prof. Lokesh Chandra.* Satapitaka Series, Vol. 68, pp. 33-42.

Yu, Chun-fang (2001). *Kuan-yin: The Chinese Transformation of Avalokitesvara.* New York: Columbia University Press.

Endnotes

1 We are deeply indebted to Dr. Peter D. Sharrock for his comments on this paper. Our thanks also to Prof. Marijke J. Klokke for her picture and the material related to Pāṇḍaravāsinī in East Java; to Mai Bùi Diệu Linh for her editing the first draft; to Hoàng Như Khoa for his pictures and the information related to the Cam sites in Bình Định province.

2 Of the 130 Cham inscriptions published, 92 worship Śiva, three Viṣṇu, five Brahma, seven are Buddhist, two are jointly dedicated to Śiva and Viṣṇu and 21 are non-sectarian (Mus 1933: 369; Majumdar 1985, I: 170).

3 The An Thái site is 10 km due east of the Đồng Dương monastery.

4 Nandana Chutiwongs (2005: 79; 2011: 12-27) proposes the statue represents the historical Buddha or a Mahāyānist primordial Ādi-Buddha, "[…] qu'il s'agisse du Buddha historique et/ou de l'incarnation du Buddha principiel primordial [Ādi-Buddha], au sens mystique du bouddhism mahāyāniste." Meanwhile, Pierre Baptiste (2005: 212-3) thought the bronze Buddha may have been erected in Enclosure III.

5 The Amitābha statue was possible located at the centre of the 'central tower' (*tour central*), as the surviving upper body was found at the same location; this assumption comes from Parmentier's diary during the excavation at the Đồng Dương site on 22 November 1902. Parmentier then reconnected the upper body with the lower legs of the statue found nearby (*Missions archaéologiques françaises en Annam: les monuments du Champa* 2005: 129).

6 The *bhadrāsana* posture is asserted as a popular posture in the Buddha statues of Southeast Asia in which both legs pendant with knees are bent into a diamond shape, one of his hands performs *vitarkamudra* or *dharmacakramudra* while the other is *abhayamudra* or *bodhyagri* gesture (Revire 2017: 279-304). However, the Buddha of Đồng Dương is sitting with both legs pendant and the two palms resting on the knees. This may be a Cam original posture of Amitābha or it may follow the Chinese tradition for portraying Maitreya. According to Grace Chiao-Hui Tu, "[B]uddha images in *bhadrāsana* are usually identified in China as Buddha Maitreya, who will descend to earth in the future, as mentioned in the Descending Sūtra. The representation of Buddha Maitreya in *bhadrāsana* made its first appearance in China under the Northern Liang dynasty (421-39 CE) as a symbol of salvation and political renewal. His importance was reaffirmed when empress Wu claimed herself to be equal to Maitreya in order to legitimize her assumption of imperial power in 690 CE." (Chiao-Hui Tu 2018: 80). There is also a large (420 cm) stone 8th century Dvāravatī Buddha seated with legs pendant and both hands on his knees who is identified as Maitreya and now worshipped at Wat Na Phra Men, Ayutthaya (Krairiksh 2012: 64-6, fig. 1.41).

7 It is likely that the Śrī Indralokeśvara *vihāra* erected by Jaya Indravarman was located in the Trà Kiệu area where a sandstone head of Lokeśvara was excavated by Jean-Yves Claeys in 1927-8 (Boisselier 1963: 188). Boisselier dated the head in the 10th century but later scholars assign it to the 11th-12th centuries (Southworth and Prior 2010: 191; Trần 2018: 222-5).

8 According to the Bình Đinh Provincial Museum the site called Xuân Mỹ by Parmentier is now named Long Triều tower by the local people (personal communication from Hoàng Như Khoa in March 2021).

9 Although Mahāmāyūrī is a goddess present in India, Odisha, Nepal, Tibet, China and Japan, she has yet to be identified as present in Campā, Cambodia or Java. This goddess is usually represented with multiple arms – one holding a peacock feather, seated on a lotus throne, and her vehicle is a peacock (Battacharyya 1958: 234; Getty 1988: 136-8; Frédéric 1995: 230-1).

10 Her attributes may have also been identified the wish-fullfilling jewel (cintāmaṇi) as same with the 10th century bronze statuette of Pāṇḍara found in East Java (Scheurleer and Klokke 1988: 98, cat. 46).

11 If the Xuân Mỹ goddess is Pāṇḍaravāsinī, she would probably not have been worshipped alone. It is more likely that she was joined by two other goddesses worshipped in the two other temples of the Xuân Mỹ complex that Parmentier reported in a collapsed state (1909: 155-7). According to the *Mañjuśrīmūlakalpa*, Pāṇḍaravāsinī together with Prajñāpāramitā and Tārā sometimes flanked Avalokiteśvara (Studholme 2002: 111).

12 Initially, the tympanum was believed to be from the Phú Lộc or Thốc Lốc temple built on top of the Châu Thành hill. The image of the goddess has been identified as Sarasvatī (Ngô and Lê 1989: 193).

13 The Vairocana, in *bodhyagri-mudrā*, is 64 cm high and is now in the Fine Arts Museum in HCMC (acc. no. BTMT. 203). The Amoghasiddhi, in *abhaya-mudrā* is 72 cm high and is displayed at the Đà Nẵng Museum of Cham Sculpture (acc. no. BTC. 194/13.7).

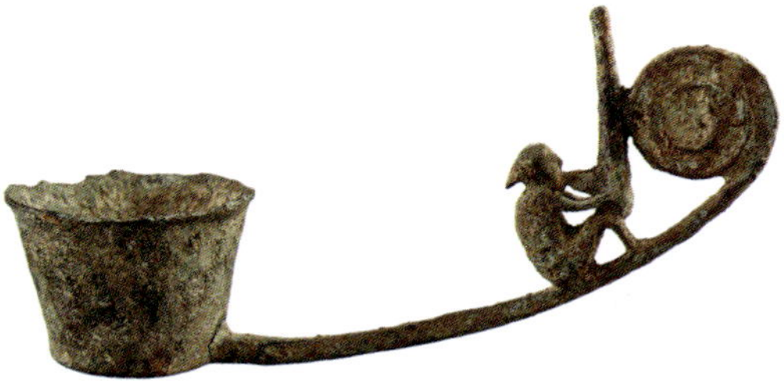